CHRÉTIEN DE TROYES

CHRÉTIEN DE TROYES

A STUDY OF
THE ARTHURIAN ROMANCES

L. T. TOPSFIELD

Fellow of St Catharine's College
and Lecturer in Provençal and
French in the University of Cambridge

CAMBRIDGE UNIVERSITY PRESS

Cambridge
London   New York   New Rochelle
Melbourne   Sydney

Published by the Press Syndicate of the University of Cambridge
The Pitt Building, Trumpington Street, Cambridge CB2 1RP
32 East 57th Street, New York, NY 10022, USA
296 Beaconsfield Parade, Middle Park, Melbourne 3206, Australia

© Cambridge University Press 1981

First published 1981

Printed in Great Britain by The Anchor Press Ltd
and bound by Wm Brendon & Son Ltd
both of Tiptree, Essex

British Library Cataloguing in Publication Data

Topsfield, Leslie Thomas
Chrétien de Troyes
1. Chrétien de Troyes – Criticism and
interpretation
841'.1   PQ1448   80-49938
ISBN 0 521 23361 5

To Valerie

CONTENTS

ACKNOWLEDGEMENTS

SOME IDEAS WHICH have been suggested in this work in the chapters on *Lancelot* and *Perceval* have been amplified in three articles of which some paragraphs occur also in this book. These articles are: 'The tourney at Noauz and the Hermit Episode in the *Lancelot* and the *Perceval* of Chrétien de Troyes', *Miscellània d'homenatge a Ramon Aramon i Serra* (Barcelona, 1979); 'Fin'Amors in Marcabru, Bernart de Ventadorn and the *Lancelot* of Chrétien de Troyes', a paper which was given in May 1978 at the VIIIth International Colloquium of the Catholic University of Louvain and is at present in press as a contribution to *Love and Marriage in the Twelfth Century* (*Mediaevalia Lovaniensia*, Leuven); 'Malvestatz versus Proeza and Leautatz in the early troubadours and Chrétien de Troyes', a contribution to a volume of troubadour studies in *L'Esprit Créateur*, XIX (1979) – a shortened version of this article was given as a paper at the *First Conference on Medieval Occitan Language* at the University of Birmingham on 2 April 1979. Reference to these articles will be found in the notes, and full details are given in the bibliography. I thank the editors of these journals and collections of studies for their agreement to the use of this material.

I am greatly indebted to the Syndics and Officers of the Cambridge University Press, and particularly to Terence Moore for his helpful suggestions. I also wish to thank Caroline Murray for the care with which she prepared this work for press, and Susan Church and Iris Little for the skill and patience with which they turned my manuscript into a typescript.

February 1980   L.T.T.

The Inheritance

AMIDST the brilliance of twelfth-century civilisation in France, the glory of Chartres, of its philosophers and those of Paris, Cîteaux and St Victor, and the early troubadours at Poitiers, not the least enduring light is that of the Grail, the imaginative high point in the five Arthurian romances of Chrétien de Troyes and the zenith of his literary achievement. This book is an attempt to consider these five romances separately and also as component parts of the whole work, and to trace the ways in which Chrétien's ideas and view of the human condition evolve from *Erec et Enide*, his earliest known romance, through *Cliges*, *Lancelot* and *Yvain* to the unfinished *Perceval* or *Le conte du Graal*.

In the sense that all great works of literature and art are inevitably the product of time, place and the creative genius, Chrétien was singularly fortunate, for he was the heir to an era of spiritual and artistic reawakening and to the two centuries of cultural stirrings which had preceded it. If, as seems probable, he composed *Erec et Enide* about 1170, he came to the fore at a moment particularly suited to his talent for assimilating, adapting and building upon some of the major innovations in thought and literature of the earlier twelfth century in France. This century was clearly one of the great formative periods in the history of European civilisation, a true age of Renaissance which had turned for inspiration directly or indirectly to Greece and Rome, to Plato and Aristotle, Virgil, Seneca, Cicero and Quintilian, to Horace, Martial and Ovid, to Boethius and St Augustine, and, with quickening interest, to the resources of Hispano-Arabic thought and science. This amalgam of new learning, especially at Chartres, was no passive clerical preoccupation.

Permeating lay society, it bore the mark of a vital curiosity, seeking models for its creative spirit, accepting ideas, themes, knowledge from all quarters, Celtic, Moorish, Classical and Christian. This was a curiosity which was concerned both with the reality of the idea and the natural phenomenon. It extended to the living reality of creation, to plants and animals as well as to their mythology and symbolical reality. It embraced the 'wholeness' of existence, the belief in the principle of *universitas*, the basic unity and oneness of God's creation. It inspired the faith and inventive genius which in the new cathedrals blended stone and glass with the vision of the infinite.[1]

This vision of the infinite, of *universitas* and supreme union with God, also found expression in the work of Bernard of Clairvaux, the son of a Burgundian nobleman, who with a following of four brothers and twenty-seven friends entered the new monastery at Cîteaux and within two years had established at Clairvaux the abbey which he made into one of the great spiritual centres of Europe.[2] Bernard, who was abbot of Clairvaux from 1115 until his death in 1153, preached and wrote 'in order to reach people's hearts', and his faith in the life of positive *caritas*, together with the warmth and brilliance of his style and imagery furnished rich inspiration to the developing literatures of Europe, and especially to the romances on the theme of the Grail.

'The lyre of poetry', says Alanus de Insulis, in his *De Planctu Naturae*, written possibly as late as 1178–80, 'sounds a false note on the superficial, literal shell of a poem, but, deeper within, it conveys to those who can hear it the secret of a higher understanding, so that, with the externals of falsehood cast away, anyone who would interpret the poem may discover the sweeter essence of truth secreted inside it' (PL, CCX, 451 C). Behind this eloquence there lies a commonplace principle of medieval, and especially twelfth-century thought. Words, however pleasing, are dross. Gold lies in the meaning which they enshrine. The art of discerning such meaning is the main purpose and joy of *lectio*, the reading and especially the understanding of what is being read.[3] In the vernacular literature of twelfth-century France, in the metaphysical poetry of the troubadours, and in Chrétien's later romances, the fictions of poetry are harnessed to the quest for philosophical truth. And this vital literary process was recognised by the learned men of the day, as witness the *Mendacia poetarum serviunt veritati* of John of Salisbury,[4] a leading thinker and administrator at the court of Henry II Plantagenet.

This alliance between the new learning of the schools, especially at Chartres, the brilliance of Christian, especially Cistercian thinking, and the literary genius of poets such as the troubadour Marcabru (c. 1130–c. 1150) and Chrétien de Troyes, constitutes a major advance in the evolution of European literature in the vernacular, introducing a new philosophical mode of poetry and narrative romance which reaches beyond Dante on the one hand and the whole Arthurian and courtly cycle of romances on the other, to the present day.

This new mode of vernacular poetry appears for the first time at the very outset of the twelfth century in the court of the first troubadour Guilhem VII Count of Poitou, IX Duke of Aquitaine. This court, which was associated with all the earliest troubadour poetry, had long been famous for its interest in learning and letters. Guilhem the Great, the third count of Poitou who reigned from 993 to 1030, was renowned throughout Western Europe for his wisdom. His literary tastes are evident in the allusive imagery which he uses in his letters to conceal confidential matters from the uninitiated. During his long and peaceful reign over the vast lands of Poitou and Aquitaine, he was on terms of friendship with Odilon of Cluny and with Fulbert, the founder of the cathedral school at Chartres, whom he persuaded to accept the treasurership of the cathedral at Poitiers. This link between Chartres and the court of Guilhem the Great was reinforced when Fulbert sent his pupil, Hildegarius, to establish the famous episcopal school at Poitiers.[5] The practical influence of the 'new' learning of Chartres, and its ideas of classical humanism and natural philosophy were not confined to the schoolroom. They are apparent in the letters of idealised love which passed between Peter Damian and Agnes, daughter of Guilhem the Great, Empress of Germany from 1043, and her sister-in-law Hermensent.[6] Reflections of these philosophical ideas are even more apparent in the poetry of the earliest troubadours.

3

Not the least remarkable quality of this poetry at Poitiers is that in its beginnings it was deeply concerned with the moral and philosophical questions of man's existence. Thematically, it was based on a series of antitheses, of conflicts between ways of life which are fruitful or sterile, ways of thinking and living which are whole or fragmented, of joys which are ephemeral or durable. It was concerned with the conflicting rules of reason and desire, order and impulse, the needs of the community and the individual, and also with the nature of carnal, mental and spiritual love, of illusion and reality, of nothingness, and the wisdom of folly.

These themes can be related to Christian and Stoic ideas, to the view of human love expressed in the *De natura et dignitate Amoris* of the Cistercian William of St Thierry, to Chartrian concepts of rational happiness and of man's awareness of his place in the natural order. They are used by the troubadour Marcabru in order to fashion both his ideal of *Fin'Amors*, a love which unifies physical and mental desire and spiritual aspiration, and his ideal of *cortesia*, the sum total and the outward expression of all the courtly virtues. These include *Jovens*, youthfulness of spirit, *Jois*, the quest for happiness in life, *Valors*, innate courtly virtue, and the concept of *conoissensa*, the power of discerning the good from the bad, the true from the false, the real from the illusory. It is this faculty of discrimination which shows a man the right path to follow and enables him through the rational quality of *mesura* to direct himself to a real life suited to his talents, his position in life and his *natura*, the essence of each individual human being as it exists within the natural order of created things. These moralising ideas of Marcabru, and especially his concepts of *Fin'Amors* and *mesura*, greatly influenced the evolution of troubadour lyric poetry, and, in so doing, supplied one of the foundation stones of European courtly literature.[7]

It is even more remarkable that many ideas from contemporary philosophical thought are apparent already in the burlesque poetry of Guilhem IX. The treatment he affords them is exactly opposite to that of Marcabru. In the quicksilver flash between laughter and seriousness, wisdom and bawdy folly, Guilhem satirises the methods of scholarly debate and the moral and philosophical terms, *Malvestatz*,

Proeza, Leis 'the natural law of all creatures', *Jovens, Amors* and *Jois*, which were almost certainly current in his day at the court of Poitiers, and even before that time if we are to judge from his satirical treatment of his aunts Agnes the Empress and Hermensent and Peter Damian in his licentious poem of the ginger cat, *Farai un vers pos mi sonelh* (v).[8]

From the poetry of Guilhem IX and Marcabru we can see that there already existed at the court of Poitiers, before 1100, a lively interest in philosophical notions about man's quest for happiness (*jois*) and an awareness of an ultimate, transcendental happiness (*lo mielhs*) which may have been an adaptation to profane love of the *summum bonum* of Boethius.[9] We can also see in both poets, though treated in opposite ways, a sense of the moral conflict in life between *Proeza*, an excellence of virtue based on order, and its opponent, the vice of recreancy and disorder which is *Malvestatz*.[10]

It was largely from the cultural traditions which had evolved over two centuries at the court of Poitiers that the noble society of Chrétien's day drew its ideal of a rational and ordered way of life based on *mesure*, the ability to act, in given circumstances, in a way most appropriate to one's temperament, qualities or status. To this ideal of *mesure*, the rational progeny of *savoir*, a gentle dose of *folie* might be added in order to salt and define its quality.[11] And behind this ideal of rational courtliness and the *folie* of fantasy and impulse, there existed in Chrétien's day the weighty *curialitas* of the functional court of Henry II, of the administrators and men of learning such as John of Salisbury who, in his *Policraticus*, advocated a morality of Roman *gravitas* based on a sense of responsibility towards oneself and the good of the community.

It is scarcely surprising that this rationally ordered society, with its own flights of fancy towards *folie*, should have found in Arthurian romance an idealised mirror-image of itself, an embellished reflection of the infinite possibilities of knightly adventure, love and heroism, observed against the exotic back-cloth of the Celtic tradition. Courtly reason and *savoir* could find release for its imagination in the Other World, the summons of a Celtic king to an earthly hero, of a fairy mistress to her lover. It could escape from the trials of *Fin'Amors* in the tragedy of the uncontrollable Tristan-type passion imposed by a *geis* or spell, in the theme of a mortal abducted to the Other World, of a fairy mistress rewarding the lover who defends her magic garden or fountain, of abundance turned into waste land.[12]

For the knightly, dynastic and Arthurian side of Chrétien's literary inheritance, and for the origins of the romance genre in French, we must turn away for the moment from the court of Poitou and move northwards to England, where the Norman usurpers sat uneasily on the throne of Edward the Confessor. It is this royalty, at first uncertainly established then immensely powerful though still torn by family dissension, which under Henry II Plantagenet was to have an electrifying effect on the literature of twelfth-century France. The Norman kings of England had clearly inherited the taste of their Viking ancestors for historico-epic narrative. They were also impatient to establish the legitimacy of their royal functions, and for this purpose they encouraged the historical endeavours of their scholars and writers. The first real landmark in this dynastic literature which sought to link the new Norman royalty with its illustrious predecessors, is the *Historia Regum Britanniae* of Geoffrey of Monmouth. His work, the inheritor of a tradition of historical narrative, is original in its flattering view of the Norman conquest as retribution meted out to the Anglo-Saxons for their invasion of Celtic Britain. Its sequence of dedications reflects the shaky state of the English crown. It was first dedicated soon after the death of Henry I in 1135 to his natural son Robert of Gloucester 'illustrious through his exploits and learning'. Following the swing of political change, it was then dedicated to Robert and to Waleran of Beaumont, a supporter of Stephen, and then, probably in 1136 and certainly before 1138, to King Stephen and Robert of Gloucester jointly. Geoffrey claims, though improbably in the view of many scholars, that his work is a plain translation into Latin of a 'very ancient book in the British language' *britannici sermonis librum vetustissimum*, given to him by Walter, Archdeacon of Oxford.[13] He uses Gildas and Bede, Livy and Nennius to sketch the story of the Kings of Britain from Brutus, who landed at Totnes in Cornwall with a band of Trojans, to the death of Cadwallader in A.D. 689. Geoffrey's main importance for us is that he introduced the stories of Lear,

Cymbeline, Merlin and Arthur, who, he says, was the son of Utherpendragon and gained victories over the Saxons, Norwegians, Gauls and Romans. Geoffrey's *Historia* supplied Arthurian material to Gaimar for his vernacular *Estoire des Engleis*, but its influence on later writings concerned with the Arthurian tradition, the so-called *matière de Bretagne*, was greatly augmented by the translated version of it, together with the new theme of the Round Table, in the *Roman de Brut* which Wace dedicated to Eleanor of Aquitaine in 1155.[14]

At this point the cultural traditions of Poitou and Britain are effectively united. In 1137, Eleanor, the grand-daughter of the first troubadour, Guilhem IX of Aquitaine, had succeeded in her own right to the immense territories of Poitou and Aquitaine which stretched from the Atlantic to Auvergne, from Poitou to the Pyrenees. It is not surprising that in this same year she was married to the young prince Louis who within a month of the wedding succeeded to the throne of France as King Louis VII. Eleanor bore two daughters by him, Marie de France who later became the Countess of Champagne and Chrétien's patroness, and Alice of Blois. Eleanor's energy and ebullience were, however, ill-suited to the ways of Louis VII, and, after their marriage was annulled, Eleanor, now at the age of thirty, wed in 1152 the dynamic young Henry, Count of Anjou and Duke of Normandy, who within two years was crowned Henry II Plantagenet of England. This tumultuous marriage, marked by bouts of active warfare, between husband and wife, father and sons, sons and sons, produced Henry the Young King, King Richard the Lion Heart, Geoffrey, Count of Brittany, and the gifted but ill-fated King John of England. By uniting England, Wales, and later Ireland with the western half of France, it also produced the so-called Angevin Empire and sowed the seeds of three hundred years of bloodshed between France and England.

For French literature, however, the marriage of Eleanor and Henry was of major importance. It joined the vigorous traditions of philosophical and courtly poetry in Poitou to the obsessive interest of the English royalty in the 'history' of its dynastic origins. It also provided through Henry II and Queen Eleanor an immensely important source of patronage and stimulus for narrative and poetic creation. Henry II, great-grandson of the Conqueror, was a brilliant man, a tire-less soldier, administrator and lawgiver, an intellectual who surrounded himself with men of great intellect. Eleanor, Queen in turn of two great countries, Duchess of Aquitaine and Countess of Poitou, an astute and daring politician, an authority on courtly behaviour, a leader, when need arose, of her troops in the field, remained true to her Viking descent from Adele, the sister of Rollo. But for our present purpose her importance lies especially in her encouragement of the love lyric of the troubadours in the Provençal tongue, or the *langue d'oc*, and of the new and evolving genre of the romance in Northern French, or the *langue d'oïl*.

The influence of Eleanor was almost certainly active in a major transformation which began to take place in trouba-dour poetry between 1150 and 1170. The early metaphysical poetry in the closed style, such as we find in Marcabru, was concerned with the problems of the human condition, with the quest for a supreme, unknowable happiness, with Fin'Amors as an abstract ideal of Love, a 'fount of goodness which illumines the world'. This allusive poetry gradually yields to the fashion for courtly compositions in the clear style, dominated by the physical presence of the idealised lady and epitomised by Eleanor's most illustrious troubadour Bernart de Ventadorn. Bernart's songs, composed between about 1145 and 1180, are intensely lyrical but have a far more restricted vocabulary than those of Marcabru.[15] For Bernart, Fin'Amors is the loyal love offered in submission to the exalted, physical lady or *domna*. It rejoices in her idealised beauty and virtues. It seeks fulfilment in equal and mutually shared physical delight (xv, 29–32).[16] Though Bernart has within him a form of *mesura* which allows him to recognise his fine folly of feeling, it is irrational feeling, the oblivion of the mind, the moment of ecstatic identification with the skylark, the nightingale or the lady, which for him is purest joy. He is the *fis amaire*, the true lover who desires, has desired and will desire one woman alone (xxx, 1–7 and 43–6), and he rejects Marcabru's concept of *mesura* as a rational force which must control these desires (xv, 33–5). The attitudes to love of Marcabru and Bernart de Ventadorn[17] are both of fundamental importance for the development of courtly literature in Europe, and it is in their concepts of Fin'Amors

8

that Chrétien de Troyes will find the inspiration for his treatment of the love affair between Guenevere and Lancelot.

Yet Chrétien's richest legacy was to be gathered from the *matière de Bretagne*, which came to him from two separate though related narrative traditions. One of these traditions took the form of Celtic lays which drew on the stories and customs of Ireland and Wales and celebrated, among other happenings, the deeds of Arthur's knights and of Tristan and Yseut. These lays had been known in France, especially in Poitou, from the later years of the eleventh century, and had spread rapidly into Italy and Catalonia.[18] We must first, however, consider briefly the cultivated and literary tradition of Arthurian and Classical narrative which, fostered by the Angevin courts of England–Aquitaine, provided a major basis for the genre of the romance in France.

Some fifteen years of rapid evolution in this genre still separated the influential *Roman de Brut*[19] or *Geste des Bretons*, which Wace dedicated to Queen Eleanor in 1155, from the *Erec et Enide* of Chrétien de Troyes. But Wace's star waned, and he abandoned the *Roman de Rou*, or *Geste des Normans*, written between 1160 and 1174, when Henry II gave the same task to his more fashionable rival Benoît de Sainte-Maure.

Though Benoît, in the 43,210 octosyllabic rhyming couplets of his *Estoire des ducs de Normandie*, carried the history of the Normans down to Henry I, he is better known for his *Roman de Troie*, again in octosyllabic couplets, composed between 1154 and 1173, and dedicated to Eleanor, 'riche dame de riche rei', between 1160 and 1170. This romance drew its material from the *Historia de excidio Trojae* written about A.D. 550 by Dares Phrygius who was reputed to have fought for the Trojans, and from the *Ephemeris belli Trojani* (c. A.D. 330) of Dictys Cretensis who, it was claimed, had fought for the Greeks. The *Roman de Troie* is usually thought to be the last of three romances by different authors which are sometimes called the *triade classique*. These romances, together with the very successful *Roman d'Alexandre*[20] and numerous lays[21] on classical themes attest the contemporary popularity in courtly circles of heroic subjects from Classical Antiquity.

The first in date of these three classical romances was the

Roman de Thèbes, composed between 1150 and 1156, and based largely on the *Thebais* of Statius,[22] though flavoured with elements from the Northern French epic or *chanson de geste*. But a yet greater influence on the development of the romance genre was exercised by the *Roman d'Eneas*, composed in ten thousand octosyllabic couplets by an unknown Norman about 1156.[23] Apart from the opening scenes and the Dido episode, the *Roman d'Eneas* strays far from Virgil's text and intention.[24] It neglects Virgil's theme of the high destiny which impels Eneas to found a new city and a new royalty to compensate for the waste land of Troy. Its characters are devitalised and empty of the affection and tenderness which Virgil lent them. Yet, despite the flatness of its narrative passages and the trivialisation of Eneas' motives, there were two major reasons why it should appeal to a contemporary courtly audience in France. Both these reasons stem from the expanded love affair between Lavinia and Eneas which the poet added to Virgil's story. In Lavinia, courtly society was offered an archetypal example of the damsel who recognises and controls the Ovidian fears and doubts of love and finds happiness through declaring herself to the beloved. In this respect Lavinia is the precursor of Fenice in Chrétien's *Cliges*. The second reason is the clear contrast which is established between the nature, quality and results of the loves of Dido and Lavinia for Eneas. Dido's uncontrollable passion compels her to forswear her vow of widowed chastity, to destroy herself and bring her country to ruin. The fresh, mutual love of Lavinia and Eneas accords with all the individual and social demands of courtly *mesure*. Though the terms of their falling in love may be Ovidian, the two lovers are shown to be wholly suited to each other by their youthful devotion, temperament and nobility of birth. Their marriage is also not only a love match but a dynastic triumph, promising order and happiness for the lands they will inherit and auguring well for a new dynasty which will rule the recently united lands of Eleanor and Henry II Plantagenet. This elementary *conjointure* or 'joining together' of the two love episodes in the *Eneas*, and the embryonic *sen* or underlying meaning which they imply, mark an important step forward in the evolving genre of the courtly romance. In these important respects, the *Eneas* points the way ahead to the art of Chrétien de Troyes in his first romance *Erec et Enide*.

What was a *roman* or romance? In the Carolingian Renaissance the word *romanice* had been used to express the meaning 'in the vernacular', as distinct from *latine*. In the twelfth century the form *romanz* is used regularly as an adverb, adjective or noun. The phrase *et en romans et en lati*, literally 'both in romance and in latin', which occurs in the first troubadour Guilhem IX,[25] implies the desire for self-expression to the limit of one's capacity, for example in prayer. Used in negative constructions, it implies complete taciturnity.

Romanz, used as a noun,[26] can refer to speech in the vernacular, to a translation into the vernacular, or a vernacular literary work. A lively twelfth-century interest in the legends of ancient Greece and Rome, of Apollonius, Alexander, Hero and Leander, Cadmus, Jason and Julius Caesar,[27] led to the commissioning of translations into romance of the latin versions of classical texts, or even of the texts themselves. Equally strongly, as we have seen, Norman and Plantagenet dynastic interest in the ancient kings of Britain encouraged translations into romance from writings such as the *Historia* of Geoffrey of Monmouth which prompted the *Roman de Brut* of Wace.

From the 'schoolroom' task of translation into romance to the creative embellishment of the text was an easy step, and so the romance as 'translation' merged inevitably into the romance as narrative literary genre. Embellishment was inspired at first by a desire to update knowledge of the past and to write for the benefit and ornamentation of present life. Twelfth-century writers and their patrons followed the great thinkers of the day in their awareness of the giants on whose shoulders they perched. Alexander, Eneas, Arthur and, more especially, his knights are re-created in their imagination as contemporary figures of knightly and courtly excellence. It is this process of adaptation of the translated work, by additions such as the Round Table in Wace's *Brut* and the expanded Lavinia episode in *Eneas*, the introduction of marvellous objects and happenings, of the carbuncle, the precious light-giving stone, of magic animals and the wealth of the Celtic tradition, which determines the character of the romance in the second half of the twelfth century. When

Chrétien writes Erec et Enide about 1170, the genre has moved beyond the state of being a translation or an adapted and embellished translation into a romance language. It may still draw its material from Byzantine sources, from Classical Antiquity, the matière de Rome, or from the matière de Bretagne,[28] but it is now ready to be fashioned, and recited or read aloud, according to the interests of its audience and its poet.[29] As a romance of love and adventure, such as Floire et Blancheflor, it may serve as a pleasing courtly diversion, and this is also partly true of the weightier and more tragic Tristan stories in the versions of Beroul and Thomas. With Chrétien de Troyes, however, a dichotomy occurs in the genre of the romance. This dichotomy has many similarities to the existing division in troubadour poetry between works composed with a courtly or a metaphysical intention. With Chrétien de Troyes a new form of romance evolves and achieves, through the creative intention and the ideas which inspire it, an independent identity which is quite separate from that of its sources and from the contemporary romans d'aventure. This higher form of romance is characterised by its sen or underlying meaning and by the conjointure, the jointing together of incidents, and of incident and dialogue, through which the sen is revealed. In this respect, this form of romance differs also from the estoire, the 'story' or 'history' and from the conte which is usually a short tale about a single happening or an aventure and its consequences.

The different roles of the estoire, conte and romanz are acknowledged by Chrétien in the opening lines of his Cliges:

Ceste estoire trovons escrite,
Que conter vos vuel et retreire,
An un des livres de l'aumeire
Mon seignor saint Pere a Biauvez.
De la fu li contes estrez,
Don cest romanz fist Crestiiens.[30]
(18–23)

This story which I wish to tell and relate to you do we find written in one of the books from the book-cupboard of my beloved lord Saint Peter at Beauvais. From this history was drawn the tale from which Chrétien created this romance.

Though the conte of Cliges was of Greco-Byzantine origin, Chrétien set his romance within the framework of the court of Arthur in Britain which we find in Geoffrey's Historia and Wace's Brut. An Arthurian framework also exists for the other four romances, but, as we shall see, it is less martial, less robust and becomes increasingly decadent. This change in attitude may have reflected Chrétien's growing disenchantment with the courtly and knightly values of the society around him. Another reason, however, was that he was drawing his *matière* or subject-matter from a separate and richer source. This was the oral and written tradition in which ancient Irish and Welsh tales were retold and refashioned without the constraints of the Norman and Angevin dynastic ambitions which had affected the 'literary' transmission of the Celtic Arthurian tradition by Geoffrey of Monmouth and Wace, among many other writers. It is from this less adulterated source that Chrétien inherits figures such as Erec, Mabonagrain, Meleagant and Giflet, and the weaknesses and vices of Kay and King Arthur, together with the whole mythology of the Celtic supernatural tradition.

Details of the written works in which the ancient Irish tales were transmitted and blended with Welsh traditions, are available elsewhere and have no place here.[31] Briefly, it may be said that they extend from the Welsh poem the *Gododdin* of about A.D. 600, through the account by Nennius (c. A.D. 800) of Arthur's victories over the Anglo-Saxons, the *Annales Cambriae* (c. 955) which record, under the years 516 and 517, Arthur's victory at Badon and his death with Medrant at the battle of Camlann; through The *Spoils of Annwn* (tenth century), The *Black Book of Camarthen*, which lists Arthur's warriors, through the prose love story *Kulhwch and Olwen* (c. 1100) to the *Vita Gildae* of Caradoc of Llancarvan, relating the abduction of Guenevere by Melvas, and the Welsh prose tales of *Geraint, Owain* and *Peredur*, which show respectively a marked similarity to Chrétien's *Erec et Enide* and *Yvain*, and a loose relationship with *Perceval*. These three Welsh romances, together with *Kulhwch and Olwen* and other tales, are found in the *Mabinogion*, in two Welsh collections, the *White Book of Rhydderch*, written down about 1300–25, and the *Red Book of Hergest*, from about 1375 to 1425.

There is evidence that tales from this Celtic tradition were transmitted orally and were popular in France from about 1100, or even earlier. William of Malmesbury, in his *Historia Regum Anglorum* of 1125, declares that trifles of the Bretons, *nugae Bretonum*, were current in his day about Arthur, 'a man worthy not to be dreamed about in false fables but to be proclaimed in truthful works of literature'.[32] He also tells of the discovery in south-west Wales, about 1087, of the tomb of Arthur's nephew Walwen (Gawain).[33] In 1155, Wace also speaks of the many tales which the Bretons tell about the Round Table.[34]

From 1100 onwards, and especially in Brittany, Poitou and its neighbours, the names of Arthurian heroes occur regularly in historical documents in France. A Gawain is attested in 1110, a Tristan in 1113, the name Arthur from as early as 814. And the references in French and German romances to Breri or Bleheris (Blihis, Bliheris, Pleherim) 'who knew the epic deeds and the stories of all the kings and counts of Brittany, and retold them to the Count of Poitiers', possibly Guilhem IX, the first troubadour, cannot be easily discounted, especially as Bleheris may be the Bledhericus whom Giraldus Cambriensis described as *famosus ille fabulator*, and may even be Bledri ap Cadivor, a Welsh nobleman allied to the Normans, who lived from about 1070 to 1140 and was given the appellation of *Latinarius* or 'interpreter'.[35]

That courtly interest in the romance in the last third of the twelfth century embraced not only the Classical but the Celtic tradition is clear from the *Tristan* of Thomas, the *Ille et Galeron* of Gautier d'Arras, and the lays of Marie de France who states her poetic purpose: 'To prevent ourselves from falling into vice, we must study and understand and begin some difficult task. So I began to think of composing some fine story and of making a translation from latin into romance. But so many others have undertaken this sort of work that I should thereby have gained little reputation' (*Lais*, Prologue, 28–32, ed. A. Ewert (Oxford, 1958)). So Marie turned her thoughts to the lays which she had heard, and in order to keep their memory fresh, retold them in a rhymed narrative, which she calls a *conte*:

> M'entremis des lais assembler,
> Par rime faire e reconter.   (Prologue, 47–8)

She defines her sources:

> Les contes ke jo sai verrais,
> Dunt li Bretun unt fait les lais
> Vos conterai assez briefment.   (*Guigemar*, 19–21)

I will relate to you, without too much amplification, the authentic stories of which the Bretons have composed their lays.

She describes her method:

> De un mut ancïen lai bretun
> Le cunte e tute la reisun
> Vus dirai, si cum jeo entent
> La verité, mun escïent.   (*Eliduc*, 1–4)

Working from a very ancient Breton lay, I will tell you the story in my own words and its whole theme, according to the authentic truth as I, in my mind, believe it to be.

Lai may come from Old Irish *laíd* or *loíd* which in Old Irish sagas denoted the passages of speech inset into the story of adventure. If this is the case, *lai* may have been originally a lyrical passage of speech as opposed to the pure narrative, the *conte* about the *aventure*. Later it came to denote the short narrative poem itself.[36] It seems probable that the older narratives originated in Ireland, and were inherited by the Bretons who made of them their lays which Marie was now rendering into *contes* in French, without undue amplification but with the sense of the story, the *reisun*, as she saw it, 'brought out' or, in other words, invented and then imposed in gentle fashion on the original tale.[37]

This particular Celtic tradition, unlike the more learned literary one, not only provided stories of individual heroes, heroines and villains, to writers such as Marie de France, Beroul,[38] Thomas and Chrétien de Troyes, but furnished them with the even more important legacy of Celtic myth. The fundamental principle of this mythology lies in the acceptance of a close and continuous relationship between this earthly human world and the Other World. No impassable barrier separates the two worlds and there is between them a frequent interchange of human and other-worldly beings. Gods, fairy maidens, can come to live in various forms in this world, especially at the seasonal festivals. Men, summoned by a fairy spirit, or by a ruler who needs assistance, may venture on a quest into the Other World.

This Other World is represented in two ways. It may be situated in the islands of happiness, youth and abundance, a place of wondrous fruits and divine drinks such as the island of Avalon. Alternatively, it may be the subterranean world of the Tuatha De Danann, a fairy people, thought to be the inhabitants of old Ireland who fled from earlier invasions. These Tuatha were believed to be guardians of the traditions of the ancient civilisation, and the custodians of the Talismans or Magic Objects which endowed their possessor with powers of sovereignty and abundance.

The Tuatha De Danann are linked with human beings by *geasha*, the plural of *geis* which means 'spell'. This *geis* is important in Celtic literature in which motivation to action comes from outside the characters. Negatively, the *geis* is a form of taboo such as the denial to a human being of the right to sleep two nights consecutively in the same place. Positively, the *geis* is extremely important, as the compulsion laid on a human to act, endure trials, undertake quests, and also to fall irrevocably in love. This element of supernatural power inflicted on a human being goes back to the eighth or ninth centuries of the Celtic tradition, and is symbolised in the twelfth century by the love potion intended for the ageing Mark which Brenguain inadvertently gives to Tristan and Yseut, this love triangle of uncle, wife, nephew being also a traditional Celtic pattern.

In Celtic literature themes involving journeys are a commonplace, and are of three kinds. There are abductions (Irish *aitheda*), journeys in a ship to the Magic Islands of the Other World (*imrama*), undertaken because of a *geis* imposed by a fairy mistress, and there are journeys to the Other World beneath the Hills (*echtrai*), in which the earthly hero may conquer palaces, help a king and return victorious with the Magic Objects or Talismans which are important for our understanding of the romance of *Perceval* (pp. 208–9).[39]

Chrétien de Troyes has a Shakespearian talent for absorbing and refurbishing the ideas he inherits, and for responding to and refashioning courtly taste. He is his own man, adept at irony, wary of the static and conventional, preferring movement and progress. Having taken hold of his materials, his 'story', the themes of the Celtic supernatural, the philosophical or religious ideas of his day and current views of courtesy and knighthood, he pares and shapes them, diminishing or increasing their importance entirely in accordance with the underlying theme or *sen* and the dramatic purpose of a particular work. And when in *Cligès* and *Erec et Enide* he adds a topical note, he appears to have adapted historical truth to suit his narrative needs.[40]

Of Chrétien's life we know little. To judge by traces of

dialect in his language, he appears to have been a native of Champagne, and his description of himself as Crestiiens de Troies in *Erec et Enide* implies that he came from Troyes, or that he lived there. A document of 1173 from the archives of the episcopal palace at Troyes has as one of its signatories a 'Christianus canonicus sancti Lupi'.[41] Can this Christianus, canon of the abbey of Saint Loup at Troyes, be the same man as Chrétien de Troyes the writer? Frappier had his doubts: 'si l'on admet cette conjecture, il faut admettre aussi qu'il était d'Eglise, ce qui, du moins en principe, se concilierait mal avec l'esprit mondain et profane de presque toute son œuvre'.[42] Yet this argument is not decisive. Though Chrétien's romances may create an appearance of profanity, his underlying ideas are not at variance with those which might have been held by a canon who had some acquaintance with the political and social life of the courts. Quite the contrary. Another canon of the Church at this time, Peire d'Alvernhe, sang of *Fin'Amors* and the Joy of the Court and was praised by Dante (*De Vulgari Eloquentia*, IX, 3) as one of the *antiquiores doctores* of eloquence, and by his thirteenth-century biographer as 'the best troubadour in the world before Giraut de Bornelh came'.[43] It is not without interest that in his poetry Peire, like Chrétien, moves away from a belief in the joy of the world to the hope of peace in the life hereafter.[44] Wolfram von Eschenbach refers to Chrétien as *meister Kristjân von Troyes*.[45] The title of *meister* implies clerical status. It may also imply his pre-eminence among the writers of his day, in the same way that Giraut de Bornelh was praised as *maestre dels trobadors* in his thirteenth-century biography.[46]

Chrétien gives us little direct information about himself. In *Lancelot* he tells us that the work was commissioned by his patroness *ma dame de Champagne*, who was almost certainly Marie de Champagne, the daughter of Eleanor of Aquitaine and her first husband, Louis VII of France. Since Marie married Count Henry I of Champagne in 1164, *Lancelot* was certainly not written before then. In *Perceval* Chrétien praises the virtues of *Li cuens Phelipes de Flandres* (13), who, he says, commissioned the work and gave him a source book for it (62–7). This patron is Philip of Alsace, the cousin of Marie de Champagne, who became Count of Flanders in 1168 and *de facto* regent of France during the minority of Philip

Augustus (1180–2). He departed on the Third Crusade in 1190, and died at Acre in 1191.

So far as the chronology of his work is concerned, Chrétien tells us in the opening lines of *Cliges* that he had already written *Erec et Enide*, together with other works which have not survived. These include: *Les Comandemanz Ovide* and *L'Art d'Amors*, which were probably translations or versions of the *Remedia Amoris* and the *Ars Amatoria*; *Le Mors de l'Espaule*, probably the story of Pelops; *Del roi Marc et d'Iseut la blonde*; and *Del Rossignol la Muance*, usually called *Philomena*, from Ovid's *Metamorphoses*, which has been preserved in updated language in a late thirteenth-century *Ovide moralisé*.[47] In *Guillaume d'Angleterre*, based on the story of St Eustace, a Chrétien names himself in the first line. If, as seems probable, this means that Chrétien de Troyes was the author, this work was almost certainly written after *Cliges*.[48] Recent research has suggested that *Erec et Enide* may date from about 1170, and *Cliges* from 1176. *Yvain* and *Lancelot* were written more or less concurrently and may date from between 1177 and 1181, and *Perceval* was composed probably between 1181 and 1191, and possibly around 1181.[49]

Of the thirty-one mss. in which Chrétien's Arthurian romances figure, two only (mss. B.N. 794 and B.N. 1450) contain all five works. *Erec* occurs in eight mss., *Cliges* in nine, *Lancelot* in six, *Yvain* in ten and *Perceval* in sixteen.[50]

Chrétien gathers in an abundant legacy from his twelfth-century predecessors, and their Classical, Christian, courtly and Celtic inheritance. From the philosophers and theologians he takes their belief in the principle of *universitas*, the basic unity of God's creation, and, within this wholeness, man as an individual of inexhaustible interest in his conflicts, temptations, and passions, his *cupiditas* and search for *caritas*. Chrétien also inherits the dialectical method of the schools in which opposites are juxtaposed, compared, contrasted and analysed. For Good to be recognised, Evil must be understood. To know wisdom, folly must be detected. And in this process honour is contrasted with baseness, reality with illusion, love of God with self-love. Such use of antithesis is a device of medieval description, found in twelfth-century Arts of Rhetoric.[51] It plays a major part in the poetry of the early troubadours, and also in Chrétien's

18

romances in which folly precedes wisdom, pride goes before humility and shame, and misery before self-knowledge and joy. In Chrétien's 'whole' view of life, comedy keeps company with sorrow, burlesque with seriousness, and irony lightens and enhances idealism. Truth may be discerned in the vision of the world upside-down. The actual world may be illumined by the supernatural world with which it co-exists. A rational man in the courtly tradition may seek security of mind and discover a higher, mystical truth which enriches or disturbs that serenity. Chrétien's acquaintance with the principles of rhetoric and dialectic, and the intellectual distance from his material which this gave him, allowed him to interweave in his romances a higher *sen* through which objects, characters and events are raised from the level of the immediate and the particular to that of the universal. This intellectual coolness which disguises personal feeling nevertheless enhances the value of Chrétien's convictions when these finally become apparent.

Chrétien's intellectual distance from the courtly and knightly values of his day becomes increasingly evident in his later works. He could scarcely have belonged to a more talented or 'courtly' court than that of Marie de France, the Lady of Champagne for whom he composed *Lancelot*. Marie was clearly well acquainted with the etiquette of behaviour which had been established at the court of her mother Eleanor of Aquitaine, and which was 'recorded' with gentle irony, probably at Marie's request, in the *De Amore* of Andreas Capellanus.[52] This *art de plaire* was essentially a projection into courtly social life of the abstract ideals of *Jois*, *Valors*, *Jovens*, *Mesura* and *Proeza* which had been extolled earlier by Marcabru (see p. 50). It cherished elegant conversation and manners and a positive and joyous attitude to life through which each individual contributed to the communal Joy of the Court. It was a system which revolved round the idealised presence of the lady or *domna*, and in its emphasis on the courtly and social rather than the metaphysical essence of *Fin'Amors*, on reputation rather than individual joy, it fashioned for itself a cadre of convention which hampered the higher and wider aspirations of mind and spirit.[53] Gace Brulé, the archetypal *amant martyr* and major lyric poet at the court of Champagne, came to terms with these constraints.

Chrétien, like many contemporary troubadours such as Peire d'Alvernhe, Raimbaut d'Aurenga and the later Arnaut Daniel, appeared to accept them outwardly while reacting quietly and effectively against them.

Despite the outward clarity of his narrative, Chrétien is an essentially enigmatic writer. He understates, implies, suggests. His negative opinions are indicated as subtly as his positive views, as his *antancion*, the direction or purpose given to each work, and the *conjointure* through which he reveals his ideas on love, knighthood and the quest for happiness, on man's relationship to man and to God. It is in an attempt to understand these ideas and the varying *antancion*[54] of his works that this book has been written.

Early romances

2

Erec et Enide and the Joy of the Court

CHRÉTIEN's reference to the *mout bele conjointure* with which he has fashioned the romance of *Erec et Enide* out of a simple *conte d'avanture* (13–14),[1] may be a commonplace of self-praise. It may also refer to his structural skill in arranging and jointing the component parts of his narrative material, for *conjointure*, like the *iunctura* of Horace, could be applied to the formal method by which a poet effected a smooth transition from the adventures of one knight to another, or from one place to another.[2] But if we go beyond the formal level of the narrative, and look at the thematic structure of *Erec et Enide*, we can see that it is precisely through this process of formal 'jointing together' that the *sen* or inner meaning of the romance, in both major and minor themes, is revealed, and that this is why Chrétien, conscious of his innovatory skill, finds pleasure in his *mout bele conjointure*.

In order to express his inner meaning or *sen*, Chrétien uses three methods which I will call linear, lateral and allusive. The linear method uses analogy and contrast to unthread an enigmatic meaning which is interwoven with the line of the narrative. Meaning is hinted at or revealed clearly through the repetition of words, phrases, incidents or situations, even after a major lapse of time. This repetitive device, which strengthens and binds up the structure of the romance, is used by Chrétien with great subtlety, not translatable into another language. Meaning may be revealed in scarcely perceptible fashion, in a slight shift of emphasis which contrasts one character or set of values with another, in a variation of word order, syntax or dialogue, in the coloured overtones of meaning in a word, in the different response to a similar situation.

The second method, which I have called lateral, is more

23

abrupt. It is an expository device and frequently takes the form of a major dialogue, or monologue, offering elucidation or the summing up of a theme which has been suggested by the linear method. Whereas the linear method is progressive and dynamic, charting the stepping stones by which a character may move towards his higher self, the lateral method is static, argumentative, a plateau of clear meaning which projects, as it were, horizontally from the upward progression of the story line. It is a statement of the poet's intention about his *sen*, a moment in which his listeners may collect their thoughts. With the linear or dialectical method the poet uses analogy, contrast and repetition to suggest the development of his major characters, their lacks and fulfilment, their weaknesses, vices and virtues. With the lateral or expository method he frequently draws wider conclusions about the meaning and morality of their actions.

With the third or allusive method the poet uses symbolical and allegorical overtones of meaning to set the narrative within the context of a universal truth, which in the later romances, *Lancelot*, *Yvain* and *Perceval*, becomes increasingly metaphysical. It may also be used to evoke the atmosphere of a mysterious Other World associated with Celtic tradition. The lateral method appeals to the mind, to the reason. The allusive method, like the poetry of the early troubadours, touches the audience in relation to the depth of their emotional or spiritual experience. For Chrétien's audiences, the death-cart, the lion, the grail, the lance, must have evoked associations which varied according to the degree of response to the different cultural traditions which they represented. To appreciate the variety of these associations[3] demands a leap of the imagination from the present-day reader, and a desire to understand, however imperfectly, the texture of a work in which Celtic and Classical traditions, and Christian, courtly, knightly and feudal values are inextricably intermingled. The diffuse overtones of Chrétien's allusive style preclude any clear cut interpretation of his work on the plane of any one of these traditions. Especially in the later works, Chrétien seeks a response on several planes of feeling and experience, and the depth of this response will depend on the difficulty or ease with which the inward eye sees through the shell of the *conte d'avanture*.[4]

These three major methods of conveying or implying meaning, the linear, lateral and allusive styles, may be used separately or together. In *Lancelot* they run together. In *Erec et Enide*, Chrétien's separate use of them may indicate a sense of novelty in this art of thematic *conjointure*.

Erec et Enide sets a formal structural pattern which Chrétien follows, in large measure, in *Lancelot*, *Yvain* and *Perceval*. A knight appears to conform to the highest standards of courtly and chivalrous conduct, but in his character there is a flaw which is indicated in the titles *Erec et Enide*, *Le Chevalier de la Charrette*, *Le Chevalier au Lion*, *Le conte du Graal*. Enide, the cart, the lion, the grail are agents associated with the tests which the knight will fail. They also represent, directly or obliquely, the strength or virtue which he needs, and they are instrumental in showing him the path to self-redemption. In simple terms, the major theme in these romances is the quest for 'wholeness' of the individual character, and, on a wider plane, the conflict between Good and Evil, Order and Disorder. This ideal of 'wholeness' takes different forms in the various romances. It may be a temporal or spiritual wholeness, or both, and it is sought and achieved within a framework of love and knightly endeavour, though knighthood and love are not Chrétien's central theme. This is concerned with the virtue and weakness of the individual character, its aspiration towards a state of wholeness, and the temporal and spiritual well-being which the achievement of this wholeness will bring to the individual character and to the community, which is not necessarily that of Arthur's court.

These romances have a clear structural pattern.[5] A knight, successful in the eyes of the world, suffers a moral or spiritual humiliation which is prefigured by earlier failures in apparently minor episodes. Seeking rehabilitation, he progresses beyond the values and reputation of his former self, and attains a degree of virtue and wholeness beyond that of the ideal Arthurian knight, such as Gawain. In the course of his adventures he may have to venture into a world which is outside that of Arthurian society and which may have Celtic associations. This Other World, as in *Lancelot*, may be the scene of a conflict between Good and Evil, and the forces of Evil from this world may invade Arthur's world and threaten it with destruction. Arthur's court may be described with either respect or derision, but it remains a pivot for the action, which, except for the unfinished *Perceval*, returns to it four times in each romance, and always at the beginning and the end of the work.[6]

In his Prologue[7] to *Erec et Enide* (1–26) Chrétien distinguishes between his work and that of other tellers of stories: 'In his proverb the peasant tells of things which are scorned but are of far greater value than people imagine. For this reason that man acts well who applies whatever knowledge he may have to the things which are good' (1–5).

Por ce dit Crestiiens de Troies	For this reason Chrétien de Troyes
Que reisons est que totes voies	says it is right and reasonable for
Doit chascuns panser et antandre	every person, in thought and
A bien dire et a bien aprandre,	aspiration, to speak of and learn
Et tret d'un conte d'avanture	about goodness. And out of a tale
Une mout bele conjointure,	of adventure he draws a fine and
Par qu'an puet prover et savoir	unified structure which allows the
Que cil ne fet mie savoir,	lesson to be proved and known
Qui sa sciance n'abandone	that no man behaves rationally un-
Tant con Deus la grace l'an done.	less he gives freely of the experi-
D'Erec, le fil Lac, est li contes,	ence he has gained, as much as God
Que devant rois et devant contes	gives him grace to do so. Of Erec,
Depecier et corronpre suelent	the son of Lac, is this story, which
Cil qui de conter vivre vuelent.	those who live by the telling of
(9–22)	tales are wont to fracture and
	corrupt.

It is through *savoir* (16) that the disorder of *folie* and self-indulgence can be defeated, so that wholeness may be achieved. In this conflict, *savoir*,[8] which gives self-knowledge, and determines and guides human conduct, is supported by its ally *sciance*, the experience and knowledge which are gained from life and then applied by the power of *savoir* to good purposes. It is this lack of *savoir* in his behaviour which Erec is made to recognise as he and Enide his wife lie in bed 'mouth to mouth, in close embrace, like people who have made much love'. Enide is awake, and he sleeps (*Cil dormi et ele vella*, 2479), and, as she admires Erec's clear face and fine body, *folie* (2488) possesses her mind:

Et plore de si grant ravine	She weeps so fiercely her tears
Que chieent dessor la peitrine	fall on her lord's breast, and she
Son seignor les lermes de li,	says: 'Alas! What grief that I
Et dist: 'Lasse, con mar m'esmui	left my land! Why did I come

26

De mon païs! Que ving ça querre
Bien moi devroit sobir la terre,
Quant toz li miaudre chevaliers,
Li plus hardiz et li plus fiers,
Li plus frans et li plus cortois,
Qui onques fust ne cuens ne rois,
A del tot an tot relanquie
Por moi tote chevalerie.
Donques l'ai je honi por voir;
Nel vossisse por nul avoir.'
Lors li a dit: 'Con mar i fus!'
(2493–507)

to seek this fate? Better the earth should enfold me, since the best of all knights, the bravest, the boldest, the most generous and courteous knight that ever was a count or king, has, for my sake, forsaken all knightly deeds. I have brought shame upon him, and this I would not have wished for all the world.' Then she addressed him: 'My love, how cruel was your fate.'

At this, Erec stirs: 'Tell me, fair, dear love. Why do you weep like this? What gives you such sorrow and grief? You must tell me. I insist. I intend to know. Tell me, sweet love, and take care to keep nothing from me. Why did you say my fate was cruel?' (2515–21).

Enide prevaricates, is made to confess: 'People mock you, and blame me. They say:

Que si vos ai lacié et pris
Que tot an perdez vostre pris,
Ne ne querez a el antandre.
Autre consoil vos covient prandre,
Que vos puissiez cest blasme estaindre
Et vostre premier los ataindre;
Car trop vos ai oï blasmer:
Onques nel vos osai mostrer.
Sovantes foiz, quant m'an sovient,
D'angoisse plorer me covient.
Tel pesance or androit an oi,
Que garde prandre ne m'an soi,
Tant que je dis que mar i fustes.'
(2563–75)

That I have so loved you and made you prisoner that you lose all your knightly fame, and seek to aspire to nothing save to my love. You must take thought and plan your deeds differently so that you may wipe away this blame and attain to the praise which once was yours. Too much have I heard you blamed. Never have I dared to reveal this to you. Many times, when my thoughts turn to this, my grief brings me to tears. So great was my sorrow just now that I could not hold myself back from saying: 'How cruel was your fate.'

Enide was symbolically awake, while Erec slept. Her *savoir* has seen their crisis, and the need for Erec to resolve it. But Enide, innocent of the world, still lacks *sciance*, and, when ordered to put on her best dress and have her best palfrey saddled, she dithers in anguish in her room, misunderstanding his thoughts, fearing to be sent away. Erec arms himself on a leopard rug, loses patience, summons her abruptly:

27

'Young man, go with all speed to the room beside the tower, where my wife is. Tell her she does keep me waiting here too long. She has taken too long to make ready. Tell her to come and get on her horse right away, for I am waiting for her' (2665–71).

At the words *Car je l'atant*, Enide's crisis is over. She knows that Erec must regain the *premier los* which he had won in the lists, but she feared that he would reject her and seek adventure on his own. She accepts the primary importance of knightly prowess. She does not realise how indispensable she will become to Erec, but she sees the possibility that married love and knightly prowess are compatible, and that such wholeness of life is their destiny. Her belief in a joint adventure, only glimpsed at this stage, will soon be put into practice. Enide, through her passion for Erec and her lack of social awareness, has erred in her role of wife and feudal lady, and must, like Erec, redeem herself. She heeded the slanderers, and hid her shame, folding it in on herself, not daring to recall Erec to knightly duty. Her social awkwardness, which is also a part of her attractive innocence, was prefigured in the scene of her embarrassment (*vergoingne*, 1755) at Arthur's court (see p. 39). Enide must now go with Erec on a mutual quest. She needs the personal and social education which life with him can provide, as much as he will need the cool direction and support of her innate *savoir*. The title of the romance, *Erec et Enide*, implies the reverse title *Enide et Erec*.

Enide develops, Erec remains static, thinking to overcome moral weakness by martial prowess. For love of his wife he has neglected his duties. His reputation is tarnished. As will happen in the case of Perceval, when he first seeks knowledge of the Grail and Lance, the path of atonement appears to lie only through knightly combat. Erec bids Enide go with him so she may observe his knightly prowess and learn to trust and obey him. He is the lord, she is the vassal. The shared joy of their early sensual love has vanished in this moment of trial. Neither truly understands the other. Both must change. Erec, and to a lesser extent Enide, see their plight with the eyes of their former selves, with the values of Arthur's court, which esteems the knight who excels in combat for the lady he loves. When they leave the court of King Lac, Erec and Enide are destined to shed their former selves, and the conventions of love and knighthood epitomised by Arthur's world. Together they are drawn into the adventure of living, of hardship, self-discovery and preparation for their royal duties.

If we now look back to the opening lines of the romance, we may see that Erec's humiliation at the court of his father is prefigured by his shaming at the court of Arthur, and for the same reasons. Erec is already moving away from the values of Arthur's court when we first meet him, arrayed in an ermine cloak, a tunic of fine silk, and silken hose, as he gallops up, radiant with good looks and armed only with a sword, to bear the Queen company at the Hunt of the White Stag. This hunt, on the worldly level, is a custom (*costume* 38) of the court. The knight who can kill the White Stag must kiss the fairest damsel in the court. Gawain fears the envy and dissension this may cause, and tries in vain to dissuade Arthur from his pastime. On a Celtic level, such an animal, like the white hind in the *Guigemar* of Marie de France, is an emissary from the Other World sent to summon a hero to adventure and love.[9] And this, indirectly, will be Erec's fate.

Erec stands aside from the Hunt. Self-indulgent in soft raiment, he is committed to no damsel who would involve him in the chase of the Stag. In the company of the Queen, he is more powerless to protect her than Kay will be when he rides out to fight Meleagant. Erec, seeking pleasure, neglects the duties imposed by *savoir* and *mesure* and is about to fail his first test. The horns, the dogs, the huntsmen pass, and, in the silent forest, Guenevere, her maids-in-waiting and Erec are confronted by a knight, a damsel and a dwarf with a whip. Guenevere asks the knight and damsel to approach but when the maid-in-waiting advances with this invitation, she is beaten back by the dwarf, and Erec likewise. The knight, *felon et desmesuré*, who will later reveal his name as Yder (1046), and his damsel, are the prototypes of Mabonagrain and his mistress who will figure in Erec's final adventure of the *Joie de la Cour*. They are the extreme form of the *accidia*,[10] the apathy and indifference to society into which Erec is drifting. In this opening scene we have a *conjointure* of the theme of Erec's weakness, his self-indulgence and lack of *savoir*, with that of the aggression and self-will of alienated knighthood which will disrupt Arthur's court and destroy its Joy. When Erec restores this Joy by his victory over Yder at the Contest of the Sparrow Hawk, he achieves on a courtly plane what he will accomplish on a far wider plane by his defeat of Mabonagrain in the *Joie de la Cour* adventure. So the *premerains vers*, or introductory part of the romance, which ends at l. 1844, contains within itself the *sen* and the thematic framework of the romance.

Despite its implicit associations with Celtic tradition, especially in the Hunt of the White Stag at the beginning, and the final adventure of the Joy of the Court,[11] the action in *Erec et Enide* is free from overt supernatural intervention and springs directly from the weaknesses, the aspirations, and sense of purpose of the two main characters. Since it is in the human problems of love within marriage and in the response of Erec and Enide to each other, and in their generosity and goodness that a great part of the attraction of this romance lies, let us look at these characters in turn as they move from spontaneous, self-interested action to a way of life which is determined by reason and will.

It is in the fine folly of feeling of a Bernart de Ventadorn[12] that Erec is startled from his state of self-absorption, as he looks on his bride-to-be, as they ride to Arthur's court after the Contest of the Sparrow Hawk. Youth and innocence fall in love:

De s'avanture s'esjoïst;	He rejoiced in his adventure.
Mout estoit liez de s'avanture;	He found great happiness in his
Qu'amie ot bele a desmesure,	good fortune. For he had a
Sage et cortoise et deboneire.	damsel of peerless beauty, wise
De l'esgarder ne pot preu feire:	and courteous and of noble
Quant plus l'esgarde, plus li plest.	disposition. His eyes cannot look
Ne puet muër qu'il ne la best.	at her enough; the more he
Volantiers pres de li se tret,	looks the more he is pleased
An li esgarder se refet.	with her. He cannot help kissing
Mout remire son chief le blont,	her. Eagerly he draws near to
Ses iauz rianz et son cler front,	her and looks at her closely
Le nes et la face et la boche,	once again. Intently he gazes on
Don granz douçors au cuer li toche.	her fair head, her laughing eyes,
Tot remire jusqu'a la hanche,	and clear brow, her nose and
Le manton et la gorge blanche,	face and lips, so that great
Flans et costez et braz et mains;	sweetness touches his heart. He
Mes ne regarde mie mains	gazes at every part of her down

La dameisele le vassal
De buen oel et de cuer leal,
Qu'il feisoit li, par contançon.
Ne preïssent pas reançon
Li uns de l'autre regarder!
(1482–1503)

to her hips, her chin and white neck, her sides and ribs and arms and hands. No less eagerly than he gazes on her does the damsel look at the young man with admiring eye and loyal heart. Neither would have taken a ransom not to look at the other.

Erec and Enide are equals in beauty and birth and passion:

Mout estoient d'igal corage
Et mout avenoient ansanble.
Li uns a l'autre son cuer anble.
Onques deus si beles images
N'assanbla lois ne mariages.
(1512–16)

Very much did they have an equal desire, and very well did they befit each other. Each one steals the heart from the other. Never did the natural law or marriage bring together two people so fair of face.

They fall in love as generously as the young lovers in Marie de France, with the shared desire so praised by Bernart de Ventadorn:

En agradar et en voler
es l'amors de dos fis amans.
nula res no i pot pro tener,
si.lh voluntatz non es egaus.
(edn Appel xv, 29–32)

In pleasing and in desiring does the love of two true lovers consist. Naught avails in love, if desire is not equal.

For Bernart true love excludes reason and moderation: like a leaf following the wind, he is bereft of power over himself when he looks into his lady's eyes. Just so do Erec and Enide fall in love on their wedding night when their eyes touch. Enide makes love boldly (2103–4) and, when they arrive in his father's land, Erec, who at Arthur's court has been acclaimed as champion of the tourney, loves Enide to the neglect of all knightly duty:

Mes tant l'ama Erec d'amors
Que d'armes mes ne li chaloit,
Ne a tornoiemant n'aloit,
N'avoit mes soing de tornoiier;
A sa fame aloit donoiier.
De li fist s'amie et sa drue:
Tot mist son cuer et s'antandue

But Erec loved her so much in his lovemaking that he cared no more for deeds of arms. He went to no tourney, for jousting he had no more care; he was wont to go and make love to his wife. He made her his love

An li acoler et beisier;
Ne se queroit d'el aeisier.
Si conpeignon duel an avoient,
Antr'aus sovant se demantoient
De ce que trop l'amoit assez.
Sovant estoit midis passez,
Einçois que de lez li levast:
Lui estoit bel, cui qu'il pesast.
(2434–48)

and his loved one. In embracing and kissing her he placed his whole heart and aspiration and he sought pleasure nowhere else. His companions were grieved by this, and often, among themselves, they regretted that he loved her far too much. Many times was it past noon before he rose from her side: he was happy, without thought for the grief he might cause others.

Erec and Enide reject the society which had welcomed them with Joy and had honoured them with gifts and the ringing of church bells. When, by their self-indulgence they have turned this Joy of the Court to grief, Enide, as we have seen, wakens Erec to the need to purge this recreancy through exile and adventure. Their passion, unlike that of Tristan and Yseut, will change and develop with experience, and will re-establish the Joy of the Court which it had threatened.

At the outset of their quest Erec treats Enide harshly,[13] as a possession, a falcon to be trained to obedience, a prize to be staked and won in combat, as he had won her before at the Contest of the Sparrow Hawk. He has no idea, at this stage, of a shared adventure, of a joint need for redemption. He has no sympathy for Enide, and orders her to keep silent. She is exposed as a lure to predators, along with the horses of the knights he defeats, which he orders her to lead and control as she rides in silence in front of him. He rejects her attempt to warn him of danger and so to share in the adventure:

Erec respont: 'Mar le pansastes[14]
Quant ma parole trespassastes,
Ce que defandu vos avoie.
Et ne porquant tres bien savoie
Que vos gueires ne me prisiez.
C'est servises mal anploiiez;
Que je ne vos an sai nul gre,
Ainz sachiez que plus vos an he.
Dit le vos ai, et di ancore.'
(2997–3005)

Erec replies: 'A curse be on you for thinking you could go against my word and do what I had forbidden you to do. And yet I knew very well you had little respect for me. This is an ill service you do me, and I thank you in no way for it. On the contrary, I hate you the more for this; know this well. I have told you this and I will tell it you again.'

There are two sides to Erec's behaviour. One is harsh anger, the other is the rational control which disciplines the impulsive word. Enide possesses *savoir* but not the experience or *sciance* which would teach her to use it, and she failed in her role as *dame* when she was upset by the scandalmongers and repeated their slander. This theme of the Spoken Word which may bring grief or happiness to the individual and the community, will be used again in more complex form in *Perceval*. Beneath his rage Erec is schooling Enide, as he later admits, in the mental control which checks impulsive response. He is ordering Enide to detach herself from his adventure and show trust in his prowess by her silence when danger approaches:

'Ancor le vos pardonrai ore,	'Once more I will pardon you,
Mes autre foiz vos an gardez,	take care not to do this again.
Ne ja vers moi ne regardez;	Do not look at me, ever, for that
Que vos feriiez mout que fole.	would be to act like a fool. I do
Je n'aim mie vostre parole.'	not care to hear any word spoken
(3006–10)	by you.'

As we shall see, Enide persists with her role in the adventure, and she changes its character. Conversely, as Erec proves his prowess, and realises the value of Enide's help, his anger abates and he accepts her as a partner. His opponents change from rapacious knights to the noble Guivret, and the two lovers are welcomed into Arthur's court which symbolically comes to meet them.

Erec's refusal, contrary to Enide's wishes, to stay longer than one night at court, may be the relic of a Celtic *geis*,[15] but on the plane of the *sen* of the story, Erec for the first time shows real *savoir* in his sense of purpose and moral courage. As Yvain refuses to stay comfortably in the castle of Noroison, Erec now takes his critical decision, and begins his new quest of self-discovery and expansion. The values of Arthur's court are not for him; to regain his *premier los* is not enough. He has been recreant in the outside world, in his father's land where he is destined to rule, and it is in the outside world that he must endure, and attain the ultimate adventure.

Erec's decision to leave Arthur's court marks the beginning of his new self. He is no longer self-absorbed, indifferent to others, passive towards the prospect of adventure, standing aside from the Hunt of the White Stag, riding behind Enide and inviting attack from rapacious knights. Henceforward, his deeds will not be accomplished in routine fashion, in conformity with an ethic of prowess which is based on self-esteem and a desire to regain his *premier los*. They will be devoted to a higher purpose, to the active need to bring help to others, to blend courage with the *caritas* of chivalry. Prowess will serve the *bien*, the well-being, of society.

Erec's desperate combat with the Two Giants, who are symbols of outrageous violence, brings joy to the damsel and to the tormented knight he has saved who sees him as a messenger sent by God (4475–7). Enide's moral victory over the lustful Count of Limors, which will be discussed later, convinces Erec of the wholeness of their mutual love. He shares his horse with Enide as they leave Limors: 'And Erec, who bears his wife away, embraces and kisses and comforts her, holds her in his arms, tightly against his breast, and says: "My sweet sister, I have indeed tested you in all ways. Fear no more, for I love you now more than I have ever done before, and I am certain and sure within myself that you love me with perfect love. Now, from this moment, do I wish to be, as I was before, completely at your command (4917–28)."'

But Erec's love, like his prowess, cannot remain as it was before. It is part of their new selves and with these it will be deepened and enriched. The trial of their new roles breaks abruptly upon them. A thousand knights and men-at-arms come riding in battle array along the moonlit path towards them. Erec, almost mortally wounded, thinks for the first time of Enide's *bien*:

Desçandre fet jus del cheval	He makes Enide dismount from
Enide delez une haie.	the horse, beside a hedge. He
N'est pas mervoille s'il s'esmaie:	has every right to be afraid:
'Remenez ci, dame!' fet il,	'Remain here, my lady', he says,
'Un petit delez cest sevil	'a little to the side of this path,
Tant que cez janz trespassé soient.	until these people have passed.
Je n'ai cure que il vos voient;	I do not wish them to see you . . .
Droit a l'ancontre aler lor vuel,	I will go straight ahead to meet
Et vos soiiez ci tote coie.	them. You, I beg, keep absolutely
Gardez que ja nus ne vos voie.'	quiet here and take care not to
(4974–80 and 4994–6)	be seen by any one of them.'

34

The theme of Enide as a prize for combat, which began symbolically with the Contest of the Sparrow Hawk, is now over. Erec, wounded but undaunted, is protective, loving and kind towards her, and when, in this episode, he is defeated by Guivret, he accepts the humiliation with composure. This is a major stage in his development.[16] He has moved beyond the stage of combat for *vaine gloire*, of prowess regained, and especially beyond the unthinking folly of Guivret, who marching loyally to rescue him from the Count of Limors, attacks him with uncontrolled violence, because he happens to be there, on the same moonlit path. The scarcely perceptible irony with which Chrétien treats this incident is a presage of his condemnation of aimless knightly violence in his later works. However, Guivret, the knight of good repute, makes amends. He offers hospitality to the married lovers, and, when Erec's wounds are healed, he and a splendid company escort them to the ultimate adventure of the Joy of the Court.

As Erec is about to enter this contest, which balances his combat with Yder, his understanding with Enide is complete:

Et cil vers Enide se beisse,	And he bends down to Enide who
Qui delez lui grant doel feisoit	was by his side, grieving deeply,
Ne porquant s'ele se teisoit;	but yet silent, for grief spoken
Car diaus, que l'an face de boche,	by the lips amounts to nothing
Ne monte rien, s'au cuer n'atoche.	unless it touches the heart.
(5828–32)	

Erec is tender, sympathetic, reassuring:

Et cil qui bien conut son cuer,	And he, knowing well the secret
Li a dit: 'Bele douce suer,	of her heart, said: 'Fair, sweet
Jantis dame leaus et sage,	sister, noble lady, true and wise,
Je conois tot vostre corage.	well do I know all that you feel.
Grant peor avez, bien le voi,	Your fear is great. I see this
Si ne savez ancor por quoi;	well, and as yet you have no
Mes por neant vos esmaiiez . . .'	reason for this. But there is no
(5833–9)	need for you to fear. . .'

In this scene, which binds up the disastrous scene in the bedroom, Erec and Enide have overcome their former selves. Enide represses her words of grief and fear, for which there is no need, since Erec, removed from his shell of self-centred indifference, understands her heart, and calls her wise. Erec's conquest of his former insouciant self is also symbolised in his defeat of Mabonagrain, the giant knight who is tyrannised by sensual love. Erec fights him, as he had fought Yder, and on each occasion a woman, or her reputation for beauty, is at stake. But when Erec chides Mabonagrain for speaking folie (5920) he is fighting symbolically to assert the primacy of savoir, of disciplined thought and rational behaviour, and as we may see when we come to look at the Joy of the Court episode, the supremacy of a sense of order and joy over mindless self-interest and its attendant violence and un-happiness.

Erec shows his new-found fitness for royal responsibility when he is summoned to the throne of his father King Lac. He gives alms and clothes to the needy, he helps poor clerics and through his charity

> Mout fist grant bien por Deu a toz. (6540)

He shows the sovereign quality of mout grant savoir (6544) when, humble and controlled, he asks Arthur to crown him. And as we may see later, the theme of savoir, of wholeness and of order, is finally bound up in the symbolism of his sceptre and coronation cloak.

Erec, the young and innocent knight, drifting, unsure of himself, though possessed of innate savoir, touches the reader with his slightly obtuse candour, his courage and innate gentleness, but it is Enide who dominates the romance, as Fenice dominates Cliges. Enide, as a damsel or pucele, is at first submissive, when she is won and instructed and tested by Erec, but, as the romance progresses, their roles are reversed. Enide, as a dame, begins to instruct Erec, though unobtrusively, and so becomes the epitome of active savoir and of constructive, selfless love within marriage.

Enide enters the romance in a state of untutored inno-cence, sheltered from the world by her father, almost as much, but not as harshly, as Perceval will be sealed off from life by his mother. Her great gift, in addition to her noble birth, and beauty (422–3), her hair lighter and fairer than that of Iseuz la blonde (424), is her savoir, the power of reasoned thought, the wisdom of heart and mind:

36

Mout est bele, mes miauz assez	Great is her beauty, but yet far
Vaut ses savoirs que sa biautez.	greater in value than beauty is
Onques Deus ne fist rien tant sage	her wisdom. Never did God
Ne qui tant fust de franc corage.	make anyone so wise, so full of
(537–40)	fine thoughts and feeling.

The world of Laluth, in which she lives, lacks this quality of *savoir*. It esteems outward show, the appearance of beauty and prowess. It acclaims Erec as immoderately as it had welcomed Yder. This city of bustling streets, real houses, and crowded tourneys, is an allegory of a world which has no sense of joy based on order, no sense of moral values, of the rational control and understanding of what is right and necessary to create this order. This lack of *savoir* is epitomised in the ruler of the city, the count who controls his subjects by threats of personal violence (801–4), who allows his sister and her husband, Enide's parents, to live in poverty, who thinks of bestowing a dowry on his niece, betrothed to the son of a king, only when his daughter, not without a touch of patronage towards Enide, urges him to do so. It is not chance, but an assertion of Erec's latent *savoir* and of respect for the poverty of Enide's parents which leads him to refuse rich garments, on Enide's behalf, and to finally turn aside, almost peremptorily, the insistent invitation of the count to leave the modest house of Enide's father and stay at court. In this dialogue, Erec reproaches the count's complacent platitudes, his lack of generosity and ill-concealed contempt for the status of Enide and her family:

Erec respont: 'Ne vos enuit!	Erec replies: 'And it may not vex
Ne leisserai mon oste anuit,	you, I will not leave my host
Qui mout m'a grant enor portee,	tonight, for he has shown me
Quant il sa fille m'a donee.	very great honour in giving me
Qu'an dites vos, sire? N'est dons	his daughter. And what, my lord,
Mout biaus et mout riches li dons?'	do you then say of this? Is this
'Oïl voir, sire!' fet li cuens;	gift not very fine and precious?'
'Mout est li dons et biaus et buens.	– 'Yes, in truth, my lord', says
La pucele est et bele et sage,	the count,' this gift is fine and
Et si est mout de haut parage:	good. The maiden is beautiful
Sachiez que sa mere est ma suer.	and wise and is also of very high
Certes mout en ai lié le cuer,	birth. You should know that her
Quant vos ma niece avoir deigniez.	mother is my sister. Be assured
Ancor vos pri que vos veigniez	that my heart is well content
A moi herbergier anuit mes.'	that you have deigned to accept

Erec respont: 'Leissiez m'an pes!
Nel feroie an nule meniere.'

(1269–85)

my niece. I beg you again to
come and stay with me tonight.'
Erec replies: 'Leave me in peace!
I would not act so under any
circumstances.'

Enide, when we first meet her, wears simple, ragged clothes, but she is well trained in manners and, at her father's bidding, offers Erec hospitable welcome, leading him upstairs to repose on beds in the main room. With equal willingness, again at her father's order, she has just groomed and fed Erec's horse:

La pucele prant le cheval,
Si li deslace le peitral,
Le frain et la sele li oste.
Or a li chevaus mout buen oste:
Mout bien et bel s'an antremet.
El chief un chevoistre li met,
Bien le torche, estrille et conroie,
A la mangeoire le loie
Et si li met fain et avainne
Devant assez, novele et sainne.

(459–68)

The damsel takes the horse, unties its breast strap and removes the bridle and saddle. Now the horse has someone who knows how to care for it. Skilfully she sets herself to the task. She puts a head-stall on it, and well does she curry-comb it, wipe it and rub it down. She leads it to the manger and places before it a feed of fresh and wholesome hay and oats.

Enide has qualities which Erec lacks, the *sapientia* which in far different circumstances Oliver offers to Roland.[17] As her sense of humility and freedom from *voluntas propria*, or self-will, are matched against the trials of life, her character and innate *savoir* begin to develop in a way which is totally opposed to the concept of a love that can be won and dominated by knightly combat. For Chrétien, who speaks through Enide, love and prowess must be selfless, and when this ideal is achieved, as it will be by Erec and Enide at the castle of Limors, love will then inspire prowess and no longer be in conflict with it. As Enide's character asserts itself and influences Erec, the idea of a love which takes its quality from prowess won by knightly violence gives way to the principle of a willing partnership of equal rights and service, which Enide, in the adventure of the Joy of the Court, will recommend to her cousin, the mistress of Mabonagrain.

Enide's wooing by Erec has a Celtic fairy-tale quality.

Touched by her beauty, he asks for her hand: 'I am the son of a rich and mighty king. My father is called King Lac. The Bretons call me Erec. I belonged to the court of Arthur, and stayed there a good three years. . . . I promise that if you equip me with arms and give me your daughter so that I may win the Sparrow Hawk tomorrow, I will take her to my land, if God grants me victory, and I will have her crowned and she will be the queen of three cities' (650–65). And the father grants her forthwith:

> 'Tenez', fet il, 'je la vos doing.'   (678)

In this first trial Enide acts as Erec's squire and servant. She arms him 'without pronouncing any spell or charm'[18] (710) and hastens to mount her palfrey, with its poor accoutrements. As they ride through the bustling throng, followed only by Enide's parents, the people wonder at their beauty, but follow their established favourites, Yder and his mistress, to the tourney.

In spite of her latent *savoir*, Enide has, at this moment, no understanding of what is happening to her. She is carried along by life even more than Erec was at the Hunt of the White Stag. After his victory over Yder, it is Erec who makes the decisions. He refuses fine clothes for her, so that she may receive her robe from the Queen, and, destined to royalty herself, receive with it some aura of royalty from Guenevere. Enide is overwhelmed by the admiration of Arthur's court:

Quant la bele pucele estrange	When the fair damsel from a
Vit toz les chevaliers an range,	strange and distant land saw all
Qui l'esgardoient a estal,	the array of knights staring at
Son chief ancline contre val,	her without respite, she bows
Vergoingne an ot, ne fu mervoille,	her head low, a sense of shame
La face l'an devint vermoille;	came over her, and this was no
Mes la honte si li avint	wonder. Her face turned scarlet,
Que plus bele assez an devint.	but this shame became her so
(1751–8)	well that her beauty was greatly
	enhanced.

When Enide is acclaimed as the ideal of beauty, and receives from Arthur the traditional kiss, and his declaration of love and courtly service (1822–40), the *premerains vers* of the romance is ended (1844), the fairy tale is complete.

Enide is at the summit of a success, which she has done little to deserve. The formal approval of her beauty, which Erec won for her with the sparrow hawk, is repeated and reinforced by the unconditional praise of Arthur's court. The Joy of the Court which was disturbed by Yder is restored since Yder and his mistress now share in its life. Possible strife about the choice of the most beautiful damsel has been avoided by the advent of Enide.

But for the lovers there is no lasting joy. When Enide weds, her name is revealed. She has a social identity[19] which, together with that of Erec, will be tested in the lands of King Lac by a society which hopes to see in them a future king and queen. When Erec fails this test, Enide, acting from natural feeling, breaks with convention, and tells her husband of his lost reputation. She heeds the slanderers, the losengier, and forces Erec to act. In troubadour terms, she speaks churlish truth (vertat vilana) instead of courtly pretence (cortez'ufana). In a similar way will Perceval be rocked out of his self-centredness when he meets his cousin after leaving the castle of the Fisher King.

Enide, as we have seen, rejects Erec's attempt to revert to their earlier relationship. She will no longer be the supreme beauty for whom he fights and wins fame. She insists on playing a full part in their quest, and, in so doing, changes and widens its character. In her humility she regrets her arrogance in appearing to doubt Erec's prowess and for this she wishes to make amends. She insists on warning him of danger, and, after the day's fighting, she rejects his orders: 'Erec orders the lady to sleep, and he will stay on watch. She will not do this: It is not just (droiz). Since he is in greater pain, he must sleep. Erec granted this, and it pleased him to do so. He put his shield under his head and the lady takes her cloak and spreads it over him from head to toe. He slept and she stayed awake (cil dormi, et cele vella). Not once did she fall asleep that night' (3090–100).

The words cil dormi, et cele vella (3099) 'he slept and she stayed awake', with which Chrétien refers back to the bedroom scene, still have their figurative meaning. Enide was mentally awake at their moment of crisis, but uncertain of Erec's reactions and of the remedy for their plight. She now examines herself and looks back with humility and guilt to

her earlier pride and arrogance (3108–12). She offers
practical help, and is about to save Erec's life in a situation
which is outside his power to control. Erec still 'sleeps'. He
is unaware of any moral weakness within him, of any failing
towards her. He treats her with scorn as he drives on, as if
impelled by a *geis*, with the knightly task of regaining his
lost prowess. Erec seeks rehabilitation through courage and
skill in combat. He is sure of success because like Tristan he
trusts in his invincibility. He does not suspect a view of life
in which prowess and fighting are ends in themselves until
Enide and he are faced with lust masquerading in courtly
attire.

The local count, a lover of beauty, visits them in their
lodging in a neighbouring town. He obtains Erec's permission to speak with Enide, and, in courtly fashion, presses
his suit. 'She cannot love a knight who inflicts such harsh
living on her' (3316–33). He offers her marriage, a more
comfortable life. He becomes urgent,[20] and, as in a *pastourelle*,
turns to threats, when Enide, like Beroul's Yseut, prefers
to die in flaming thorns rather than think of treachery or
deceit (3336–41). Although marriage is offered, this is the
only situation involving a declaration of 'courtly love' in
the romance, and it is noteworthy that this plea to the
married lady to accept a lover is shown, as in the *Equitan* of
Marie de France, to be self-seeking and treacherous. The
courtly veneer here, as in *Equitan*, is hypocritical, a false
courtoisie which seeks to disrupt a love in which the partners
are suited to one another according to *mesure* 'the essential
fitness of things'.

When the count threatens to kill Erec, and to break
Enide's pride with shame and insult, she dissembles: 'I was
testing your love. If you kill my husband openly here, you
will be blamed and my reputation will suffer. Send your
knights and soldiers tomorrow in the morning, to seize me
and slay my husband when he defends me. I have led this
sort of life too long. I no longer desire my husband's
company. I would like to feel you, as we lie naked in a bed.
I assure you of my love' (3360–401). Enide also ensures a
safe night of sleep for Erec by demanding the count's word
of honour on this bargain. Again she keeps vigil: (*tote la
nuit vellier l'estuet*, 3455). Before daybreak she reveals her plot

to Erec, and they escape, but not before Erec has slain the count who pursues them too hotly.

In this episode the roles of the lovers are reversed. Erec is the pawn and Enide takes over the function he had claimed of deflecting attacks against her. Enide not only shares the adventure, but by using her wits (*savoir*) to understand and defeat the enemy, she shapes and develops it. She is also supporting Erec as the lion will support Yvain, and this analogy becomes very close after the fight with the Two Giants when, believing that Erec, who has fallen from his saddle, is dead, she suffers for love of him as the lion will suffer for Yvain. Blaming herself for speaking the original fateful word, she draws Erec's sword in order to kill herself (4670). With Erec's head on her knees, she laments his death in the style of the epic or the Provençal *planh*: 'Beauty was mirrored in you, Prowess had proved itself in you. Wisdom (*savoirs*) had given you its heart. Generosity had crowned you.' She bears the guilt for his death. She faints, recovers. She must avenge her crime, on herself. In extreme distress, she is stopped in her intention by a count and his retinue of knights, and is led away, with Erec's 'corpse' carried on a bier, to the castle of Limors (4635–719).

Here, isolated, threatened and struck by the lustful count, who wants her for wife, she expresses absolute love for Erec whom she believes to be dead, as earlier, secure and surrounded with comfort in the bedchamber, she had admired Erec's naked body, but had doubted him and her part in his life. This test of seduction is more severe than the first, which prefigures it, because, believing Erec dead, she cannot outwit the Count of Limors and escape once more at dawn with her husband. Faith must support *savoir*. Her love for Erec is now as complete and unselfish as that of the lion for Yvain, and when she resists attack she defends this love and her own integrity of purpose. Like Yseut and Fenice she proves her constancy in love against physical violence. She resists the blows of this count who is maddened by possessive lust:

'Ha! fel', fet ele, 'ne me chaut 'You wretch, I scorn your words
Que tu me dies ne ne faces!   and deeds. I do not fear your
Ne criem tes cos ne tes menaces. blows or threats. Beat me, strike

Assez me bat, assez me fier !   me. I shall never think you so
Ja tant ne te troverai fier   fierce that I will do any more
Que por toi face plus ne mains,   or any less for you, even if now
Se tu or androit a tes mains   with your own hands you were
Me devoies les iauz sachier   to pull out my eyes or flay me
Ou trestote vive escorchier.'   alive.'
          (4844–52)

Her defiant words rouse Erec, as her tears had done in the bedchamber. 'Bemused and amazed – and no wonder' (4856), he rises from the bier, slays the count, scares and harries his followers who flee in panic before the devil which they believe has entered Erec's corpse. Enide seizes Erec's lance (4888) and joins in the fray, which, with burlesque humour, offers relief to the previous episode of Enide's sufferings and to the ensuing romantic scene in which the lovers ride away from Limors, in the moonlight, on the same horse. With this accord, the testing of Enide's love which began in the bedchamber is now over. The 'false' death of Erec inspires her to express absolute love as that of Yvain and Lancelot will inspire the lion and Guenevere. In ultimate adversity Enide has proved her constancy, and her feeling of guilt is removed when Erec, in feudal form, offers forgiveness for the word she spoke against him:

'Tot a vostre comandemant   'Henceforth I wish to be entirely
Vuel estre des or an avant,   submissive to your command,
Aussi con j'estoie devant.   as I was before. And if you have
Et se vos rien m'avez mesdite,   done me injury by what you have
Jel vos pardoing tot et claim quite said, I give you complete pardon
Del forfet et de la parole.'   and have no further claim against
          (4926–31)   you for this misdeed and the
                            word that was spoken.'

Enide and Erec have found wholeness in love, and mutual trust. And so they actively share the next adventure in which Erec, weak from his wounds, is unseated by Guivret. Enide leaps to his aid, seizes the reins of Guivret's charger:

'Chevaliers, maudiz soies tu !   'Sir knight, a curse upon you
Qu' un home seul et sanz vertu, for attacking a lone man, weak
Doillant et pres navré a mort,   and in pain, almost dying of
As anvaï a si grant tort   wounds; and for acting so
Que tu ne sez dire por quoi.'   wrongly, in that you can give
          (5029–33)   no reason for this deed.'

43

Enide supports Erec with her moral courage, as the lion, with his strength and bravery, will help Yvain. And more than this, she speaks against purposeless violence committed in the name of prowess. In so doing, she speaks for Chrétien, as, in more clearly expository style, she will do when she condemns socially disruptive, self-indulgent love in the Joy of the Court adventure. Enide has been tested in love and constancy, as Lancelot will be on his journey to the Sword Bridge. Her lapse into 'folly' has been redeemed, and she is now the symbol of *savoir*, or moral courage, and happiness through order, as Erec is the personification of prowess and courage applied to virtuous ends. Erec and Enide mark the end of their quest of mutual self-discovery, and of the linear development of their interdependent characters, by once more sharing their bed, each striving to please the other with joy in their new selves:

Or fu acolee et beisïee,
Or fu de toz biens aeisïee,
Or ot sa joie et son delit;
Que nu a nu sont an un lit
Et li uns l'autre acole et beise;
N'est riens nule qui tant lor pleise.
(5245–50)

Now was she embraced and kissed and provided with all happiness. Now did she have her joy and her delight, for naked together they lie in one bed and embrace and kiss each other. Nothing else has such pleasure for them.

With this reunion, the theme of their estrangement, which began and now ends in bed, is bound up. Erec and Enide have been tested in turn, and Chrétien turns his attention from the evolution of their characters, and the linear unthreading of his *sen* on the individual level, to the two major episodes which are the culmination of the romance, the widespread branching out and burgeoning of the tree which has grown. These two episodes, the Joy of the Court and the Coronation, demonstrate the wider practical value of the wisdom and moral qualities which Erec and Enide have discovered, and the joy and sense of order which these qualities will bestow on their society and kingdom. Within the framework of Chrétien's *conjointure*, these episodes have the common purpose of defining and binding up the major themes of the romance. The binding-up of the *sen* is accomplished through a continuation of the linear method of analogy and contrast, as in the implied

44

comparison between Yder and Mabonagrain, whom he prefigures, and in the contrast between the humiliation of
Erec at the Hunt of the White Stag, and his fight on behalf
of the community in the adventure of the Joy of the Court.
The defining of the *sen* is achieved through the lateral or
expository method which is apparent in Enide's advice to
her cousin and in the ceremonial and intention of the
Coronation. In these scenes we may also detect glimpses of
the subtle and enigmatic use of imagery which, in the later
romances, will develop into the rich allusiveness of the
Cart, the Lion and the Grail.

In background and presentation the two episodes are
different. The setting of the Joy of the Court is allegorical,
veiled with the Celtic mystery inherent in the Wall of Air,
the heads set on pikes and the horn which the victor must
sound;[21] that of the Coronation, despite its symbolic
imagery, is concerned with the reality of this world, possibly
even with events in the reign of Henry II Plantagenet (see
p. 58). In the Joy of the Court, Chrétien lifts the imagination, so that it may admire the heights of courage, self-
sacrifice and devotion in love; in the Coronation scene he
presents the benefits and happiness granted by government
which is wise, splendid and just.

The adventure of the Joy of the Court takes place at
Brandigan, the island realm and castle of King Evrain, impregnable, rich and fertile in fruit and corn and wine, but
beset symbolically by deep, tumultuous waters (5373–5).
The court and town are condemned to grief by an adventure
from which no knight returns alive, the Joy of the Court
which Erec recognises as his ultimate task. He attempts to
still Guivret's fears for his safety:

'Deus, an joie n'a se bien non!'	'In God's name! In joy there is
Fet Erec; 'ce vois je querant.	nought but good, and that is
Ja ne m'alez desesperant,	what I seek. There is no need to
Biaus douz amis, de ce ne d'el,	despair on my behalf, fair friend,
Mes feisons prandre nostre ostel;	in this or any other matter.
Que granz biens nos an puet venir.	Let us take lodgings, for great
Riens ne me porroit retenir	goodness can come from this
Que je n'aille querre la joie.'	adventure. No one could restrain
(5466–73)	me from the quest for this joy.'

Por ce fet bien qui son estuide
Atorne a bien . . .

said Chrétien in his Prologue (4–5), and it is this *bien*, the goodness, which the new Erec sees can be found in life and which he seeks as his destined role. Erec gathers heartfelt admiration for his good looks from knights, ladies and damsels, and prayers that God may save him from death. King Evrain welcomes him as a *cuens ou rois* (5546) and the repetition of this phrase from the bedroom scene (2502) is not fortuitous. Erec's reputation is now secure, and this appears in his confident manner. Unlike Perceval, he does not hesitate to speak the word which will unlock the way to his greatest adventure: 'My lord, I must tell you my reason for coming here. I can conceal this no longer. I ask for the Joy of the Court and desire nothing so much. Grant me this adventure, whatever it may be, if this lies in your power' (5599–607).

The King grants the boon with prophetic words:

'Se vos a joie an espleitiez,
Conquise avroiz si grant enor
Qu'onques hon ne conquist greignor,
Et Deus, si con je le desir,
Vos an doit a joie partir.'
(5664–8)

'If you accomplish your deeds with joy, you will have won greater honour than any man ever won before. And may God, as I desire he may, grant that you may come out of this with joy.'

Erec will now fight as the champion of King Evrain, who gives him arms, and of the people, great and small, who go with him to the adventure:

A l'esmovoir a mout grant noise
Et grant bruit par totes les rues;
Car les granz janz et les menues
Disoient tuit: 'Hai! hai!
Chevaliers, joie t'a traï,
Cele que tu cuides conquerre;
Mes ton duel et ta mort vas querre.'
Et n'i a un seul qui ne die:
'Ceste joie, Deus la maudie!
Que tant prodome i sont ocis.'
(5702–11)

As they set out, a great tumult and uproar rises in the streets, for all, great and small, say: 'Alas! Alas! Sir Knight, Joy has betrayed you, this very Joy which you imagine you can win. But you are going to seek your grief and your death.' Not one single person but says: 'May God curse this Joy, for which so many excellent men have been slain.'

These ambivalent undertones continue as Erec, puzzled by this grief and fear, comes to an orchard enclosed by a wall of air, with but one entrance. This is an orchard of abundance, of spices and herbal remedies, of perpetual flowers and ripe fruits. These fruits may be eaten within the garden, but anyone seeking to carry them away will not find the exit until the fruits are replaced on the tree (5739–54). On the plane of Byzantine wonder, this orchard is the type of exotic, magic garden which becomes a common-place of medieval romance.[22] On the Celtic plane, the wall of mist is one of the entrances to the Other World, and this island of fertility, sealed by a magic spell from the world outside (5742), resembles the Celtic islands of abundance and eternal youth.[23] On the courtly plane, the orchard is an allegory of the *biens*, the joy and happiness which is the aim of courtly man, but which is exiled from his society by the vices of self-interest and violence.

As Erec, with lance at rest, enters the orchard with his companions, he rejoices in its promise of happiness:

Qui mout se delitoit el chant	for great was his delight
Des oisiaus qui leanz chantoient;	in the song of the birds
Sa joie li represantoient,	which were singing there and
La chose a quoi il plus beoit.	offered him his Joy, the very
(5770–3)	thing to which he most aspired.

Abruptly he sees the Death which the Quest for Joy offers, the heads of defeated knights impaled on stakes. One stake alone is vacant, save for a horn which Erec, if victorious, must sound so that all may come to do him honour.[24]

Erec rides on, borne along by the love 'which makes him fear no man in battle' (5855–62). On a splendid bed of cloth of gold, under a sycamore tree, he comes upon a damsel, and, in courtly fashion, sits with her in converse. Although the damsel, in knightly and Celtic terms, is the lure for combat,[25] Erec will not fight, as Yvain will, to possess the damsel and her 'territory'. The new Erec fights to restore the orchard, and hence the allegory of happiness and fecundity, to society, and to free the knight, who now challenges him, as he had freed Yder, from the *folie* of sensual love which displaces *savoir*, from the enchantment of the damsel who commands him entirely.

The defeated knight tells his story: 'I am the nephew of King Evrain. This damsel and I loved each other from childhood. I granted her any boon for which she might ask[26] . . . she said, when I was knighted in this orchard by King Evrain, I should not leave this place until a knight should come who would defeat me in combat. I would not be untrue to my word, which I should not have given' (6052–81). He epitomises knighthood enslaved by love and misapplied to useless ends. Refusing to be churlish and unfaithful, he would not seek escape through defeat. Unwillingly he has gone the round of proving his prowess, until Erec sets him free and restores him to Joy:

'Mout avez an grant joie mise	'You have given great joy to
La cort mon oncle et mes amis,	the court of my uncle and my
Qu'or serai fors de ceanz mis;	friends, for now I shall be free
Et por ce que joie an avront	to go into the world. And
Tuit cil qui a la cort seront,	because all who come to this
"Joie de la cort" l'apeloient	court will receive joy from it,
Cil qui la joie an atandoient.'	those who were expecting to
(6118–24)	to find joy here called it the
	Joy of the Court.'

The contrast between the knightly purpose of Erec and Mabonagrain's lack of purpose is balanced by the contrast between the loves which inspired them, the love of Erec for Enide and the enthralment of Mabonagrain by his mistress. She is repelled by the Joy which Erec has restored to Mabonagrain and to the court. Enide, and the damsels and ladies of the court, *por amor et por conpeignie* (6212), seek to comfort her, and when Enide reveals that she is the niece of the Count of Laluth and the damsel's cousin, 'her heart stops for the happiness she feels, and she can no longer conceal her joy' (6246–57).

When the two women speak of their loves, Enide praises the quest for mutual love in a marriage approved by society. Her monologue is an exposition of the two contrasting types of love, and the two ways of thought and life in the romance, the one wilful, self-indulgent, anti-social, sterile in good works and even destructive, the other ruled by *savoir*, mutual humility and care, subjected by the condition of marriage to harsh experience which brings Joy to the individual and to society.

The *Joie de la Cour* is now celebrated in its literal sense of the courtly Joy of the *vergier d'amour* of Guillaume de Lorris, of happiness as a way of life which is individual and shared:

Mabonagrains grant joie fet	Mabonagrain brings great joy to
D'Enide, et ele aussi de lui.	Enide, and she also to him. For
Erec et Guivrez anbedui	their part, Erec and Guivret
Refont joie de la pucele.	bring joy to the damsel. They
Grant joie font et cil et cele,	celebrate great joy, and kiss and
Si s'antrebeisent et acolent.	embrace one another.
(6352–7)	

Erec sounds the victory horn and summons all the people to the Joy of the Court, for which the ladies have composed le lai de joie (6188). The celebration of Joy, accompanied by all possible manner of harmony (6384–5), lasts for three days. The harmony is not limited to music and song. It belongs to the mind, and, spreading from the personal happiness of Erec and Enide to the Joy of Evrain's court, it will be carried to the world outside, and so to the court of Arthur which is in sorry plight: 'on the day before (the arrival of Erec and Enide and Guivret) the king had been bled, privately in his rooms. Together with him there were only five hundred barons of his household. Never before at any season was the King to be found in such solitude, and he was sorely troubled by the lack of people at his court'[27] (6416–23).

Erec and Enide and Guivret now have the gift of bestowing Joy on others, and the mark of this Joy, as at Evrain's court, is the exchange of courtly embraces and kisses and mutual delight (6459–69). And so Joy is brought to Arthur and Guenevere, and to their court.

The Joy of the Court in Erec et Enide[28] has a literal and an allegorical significance. It is, at one particular court, a tangible delight in a communal happiness in which each individual feels joy within, and a desire to share this with others.[29] Any court with this sense of joy will be well attended. The court without it, as we have seen from Arthur's court, will be desolate, the king will fall sick, and knights and ladies will remain absent. Erec and Enide, Guivret, Mabonagrain and his mistress, now feel this positive joy and, wishing to share it, they bring Arthur and his ailing court back to life. On a wider plane, this Joy of the Court is an allegory of the personal and social happiness which is granted by the courtly virtues and tarnished by the courtly vices. The pursuit of Joy, especially in the first half of the twelfth century, appears to have been a principal aim of the courtly ethic, more important than and at times even separate from the pursuit of Love. We find this ideal of supreme, intangible happiness in the poetry of the earliest known troubadours, who were all linked with the court of Poitiers and with Aquitaine: Guilhem IX, Jaufre Rudel, and Marcabru.[30]

Marcabru's recipe for happiness, for the individual and society, was Roman in its logic and principles. Avoid disruptive self-indulgence. Through mental control and *mesura* create order and mental serenity within yourself. *Mesura*, which in later troubadours such as Peire d'Alvernhe is referred to as *sabers*, is the ability to order one's actions according to one's talents and temperament, and one's position and responsibilities in society. The man who guides his life in this way, says Marcabru, will possess *cortesia*, which is the sum total of the courtly virtues and the way in which they are expressed in society. These virtues are generosity of mind and spirit (*Jovens* 'Youth'), an active search for happiness (*Jois*), the ability to distinguish between right and wrong, true or false (*Conoissensa*), the regard for the personal courtly virtue within oneself (*Valors*), the desire for reputation in society (*Pretz*). A man with these qualities will love with *Fin'Amors*, in which the mind controls sensual desire and channels it into spiritual as well as physical aspiration. He will avoid the undisciplined love of the senses, the 'foolish burden' of unformulated desires which disturb the happiness of individuals and of society. He will live *letz, cortes e sapiens*; *letz* 'happy', because of the order within him, *cortes*, because he nurtures and is guided by the courtly virtues, *sapiens* because he thinks positively about his way of life, and so determines the path he will follow.

For Marcabru, actions which spring from spontaneous feelings are classed as folly or *foudatz*, and must be excluded from the ordered way of life. But in the second half of the twelfth century, and at about the time that Chrétien was writing *Erec et Enide*, other troubadours proclaimed the virtue of folly in the sense of obedience to the impulsive desire which springs from the joy within. Of these, the most famous was Bernart de Ventadorn, whom Chrétien may have known personally and with whose ideas he appears to have disagreed in the poem *D'Amors qui m'a tolu a moi*, which we shall discuss later (p. 68).

Other troubadours followed Marcabru in rejecting the tyranny of mindless desires. Such were Raimbaut d'Aurenga and Peire d'Alvernhe who were both composing about 1170. Joy for Raimbaut lay in the mentally active quest for happiness and the rejection of *flacs volers* or unformulated sensual longings. For Peire d'Alvernhe, a disciple of Marcabru, Joy proceeds directly from *sabers*, the rational power that he applies to his life and which appears to have the importance for Peire that *mesura* had for Marcabru. For Peire it is the wisdom of *sabers* alone which guarantees poetic and courtly success, and the happiness of a serene mind. From *sabers* comes Jois with all its good results:

Deiosta·ls breus iorns e·ls loncs sers, qan la blanc' aura brunezis, vuoill que branc e bruoill mos sabers d'un nou ioi qe·m fruich' e·m floris.[31]
(VII, 1–4)

At the approach of the short days and the long evenings when the white air grows dark, I want my wisdom to branch and bud with a new joy which bears fruit and blossoms for me.

Joy in this context is a rational, positive attitude to life and a belief that happiness is to be found through what Peire d'Alvernhe calls *sabers* and Chrétien calls *savoir*. Peire rejoices in the courtly accomplishments of his lady, her high social reputation and the supreme Joy of the Court which she offers (VII, 42–9). But Peire, as Chrétien will do in his later romances, reaches the point where he turns his back on the joy of this world, of the lady and the court, and seeks in its place the joy which comes from love of God. He and many major troubadours[32] refuse, like Chrétien, to see the courtly ethic as a self-contained set of values centred in the lady and the happiness and reputation which she and the court may bestow. For Peire, such adherence to courtly ideas, expressed in 'clear' language on the single plane of the senses is 'fragmented' or *fraich*, in contrast with his own poetry which is 'whole' or *entiers*, rounded by the discipline of the courtly virtues of *Jovens, Jois* and *Mesura*, and complete, *complitz*, when it is enriched with overtones of higher meaning, or interwoven with some moral or Christian truth.[33]

It is in the context of such controversy about reason and feeling, and whole and fragmented poetry, which, as we shall see, reflects philosophical arguments of the day, that the deceptively simple plot of *Erec et Enide* should be considered. Chrétien is advocating the value of reason, of *savoir*, as the guiding principle for the good life, not in the hermetically sealed environment of the lady, of Guenevere and of Arthur's court, but as the key to mutual love in marriage, and to happiness which brings its 'fruits', its good results to the individual and society. Chrétien's thought is not as 'complete' as it will be in *Le conte du Graal*, for it is still contained within the values of this world. But it is whole and not 'fragmented', since Chrétien, like Marcabru, sees beyond the situation in which courtly virtues are practised and developed in sole relation to the lady. The importance of courtly values in *Erec et Enide* is that they are not related to so-called 'courtly love', but to the ordered way of life, the happiness and good government which they can give to the individual and to society. This is apparent in the Coronation scene in which Chrétien clearly cherishes the virtues of reason, and of service and deeds which are devoted to an enlightened purpose, in particular to good government. When courtly virtues are applied in this way, they are the qualities of the man who takes part in the administrative life of the court which was, after all, its main function. The combination of these qualities provides the *curialitas* which was taken over from the civic virtues of Ancient Rome with an admixture of Christian principles, and which we find in the great ecclesiastics and men of letters and action, the moralists, practical thinkers and chroniclers who adorned the court of Henry II and often held high administrative office. Chrétien may not have belonged to the court of Henry II, but his approval of love within marriage, and of a knighthood which prefers service to jousting, is close to the ideas in the *Livre des Manières* of Etienne de Fougères,[34] chaplain to the turbulent, promiscuous but efficient Henry II. And the depiction of the courtly virtues, and their practical application for the communal good in *Erec et Enide*, are close to the ideas in the *Policraticus* which John of Salisbury presented to his friend and patron, the then Chancellor of Henry II, Thomas Becket.

John of Salisbury was born between 1110 and 1120. He studied in Paris, and probably at Chartres, and was versed in Cicero. About 1147, on the recommendation of Saint Bernard, he was appointed secretary to Thibaut, Archbishop of Canterbury. In 1164 he followed Thomas Becket into exile and urged him in vain to be reconciled to the king. He was present at the murder of Thomas in the cathedral, but was later appointed secretary to Henry II. In his *Policraticus*, which was sub-titled *De nugis curialium et vestigiis philosophorum* 'On the frivolities of courtiers and the tracks of philosophers',[35] he sought to correct the mindless pleasure-seeking of the court and to instil a belief in thought, inherited from the philosophers, as the inspiration and guide to good and fruitful deeds.

John attacks the evil of self-indulgence which 'destroys manly vigour, moulds both sexes to the command of Venus and combats the rule of law and order' (*ibid.*, VIII, 15). He praises generosity, which in its best form disregards reward, and which is inspired by compassion, *caritas* even, and a desire to share one's possessions (*ibid.*, VIII, 13). Moral rectitude must be sought above all things (*ibid.*, VIII, 15). Self-interest, on the other hand, pours out a flood which extinguishes charity and almost submerges the world; it leads to the love of possession, the lures of self-indulgence, it becomes a tyranny and strives for fame in a combat swollen with deceit (*ibid.*, VIII, 16).

On the subject of Joy, John condemns the search for happiness through self-indulgent pleasure. For him the way to happiness is the path of virtue, which is followed by those who love God, and which is bounded by the knowledge and practice of goodness. To know goodness and not to practise it leads not to happiness but to damnation (*ibid.*, VIII, 25). Even in the exercise of virtue, a sense of moderation is essential (*ibid.*, I, 4). Acts are criminal not in themselves but by reason of their intention. No display of virtue lends distinction to an act which derives from pleasure (*ibid.*, I, 4). Excess of pleasure impairs the human mind and undermines reason itself (*ibid.*, I, 4).

On the subject of *mesura*, John quotes Cicero *De officiis* I, XXXI, 113: *id enim maxime quemque decet, quod est cuiusque maxime suum*; 'For the more peculiarly his own a man's character is, the better it fits him.'[36] In other words, according to Cicero (*ibid.*): 'it is the duty of each man to consider well the nature of his own particular traits of character, to order these properly, and not to want to experiment to see how another man's would suit him'. Such is the quest of Enide, and to a lesser degree of Erec, for self-discovery.

Duty, for John of Salisbury, is the natural destiny of certain men: 'That which does not accord with the principles of nature or duty is alien to man's proper nature. The principles of nature apply in like measure to all men, the consideration of duty applies to particular individuals . . . transgression of this rule is always a crime' (Policraticus, I, 2).

The underlying ideas of Chrétien's Erec et Enide which concern goodness, virtue, joy, self-knowledge and duty, are close to the precepts which we find in the Policraticus of John of Salisbury and the De officiis of Cicero. Chrétien may have been inspired directly by the great moralists of his day, such as John of Salisbury, but these ideas, many of which can be found in the poetry of Marcabru and Peire d'Alvernhe[37] must have formed part of the common intellectual currency in the great courts of his day. They are the moral and social values of courtoisie, of curialitas, independent of any association with so-called 'courtly love', or Fin'Amors.

If we return to the episode of the Joy of the Court, we see that Joy for the people of Brandigan lies in the return of the king's nephew to society, and in the freedom to re-enter the allegorical garden of joy and fertility which he had denied them. In this idea of a 'waste land', of a joy which has been lost in the garden and the surrounding countryside, and of fertility and happiness restored, the garden and the wall of air retain traces of Celtic tradition[38] and are also an early presage of the Grail theme. Joy for Erec lies in the victory over his former self, symbolised by Mabonagrain's enslavement to his mistress. By defeating Mabonagrain he is freed from the image of this former self in his mind, as Enide was freed from her sense of guilt by Erec's act of forgiveness at Limors. Joy for Erec and Enide lies in their knowledge of harmony within themselves, within their marriage and with society. The symbolical 'wall of air' which surrounded them when they left the court of King Lac, and which thinned as their quest progressed, has now disappeared. Their newly found joy is an assertion of life, and so, with Guivret, Mabonagrain and his mistress, they bring this Joy to King

Arthur. But to retain this Joy as a source of personal and communal delight within Arthur's court would, for John of Salisbury and Chrétien, be self-indulgence. This Joy is an affirmation of life, which no wall of air may resist. It is not to be contained within Arthur's court, in which courtly virtue and knightly excellence find a home but no good purpose for their use. Joy and Prowess come to the court in the company of knights who have done noble deeds in the outside world, and who have sent their defeated prisoners to court to join the pool of knighthood. Arthur's court is inactive, except in a restricted courtly sense, a sponge which fills with Joy when well attended, and shrinks into Grief when its knights depart. This view of Arthur's court is made clear in Chrétien's later works by the contrast between the static Gawain and the progressive, 'charitable', Lancelot, Yvain and Perceval. In Erec et Enide, Chrétien appears to respect Gawain and Arthur's courtly establishment, despite the implied preciosity of the Hunt of the White Stag and its sequel. In the later romances, his ideas harden about the futility of purposeless action, and Arthur's world is shown in an increasingly less favourable light. It is the Coronation scene in Erec et Enide which allowed Chrétien to move from behind the wall of marriage, love, chivalry and courtliness, and to apply the moral truth, which is the sen of the romance, to the theme of good government.

Erec is ready for this role. Through the sciance of experience and through savoir, mental control to which self-indulgence must submit, he has found harmony between the demands of marriage, love, chivalry and social duties.[39] He, like Enide, is now fitted to rule, and his coronation is the ultimate purpose to which he has been progressing since, at Guenevere's side, he listlessly observed the Hunt of the White Stag.

The Coronation scene has a literal and an allegorical meaning. It closes past adventure, and opens future promise. The scene is set when Erec hears that his father is dead. He 'swiftly acts as a king should':

La ou il iert a Tintaguel	There at Tintagel, where he was
Fist chanter vigiles et messes,	staying, he caused vigils and
Promist et randi ses promesses	masses to be chanted. He gave
Si com il les avoit promises,	promises, and fulfilled them as

As meisons De et as eglises;
Mout fist bien, quanque feire dut:
Povres mesaeisiez eslut
Plus de çant et seissante et nuef,
Si les revesti tot de nuef;
As povres clers et as provoires
Dona, que droiz fu, chapes noires
Et chaudes pelices dessoz.
Mout fist grant bien por Deu a toz . . .
(6528–40)

he had promised, to the houses of God and the churches. Very well did he carry out all those things which it was his duty to do. He chose more than one hundred and sixty-nine poor wretches and gave them comletely new garments. To the poor clerks and priests he gave, for this was right, black hooded cloaks lined with warm furs. For the sake of God, he brought happiness to all through his acts of great goodness.

Quant departi ot son avoir,
Aprés fist un mout grant savoir,
Que del roi sa terre reprist;
Aprés si li pria et dist
Qu'il le coronast a sa cort.
(6543–7)

When he had shared out all his wealth he then acted with very great wisdom, for he took back his land in fealty from the king, and entreated him then to crown him at his court.

Arthur orders the royal ensign, the crown of gold and the sceptre to be taken to Nantes in Brittany, where, on Christmas Day, Erec and Enide will be crowned. The summons to court goes out from Arthur and Erec. Enide joyfully welcomes her parents (6632–40). The court is complete: 'There were counts and dukes and kings, Normans, Bretons, Scots, Irish. From England and from Cornwall came many mighty barons. So that from Wales to Anjou, and in Maine and Poitou, no knight of great standing or noble lady of high birth stayed behind so that the best and the most accomplished might not all be present at the court at Nantes' (6645–54).[40]

Arthur dubs four hundred knights and more, richer and more generous at this coronation court than Alexander or Caesar or any king of any *chanson de geste* (6660–82). Rich cloaks are spread throughout the rooms, and bushels of sterling coins, so that each man may help himself. Arthur and Erec, in his coronation robe, sit on twin seats of pure ivory which have two carved legs in the shape of leopards, and two as crocodiles (6713–29).[41]

Enide is late, but no squire now brings her an abrupt summons. Gawain and the Queen, Guivret and Yder and more than a thousand nobles act as her escort. Enide sits enthroned beside Erec as their two crowns, ablaze with

56

light, are brought forward. When Erec is anointed and crowned:

L'evesques de Nantes meïsmes,	The Bishop of Nantes himself,
Qui mout fu prodon et saintismes,	an excellent and most holy man,
Fist le sacre del roi novel	anointed the new king in most
Mout saintemant et bien et bel,	sacred and proper ritual, and
Et la corone el chief li mist.	placed the crown on his head.
(6865–9)	

Arthur hands Erec a sceptre of a single pure emerald, richly worked with the images of all known fish and beasts, and men and birds, and Erec, in his turn, crowns Enide. Bells for mass ring from the cathedral, and on their way to prayer, Erec and Enide are greeted by a procession of all the clergy, coming towards them, bearing all the holy relics and treasures of the Church. Amidst joyful song as they enter for mass, Erec and Enide have accomplished their quest. The microcosm of personal joy which they found together in the castle of Guivret and which they extended, through the Joy of the Court adventure, to the worlds of Evrain and Arthur, now becomes part of the macrocosm of the divine *ordo*, temporal, natural and Christian, into which they are welcomed in the cathedral at Nantes. Erec and Enide are now *leals* in the sense that they represent and uphold the *loi*,[42] the temporal law and religious responsibilities, which, for Chrétien's audience, are part of the natural order of things, and which, administered by the right rulers, can create order and happiness.

Erec is now in the royal situation which Arthur had described:

'Je sui rois, ne doi pas mantir,	'I am king, and I must not lie or
Ne vilenie consantir,	condone any churlish act, or
Ne faussté ne desmesure:	falseness or outrageous or
Reison doi garder et droiture.	inappropriate deed. I must hold to
Ce apartient a leal roi	the practice of reason and justice,
Que il doit maintenir la loi.'	for it befits a true king to uphold
(1793–8)	the "law".'

Erec and Enide are both equipped to use their knowledge (*sciance*) and wisdom (*savoir*) 'tant con Deus la grace l'an done' (18).

Why does Chrétien linger with such admiration and hope for the future over the crowning of the 'new king'? Is his enthusiasm merely a device to please his audience with an event of courtly brilliance? Had he heard an account, or been the witness of such a coronation? And why does he locate it at Nantes on Christmas Day? The evidence is slight, but it is possible that Chrétien may have been influenced by contemporary events, as he was when he came to write *Cliges*.[43] Laudatory references to current happenings might attract favour, reward and patronage, and Chrétien would have a precedent in this matter in the *Couronnement de Louis* in which the coronation scene of Charlemagne's son, Louis the Pious, draws on contemporary accounts of the crowning of Louis VII in 1131.[44]

The Coronation scene in *Erec et Enide*, which is not in the Welsh *Gereint*, imitates a similar scene in Wace's *Brut*,[45] but has features which are unique. Wace, for Arthur's coronation, brings together guests from many provinces. Chrétien, in some versions of the text, limits himself for Erec's coronation to the lands of Henry II.[46] Secondly, Henry held court in Nantes on Christmas Day 1169, when barons rendered joint homage to him and his son Geoffrey, who in 1166 had been betrothed to Constance, the five-year-old heiress of Conon IV Duke of Brittany. Objection can be made that Christmas Day was not an unusual day for coronations, and that the affair at Nantes in 1169 was not a coronation but an acceptance. Yet, even without further evidence, the thought must persist that when Chrétien placed Arthur and Erec on identical ivory thrones, with two of the legs carved in the shape of leopards, emblem of the Angevin Plantagenets, at a ceremony intended to symbolise the coming splendour and happiness of Erec's reign, he may well have had in mind the joint homage received by Henry II and his son Geoffrey, and the hopes offered thereby to the Breton nobles for the future of their land. If one also considers Chrétien's custom of adapting and amalgamating, sometimes reversing, as in the Byzantine offer of marriage in *Cliges*, the material which he acquires, it is not impossible that he may also have had in mind the coronation of Henry II's eldest son, Henry the Young King, in Westminster Abbey in June 1170, a ceremony which created some furore because it was carried out by the Archbishop of York instead of by Thomas Becket, Archbishop of Canterbury.[47] The promise of the *novel roi*

(6867) in *Erec et Enide* would accord well with the gifts and promise of the Young King, of which Bertran de Born was to sing. Chrétien's praise of Arthur's generosity (6677–82), which is far less subtle than but not entirely unlike his praise of the Count of Flanders in *Le Conte du Graal*, may just possibly have been directed, in any case probably in vain, at Henry II.

Whether or not the Coronation scene was related to the Plantagenet celebrations of 1169 and 1170, it could scarcely fail to please a courtly audience, especially in the description of Erec's coronation robe which Chrétien begins to describe when Erec is seated, beside Arthur, on his twin ivory throne:

Macrobes m'ansaingne a descrivre,
Si con je l'ai trové el livre,
L'uevre del drap et le portret.
Quatre fees l'avoient fet
Par grant san et par grant mestrie.
L'une i portrest geometrie,
Si com ele esgarde et mesure,
Con li ciaus et la terre dure,
Si que de rien nule n'i faut,
Et puis le bas et puis le haut,
Et puis le le, et puis le lonc;
Et puis esgarde par selonc,
Con la mers est lee et parfonde,
Et si mesure tot le monde.
Tel oevre i mist la premerainne.
(6741–55)

Macrobius instructs me how to describe the working on the cloth, and the imagery, as I have found it in the book. Four fairies had done this work, with great wisdom and great skill. The one portrayed Geometry and showed the faultless way in which it observes and measures the extent of the sky and the land, and then the depth, and then the height, width and length, and then observes how wide and deep the sea is, and so it measures all the world. Such work did the first fairy put into the robe.

As Geometry holds the notion of the world and the universe in balance through its measure, so does Arithmetic, which is the second portrait on the robe, number everything in life, the days and hours, the drops of the sea, the stars and the leaves in the wood, without lie or deceit, for the second fairy put all her effort into this (6756–69). The third portrait is of Music, which provides Joy and harmony, which brings together all delights (6770–6). The fourth fairy put into the robe the best of the arts, Astronomy, which takes counsel with the stars, and the moon and the sun (6777–83):

An autre leu ne prant consoil
De rien qui a feire li soit;
Cil la consoillent bien a droit.
De quanque ele les requiert,

In no other place does it take counsel about anything which it may have to do. They give it counsel, right and true. They tell

Et quanque fu et quanque iert,
Li font certainnemant savoir
Sanz mantir et sanz decevoir.
(6784–90)

it, without lies or deceit, about
whatever it asks them, about
whatever was and whatever will
be.

In his Prologue Chrétien speaks of the value of knowledge
and of the duty of each individual to cultivate his or her
talents to the utmost. On the superficial level, this theme is
bound up by the portraits of the four arts of the quadri-
vium, which, linked with the theme of the coronation,
symbolise Erec's *savoir* and *sciance*, his wisdom and practical
knowledge of life, and his promise as future king. On a
higher level, the way in which the four arts are described
may indicate that the robe is also intended as a symbol of
the divine ordering of the universe. God has disposed all
natural things in a harmonious measure; this is geometry.
He has numbered and set them in their station, and this is
arithmetic. He has provided them with the harmonies of
music which depends on the mathematics of natural law
and which, according to John of Salisbury, 'embraces the
universe; that is to say, it reconciles the clashing and dis-
sonant relations of all that exists and of all that is thought
and expressed in words by a sort of ever varying but still
harmonious law derived from its own symmetry. By it
[music] the phenomena of the heavens are ruled and the
activities of the world and men are governed.'[48] God has
made available to man the influence, wisdom and advice of
the well ordered firmament of the sun, stars and moon.
Just so in Chrétien's description of the robe is music followed by astronomy, by which God offers knowledge of the
universe, past and future.

This idea of the natural order as a pattern for human
society is basic to the twelfth-century thought of the school
of Chartres, and especially of Bernardus Silvestris.[49] In vernacular poetry it is found in the *trobar naturaus* or 'natural'
style of Marcabru, who saw in the well regulated life of
Nature a model for the troubled world around him.[50] The
central belief that this order which exists in nature, and
which can be attained in human society, is appointed and
directed by God, is exemplified by the multitude of exegeti-
cal comments, from St Augustine to the twelfth century, on
the quotation from the wisdom of Solomon: *omnia in mensura*

et numero et pondere disposuisti (Lib. *sap.* XI, 21). The essence of
this exegesis is that everything is subject to the workings of
God and so part of the divine *ordo*. Since God is the *mensura*
or measure of all things, nothing exists outside this creation
and the purpose He gives it. All creation has its constant
place in the hierarchy of the cosmos, and *numerus* stands for
the numerically arranged ordering of the cosmos from in-
organic to organic, to the human world and then to the
world of the angels, and finally to God. The higher the
numerical step in the order, the greater the fullness of Being;
the lower the number, the further from the image of God
and the sense of Being. All creation is bound to its situation
by its number in the hierarchical order, but it desires to
strive towards and reach its place of origin, to achieve the
likeness to God.[51]

If we accept this idea of a higher enigmatic meaning to
the Coronation scene, we may see that Erec, as anointed king,
endowed, through the symbolical imagery of the sceptre,[52]
with authority over God's natural creatures, represents the
ideal synthesis of the Christian establishment of his day, the
blending of chivalry and *curialitas* within the God-given
order. To this affirmation of a belief in the triumph of
Goodness over Evil, in the high purpose of knighthood, the
strength and benefits of loyal mutual love, and the social
virtues, largely inherited from Roman antiquity, which
guide his characters, Chrétien adds his humane trust in the
individual, who, standing aside from social convention,
develops within himself those qualities which are particularly his own, and, by using these qualities for the communal good, defeats the forces of Evil and restores Goodness, Order and Joy to society. Chrétien's belief, which reflects the courtly idea that reason, moderation, and a sense
of fitness can create order from the anarchy of feeling, is
basically Ciceronian. In the *De finibus bonorum et malorum*[53] we
read: 'Man's end is the perfection of his whole being' (v,
xiv); 'man attains only gradually to a knowledge of his
nature' (v, xv); 'to know ourselves the whole of nature must
be studied. The perfection of the whole self is therefore the
Chief Good' (v, xvi). And in the *De officiis*, on the subject of
reason, moderation and order: 'And it is no mean manifestation of Nature and Reason that man is the only animal that

has a feeling for order, for propriety, for moderation in word and deed. And so no other animal has a sense of beauty, loveliness, harmony in the visible world; and Nature and Reason, extending the analogy of this from the world of sense to the world of spirit, find that beauty, consistency, order, are far more to be maintained in thought and deed' (I, iv), and, even more aptly: 'This then ought to be the chief end of all men, to make the interest of each individual and the whole body politic identical. For, if the individual appropriates to selfish ends what should be devoted to the common good, all human fellowship will be destroyed (III, vi)'.[54]

The Coronation scene is distinguished by its praise of worldly splendour, and knowledge, its belief in the God-given harmony of the natural order and man's ability to discover and imitate this. This optimistic view of man's powers and possibilities, which is characteristic of twelfth-century writers such as the later Alanus de Insulis,[55] is hinted at in the symbolism of the coronation, of the robe and sceptre, which is part of Chrétien's allusive style. It is also confirmed in the rest of the romance by Chrétien's confidence in the ability of Erec and Enide to reject the forces of disorder and folly, in order to discover harmony and joy within themselves and in each other.

The remarkable quality of *Erec et Enide* derives from this pervading sense of *biens*, the spontaneous innocence and creative goodness, which radiates from Enide and enhances Erec's knightly courage. It derives also from the structural order and harmony which reflects and strengthens the inner meaning of the romance. Chrétien integrates thematic and narrative structure more clearly here than in his other romances, and in this his task is made easier because, in large measure, the action and *sen* proceed directly from the motivation of the two main characters, and are concerned with temporal, and not metaphysical aspirations, or 'supernatural' interventions.

Order and harmony are evident in Chrétien's use of the three ways of revealing his *sen* to which earlier reference has been made in this chapter. The linear method of analogy is of major importance and runs through the whole narrative; the lateral method of exposition, or summing up, is assigned to Enide, and is limited mainly to the beginning and end of the quest, her warning to Erec in the bedchamber and her counsel to her cousin, the mistress of Mabonagrain; the allusive method of coloured meanings, of symbol and allegory, is evident in the three great occasions of the Hunt of the White Stag, the Joy of the Court and the Coronation. Traditional symbols of the Celtic supernatural, such as the White Stag and the Wall of Air,[56] are made to blend harmoniously with the courtly attitudes of Chrétien's time and the day-to-day atmosphere in which events and trials, however exceptional, befall Erec and Enide.

The skill and harmony of the narrative *conjointure* is self-evident in the balance and progression of episodes, speeches, phrases, trials and triumphs. In the thematic *conjointure*, there is a close linking between the individual roles of Erec and Enide, their social performance, and the universal significance of the virtues which finally fit them for their royal destiny. Moving easily between these three levels, individual, social and universal, Chrétien binds up his themes of reason and folly, of purpose or vanity in life, of true prowess and vain-glory, of the claims of knighthood and love, of marriage and social duty, of sensual love and love in the heart and mind, of understanding between lovers and the lack of this, of self-indulgence and discipline, of joy which is selfish and ephemeral, or lasting and productive, of chaos and order, of attitudes to life which are static and positive, of the spoken word which brings good and evil, of the victory of *savoir* and *sciance*, the triumph of good over evil, and the goodness of man guided by reason and wisdom.

Chrétien's apparent belief in the joy of this world will retreat, in the last three romances, before the fear that the forces of evil, and human folly, are ineradicable.[57] But before this gathering despair about the ills of society came upon him, Chrétien wrote another dynastic and worldly romance, *Cliges*.

3

Cliges

WITH *Cliges* Chrétien's attitude to his art has changed. It is now more distant, objective and ironical. He sees no certainties in this worldly existence. He praises reason and common sense, and mocks them. *Savoir* now has its part of folly which impairs its achievement, truth must coexist with illusion. Even the happy dynastic ending has an ironical twist. With this intermediate romance which precedes the great trio of *Lancelot, Yvain* and *Perceval,* Chrétien is stretching his imagination sideways so that he may also see the reverse side of his narrative. In adopting the twelfth-century view of life as an amalgam of opposites, he begins to reveal doubts which he will amplify in *Perceval.* In *Cliges* Chrétien is not only offering us a blatant comedy of situation, an essay in literary and social satire and an Art of Love, but behind all this, he begins to uncover a subtle and intellectually minded view of the human condition.

The narrative structure of *Cliges* is straightforward. The first act (0–2623),[1] which corresponds to the *premerains vers* of *Erec et Enide,* is a self-contained introductory romance in which the marriage of Alexander and Soredamors is a paradigm of ideal harmony, love, prowess and wisdom.[2] This section is a copybook exercise, sensitively written, of the art of falling in love in a courtly society, of love in marriage, and the founding of a dynasty. In the second 'act', which is the main part of the romance (2624–6744), Cliges, the son of Alexander and Soredamors, overcomes, under the guidance of Fenice, all obstacles in the path of their love, and, in a brief third 'act' or epilogue (6745–84), these lovers attain the ideal of love exemplified in the first act, together with the dynastic succession to the Greek Empire.

In this basic pattern of lovers separated and reunited *Cliges* accords with the narrative structure of many works such as the *Guigemar* of Marie de France[3] and the contemporary *Roman de Horn* by Thomas.[4] This tradition, which is parodied gently in the thirteenth-century *Aucassin et Nicolette*, is enriched in *Cliges* by the switching of scene from Byzantine Greece to Arthurian Britain, to Greece, to Imperial Germany, to Britain, to Greece, to Britain, and finally to Greece for the coronation at Constantinople. Chrétien, unlike Beroul who 'explains' the return of Yseut to Mark by the waning power of the love potion and the ritual offer of glove, ring and sword, scorns to rationalise the vicissitudes of fate which afflict his lovers. Alis dies at the most opportune moment, the 'secret' tower and 'enchanted' garden are discovered when the lovers' idyll must end.

The work in which Chrétien claims to have found his story in the book-cupboard of the cathedral of Saint Peter at Beauvais (18–25), may have contained the central theme of feigned death which is found in Slavonic, German and Portuguese folklore, in the lay of *Eliduc* by Marie de France, in *Amadus et Idoine* and in the fourteenth-century romance of *Perceforest*. It persists in Italian short stories by Luigi da Porto and Bandello, and sixteenth-century French imitations of these may have brought the theme to England for Shakespeare to use in *Romeo and Juliet*.[5] In *Eliduc* the *Fausse Mort* occurs unexpectedly. In *Cliges*, 'feigned death' is induced, and this version may derive from the story of Solomon's wife, who, anxious to leave him, feigned death and was tortured by doctors who poured molten lead – and, in some versions, gold – into her hand. The wife does not flinch, is pronounced dead, is buried and abstracted from her tomb by her lover. This oriental, and probably Hebrew, story was applied in a Byzantine version to an Emperor and Empress of Constantinople, and recurs in the eleventh story of a romance called *Marques de Rome*, which, in a thirteenth-century text, provides a version of the story of Cliges, independent of and possibly earlier than Chrétien's romance. In this version, Cliges falls in love with the Empress and they consummate their love. In order to be together night and day, they adopt the use of feigned death. The Empress resists the torture of hot lead poured into her palms on the order of her suspicious husband. She is buried 'alive', disinterred and rescued from the tomb, and dwells for a long time, freed from her husband, in a fine house with a large orchard outside Constantinople, where Cliges visits her freely.[6]

When Chrétien came to write *Cliges*, he was master of the theories of love current in his day. He was interested, as we shall see, in troubadour poetry, and almost certainly knew the love scenes in the *Roman d'Eneas* and the *Roman de Troie*. He tells us, in the opening lines of *Cliges* (1–7), that, as well as writing *Erec et Enide*, he had immersed himself in Ovid.[7] He had translated the *Remedia Amoris* and the *Ars Amatoria*, and had composed a work on the terrible story of Tereus, Procne and Philomela (*Metamorphoses*, vi, 412–674), who are changed respectively into a hoopoe, a swallow and a nightingale. It is probably this poem by Chrétien which survives as *Philomena*, a poem in the late thirteenth-century *Ovide moralisé*. Nothing else remains of Chrétien's work on Ovid, of his *Le Mors de l'Espaule* (4), probably on the story of Pelops and his ivory shoulder (*Metamorphoses*, vi, 404), or of his *Del roi Marc et d'Iseut la blonde* (5).

Love and knighthood alternate separately as major themes in *Cliges*. They may merge on occasions, as in the thread of gold in the shirt prepared for Alexander's knighting, and in the rescue of Fenice from the Saxon ambush, but they are never in conflict. The quest for knighthood, in war or joust, reinforces love and is never at variance with it. Conflict arises from the opposing claims which *savoir* and *folie* make on the individual and on society. These conflicting demands by reason and folly are made on the individual in terms of love, knighthood and social duty. They are made on society. in particular on that of Arthur and of the Emperor, in terms of the ability to recognise reality and illusion, and to react accordingly.

In *Cliges*, the themes of love, knighthood, social behaviour, reality and illusion, become more important than the individual development of the main characters. Cliges and Fenice do not progress in a moral sense towards an ideal of rounded perfection, like Erec and Enide. Their development can only be measured by their pragmatic responses to the promptings of reason and folly, the wish for ultimate social acceptance and succession to the Empire, and the promptings of the passion which fired Tristan and Yseut.

Chrétien's thematic *conjointure* in *Cliges* is not a well defined linear development, bound up with the evolution of the main characters, as in *Erec et Enide*. It depends on a structure in which the four main areas of thematic exposition, love, knighthood, social behaviour, reality and illusion, are juxtaposed and sometimes superimposed, and in which the total effects of the conflict between *savoir* and *folie* on all these levels may be treated simultaneously. This form of *conjointure* still depends, however, on a system of analogy and contrast. In the treatment of the main theme of love, there is analogy and contrast between the love and marriage of Alexander and Soredamors, and that of Cliges and Fenice. The one is ideal, enjoyed in most favourable conditions, the only hindrance to love being the natural reticence and timidity of the lovers, which, in the guise of *peors*, is part of the courtly convention in wooing; the other is so beset with trials and problems that true love, as in *Flamenca*, pursues the Ovidian path of deceit. There is analogy and contrast between the love triangle of Cliges, Fenice and Alis, and that of Tristan, Yseut and Mark. In this particular instance, the *conjointure* of absolute contrast reaches its climax in the commonplace of the world upside-down on Alis' wedding night, after Fenice has refused to follow Yseut's example and share her body with husband and lover. On the levels of knighthood, social behaviour and reality and illusion, there is analogy and contrast in the behaviour of Arthur's court during the visits of Alexander and of his son, Cliges, and between Arthur's court and that of Alis. This theme of contrast is most evident in the characters of Thessala and Jehan, the two retainers who exemplify the extremes of illusion and reality, falsehood and truth. It is also apparent in Fenice and Cliges, the one inclined initially to *savoir* and the other to *folie*, but who both agree to pursue the path of *savoir* and are nevertheless involved, in Ovidian fashion, in deceits which spread illusion.

For Chrétien, faced, as in *Lancelot*, with this coexistence in life of good and evil, truth and illusion, the choice is clear. The distinction between truth and illusion may be blurred, and illusion will always persist, but the hope of happiness for the individual and society must depend on the rational ordering of life. In this connection, mention may be made of Chrétien's possible contribution to a poetic controversy about the conflict in love between the powers of reason and feeling, in troubadour terms between *sen* and *foudatz*. In the poem *D'Amors qui m'a tolu a moi*, which is almost certainly correctly attributed to him,[8] Chrétien appears to offer a riposte to the troubadour Bernart de Ventadorn who in his *Can vei la lauzeta mover* had said of his beloved:

> tout m'a mo cor, e tout m'a me,
> e se mezeis e tot lo mon.
>
> (edn Appel, XLIII, 13–14)

She has stolen my heart from me and has stolen myself from me, and herself and the whole world.' Bernart continues: 'And when she stole herself from me, she left me nothing except desire and a heart filled with longing. Never did I have control over myself, nor was I my own master from that moment when she let me look into her eyes, into a mirror that pleases me greatly' (15–20).[9] In *D'Amors qui m'a tolu a moi*, in which the first line takes up l.13 of Bernart's poem, Chrétien rejects this *folie* of feeling which is free from mental control.

Onques del bevraje ne bui	Never did I drink of that drink
don Tristans fu anpoisonez,	with which Tristan was poisoned,
mes plus me fet amer que lui	yet a true heart and a true desire
fins cuers et bone volantez.	make my love greater than his.
Bien an doit estre miens li grez,	The pleasure from this must
qu'ains de rien esforciez n'an fui	indeed be mine, for I was never
fors de tant, que mes iauz an crui	constrained in any way, except
par cui sui an la voie antrez,	in so far as I believed my eyes,
don ja n'istrai n'ains n'i recrui.	through which I have entered
(ed. Bartsch, *Chres*, XXXII, 28–36)	the path from which I shall never
	stray, and from which I was
	never recreant.

Chrétien's love, which is inspired by a true heart and a noble determination, is superior, he believes, to that of Tristan, and, by implication, of Bernart. Chrétien will not show recreance to his lady and to society, as Bernart did in his poem (XLIII, 54–6). He accepts the courtly precept that the mind of the lover must control the disorder of the senses which leads to a loss of self-identity. He attacks Tristan's passion which, born of a potion and not of the heart or the inclination of the will, disregards all laws, social order, and even death.[10] Another troubadour, Raimbaut d'Aurenga, composing before 1173, appears to take up Chrétien's challenge in his *Non chant per auzel*, in which *Carestia* in the envoi may be a pseudonym for Chrétien:

De midonz fatz domn' e seignor	I make of my lady my feudal
Cals que sia·il destinada.	lady and lord, whatever may be
Car ieu begui de la amor	my fate. Since I have drunk of
Ja·us dei amar a celada.	that love, I must love you with
Tristan, quan la·il det Yseus gen	secrecy. Tristan, when the fair
E bela, no·n saup als faire;	and gracious Yseut gave him this
Et ieu am per aital coven	love, could not do otherwise.
Midonz, don no·m posc estraire.	And in just such a way as that
(edn Pattison, XXVII, 25–32)	do I love my lady from whom
	I cannot part.

Raimbaut ironically uses the image of the shirt which Yseut gave Tristan as a symbol of virginity. May he be granted the same, and may his lady, like Yseut, make her husband believe that no man born of woman has ever touched her (XXVII, 33–48).

In *Cliges*, Chrétien denigrates the all-consuming, self-absorbed passion of Tristan and Yseut. Such *folie* in love destroys the individual, disrupts society. In contrast to this, Fenice and Soredamors are courtly paradigms of the mental control of desire, of the supremacy of *savoir*. Because of this role, Fenice, and to a lesser degree Soredamors, is used by Chrétien to determine the love theme in the narrative. The same role will be given to Flamenca in the romance of that name, a century after Chrétien.

Cliges is primarily an entertainment. But it is also an Art of Love in dramatic form. This is especially true of the Ovidian awakening and recognition of love between Alexander and Soredamors, which is more gentle, more lyrical than that of Lavinia and Eneas. Soredamors, disdaining love (446), is smitten on the ship bearing Arthur and his retinue, and Alexander, son of the Greek Emperor, to Brittany. The Ovidian wound in the heart removes all control:

Bien a Amors droit assené,	Love has indeed struck true,
Qu'el cuer l'a de son dart ferue.	piercing her heart with his arrow.
Sovant palist, sovant tressue	Many times she grows pale, many
Et maugré suen amer l'estuet.	times she sweats; despite herself
A grant painne tenir se puet,	she is forced to love. Only with
Que vers Alixandre n'esgart.	a great effort can she hold herself
(460–5)	back from looking at Alexander.

For his part, Alexander soliloquises at length about the pains of love which torment him. He is terrified, ill, out of his wits. Can Love, who is gentle and well-bred, do this? He will not be recreant. Sickness may be cured. Happiness may follow (616–872).

Despite Love's torments, reason begins to assert itself in Soredamors:

Tote nuit est an si grant painne,	All night she is in distress so
Qu'ele ne dort ne ne repose.	great that she cannot sleep or
Amors li a el cors anclose	rest. Love has imprisoned within
Une tançon et une rage,	her heart a contention and a
Qui mout li troble son corage	madness which disturbs her
Et qui si l'angoisse et destraint,	thoughts, constrains and oppresses
Que tote nuit plore et se plaint	her so that she spends the night
Et se degiete et si tressaut,	in tears, laments, jerks in torment
A po que li cuers ne li faut.	with sudden tremblings so that
Et quant ele a tant traveillié	her heart almost fails. And when
Et sangloti et baaillié	she has endured such trials and
Et tressailli et sospiré,	sobs and wakefulness and tossing
Lors a an son cuer remiré,	about and sighs, she looked into
Qui cil estoit et de ques mors,	her heart to see who this was,
Por cui la destreignoit Amors.	and what manner of man, for
(876–90)	whom Love constrained her.

She is more positive than Alexander. She analyses her distress in lyrical passages:

'Mes Amors m'a si anvaïe,	'Love has so invaded me that I
Que fole sui et esbaïe,	am foolish and out of my mind.
Ne deffanse rien ne m'i vaut,	No defence avails me now and
Si m'estuet sofrir son assaut.'	I must suffer its assault.'
(933–6)	

True to her name 'gilded over with love' (980) she will accept Love's teaching and do his pleasure:

'Por neant n'ai je pas cest non,	'It is not for nothing that I bear
Que Soredamors sui clamee.	this name, that I am called
Amer doi, si doi estre amee,	Soredamors. I am destined to love
Si le vuel par mon non prover.'	and to be loved, and I will prove
(962–5)	this through my name.'

Her love is no idle fancy:

'Par moi meïsmes le sai bien:	'I know this through my very
Car onques n'an poi savoir rien	being, for never could I know
Par losange ne par parole.'	anything about it through
(1025–7)	flattery or through spoken words.'

Yet Alexander may not know about love:

Qu'or an sai plus que bués d'arer.	Now I know more about love
Mes d'une chose me despoir,	than the ox knows about
Que cil n'ama onques espoir;	ploughing. But of one thing do
Et s'il n'aimme ne n'a amé,	I despair, that he perhaps has
Donc ai je an la mer semé,	never loved. And if he does not
Ou semance ne puet reprandre.	love, and has not loved, then I
(1032–7)	have sowed in the sea where no
	seed can take root.

If this is so, she will still love, will lead him on with looks and covered words:

Tant ferai que il sera cerz	I will do this until he is sure of
De m'amor, se requerre l'ose.	my love, and dares to ask for it.
Donc n'i a il plus de la chose,	So there is nothing more to this
Mes que je l'aim et soe sui.	than that I love him and am his.
S'il ne m'aimme, j'amerai lui.	If he loves me not, I will love
(1042–6)	him.

Soredamors sets the pattern for Fenice. She loves with *fin cuer* and *bone volantez*. Using thought and reason on herself, she is far more courtly than Enide who won understanding of love through the shared experience of life. Soredamors had disdained love (445–6), had wanted to rid herself of desire for Alexander, but, says Chrétien, *Ceste amors fust leaus et droite* (536) 'This love would be natural and right', and Soredamors comes to terms with it.

The themes of love and knighthood intertwine when Alexander is knighted. Guenevere who rejoices in seeing young men (1202–8) and 'loves, praises and esteems Alexander' (1149), will give him a fine shirt of white silk, with every thread of gold and silver. Soredamors, sewing into it a thread of her golden hair, does not know it is intended for Alexander. He does not know that the shirt was sewn by her. Had he known:

. . . an eschange n'an preist	He would not have taken the
Tot le monde, einçois an feïst	whole world in exchange. Rather
Saintüeire, si con je cuit,	would he have made a holy relic
Si l'aorast et jor et nuit.	of it, and would have adored it,
(1193–6)	as I believe, day and night.

Alexander loves a damsel with a *Fin'Amors* as exalted as Lancelot's adoration of Guenevere, quite separate from the physical attraction of Erec and Enide when they first fell in love. Alexander loves with love of the imagination, an *amor de lonh*, which Chrétien treats with humour and gentle irony, especially when Alexander, having been told about the thread of golden hair, kisses it and embraces the shirt all night (1640). Chrétien offers a kindly nod:

Bien fet amors de sage fol,
Quant cil fet joie d'un chevol.
(1643–4)

Love indeed makes a fool of a wise man when he finds his joy in a strand of hair.

Alexander, in the campaign against the usurper Angres, captures the castle of Windsor, and is granted the victor's gold cup and any boon except the crown and the queen. He gives the cup to Gawain. He dares not ask the king for Soredamors:

Alixandres de ceste chose
Son desirrier dire nen ose,
Et bien set qu'il n'i faudroit mie,
Se il li requeroit s'amie;
Mes tant crient, qu'il ne despleüst
Celi, qui granz joie an eüst,
Que miauz se viaut sanz li doloir,
Que il l'eüst sanz son voloir.
(2221–8)

Alexander dares not tell of his desire in this matter, and he knows well he would not be refused if he asked him for the hand of the maiden he loves. But he fears so much that he might displease her, who would have had great joy from this, that he would rather grieve without her than possess her against her will.

Valiant in war, timid in love, Alexander has the humility of the true courtly lover. Soredamors is no prize for courage in combat; he will wait until his desire is matched by hers. When she pines at this delay, Chrétien soothes his audience, for delay in love is the essence of his exposition:

Par tans avra ce qu'ele viaut;
Car anbedui par contançon
Sont d'une chose an cusançon.
(2246–8)

Soon she will have what she wants, for both of them are contending with the same desire.

Guenevere brings the lovers together: 'I will teach you about Love. Take good care to conceal nothing from me, for I see from your faces that your two hearts are one' (2290–7).

She delivers a homily on the virtues of marriage:

'Or vos lo que ja ne queroiz
Force ne volanté d'amor.
Par mariage et par enor
Vos antraconpaigniez ansanble.
Einsi porra, si con moi sanble,
Vostre amors longuemant durer.'
(2302–7)

'Now I advise you not to seek
tyranny or self-will in love.
In marriage and honour may you
bear each other company
together. So, I believe, your love
will be long lasting.'

It is Guenevere's duty to ensure a good marriage for her niece. A courtly audience would scarcely fail to see the irony of Guenevere's praises of that unity of heart and body in marriage which will later become the aim of Fenice.

Alexander's joy and honour are complete, for three reasons: his capture of the castle, Arthur's promise to give him the finest kingdom in Wales, and his marriage to Soredamors who will be the queen of the chessboard of which he is king (2361–73). Yet abruptly their idyllic love is disturbed after their son Cliges is born. The Emperor dies. False news of Alexander's death is carried to Constantinople, and his younger brother, Alis, succeeds to the Empire. On Alexander's return to Greece, Alis vows not to marry and so impair Cliges' rights to the throne (2577–80). The love of Alexander and Soredamors, which has flourished in dream-like serenity, ends with their shared death, Soredamors, like Yseut, dying of grief.

When Cliges and Fenice fall in love, they face a situation fraught with difficulty. Fenice, the daughter of the German Emperor, is already the betrothed of his uncle Alis, who, breaking his vow, has brought an army to Cologne to escort his bride to Constantinople.

The good looks of Cliges and Fenice, as beautiful as the phoenix from which her name is derived, radiate a light which lights the palace, as the sun with its vermilion brilliance lights the world anew at dawn (2754–60). Cliges in the flower of youth, more beautiful and pleasing than Narcissus (2764–7), has golden hair, tall stature, and greater skill at fencing and the bow than Tristan, the nephew of King Mark. He is endowed with *san*, *largesce* and strength, and abundant *savoir* (2761–90).

73

Love is instantaneous, and so is his courtly discretion:

Mes Cligés par amor conduit	But Cliges, in obedience to love,
Vers li ses iauz covertemant	moves his eyes covertly towards
Et ramainne si sagemant,	her and then discreetly away
Que a l'aler ne au venir	that neither in their passage to
Ne l'an puet an por fol tenir.	and fro could anyone think of
(2800–4)	him as an untutored fool.

Fenice unlike Soredamors does not delay:

Par buene amor, non par losange,	In true love, and without deceit,
Ses iauz li baille et prant les suens.	she gives him her eyes, and
(2808–9)	accepts his.

She knows nothing except that he is fair, and that she will find no one as handsome:

Ses iauz et son cuer i a mis	She has given him her eyes
Et cil li ra le suen promis.	and her heart, and he has pledged
Promis? Mes doné quitemant.	his to her. Pledged? Rather given
(2817–19)	outright.

Chrétien jests lightly with the theme of two hearts in one body (2825–6), but Cliges and Fenice, with shared desire, belong together (2833–42).

It takes Cliges and Fenice fifty lines to accomplish the process which had cost Alexander and Soredamors several hundred, and infinite heart searching. But on this occasion, time cannot wait. The erstwhile suitor of Fenice, the Duke of Saxony, is approaching with an army. Fenice, a pawn in this game of power, is saved by Cliges. Like Guenevere in *Lancelot* and Lavinia in *Eneas*, she watches from a window as Cliges defeats the Saxon emissary, and rewards him with another exchange of glances (2894–962).

Fenice presents her predicament, lucidly and directly, to Thessala, her teacher and nurse who is skilled in magic (3002–4). Fenice knows that the Emperor Alis will marry her, but she insists that she must have the nephew. If Alis enjoys her, she will have lost joy for ever (3138–43). Again, there is no room for delay, Thessala must act:

'Miauz voldroie estre desmanbree,	'I would rather have my limbs
Que de nos deus fust remanbree	torn from me than that our love
L'amors d'Iseut et de Tristan,	should be remembered like that
Don tantes folies dit l'an,	of Yseut and Tristan, of which
Que honte m'est a reconter.	so many unbecoming stories are

74

Je ne me porroie acorder
A la vie, qu'Iseuz mena.
Amors an li trop vilena;
Car ses cors fu a deus rantiers
Et ses cuers fu a l'un antiers.
Einsi tote sa vie usa,
Qu'onques les deus ne refusa.
Ceste amors ne fu pas resnable;
· Mes la moie est toz jorz estable,
Ne de mon cors ne de mon cuer
N'iert feite partie a nul fuer.
Ja voir mes cors n'iert garceniers,
Ja n'i avra deus parceniers.
Qui a le cuer, si et le cors,
Toz les autres an met defors.'
(3145–64)

told that I am ashamed to speak of them. I could not agree to lead the life that Yseut led. Love became too churlish in her, for her body was hired out to two men, and her heart belonged entirely to one. Thus she spent all her life, never refusing these two. This love was not rational, but mine is forever stable. Neither my body, nor my heart will be shared, not in any way. In truth my body will never be common property; it will never have two men to share it. Let him have the body, who has the heart. All the others I put outside.'

Chrétien's purpose is more positive than mere criticism of Yseut. Fenice is advocating the type of balanced, lasting love which comes from mental control and mutual desire, while Yseut exemplifies life wasted by an irrational love which lacks order, moral values and social approval. Behind the vows which Fenice utters, there is an implicit attack on the concept of Fin'Amors addressed by the courtly lover to the married lady which we find, for example, in the songs of Bernart de Ventadorn and in the De Amore of Andreas Capellanus. Joy for Fenice comes from the pleasure of the heart and body which are shared with one person alone, and there is no exception to this rule. It is wrong, in her eyes, to share the heart with a lover and the body with the husband, as a courtly dame might do, or to give the heart to the lover and the body to both, as Yseut had done, and as Guenevere will do in Lancelot.

Anguish turns to comedy when Thessala rescues her mistress, and, with her magic, turns the world 'upside-down'. She brews a potion which will give Alis the illusion of enjoying Fenice on the wedding night, and afterwards. 'This potion', says Thessala, 'will be like a wall between you':

'. . . quant il dormira formant,
Avra de vos joie an dormant
Et cuidera tot antreset,
Que an veillant sa joie an et.'
(3209–12)

'When he will be fast asleep he will have his joy of you in his sleep and will imagine he is awake at the same time as he has his joy.'

75

This device will also preserve Cliges' rights to the Empire (3227–8).

The plan works perfectly. Cliges, who does not share the secret, gives the potion, at Thessala's request, to Alis who 'trusts him greatly' (3312–15). The nuptial bed is blessed by bishops and abbots with the sign of the cross (3330–1), and Alis enters the land of Tore Lore in love:

Quant ore fu d'aler gesir,
L'anperere, si come il dut,
Avuec sa fame la nuit jut.
'Si come il dut', ai je manti,
Qu'il ne la beisa ne santi;
Mes an un lit jurent ansanble:
La pucele de primes tranble,
Car mout se dote et mout s'esmaie,
Que la poisons ne soit veraie.
Mes ele l'a si anchanté,
Que ja mes n'avra volanté
De li ne d'autre, s'il ne dort.
Mes lors an avra tel deport,
Con l'an puet an sonjant avoir,
Et si tandra le songe a voir.
Neporquant cele le ressoingne,
Premieremant de lui s'esloingne,
Ne cil aprochier ne la puet;
Car maintenant dormir l'estuet.
Et dort et songe et veillier cuide,
S'est an grant painne et an estuide
De la pucele losangier.
Et cele mainne grant dangier
Et se deffant come pucele:
Et cil la prie et si l'apele
Mout soavet sa douce amie,
Tenir la cuide, n'an tient mie;
Mes de neant est an grant eise:
Neant anbrace et neant beise,
Neant tient et neant acole,
Neant voit, a neant parole,
A neant tance, a neant luite.
Mout fu bien la poisons confite,
Qui si le travaille et demainne.
De neant est an si grant painne,
Car por voir cuide et si s'an prise,
Qu'il et la forteresce prise.
Einsi le cuide, einsi le croit,
Et de neant lasse et recroit.

(3332–70)

When the time for bed had come, the Emperor, as he should, lay that night with his wife. 'As he should', with that I have lied, for he did not kiss or caress her. But they lay together in one bed. At first the maiden trembles for she is frightened and troubled that the poison may not work. But it has so bewitched him that he will never again have his will of her or any other, unless he is asleep. But then he will have such delight as one can have by dreaming, and he will believe the dream is true. None the less she is on her guard and at first moves away from him; he cannot approach her, for immediately he is forced to sleep. And he sleeps and dreams and believes he is awake, and that with much effort he is trying to flatter the maid. And she shows great fear and defends her maidenhood; and he entreats her and very gently calls her his sweet love. He believes he holds her; he holds no part of her. But with nothing he is very happy. He embraces nothing, and kisses nothing, he holds nothing, and clasps nothing, he sees nothing, speaks with nothing, disputes with nothing, struggles with nothing. Well indeed was that poison prepared which so works in him and masters him. For nothing does he strive with such effort,

for he imagines, and esteems
himself thereby, that, in truth,
he has taken the fortress. Thus
he imagines it, thus he believes
it. It is of nothing that he
wearies, from nothing that he
desists.

The repetition of *neant* 'nothingness' in ll.3359 to 3363 provides the upside-down climax for this *fabliau*-type wedding night. But the passage has overtones of literary, and possibly philosophical satire. Nothingness was a subject of medieval discussion on which Alcuin's pupil, Fredegisus, had written a treatise, *De nihilo et tenebris*, which had been attacked by Agobard. The first troubadour, Guilhem IX, grandfather of Eleanor of Aquitaine, in his poem *Farai un vers de dreyt nien* had praised, with some self-irony, the 'reality' of nothingness, the unblemished though ephemeral happiness he could find by losing awareness of his sentient self.[11] Jaufre Rudel, about 1147, had found 'wondrous joy' in the dream illusion of possessing his lady.[12] In the lays of Marie de France similar dream-like states change, in a sort of wish fulfilment, into the 'reality' of the beloved or lover from the Other World. The unhappy Lanval is taken to his fairy mistress, and in *Yonec* the discontented wife receives her bird lover.

In twelfth-century troubadour poetry, *nien* 'nothingness' and *cuda* 'fantasy' became key words in a controversy about the conflicting roles of reason and of feeling and fantasy in love, and in life. *Nien* was equated with the vanity of dream-chasing escapism, *per cuda* with the process of inducing this fantasy. So Marcabru, the apostle of *sen* 'good sense' and *mesura* 'the rational sense of what is fitting':

De nien sui chastiaire
E de foudat sermonaire.
(v, 31–2)[13]

I censure the theme of nothingness and I reprove the theme of
folly.

and Raimbaut de Vaqueiras (*c.* 1180–1207), who mocks the imagined *per cuda* love of earlier poets:

Con er perduda
ni m'er renduda

How shall my lady be lost to me
or given back to me, if I have

77

donna, s'enanz non l'ai aguda?
  Qe drutz ni druda
  non es per cuda.
      (xv, 29–33)[14]

not had her already, for a man is not a lover, nor a lady his beloved through imagining it to be so.

In this context, Chrétien, the poet of *sen* and *bone volantez*, gently mocks poetry of *cuidier* and *neant* in this illusory wedding-night romp enjoyed by Alis. He also satirises the inflammatory effects of the love potion of Tristan and Yseut, and Mark's connubial bliss with Brenguain acting as the surrogate Yseut.

Burlesque persists in the reality of the Saxon war when Cliges rescues the abducted Fenice, and love and prowess are united:

Or li est vis que buer fu nez,
Quant il puet feire apertemant
Chevalerie et hardemant
Devant celi qui le fet vivre.
      (3756–9)

Now he feels that fortune smiles, when he can accomplish deeds of chivalry bravely and openly in the presence of her who gives him life.

Love has no part in this German marriage. Alis and Fenice feel no mutual attraction, and, like the husband and wife in Marie de France's *Guigemar* and *Yonec*, they are unsuited by age. Chrétien, like Marie de France, opposes such marriage which, in their view, contravenes *mesura* and the natural order of things. Accordingly, Fenice and Cliges move towards Chrétien's earlier ideal of love in marriage when, in the Saxon campaign and especially in the ambush scene, Fenice shares in the hazards of war. Like Enide, and unlike Soredamors, she will attain happiness only through the trials of life. Yet Love, in courtly fashion, is timid (3817–914):

Des iauz parolent par esgart;
Mes des langues sont si coart.
      (3835–6)

They speak with looks from their eyes; with words from their tongues they are too cowardly.

Chrétien, in good humour, mocks himself when he chides Cliges for this timidity, and satirises the commonplace of the upside-down world of love which disturbs the natural order of things.[15] If Cliges is really a coward:

A ce me sanble que je voie
Les chiens foïr devant le lievre
Et la tortre chacier le bievre,
L'aignel le lo, le colon l'egle.
. . . . .

It seems to me that I see the hounds flee before the hare, and the fish hunt the beaver, the lamb the wolf, the dove the eagle . . . and the stag chase the

Et le lion chace li cers,
Si vont les choses a anvers.
(3848–51, 3857–8)

lion, so does everything go in reverse.

When Cliges fights the Duke of Saxony, Fenice knows that should he die, she will die, for without him there can be no pleasure in life (4055–8). When he falls, she falls likewise:

tant fu esbaïe,
Qu'ele ne criast: 'Des! aïe!'
Au plus haut que ele onques pot.
Mes ele ne cria qu'un mot;
Qu'erranmant li failli la voiz
Et si cheï pasmee an croiz,
Si qu'el vis s'est un po bleciee.
(4101–7)

she was so terrified she could not help crying out: 'God! Help him!' as loud as she could. But that was all she uttered, for her voice failed her at that very moment, and she fell forward with outstretched hands and hurt her face slightly.

Cliges defeats the Duke of Saxony and sets out for Britain to win fame, like his father, at the supreme court of Arthur. He takes leave of Fenice as he would of his courtly lady:

Devant li vient, si s'agenoille
Plorant si que des lermes moille
Tot sun blïaut et son ermine,
Et vers terre ses iauz ancline;
Que de droit esgarder ne l'ose.
(4293–7)

He comes into her presence, kneels down before her, weeping so much that his tunic and ermine are damp from his tears, and he keeps his eyes turned to the ground for he dare not look at her directly.

Fenice, overcoming fear and timidity, replies:

'Amis, biaus sire! levez sus!
Seez lez moi, ne plorez plus
Et dites moi vostre pleisir.'
'Dame! que dire? que teisir?
Congié vos quier.'
(4305–9)

'My friend, fair sir! Rise, and sit beside me, weep no more, and tell me your pleasure.' 'My lady, what is there to say, or to be silent about? I seek your leave to depart.'

Fenice's words befit a *dame* but offer hidden encouragement. The courtly façade, which has begun to crumble, is re-imposed by the skill with which Cliges practises the art of courtly concealment (*celer*):

... droiz est, qu'a vos congié
    praingne
Come a celi cui je sui toz.'
(4326–7)

'It is right that I should take leave of you as of that person to whom I belong entirely.'

Despite the lovers' sighs suppressed, no eyes at court are open enough, no hearing is clear enough to guess that love exists between these two (4328–34).

Chrétien, using the phrases of amorous concealment which he will repeat for Lancelot and Guenevere, is flattering the courtly taste of his audience. He is also amusing it by turning the courtly love situation upside-down. Fenice, in the eyes of a society given to illusion, is, to all appearance, a *dame*, who, on her arrival in Greece, is honoured as Empress at Constantinople (4344–5). On the plane of reality, however, she is a damsel whose youthful heart is entirely with Cliges. She must die if he does not return it to her in person (4340–50). Cliges has offered Fenice his adoration, as Alexander adored Soredamors and as Lancelot will adore Guenevere, and she remembers his wan face and tears:

Qu' aussi vint devant li plorer,	for so did he come with tears
Con s'il la deüst aorer,	into her presence as if he were
Hunbles et sinples a genouz.	impelled to worship her, kneel-
(4367–9)	ing in humility and innocence.

Fenice stores his words in her heart: 'What does "Je sui toz vostre" mean (4411)? Does he love me (4412)? Or did he say it to flatter and deceive me, *por moi losangier* (4441)? He has stolen my heart and me, but does he love me (4464–7)?'

Fenice is beset by humility (4416–7) and doubt. 'If Cliges loved me, as I love him, he would not leave me now. If my heart took company with his, it would never leave' (4486–8). But their hearts, she believes, are different and contrary:

'Li suens est sire, et li miens sers,	'His is the lord, and mine is the
Et li sers maleoit gre suen	serf, and the serf, despite himself,
Doit feire a son seignor son buen	must render good service to his
Et leissier toz autres afeires.'	lord and forsake all other
(4498–501)	personal interests.'

Transient doubt, a feeble antecedent of *Dangier* in the *Rose*, gives her pause: 'Could she not rescue her heart from its captivity?'

'Ramenasse? Fole mauveise,	'Rescue it? Foolish, wicked
Si l'osteroie de son eise,	woman; so would I remove it
Einsi le porroie tuër.	from its ease, so would I cause
La soit! ja nel quier remuër,	it to die. Let it remain there!
Ainz vuel qu'a son seignor remaingne	I do not seek to move it. Rather
Tant que de lui pitiez li praingne;	do I wish it may stay with its
Qu'einçois devra il la que ci	lord until he takes pity on it.
De son serjant avoir merci,	For, because they are in a foreign
Por ce qu'il sont an terre estrange.'	land, he will have mercy on his
(4516–24)	servant sooner there than here.'

In this reversal of the courtly love situation and of its terminology, the lady, whom her suppliant lover, concealing his love, has adored on his knees, declares that her heart is bondman (*sers*) to his. As Fenice, the damsel, waits for clemency, her self-abnegation, like that of Enide, contrasts with the pride of the *dame* which Guenevere will show to Lancelot. Chrétien has reversed the theme of the lover who surrenders his heart to the lady who holds it captive. In a remarkable passage, he now goes further, and through Fenice, mocks the hypocrisy and servility of courtiers, and, by implication, the courtly way of life. Just as Fenice's life at court is based on a lie, so she hopes her captive heart will flatter and please its lord:

'S'il set bien servir de losange,
Si come an doit servir a cort,
Riches sera ainz qu'il s'an tort.
Qui viaut de son seignor bien estre
Et delez lui seoir a destre,
Si come ore est us et costume,
Del chief li doit oster la plume,[16]
Nes lors quant il n'an i a point.
Mes ci a un mout mauvés point:
Quant il l'aplaingne par defors,
Et se il a dedanz le cors
Ne mauvestié ne vilenie,
Ja n'iert tant cortois, qu'il li die,
Ainz li fet cuidier et antandre,
Qu'a lui ne se porroit nus prandre
De proesce ne de savoir,
Si cuide cil qu'il die voir.
Mal se conoist, qui autrui croit
De chose qui an lui ne soit.'
(4526–44)

'If it knows well the language of flattery, which one must use at court, it will be rich before it comes back. Anyone who wishes to be in favour with his lord, and to sit by him on his right hand, must, as is now the fashion and custom, cull the down from his head even when there is none there. But herein lies a great evil: when he smooths him on the outside, and the lord has within himself wickedness and baseness, he will never be so courteous as to tell him this. On the contrary, he gives him the illusion and understanding that no one could compare with him in prowess and wisdom. And the lord imagines that he speaks the truth. Little does that man know of himself who believes another's word about virtues he does not possess.'

Chrétien returns from his attack on the lies of courtiers, worthy of John of Salisbury, to Fenice's hopes of her captive heart:

'Qui les corz et les seignors onge,
Servir le covient de mançonge.
Autel covient que mes cuers face,

'Anyone who frequents courts and lords, must render service with a lie. So must my heart

S'avoir viaut de son seignor grace.'   do, if it desires to receive
      (4561–4)   favour from its lord.'

'But', says Fenice, 'Cliges is so handsome, noble and loyal, that my heart in praising him will never lie, for in him there is nothing which can be improved' (4566–70). Again the courtly situation is reversed. Fenice in the *simplece* of love repeats the conceit which a courtly poet would address to his lady. In courtly society, fulsome praise of a high born lady is a form of blame. Applied to Cliges, it levels gentle irony at Fenice's immoderate enthusiasm, and, as in the poet's excessive praise of Guillem de Nevers, paragon of all the virtues, in *Flamenca*, there is an undertone of mockery at the vanity of words void of true meaning, of the 'speech false and gilded' which Marcabru had attacked. Chrétien ends this scene with a proverb: 'Anyone is evil who entrusts himself to a man of excellent virtue and does not improve in his company' (4573–4). So, Fenice hopes, will her suppliant heart be improved.

Cliges is recognised by Arthur's court as the flower of chivalry, but, unlike Yvain, he does not forget love of the distant Fenice. The turmoil of his thoughts impels him to return to Constantinople where Chrétien receives him with cool humour:

An la cité vint la novele: The news [of his return] came
S'ele fu l'anpereor bele   to this city. No one could ever
Et l'anpererriz çant tanz plus,   doubt – unless he were out of
De ce mar dotera ja nus.   his mind – whether this pleased
       (5111–14)   the Emperor, and gave the
                          Empress pleasure a hundredfold.

In public, Fenice and Cliges can scarcely refrain from embracing and kissing, but this, says Chrétien, would have been folly (5127–31). In a moment, aside from society, they declare their love, Fenice begins: 'Did he love any lady or damsel in Britain?' (5172–3):

'Dame!', fet il, 'j'amai de la,   'My lady', he says, 'I did love
Mes n'amai rien qui de la fust.   there, but I loved no one who
Aussi come escorce sanz fust   belonged there. Like the bark
Fu mes cors sanz cuer an   without its tree, so was my
Bretaingne.'   body without its heart, in
       (5178–81)   Britain.'

'In me nothing is left but the bark: without a heart do I live,
without a heart I exist' (5204–5). He hears that the heart of
Fenice was present there with him: 'God! Why did I not
know it? Why did I not see? God! That I did not know it!
Had I known it, for sure my lady, I would have borne it
noble company' (5218–21).

Chrétien moves from frivolity to seriousness when Fenice
states her position in the love triangle. The falling-in-love is
ended. The scene is set for the next stage, which Fenice
directs:

'Et sachiez bien, se Des me gart,
Qu'ains vostre oncles n'ot an moi
    part,
Que moi ne plot ne lui ne lut.
Onques ancor ne me conut
Si come Adanz conut sa fame.'
            (5235–9)

'And know well, as God may
protect me, that your uncle
never had any share in me, for
to me this was displeasing, nor
was he given the opportunity.
He has never yet known me as
Adam knew his wife.'

She confesses the secret of her false situation as *dame*, her real
love for Cliges: she belongs to him in heart and body.

Chrétien cannot allow Fenice, even in her false role of
dame, to offer herself, like Guenevere, to her lover. Fenice
states her case in a major monologue. She insists on a solution to their problem, which will be acceptable to herself,
to her integrity (Provençal *carestia*), to her sense of the fitness
of things, and to the judgement of the Greek society over
which Cliges is destined to rule. For her, Yseut is the
paradigm of what she refuses to become:

Vostre est mes cuers, vostre est mes
    cors,
Ne ja nus par mon essanpleire
N'aprandra vilenie a feire.'
            (5250–2)

'Yours is my heart, yours is my
body, never through my
example shall anyone learn to
act basely.'

And:

Se je vos aim et vos m'amez,
Ja n'an seroiz Tristanz clamez,
Ne je n'an serai ja Iseuz;
Car puis ne seroit l'amors preuz.'[17]
            (5259–62)

'If I love you, and you love me,
you shall never be called Tristan,
nor I Yseut, for this love would
then lose its nobility and virtue.'

What should be done? Cliges advises flight to Britain, to
Arthur's court, for, and his example is unfortunate, 'Helen
was not received at Troy with such great joy, when Paris

brought her there, as that which the land of my uncle, the king, will feel for you and me' (5299–304). Cliges has no moral sense, or long-term plans for their life at Constantinople. He speaks from *folie*. Fenice, more openly than Enide had done, takes control of their destiny:

'Ja avuec vos einsi n'irai;
Car lors seroit par tot le monde
Aussi come d'Iseut la blonde
Et de Tristan de nos parlé,
Quant nos an seriiens alé;
Et ci et la, totes et tuit
Blasmeroient nostre deduit.'
(5310–16)

'Never will I go away with you like that, for then people would speak of us, throughout the world, as they do of Yseut the Fair and Tristan. And near and far, every man and woman would find fault with our delight.'

The conflict, as Fenice sees, is once more between *savoir* rational control and social duty, and *folie*, the yielding to the demands of feeling. Fenice, like Lavinia, will use *savoir* and found a dynasty; she rejects the folly of passion which destroyed Dido, forsworn to her dead husband. If we run away to Arthur's court, she says, no one would believe, or have the right to believe, that the situation, as it now exists, is true No one would believe I am still a maiden, and not a *dame*:

'Por trop baude et por estapee
Me tandroit l'an et vos por fol.'
(5322–3)

'They would think me a loose woman, out of her senses, and you they would consider a fool.'

Her rhetorical example, not without irony, is St Paul.

'Qui chastes ne se viaut tenir,
Sainz Pos a feire li ansaingne
Si sagemant, que il n'an praingne
Ne cri ne blasme ne reproche.'
(5326–9)

'If anyone does not wish to remain chaste, Saint Paul instructs him to act with such wisdom that he may attract thereby no criticism or blame or reproach.'

Fenice proposes her solution. She will feign death, be buried and rescued. Cliges must prepare the tomb and the bier, and their future dwelling. Fenice confesses her love to Thessala, enlists her aid and her promise to provide a magic potion:

'Et si ai je trové mon per;
Car se jel vuel, il me reviaut,
Se je me duel, il se rediaut
De ma dolor et de m'angoisse.'
(5428–31)

'Now have I found my equal in love, for as I desire him, he desires me in return, and, as I grieve, so does he grieve for my pain and my sorrow.'

Fenice and Cliges, unlike Enide and Erec, attain, from the beginning, this ideal of whole and shared love, and Fenice expounds in brief words what Enide had expressed in the monologue to her cousin at the Joy of the Court.

With humour, restraint and irony, Chrétien prepares a light confection with which to begin this central episode. As Cliges and his servant Jehan return from viewing the tower which will give refuge to the lovers, they hear the people lamenting the 'illness' of the Empress: 'May the Holy Spirit grant health to that noble and wise lady who lies suffering from her great affliction' (5660–2). Again the world is upside-down. Fenice, pretending to be distressed by what really pleases her, orders her chamber to be cleared. Cliges goes around, in delight, with a gloomy face (5693–5).

Fenice refuses a doctor, and misapplying a cliché which normally refers to the lady as the only healer of the lover' ills:

Qu'ele dit que ja n'i avra	She says that she will never have
Mire fors un qui li savra	any doctor save one who will
Legieremant doner santé,	know how to return her to
Quant lui vandra a volanté.	health, easily, when he will
(5707–10)	want to do so.

Nevertheless the doctors enter, inspect the sample of urine which Thessala has thoughtfully obtained from a sick woman:

L'orine voient pesme et pale,	They see the urine, foul and pale,
Si dist chascuns ce que li sanble,	and each one gave his opinion,
Tant que tuit s'acordent ansanble,	until they are all agreed that she
Que ja mes ne respassera	will never recover and will not
Ne ja none nes ne verra,	even see three o'clock that
Et se tant vit, lors au plus tart	afternoon. And if she lives that
An prandra Des l'ame a sa part.	long, it is then at the latest that
(5750–6)	God will take her soul to
	Himself.

These quacks, ignorant, dogmatic, buffoon, qualifying their verdict as soon as it is delivered, are replaced amidst the general lamentation by three ancient physicians from Salerno, who rapidly show their mettle in the pursuit of truth. They see through Fenice's pretence, and, remembering the story of Solomon's wife who deceived her husband by

feigning death (5876–8), they cajole and beat her (5963);
'have no fear of us', they say:

'Ainz que plus vos aiiens bleciee,   'Before we do you further harm,
Vostre folie descovrez,   tell us of the foolish plan which
Que trop vilainnemant ovrez;   you so basely are carrying out.
Et nos vos serons an aïe,   And we will give you aid,
Soit de savoir ou de folie.'   whether your plan springs from
      (5978–82)   wisdom or folly.'

When Fenice endures in silence, they whip her (5984–8),
pour molten lead in her palms (6006) and, as a final cure,
are preparing to grill her on the fire, when a thousand women
and more, led by Thessala, break in and hurl the ancient
doctors over a balcony to their death. 'Never did ladies do
better deed' (6050), adds Chrétien. But the remark is double-
edged. Society believes the false, ignorant doctors in order
to preserve its illusion about the noble and tragic death of
the Empress; it destroys wise men who seek the truth.

There follows a comic-opera scene in which thirty knights,
who are guarding the tomb, lock the gate of the cemetery
from the inside, and fall asleep. Cliges, unable to get in,
scrambles up the wall, 'for Love exhorts and summons him'
(6191), and then down a tree on the other side in a prototype episode for the discovery of the lovers by the hapless
Bertran.

In the 'secret' tower, Cliges believes his beloved is truly
dead. Fenice, in her coma, hears his lament, and her heart
nearly dies of grief:

'M'amie est morte, et je suis vis!   'My love is dead, and I am alive.
Ha, douce amie! vostre amis   Alas! sweet love, why does your
Por quoi vit et morte vos voit?'   love live and see you dead?'
      (6245–7)

In a parody of 'death through love' in Bernart de Ventadorn,[18]
and Tristan, Cliges confesses his guilt:

'Amie! donc sui je la morz   'My love, I am that death which
Qui vos a morte. . . .'   has slain you. . . .'
      (6251–2)

Since their hearts are joined, and her heart lies within him,
he too must die (6265).

The desire to share the 'death' of the beloved is found in

Erec et Enide, Yvain, Lancelot and *Perceval,* as the sign of ultimate love, but here the theme is treated lightly. Fenice stirs:

'Amis, amis! Je ne sui pas
Del tot morte, mes po an faut.'
(6268-9)

'My love, my love, I am not completely dead, though nearly so.'

Cliges and Fenice disport in love with equal desire and joy, in the tower where Cliges ostensibly visits his 'moulting hawk'.

Mes n'est chose que li uns vuelle,
Que li autre ne s'i acuelle.
Einsi est lor voloirs comuns,
Con s'il dui ne fussent que uns.
(6343-6)

There is nothing which the one may desiré which the other does not welcome. So their desire is mutual, as if they were both one.[19]

When Fenice, not having seen the sun or the moon for fifteen months, asks for a garden, Jehan promptly opens up a secret door on to an orchard enclosed by a wall, and here under a vast tree, with props for its branches, the lovers lying naked together are discovered by Bertran, a luckless courtier who is chasing his lost hawk.

In Beroul, the adulterous lovers, clothed and with the sword between them, appear to be chaste when Mark discovers them.[20] In Chrétien, the reverse is true, and the lovers, who are not formally adulterous, are found in an apparently adulterous bed. But what was imminent tragedy, tinged with irony, in the forest of Morois, becomes in *Cliges* light comedy and satire. Bertran cannot believe his eyes. It must be an illusion. 'God. What has happened to me! What wonder do I see. Is this not Cliges? Yes, in faith. Is this not the Empress with him? No, but she looks like her. . . . Such a nose, and mouth and forehead, as my lady the Empress had. Never could Nature create two persons in the one likeness better than this. . . . If she were alive, I would say that it was truly her' (6452-65).

A tant une poire destele,
Si chiet Fenice lez l'oroille.
Cele tressaut et si s'esvoille
Et voit Bertran, si crie fort:
'Amis, amis! nos somes mort!'
(6466-70)

Just then a pear falls down and drops beside Fenice's ear. She starts, wakes, sees Bertran, shouts aloud: 'My love, my love! We shall die!'

Bertran realises he must leave (6476). Cliges leaps up, snatches his sword from in front of the bed, intercepts Bertran who is almost over the wall, cuts off his leg below the knee 'like a twig of fennel'. Bertran, halt and maimed, is conveyed to court where, like the physicians, he is disbelieved and mocked for telling the truth. Set ideas must not be changed, and Bertran, who claims to have seen the Empress lying naked in the orchard, is a *jeingleor* (6512), a trouble-maker, disturber of the peace.

The love idyll in the tower and garden is over. The 'Wall of Air' of solitary illusion has gone, and the lovers, as in all courtly romances, must return to society. This transition could be effected in different ways. In Beroul, there is an attempt to rationalise the sudden reversal of situation through the device of the time limit placed on the working life of the love potion. But such an explanation was not essential. This sudden twist of fortune, characteristic of many romances, *fabliaux*, and *chansons de geste*, appears to have found favour as a stylistic device with courtly audiences, and to have been accepted as such by courtly poets. In *Flamenca* the lovers are restored to society through Archimbaut's abrupt and unexplained conversion to 'sanity' and trust in his wife. In *Cliges*, the secret tower and garden, which Cliges has been visiting openly, is discovered fortuitously as soon as narrative necessity demands this, and poet and audience accept the make-believe, fairy-tale quality of their isolation and their 'secrecy'.

Cliges, Fenice and Thessala flee to Arthur's Britain, and Jehan, the repository of honesty, loyalty and truth, remains to face the Emperor's wrath.

'I will never lie', he says, '. . . and if I have sinned, it is right for me to be made captive':

'Mes por ce me vuel escuser,
Que sers ne doit rien refuser,
Que ses droiz sire li comant.
Ce set l'an bien certainnemant,
Que je sui suens et la torz soe.'
'Non est, Jehanz! einçois est toe.'
'Moie, sire? Voire, aprés lui,
Ne je meïsmes miens ne sui
Ne je n'ai chose qui soit moie,
Se tant non, come il le m'otroie.'
(6549-58)

'But my defence is that a servant may not refuse to do anything his lord commands. People know, for sure, that I am his, and the tower is his.' 'Not so, John. Rather is it yours.' 'Mine, sire? In truth, yes, after him. I do not even belong to myself, nor do I have anything which is mine, unless he grants it to me.'

Jehan cannot be bullied out of his sense of reality. He accuses the Emperor of breaking his vow not to marry, and declares himself ready to die, if necessary, for Cliges, 'but', he adds in an aside in the manner of Yseut, 'he will avenge my death'. As the Emperor, sweating with anger, consigns him to prison, Jehan releases him from his world of illusion, of *neant*:

'Mes de neant estes jalos!
Ne criem pas tant vostre corroz,
Que bien ne vos die oiant toz,
Comant vos estes deceüz,
Et si n'an serai ja creüz.'
(6606–10)

'But you are jealous of an illusion! I do not fear your anger so much that I will not tell you, in the hearing of all people, how you are deceived. And yet I shall never be believed.'

Were he to be burnt or hanged, Jehan would not bear witness against his lord (6628–30).

The Emperor hears this voice of sanity:

Lores a primes s'aparçut,
Qu'onques de sa fame n'avoit
Eü joie, bien le savoit,
Se il ne li avint par songe;
Mes c'estoit joie de mançonge.
(6634–8)

Then, for the first time he realised that he had never enjoyed his wife, and this he knew well, unless it had happened to him in a dream; but this was a joy which had lied to him.

When the Emperor has died of rage and madness and his fruitless search for Cliges, it is the presence of Jehan in the embassy to Arthur's court which guarantees the truth of their message (6711–14), though his fellow emissaries are drawn from the highest Greek nobility. Arthur calls off his plan to invade Greece, to the chagrin of those nobles who would have chosen a purposeless war (6736–8), and Cliges and Fenice return to Constantinople, and are married and crowned:

Et s'amie a fame li donent;
Andeus ansanble les coronent.
De s'amie a feite sa fame,
Mes il l'apele amie et dame,
Ne por ce ne pert ele mie,
Que il ne l'aint come s'amie,
Et ele lui tot autressi,
Con l'an doit feire son ami.
(6751–8)

And they give him his beloved to wife. They crown them both together. He has made his beloved his wife, but he calls her beloved and lady, and she does not lose thereby, for he still loves her as his beloved, and she, in the same way, loves him as one should love one's lover.

And so they live happily ever after, without quarrelling. And Fenice was never shut away from society (6761–2). In this, says Chrétien, she was more fortunate than her successors as Empress, for there was never an Emperor who did not draw the lesson from Fenice's betrayal of Alis, and so imprison his wife in her chamber, with eunuchs as her sole male company. The happy ending is reversed; present joy will not endure.

This bitter-sweet twist to the story may have been taken from the narrative which Chrétien tells us he was using. It also balances his opening praise of *chevalerie* and *clergie* in France in contrast to the uncourtly, unchivalrous ways of the Greeks (30–44). It also forms the antithesis of the ideal of love achieved by Alexander and Soredamors, and so puts the final touch to the system of contrasts on which *Cliges* is constructed.

The theme of love in *Cliges* appears to be treated on four different planes: the narrative necessity of the original story with its bizarre theme of feigned death; the perfection of shared love in dynastic marriage, attained by Alexander and Soredamors in ideal circumstances; the attainment of this same ideal by Cliges and Fenice, who, through *science* and *savoir*, overcome the trials of real life; the conclusion that life is a paradox, and truth and love a passing illusion, and that in real life deceit goes hand in hand with virtue and sows evil results. The Art of Love exemplified by Alexander and Soredamors can be squeezed into the mould of real life as happens in the case of the love and marriage of Cliges and Fenice, but this is an extraordinary event. Ideal and reality are not normally to be matched.

The love affair of Cliges and Fenice is also an Art of Love, a *summa* of the various forms of love and of controversies about love which would engage the attention of Chrétien's audience. We are shown how Cliges and Fenice fall in love through physical attraction and shared dangers, and how they endure the trials of distant love or *amor de lonh*, and the equal desire of mind and body. We see how their love, when this desire is controlled by *savoir*, develops into *Fin'Amors*. In contrast to this ideal development of perfect love, Chrétien demonstrates the constraint on feeling imposed by the feudal and political marriage of a young girl to an old

ruler, and the lies and deception to which young lovers justi-
fiably resort to defeat such a marriage. Although Chrétien
hints with humour and cool irony at the effects of such
deception, he shows no disapproval of the sexual love of
Cliges and Fenice at a time when Fenice is still 'married' to
Alis.

In this he is close to the attitude of Marie de France in
Guigemar and *Yonec*, and hence probably of contemporary
society at the courts of the Plantagenets. Adultery as such
has little interest for Marie. In an arranged marriage, in which
the husband, old, cruel and suspicious, confines his young
wife to the castle, the wife, she believes, is entitled to seek
a love of equal desire with a lover of noble birth with whom
she may find happiness. This rule of *mesure* has two applica-
tions with Marie de France: adulterous love, born of equal
desire, must redress an unhappy arranged marriage (*Guigemar*,
Yonec); it should not, however, disturb a marriage which is
already happy (*Equitan*, *Bisclavret*).

In *Cliges*, Chrétien rejects the reality but not the illusion
of adulterous love. Through Fenice he attacks the irrational,
adulterous passion of Tristan and Yseut, but he condones
the lies and ruses with which Fenice preserves her virginity
and the physical reality of her 'single' love for Cliges. It may
be argued that, in real life, ruses in love are inevitable, and
that in any case Enide used deceit and lies to fool the lustful
count. Yet Fenice and Cliges also deceive the society to
which they belong, in the manner of Tristan and Yseut.
Although the basic theme of *Cliges* is similar to that of *Erec
et Enide*, Chrétien approaches it from a wider viewpoint. The
optimism of *Erec et Enide* becomes muted in *Cliges*. Such hopefulness could not endure in a work, which, though a comedy,
looks at love and life in the round. Fenice brings her story
and that of Cliges to a happy conclusion, but the happiness
promised at the end of *Erec et Enide* is marred in the closing
lines of *Cliges*. Life for Fenice and Cliges is not as straightforward as it was for Erec and Enide, or for Alexander and
Soredamors. In the individual, reason fights with folly and
self-indulgence, truth with illusion and deceit, good with
evil. For lovers fighting against Fortune's blows, there is no
absolute solution. Reason, applied by Fenice to her own ends,
leads her to deceive and betray Alis (6769–71), and the

happiness which she gains for herself and Cliges brings sorrow to her successors.

Similarly there are two contrasting sides to knighthood and the court of King Arthur, the one robust and praise-worthy, the other courtly and effeminate.

Arthur's court, we are told, is renowned throughout the world (68–73). Alexander leaves Constantinople to seek knighthood and fame there, by his own efforts, and not because of his position as son of the Greek Emperor. Endowed with modesty and *mesure*, he sees knighthood as a search for reputation, inimical to the stagnant ways of those who amass wealth at home:

'Maint haut home par lor peresce
Perdent grant los, que il porroient
Avoir, se par le monde erroient.
Ne s'acordent pas bien ansanble
Repos et los, si con moi sanble;
Car de rien nule ne s'alose
Riches hon, qui toz jorz repose.'
(154–60)

'Many men of high nobility lose, through their idle ways, the great reputation which they could have if they journeyed in the world. Fame does not go well with a life of ease, or so it seems to me. For a man who has wealth and power, and takes his rest every day can accomplish no deeds worthy of praise.'

and:

'Et cil est a son avoir sers,
Qui toz jorz l'amasse et acroist.'
(164–5)

'That man is the serf of his riches if he increases and heaps them up every day.'

His father exhorts Alexander to cultivate largess,[21] the supreme virtue, greater than high birth, courtesy, wisdom (*savoir*), gentility, money, strength, chivalry, boldness, presence, beauty, or anything else (202–7).

Alexander, gifted with eloquence, addresses Arthur in elevated, epic style: 'King, unless the reputation which spreads your renown is a lie, no god-fearing king of such power as yours has been born, since God created man. King, your wide renown has brought me to your court . . . engage me in your service, king of great virtue, and my companions who are with me here' (342–8, 358–9).

This epic note continues when Arthur, in France, learns of the treachery of the usurper Angres in Britain. He responds like a king. His barons had advised him to entrust his land to a traitor, worse than Ganelon. He blames them so bitterly that they swear to deliver the traitor to him or never again to hold land from him (1067–92). And Arthur, summoning his army and preparing his ships, is no centrepiece of a grand but limited court. He is a royal and mighty ruler of vast lands. The knighting of Alexander and his twelve comrades is no idle gesture of approval, but a preparation for war. The ritual cleansing occurs in the sea, when the ships are ready to sail, and fame is to be won in battle, and not in the lists. The combat in which the Greek knights engage before the siege of Windsor is epic rather than chivalrous. Alexander addresses his peers:

'Nostre escu por quoi furent fet?
Ancor ne sont troé ne fret.
C'est uns avoirs qui rien ne vaut,
S'an estor non ou an assaut.
Passons le gué, ses assaillons!'
Tuit dïent: 'Ne vos an faillons.'
Ce dit chascuns: 'Se Des me saut,
N'est vostre amis, qui ci vos faut.'
                    (1303–10)

'For what purpose were our shields fashioned? As yet they bear no hole or fracture. They are possessions which have no value except in attack or assault. Let us cross the ford, and engage them!' 'We shall not fail you', they reply as one man, and they each say, 'As God give me salvation, anyone who fails you here, has no love for you.'

When the enemy are routed, Alexander presents four captive knights to the Queen, for fear that Arthur might hang them. Here Chrétien brings the knightly and feudal codes into conflict, almost in the form of a courtly debating point: How should the chivalrous knight behave in war? Is his duty to the Lady, the Queen to whom par corteisie he offers the prize of his premiere chevalerie (1349–1350), or to the King in whose army he fights? In this campaign the present-day reader and presumably Chrétien's audience can scarcely fail to see in Arthur a suggestion of Henry II as a political animal, an energetic king fighting for his land. In this depiction of Arthur Chrétien was probably influenced by Wace, but his probable purpose is also to use him as a contrast to Alis, the feckless Emperor of Greece. Opinion favours Alexander:

Tuit dïent que mout est cortois
Alixandres et bien apris
Des chevaliers qu'il avoit pris,
Quant au roi nes avoit randuz;
Qu'il les eüst ars ou panduz.
                    (1358–62)

They all say that Alexander acted in very courteous and accomplished fashion in not surrendering the knights, whom he had captured, to the King, who would have had them burned or hanged.

But the King is not playing at war, nor is he the poltroon of *Yvain* and *Perceval*. He summons the Queen to deliver the traitors. Chrétien lightens this moment of crisis, when the attention of his audience would be fully engaged, by a swift change of mood. He reintroduces his love theme as Sore-damors, sitting near Alexander, spies the thread of her golden hair which she sewed into the arm and neck of his shirt. How should she address a knight? Should she call him *ami*, use his name? But Arthur condemns the traitors to Ganelon's death, to be dragged apart by horses. As compensation for the loss of his knightly captives, Arthur gives Alexander five hundred Welsh knights and a thousand foot soldiers, with the promise of the finest kingdom in Wales, when the war is done (1363–461).

When victory is won, thanks to Alexander's device of disguising himself in enemy armour, and to the divine aid which causes the moon to appear during a surprise attack, Alexander advises the enemy to yield. Arthur will be merciful: 'Go forth disarmed to my lord the King . . . you will not die thereby, for my lord the King will forget all his wrath and anger, so gentle and courteous is he' (2182–9). Epic reality persists when Alexander sends his emissary, Acori-onde, to challenge the false Emperor's right to the crown:

Jusqu'a l'anpereor ne fine,
Il nel salue ne l'ancline
Ne anpereor ne l'apele.
'Alis!' fet il, 'une novele
De par Alixandre t'aport,
Qui la defors est a cest port.
Antant que tes frere te mande:
La soe chose te demande,
Ne rien contre reison ne quiert.
Soe doit estrë, et soi iert
Costantinoble que tu tiens.
Ce ne seroit reisons ne biens,
Qu'antre vos deus eüst descorde.
Par mon consoil a lui t'acorde,
Si li rant la corone an pes. . . .'
(2479–93)

He does not pause until he finds the Emperor. He neither greets him, nor bows, nor calls him emperor. 'Alis', he says, 'I bring you news from Alexander who is out there in the harbour. Listen to the message your brother sends. He demands what is his, and seeks nothing which is not rightfully his. Constantinople, which you hold, must be, and shall be his. It would not be right or seemly that there should be discord between you two. Take my counsel. Seek an agreement with him. Give him back the crown in peace. . . .'

When Alis prevaricates, Acorionde utters the *desfi*: 'Alis, may God destroy me, if the matter rests here. I defy and challenge you in the name of your brother. And in his name, as is my duty, I summon all those whom I see here to leave you and join him, for it is their duty to take him as their lord. Let the loyal man show his loyalty' (2516–24). But the brothers compromise: Alexander shall rule the land and allow Alis to enjoy the honour and title of Emperor (2555–63). This solution, to an audience of 1176 or thereabouts, can scarcely have failed to bring to mind the tense situation and rivalry between Henry II's eldest son, Henry the Young King, who in 1170 had been crowned King of England, but was granted no lands to rule, and his younger brother, Richard, Duke of Aquitaine.

Cliges receives his baptism of war in the fighting against the Duke of Saxony. His preliminary mass joust with the Saxon emissary and his followers, modelled on that of Alexander at Windsor, ends with a ferocity to match that of Beroul's *Tristan*. He kills the Duke's nephew, and defeats the Saxon knight who has sworn to have his head in revenge. Cliges cuts off the head of the Saxon knight and sticks it on his lance. Comedy goes with ferocity, as in the *Chanson de Guillaume* (2238–98).[22] Disguised in the dead knight's armour and riding his warhorse, Cliges, pursued by his own men in a scene worthy of *Aucassin et Nicolette*, is admitted to the Saxon ranks. 'Here comes our knight! On the point of his lance he bears the head of Cliges, and the Greeks are in close pursuit. To horse, to bear him aid' (3545–9). As Cliges charges with epic fury at the Saxons who are galloping to his aid, the situation is reversed in which Guivret attacked Erec whom he sought to rescue:

Criant s'esleisse vers un Sesne,	Shouting a war cry he hurls
Sel fiert de la lance de fresne	himself at a Saxon and with his
Atot la teste anmi le piz	lance of ash strikes both his head
Si que les estriers a guerpiz,	and the middle of his breast and
Et crie an haut: 'Baron! ferez!	knocks him out of his stirrups.
Je sui Cligés que vos querez.	He cries aloud: 'Strike, my lords
Or ça, franc chevalier hardi!	and noble warriors, I am Cliges
Ne n'i et nul acoardi;	whom you seek. To the fight,
Car nostre est la premiere joste!	my noble and daring knights.
Coarz hon de tel mes ne goste.'	Let no man flinch, for the first
(3561–70)	affray is ours. No coward can
	relish such a feast.'

Cliges again tricks the enemy with his disguise when he rescues Fenice from abduction on the battlefield, but his acts of deceit do not impair his prowess as victor over the Duke of Saxony. Yet when Cliges arrives in Britain, his fighting becomes the self-interested jousting of a knight in the lists. At the Oxford tournament, he again adopts a disguise, this time of different coloured armour, black, green, and scarlet, and finally the white armour and the warhorse which he had when he was first knighted.

Disguise in battle is an epic, and sometimes humorous, stylistic device. But why this disguise in the lists? Was it for the symbolical value of the different colours?[23] Was it to show that Cliges has no identity at Arthur's court? Or did it have the literary purpose, as in *Lancelot*, of amusing an audience and lending dramatic suspense to a characterless episode? All these considerations appear to have secondary validity. The true explanation probably lies in the contrast between the use of armour as a disguise to gain an advantage in a just war, as practised by Cliges in the Saxon war, and Alexander at Windsor, and as a device with which to pique the curiosity of the whole concourse at the Oxford tournament and so to mock knightly addiction to fine equipment and the precious remarks inspired by this, similar to the irony which Shakespeare uses against the French nobility before Agincourt.

Certainly, Arthur's world has undergone a deep sea-change. Emaciated and precious, it feeds on illusion and eschews reason. Arthur is no longer the successful general who had his enemies drawn alive by horses. When Cliges, disguised as the Black Knight, 'disappears' after the first day, Arthur crosses himself in supernatural fear:

'Par foi!' fet il 'ne sai qu'an die,
Mes a grant mervoille me vient.
Ce fu fantosmes se devient,
Qui antre nos a conversé.'
(4748–51)

'In faith', he says, 'I know not what to say about this. But it seems a very wondrous thing to me. Perhaps it was a phantom which was among us.'

He frees the defeated knights from their oaths of submission to the 'phantom', but, says Chrétien, he might just as well have kept quiet (4758).

Cliges, disguised as the Green Knight, is described with Chaucerian clarity:

A tant ez vos Cligés batant
Plus vert que n'est erbe de pre,
Sor un fauve destre comé.
        (4768–70)

Behold withal Cliges galloping
fast, greener than meadow grass,
on fallow red steed with mane
falling to the right.

and Chaucerian humour:

Et de l'une et de l'autre part
Dïent: 'Cist est an toz androiz
Assez plus janz et plus adroiz
De celui d'ier as noires armes,
Tant con pins est plus biaus que
    charmes,
Et li loriers plus del seü.'
        (4774–9)

And on all sides, they say:
'This knight, in every respect, is
more graceful, more skilful than
he who yesterday bore the black
arms, just as the pine is more
beautiful than the silver beech,
and the laurel than the elder.'

Chrétien uses the jape of the changing armour to point
up courtly preciosity and trust in illusion. He also appears
to be mocking the conventional symbolism of colours:
'green is goodness, fertility, so a Green Knight is better than
a Black Knight'. As the Green Knight, Cliges defeats Lancelot,
as the Scarlet Knight he takes Perceval prisoner, and as the
White Knight he proves himself a match for Gawain. Then
he must suffer the conventional hyperbole of the courtly
flatterers. This Chrétien also mocks:

'Tot autressi con li solauz
Estaint les estoiles menues,
Que la clartez n'an pert es nues,
La ou li rai del soloil neissent:
Aussi estaingnent et abeissent
Noz proesces devant les voz;
Si soloient estre les noz
Mout renomees par le monde.'
        (5008–15)

'Just as the sun dims the light of
the little stars so that their
brightness cannot be seen in the
sky when the rays of the sun are
new, so are our deeds of prowess
dimmed and abased in the
presence of yours. Yet ours were
wont to have great fame
throughout the world.'

Such language is beyond Cliges:

Cligés ne set qu'il lor responde;
Que plus le loent tuit ansanble
Qu'il ne devroient, ce li sanble;
Mes bel li est et s'an a honte;
Li sans en la face li monte
Si que tot vergoignier le voient.
        (5016–21)

Cliges knows not what to say in
reply, for all of them in
concourse praise him more than
his due, it seems to him. But it
pleases him, and yet he feels
shame; the blood rises to his
cheeks so that all can see his
modesty of feeling.

Although Chrétien tells us that Cliges accomplished 'many a knightly deed' in Arthur's service in Brittany, France and Normandy, he shows us Arthur's court on this occasion as a self-contained storehouse of knightly prowess, reputation, and precious manners. He may have wished to use it as a contrast to the faithlessness and injustice rife in the Greek court at Constantinople, especially in the person of Alis. But Arthur and his court are given this static role in Chrétien's other works, and it is only in *Cliges* that he puts on the mantle of the warrior king. To this part he reverts once more at the end of the romance when he espouses the cause of Cliges against Alis. He summons his forces for war (6692–8), yet with conspicuously less fire and zest than he had showed in the campaign against Angres.

This treatment of Arthur as both dynamic feudal ruler and the centrepiece of a court given to knightly pastimes and trivial speech is unique in Chrétien's romances, and is part of the duality of thematic construction which is peculiar to *Cliges*. Such duality, depending on a juxtaposition of opposites, *savoir/folie*, fertility/sterility, order/confusion, Fin'*Amors/amour-passion*, reality/illusion, provides the *sen* which Chrétien gave to the basic story he inherited. Such clear juxtaposition of opposites was a characteristic of the troubadours who had composed at Poitiers in the early decades of the twelfth century. Guilhem IX sings of idealised and bawdy love, of sensual reality and the reality of nothingness, and Marcabru (1130–c. 1150) mocks the knights and ladies, who in their cocoon of courtliness, void of *mesura* 'as the Ancients taught it', take a gadfly for a hawk and gape at the painted image (*peintura*) of life.[24] This duality of approach also led poets to use the device of the world upside-down and examples of this can be found in the troubadour poetry of Chrétien's day. Wisdom and folly, reality and illusion, churlish truth and courtly pretence are given reversed roles for the purpose of mockery, humour, moralising, irony or parody.

Although the forces of evil, in the person of Alis, appear to be defeated in *Cliges*, and the virtue of *savoir* in the person of Fenice appears to be victorious, there is less moralising intention in *Cliges* than in Chrétien's other romances. Absolute happiness, order, and harmony are not to be attained through reason (*savoir*) in real life. Truth and illusion persist, even for Fenice, for whom love for Cliges must be 'whole', must be approved by society and so result in the happiness of a dynastic marriage. But to achieve this 'real' life, she creates a world of deceit and illusion for others, for Alis through the 'love' potion, and for Alis and society through her feigned death. In her soliloquy of distant love for Cliges (4526–64), she looks with a cool eye at the flattering and lying ways of the world, yet adds to these lies with the deceptions with which she, like Flamenca, directs her love affair to success.

Such sen as there is in Cliges appears to be that savoir, which recognises truth, is far better than folie, which condones illusion, but that, in the real world, savoir is not free from folie, and must coexist with it as part of the human condition. Fenice, the epitome of savoir and the ability to manipulate the folie of others for her own ends, is contrasted with Alis who inhabits a self-induced state of illusion: 'I did not mean to deceive Cliges with my marriage' (6594). Jehan, the apostle of truth and reality, is contrasted with Thessala, who fabricates illusion. Arthur's court delights in the illusion offered by Cliges with his four suits of armour at Oxford, and the Greek court is a land of Tore Lore in its insistent belief in the reverse of the truth. Even the armies of Arthur and Alis in the field are deceived by the supposed death, the fausse morte theme in a different guise, of Alexander and Cliges, who for tactical advantage assume enemy armour and leave their own to be discovered with lamentations on the field of battle.

Chrétien mocks lightly the folly of those who accept an illusory view of life, the peintura as Marcabru called it, and like the later poet of Flamenca, whose tolerance he shares, he sharpens his depiction of it by the reality of the setting which he fashions.[25] In the case of Cliges, this reality has a geographical and historical basis. The localities of Celtic tradition are replaced by the place-names of England; Winchester, 'a short ride by the straight road from Southampton' (291–305), Windsor, Wallingford, Oxford, London, Shoreham, the Thames, Dover and Canterbury; of Athens and Constantinople; and of Germany, Cologne, the Black Forest, Saxony, Ratisbon and the Danube. The political marriage of Alis and Fenice almost certainly reflects a historical event of the time, which Chrétien, characteristically in this romance, turns upside-down. On 24 May 1170, Frederick Barbarossa, at the height of the struggle between Papacy and Empire, sought an alliance with Constantinople. In response to an embassy which he sent there from Ratisbon, Greek emissaries arrived in Cologne in June of the following year to arrange for the marriage of Barbarossa's eldest son to Maria, only daughter of the Greek Emperor. This great match, linking the Empires of East and West, failed, largely because of the opposition of the Duke of Saxony and Bavaria, at a final meeting with the Greeks at Ratisbon. Chrétien preserves the geographical sequence of Ratisbon, Cologne, Ratisbon, and, almost certainly, uses the historical Duke of Saxony as prototype of the Duke of Saxony who opposes the marriage of Alis, claims the hand of Fenice and is foiled by Cliges. But Chrétien reverses the roles of the Greeks and Germans. In Cliges it is the Greeks who approach the Germans in seeking the marriage and the alliance.[26]

Are all these paradoxes more than coincidental? Was it Chrétien's intention to make Cliges so many-sided, a court entertainment, a comedy, a royal fabliau, a dramatised Art of Love, a twelfth-century summa, in partly burlesque form, of current attitudes to Love? And does Cliges then have a place in Chrétien's development as a composer of romances, and in the evolution of the genre? The answer is almost certainly 'Yes'. Cliges is a highly inventive, original work in which Chrétien displays the ideas, attitudes, and literary themes current in the courts of his day. He gathers style and incident from the chanson de geste, the topics of reality/appearance, truth/illusion, savoir/folie, probably from the early troubadours, the art of falling in courtly love from the Roman d'Eneas, from Ovid, among other sources.[27] To the tender restraints of this psychological art, he adds the sexual delight of the unmarried Cliges and Fenice, in the style of Marie de France, and denigrates the love of Yseut and Tristan. It is a mark of the courtly romance, as of the best courtly lyric, the canso, tenso and sirventes, that it should present a problem, to puzzle and intrigue its audience. Chrétien usually does this in a subtle and philosophical manner. He is closer to Seneca and Cicero than to Andreas Capellanus. But in Cliges he presents his audience with a variety of courtly and uncourtly topics, adds more than a dash of philosophy, irony and burlesque, and, probably unwittingly, ensures the great success of this joyous work, and its direct ancestry of the greater romance of *Flamenca*.

Although its influence is perceptible in *Lancelot* and *Perceval*, *Cliges* appears to lie aside from the main path of Chrétien's development. It provides a pause in his progress in which he widens his structural methods, his range of mood, his philosophy of life which now doubts the optimistic certainties of *Erec et Enide*, the attainable ideal of an integrated joy and goodness within the individual and society. *Cliges* is an antidote to this hopefulness. Although it deals, in more courtly fashion, with the theme of *savoir/folie* and the trials of love before marriage and not within marriage as in *Erec et Enide*, it is less Arthurian, less idealising, and less concerned with the moral problem of absolute good and evil. *Erec et Enide* ends with a triumphal flourish at the prospect of dynamic prosperity and general happiness, *Cliges* finishes on a muted, ironical note. *Cliges*, composed in a restrained mood of amused tolerance, is more complex, sophisticated, worldly. The apparent *sen* of *savoir/folie* is presented boldly to the audience, not unfolded enigmatically. But the true *sen*, such as it is, is conditioned by Chrétien's descent from the idealised world of Erec and Enide, to the real life of war, of ruse and deception as practised by Alis, Cliges and Fenice. The true *sen* lies in the recognition of human frailty, the uncertainty and absurdity of human existence. In *Erec et Enide*, *savoir* overcomes *folie*, virtue defeats self-interest, and the individual, the general and the universal planes are fused, in the Joy of the Court and the Coronation, into an integrated 'wholeness' in which the ideal becomes reality. *Cliges* has no such single-minded intention. The disparate elements, ideas and topics are presented in clear, expository, sometimes burlesque and ironical fashion, but it is not Chrétien's intention to reconcile them. They must remain 'fragmented', in unresolved conflict. In this sense, *Cliges* is a debate about problems to which the answers are all qualified. With this innovatory approach, Chrétien is indulging the taste of a courtly society which delighted in diversity of mood, theme and style, which took pleasure in seeing folly juxtaposed with wisdom, the *Roman de Renart* with the romances and epics which it satirised, the *pastourelle* and *chanson de toile* with the *canso*, and the bawdy pun concealed in the heart of a lyric of idealised love[28] – a society which also found delight in questions of behaviour, of courtly casuistry in love, such as we find in the *De amore* of Andreas Capellanus.

Chrétien's breadth of approach and sense of distance in *Cliges* is especially evident in his use of what may be called 'multiple incidents', which combine a variety of moods and styles, as in the episode of feigned death. This Shakespearean type of device, in which comedy jostles tragedy, and thereby mocks and enhances serious intention, and is then removed from the stage, becomes a major stylistic device in Chrétien's later romances, especially *Lancelot* and *Perceval*, in which the 'fragmented' incidents of folly, of the 'world upside-down', can be understood more clearly in the context of Chrétien's development as a writer in *Cliges*. This work, with its almost thirteenth-century attitude of detached irony and tolerance, was important for the development of the romance genre. But its major importance lay in the influence of its 'fragmented' view of the insoluble problems of life, of human weakness and evil. It is the juxtaposition of this view with the aspiration to the 'wholeness' of the ideal life, and the conflict, in different forms, between these extremes, which provides the width, colour and richness of the later romances, and especially of the supreme Quest for knowledge of the Grail.

Later romances

4

Lancelot and the quest for Fin' Amors

Le Chevalier de la Charrette or Lancelot is a landmark in Chrétien's work. Previously, he was concerned with lovers who are destined to rule. Their ordered love, made secure within marriage, offered stability to society and to their dynasty, and their wisdom and experience promised good government for their subjects. This macrocosm of the general good depended directly on the individual trials which prepared the lovers for sovereignty. In the later romances this situation is reversed. The heroine, decisive, abounding in mesure and endurance, guiding the action towards happiness for herself, her lover and society, disappears. These later romances centre on a man and his lacks and failures which are symbolised in the titles, Le Chevalier de la Charrette, Le Chevalier au Lion, Le Conte du Graal. Erec and Enide, Cliges and Fenice formed complementary social units. Lancelot, Yvain and Perceval are isolated. They must achieve an ideal of 'completeness' within themselves, by their independent actions, and their fitness for this task is in ratio to their separation from the conventional values of Arthur's world. Benefits may accrue to society from the quests by which they redeem failure and find 'wholeness'. Prisoners will be freed from the land of Gorre, damsels will be rescued from slavery by Yvain, the Waste Land may grow fertile and Grief turn to Joy if Perceval finds the explanation of the Lance and Grail. But Chrétien has moved away from the aims and values of the courtly society for which he writes. The ideal of reason and experience as a basis for temporal happiness is replaced by a quest, which leads through self-knowledge, to humility, caritas, inner peace, and ultimately, in Perceval, to knowledge of God. Chrétien moves beyond the classical humanism of thinkers such as John of Salisbury, and the Platonic and Ciceronian ideal of a life devoted to the social good, and progresses step by step towards Cistercian ideals. Topical allusions to everyday life in the early romances give way to a much wider use of the Celtic supernatural background. A higher, universal meaning transcends by far the *sen* of the narrative line of the story and of the actions or quests of the characters for which it provides an overall framework. These changes are clearly evident in *Yvain* and *Perceval*. In embryonic form they play a major part in the shaping of *Lancelot*.

In this process, Chrétien's thought has changed from what some troubadours of his day would have called a 'fragmented' view of life to one that is 'whole'. 'Fragmented' works were concerned with the here-and-now plane of temporal values and courtly doctrine. 'Whole' works brought the planes of sensual, mental and spiritual experience into harmony, and, transcending the temporal, might aspire, through allusive imagery, symbolism and allegory, to values which were close to or identical with those of the Christian experience. The controversy between 'fragmented' and 'whole' writing, and the 'clear' and 'dark' styles in which they were expressed, reached a climax about 1170 in the poetry of Peire d'Alvernhe, who, as Chrétien appears to do in the later romances, clearly rejected the Joy of the World for the Joy of God and his hope of salvation.[1] There is no evidence that this controversy in troubadour poetry affected Chrétien directly, but it is probably between 1177 and 1181 that he composed the two works, *Lancelot* and *Yvain*, in which his changed outlook becomes increasingly apparent.

It is the quality of *Lancelot* as a transitional work which especially engages our attention. The theme of Lancelot's love for Guenevere is given perspective and distance by the allegorical conflict between Good and Evil into which it is finally absorbed. This wider moral conflict, unlike the theme of Lancelot's love, can be and is determined, at least temporarily, at the end of the romance. So there is within *Lancelot* a dichotomy of thematic levels. There is contrast and also assimilation between the literal theme of profane *Fin'Amors* and the allegorical plane of universal moral values in which true honour and integrity is set against its illusory appearance, and in which goodness is set to fight its quiet, incessant battle against flamboyant and omnipresent evil. This

thematic dichotomy is enhanced by a dichotomy of atmos-
pheres, courtly and Celtic, a duality of background in which
the circumscribed world of Arthur's court is juxtaposed
with the land of Gorre, with its limitless sense of the unknown, of the Other World and the supernatural happenings
which Lancelot encounters on his quest. This diversity of
atmosphere and of thematic intention gives the *Lancelot* an
incomplete and timeless air, suspended in a world of
mystery in which the unexpected may be expected at any
moment.

In *Cliges* Chrétien had already used a thematic construction
based on the juxtaposition of opposites. It is not surprising
that he should wish to extend this method in *Lancelot*, and
apply it to wider issues, especially if, as has been suggested
above, his inspiration was inclining away from worldly to
universal values. It is possible that Marie de Champagne,
perhaps unwittingly, may have given him the impetus to
enlarge the scope of his work by the nature of her commission which Chrétien describes: 'Since my lady of Champagne
wishes me to work on the composition of a romance, I will
undertake this right willingly, as a man should who, in all
that he can achieve in this world, belongs entirely to her.'
He has no desire to flatter her: 'Shall I say that the worth of
the countess is greater than that of queens, as the diamond
is more valuable than precious stones and the sardonyx?
No! I will say nothing of this, even if, despite my silence,
it is true' (1–6, 16–20):

Mes tant dirai je que miauz oevre	But this much I will say, her
Ses comandemanz an ceste oevre	instruction is of more moment
Que sans ne painne que j'i mete.	in this work than any meaning
Del Chevalier de la Charrete	or effort which I put into it.
Comance Crestiiens son livre;	Chrétien begins his book about
Matiere et san l'an done et livre	the Knight of the Cart. The
La contesse, et il s'antremet	subject-matter for this, and the
De panser si que rien n'i met	treatment of it, and its meaning,
Fors sa painne et s'antancion.	are given and supplied to him
(21–9)	by the Countess, and he turns
	his mind to careful thought so
	that he puts nothing into this
	work other than his effort and
	his elaboration of the meaning.

The last two lines of this passage are ambiguous. If we accept *painne* as a combination of 'effort' and 'purpose', as F. D. Kelly has suggested, and *antancion* as synonymous with *gloser*,[2] a possible translation would be: 'and he turns his mind to careful thought so that he puts nothing into this work other than her intention and interpretation of the meaning'.

The *matiere* which the countess provided, may have had two component parts. The first was the abduction of Guenevere which existed in various forms. The best known of these abductions or *aitheda* belongs to the Celtic tradition from the *Vita Gildae* attributed to Caradoc of Llancarfan. In this story Maelwas, king of the South (Somerset) steals Guennuvar, a name which can also mean 'White Fairy', and takes her to Glastonbury (*urbs vitrea*). When Arthur comes to her rescue with a large army, Maelwas heeds the advice of the abbot and of Gildas, and returns her to the king. The second component was probably Lancelot's quest for Guenevere, their adulterous love, Lancelot's victory over Meleagant and Guenevere's safe return to Arthur. An early version of Guenevere's abduction in which Lancelot saves her from danger, without there being any adulterous love between them, forms the basis of the *Lanzelet* of Ulrich von Zatzik-hoven.[3]

Marie de Champagne may have given Chrétien the idea of treating this story of abduction, quest and rescue as a form of initiation into Love, an acting-out in romance form of the conventional themes and love situations associated with *Fin'Amors*[4] such as had inspired Bernart de Ventadorn when he sang at the court of her mother, Eleanor of Aquitaine. In this case *Lancelot* may have been intended by Marie as a sequel, and possibly a riposte, to Chrétien's advocacy in *Cliges* of true love within marriage. It may also have been meant as a companion piece to the *De amore*, composed by Andreas Capellanus most probably at the court of Champagne, which codified, with good-humoured irony, the courtly ideas which had been current at the court of Eleanor, including the second rule of Love that Love within marriage is impossible. Chrétien may possibly have been grateful for the opportunity of treating the full theme of *Fin'Amors* after the 'pseudo-adultery' of Cliges and Fenice, and of adapting it to the wider purposes of his work.

Fin'Amors in courtly poets such as Bernart de Ventadorn, some of whose works survive in Northern French translations,[5] demanded complete obedience and submission to the lady who in her lover's eyes was the image of beauty, the ideal of all courtly virtues, the source of true joy and the cure for the suffering she inflicted. Love might derange the lover and deprive him of self-control, but reason and moderation and a sense of social fitness in his role of lover must overcome this folly and bring sensual desire into harmony with mental and spiritual aspiration. In this respect, Bernart de Ventadorn diverges from the norm. He chooses to welcome and not to control the 'folly' of rapturous feeling which bears him along 'like a leaf following the wind', a lack of volanté or commitment for which Chrétien, as we have seen, appears to chide him (see p. 68). Such Fin'Amors in the lyric poetry of the troubadours and in the De amore might be rewarded with a love token, a sleeve or ribbon, a kiss and a promise, and possibly a nude embrace which excluded the sexual act. Desire depended on aspiration, and on distance which was inspired either by the lady who set tests for her lover, or by the lover himself, when, like Jaufre Rudel, he sought refuge from physical desire in the mental joy of distant love or amor de lonh. Such a controlled love as this type of Fin'Amors with its attendant courtly virtues of restraint, patience, humility and service, may have provided that love, in the sense of amicitia, which was not normally the mainspring of a feudally arranged marriage. In a less courtly form, it was recognised by Marcabru, who sang at the court of Eleanor's father, as an antidote to the sexual licence of the nobility, a source of serenity in a world of moral confusions. Fin'Amors, as a pattern of ordered behaviour, also provided courtly society with an antidote to socially disruptive passion such as that of Tristan and Yseut. In these two contrasting attitudes to love, reason and mental control are directly opposed to the 'folly' of unrestrained feeling.

The adulterous love of Lancelot and Guenevere imposed problems of thematic treatment on Chrétien. He had to differentiate their Fin'Amors from the disruptive passion of Tristan and Yseut which he had attacked in Cliges. He may have had no qualms about the night of passion which Lancelot and Guenevere spend together, since in Cliges he had accepted the notion of adulterous love, however hedged around by the device of the magic potion, and in *Perceval* he describes the sensual love of Perceval and Blancheflor. Like Marie de France, he accepts that lovers who suit each other are entitled to the happiness or *le bien* of consummated love, provided that this involves no *vilenie* or injury to an innocent third party, as in Marie's *Equitan* or *Bisclavret*. In *Cliges*, the deceived husband, Alis, is no innocent third party but a perjured opportunist. Is Arthur also culpable towards Guenevere? He treats the Queen with scorn when he orders her to abase herself before the seneschal, and with indifference when he entrusts her to the care of Kay. In the eyes of Marie de France, and probably of Chrétien, this harshness would justify Guenevere's acceptance of Lancelot as her lover. It has been suggested that Chrétien, the apostle of married love in *Erec et Enide*, may have had reservations about a romance with a central theme of adulterous love, and that for this reason he failed to finish the work. This view is almost certainly too extreme. Chrétien would have seen Lancelot's devoted passion and Guenevere's adultery as two of the many different aspects of love which he treats in his romances. To his balanced mind the sexual love of Lancelot and Guenevere would provide a counterpart to the married passion of Erec and Enide. In similar fashion, we see a balanced and contrasting treatment of the theme of love in Marie de France.[6]

In *Cliges*, the Queen in her social role praises the merits of marriage to Alexander and Soredamors. In *Lancelot* she commits adultery. Is there a connection? Did Chrétien, seeing Guenevere as a queen with duties, like those of Yseut, to the damsels at her court, also wish to show her as a woman of Didoesque passion? Or was this complicated Guenevere, aloof and courtly, but with fire raging in the marrow, imposed on him by Marie de Champagne? We cannot know the answer to such questions, but, if Chrétien meant what he said in Fenice's attacks on Yseut, Guenevere could belong in heart and body either to Lancelot or to Arthur, but not, like Yseut, to both lover and husband, and he must have had doubts about the love triangle at Arthur's court after Lancelot's return from the land of Gorre. Seeing her lover, the Queen can scarcely restrain her passion in public and there is no evidence that Lancelot, as has been suggested, had fallen out of love with her. In this light, it is understandable that Chrétien should leave Lancelot imprisoned in the tower, in the amorous impasse of consummated Fin'Amors, the very situation which the unrequited lover in Guillaume de Lorris desired so ardently as he languished outside the tower of Bel Acueil. The possibility that Chrétien wished to avoid the inevitable return of Lancelot, like Tristan to the court of Mark, is a good reason, though not the only one, why he should instruct Godefroy de Leigni to finish the work in accordance with the plans, and, most probably, the draft he had prepared.

The subject-matter of Lancelot imposed on Chrétien the necessity for a narrative construction different from the two-part structure of Erec et Enide and Yvain.[7] Lancelot goes on a round trip from Arthur's court to the land of Gorre and back again, and these two journeys, with the central love episode of Guenevere and Lancelot, form the substance of the plot, of which the three main divisions are:

1 Meleagant's challenge and Lancelot's quest (1–3020)[8]
2 The events at Bademagu's court (3021–5115)
3 Lancelot's imprisonment, and his defeat of Meleagant (5116–7134).

During Lancelot's quest, obstacles are placed in his path to prevent him from entering the land of Gorre and so reaching Guenevere. After the central love episode, obstacles are put in his way to prevent him from leaving the land of Gorre and meeting Meleagant at Arthur's court.[9]

This horseshoe-type structure of two journeys and a central episode follows naturally from the traditional tripartite framework of abduction, rescue and return. It accords remarkably well with the thematic structure of the two levels of sen which Chrétien interweaves in the story. On the level of Fin'Amors, Lancelot's quest is divided between his journey to the land of Gorre, and his victories and consequent imprisonment in that land. In the first part he is faced by trials which test his devotion and love for Guenevere. In the second part, his courtly virtues of patience, constancy, obedience to love and disdain of vaine gloire, are tested by Guenevere and by the trials imposed on him by Meleagant. The higher sen, which is symbolised by the plight of

Meleagant's prisoners in the land of Gorre and their final freedom, is unfolded through the revelation of Lancelot's moral excellence on a plane of human values which is less self-enclosed than the courtly plane and in absolute opposition to the Evil symbolised by Meleagant. This moral *sen* is brought out initially by the superiority of Lancelot's character to that of Gawain, the epitome of courtly conventionality, and then on a wider, universal level, by his role as the Elect who conquers Meleagant and the self-love, purposeless violence, treachery and cruelty which he personifies.

These two thematic levels predominate at different times. On the journey out to the land of Gorre, Love is paramount; on the return journey Love withdraws to second place and the forces of Good represented by Lancelot, Bademagu and his daughter, are pitted against Evil incarnate in Meleagant. Both themes, the triumph of *Fin'Amors* and the victory of Good over Evil, are woven together in the unifying central episode at Bademagu's court. Both levels of meaning are closely bound into the character of Lancelot and his achievements, through which they are revealed. The truly devoted *fis amaire*, humble, obedient, courageous, is finally so purified of self-love that he personifies the Goodness for which he fights symbolically against Meleagant. This dual role given to Lancelot is apparent in the episode of the death-cart in which Lancelot's hesitation can be seen as the self-love of knighthood which hinders *Fin'Amors*, or as the self-love which impedes Christian humility. In this and other episodes, the linear treatment of the *sen*, which depends on Lancelot's character and its interplay with the characters he meets on his quest, is interwoven with images, such as the death-cart, the Sword Bridge, the land of Gorre and the tower, which convey allusive overtones of supernatural, mythical, Celtic and Christian values. Chrétien's other method of revealing his *sen*, which we have called expository or lateral, is contained in the important monologues and dialogues of Lancelot, Guenevere, Meleagant and Bademagu. It is in *Lancelot* that Chrétien's art of *conjointure* finds its richest and most imaginative expression.

The romance begins, as it ends, with Meleagant's abrupt threat to Arthur's world. A sudden apparition, he throws down the gauntlet. 'Let the King free his knights, ladies and damsels, whom I hold prisoner.' He scorns Arthur's impotence:

'Que tu n'as force ne avoir, Par quoi tu les puisses avoir. Et saches bien qu'einsi morras Que ja eidier ne lor porras.' Li rois respont qu'il li estuet Sofrir, s'amander ne le puet; Mes mout l'an poise duremant. (59–65)	'You have not the strength or the means with which to possess yourself of them. Know this well, you will die before you can bring them aid.' The king answers that he must suffer this, since he cannot change it for the better. Grief weighs him down.

Kay, the symbol of *orguel* in knighthood, of *outrage et desreison* (188), is, in feeble fashion, the Arthurian counterpart of Meleagant. By a devious ruse, he gains the King's permission to fight Meleagant for the prisoners against the stake of Guenevere, who, like Enide, is put forward as a prize in combat. Kay is granted this boon, which by common consent he does not deserve, in a remarkable incident in which courtly values are turned upside-down. The Queen, at Arthur's bidding, begs Kay for Arthur's sake not to leave the court, as he has threatened to do. When she is faced with his obdurate refusal, she prostrates herself at his feet.

Why does Kay behave in this way? Is this a device in an original story whereby Guenevere can be successfully abducted? Is Kay impelled to leave a court which is powerless against the threat symbolised by Meleagant who has hinted that his prisoners are held in the Other World? Or is this, as Frappier has suggested,[10] an example of the boon exacted under duress by a knight who, to gain his ends, will endanger the Queen, the court and the realm? If this is true, is Kay already afflicted by the *Mauvestié* of recreancy which, as we shall see, is personified by Meleagant?[11]

Whatever the answer to these questions, this incident is used skilfully as the first part of a 'double episode' in which a minor happening foreshadows a major one. The Queen, obedient and full of good will towards Arthur, reveals without a second thought the selfless humility which Love will demand of Lancelot when he reaches the death-cart:

'Del remenoir proiier vos vuel: Remanez! que je vos an pri.' 'Dame', fet il, 'vostre merci! Mes je ne remandroie mie.'	'I would entreat you to stay. Stay! I beg of you.' 'Lady', he says, 'and it please you, I will not stay.' Again the Queen

La rëine ancore l'an prie,
Et tuit li chevalier a masse.
Et Kes li dit qu'ele se lasse
De chose qui rien ne li vaut.
Et la rëine de si haut
Com ele estoit as piez li chiet.
Kes li prie qu'ele se liet;
Mes ele dit que nel fera:
Ja mes ne s'an relevera
Jusqu'il otroit sa volanté.

(142–55)

entreats him, and with her, all the knights who press around him. Kay tells her she does trouble herself with that which is not her concern. The Queen, from her full height, falls at his feet. Kay begs her to rise. She says she will not. She will never rise again until he grants her wish.

To a twelfth-century audience this incident could be as dramatic as if Marie de Champagne or Eleanor of Aquitaine had prostrated herself before a recalcitrant knight. Chrétien, possibly at Marie's instigation, is showing that Guenevere, who will demand self-humiliation from Lancelot, is also capable of this sacrifice. Kay's churlishness to the Queen in telling her she has no right to be concerned with this matter (148–9), finds expression in *Yvain* in outright insult, and, as we shall see, Arthur's court there presents an even sorrier state of stagnation and confusion.[12]

In words to an unknown knight which she whispers to herself as she sets out with Kay and the victorious Meleagant, the Queen knows well the contrast between this knight, presumably Lancelot, and those around her, especially her husband the King:

Dolante et mate et sospiranz
Monte la rëine et si dist
'An bas por ce qu'an ne l'öist:
'Ha! Ha! se vos le sëussiez,
Ja, ce croi, ne me leississiez
Sanz chalonge mener un pas!'

(208–13)

Full of grief and sorrow, the Queen mounts her horse, sighing and speaking low to herself, so as not to be heard: 'Alas! had you known of this, you would never, I do truly believe, have allowed me to be taken from here with impunity.'

The court is sunk in apathy:

Mes a nelui n'an pesa tant
Que del siure s'antremëist.

(224–5)

But there was nobody who was troubled enough to set out and follow her.

It is Gawain who chides Arthur's childish folly (mout grant anfance, 228), and they set out in pursuit. At the sight of the seneschal's riderless horse, Gawain gallops ahead, and at this moment, far from the court, a knight appears like a whirl-

wind from nowhere, at full stretch riding his horse to death.
The knight courteously asks Gawain for one of his two
horses, since he has one spare, possibly for the return of the
Queen. Choose the one, says Gawain, which pleases you
best. The knight has no time for thought, as he will have
when he reaches the cart. He takes the nearest, spurs furiously on, and disappears in the distance ahead. Gawain comes
upon this horse dead amidst signs as of a great combat between several knights, and he sees the knight alone, on foot,
behind a cart, with helmet laced but with no lance.

This is the moment of crisis for the unknown knight, who
is later revealed as Lancelot, and the first of a series of trials
which test his love for Guenevere and his fitness as the Elect
who will free the Queen and the prisoners from the land of
Gorre. Lancelot, humbled in mysterious combat,[13] presumably by Meleagant, is destined to start his quest without
steed or lance. He walks behind the cart and courteously
addresses the dwarf who is perched on the shafts:

'Nain', fet il, 'por Deu! car me di	'Dwarf', he says, 'in the name of
Se tu as vëu par ici	God tell me if you have seen my
Passer ma dame la rëine.'	lady the Queen pass by here.'
(353–5)	

The drawf, *cuiverz de pute orine*, offers curt reply:

'. . . Se tu viaus monter	'If you will get in this cart
Sor la charrete que je main,	which I am driving, you will
Savoir porras jusqu'a demain,	know by tomorrow what has
Que le rëine est devenue.'	become of the Queen.' Forth-
Tantost a sa voie tenue,	with, he went on his way
Qu'il ne l'atant ne pas ne ore.	without pause or moment's
(358–63)	delay.

and Lancelot fails the test:

Tant solemant deus pas demore	The knight delays, for two steps
Li chevaliers que il n'i monte.	only, before getting in. Ill fated
Mar le fist, mar i douta honte,	was he in this, ill fated to fear
Que maintenant sus ne sailli;	the shame and not jump in at
Qu'il s'an tandra por mal bailli.	once, and for this he will later
(364–8)	think himself ill used.

It is *Reisons*, the symbol of courtly and knightly convention,
which holds him back:

Mes reisons qui d'amors se part
Li dit que de monter se gart,
Si le chastie et si l'ansaingne
Que rien ne face ne n'anpraingne,
Don il et honte ne reproche.
N'est pas el cuer, mes an la boche
Reisons qui ce dire li ose;
Mes amors est el cuer anclose,
Qui li comandë et semont
Que tost sor la charrete mont.
Amors le viaut, et il i faut;
Que de la honte ne li chaut
Puis qu'amors le comande et viaut.
(369–81)

But Reason, which is separate from Love, tells him to beware of getting in, and admonishes and instructs him not to do or to undertake anything which may bring him shame or reproach. Reason which dares to tell him this, is not in the heart, but in the mouth. But Love, which orders and bids him to climb at once into the cart, is enclosed within the heart. Love desires this, and he must do this, for he cares nothing about the shame of it, since Love orders and wishes it.

Gawain's self-assurance offers immediate contrast to the self-doubt and humility of the *chevalier tot seul a pié*:

Et mes sire Gauvains s'esquiaut
Aprés la charrete poignant,
Et quant il i trueve seant
Le chevalier, si s'an mervoille;
Puis dist au nain: 'Car me consoille
De la rëine se tu sez.'
Et cil dist: 'Se tu tant te hez
Con cist chevaliers qui ci siet,
Monte avuec lui, se il te siet,
Et je te manrai aprés li.'
(382–91)

And my lord Gawain presses on, spurring after the cart, and he wonders greatly when he finds the knight sitting in it. Then he said to the dwarf: 'Tell me now if you know any news of the Queen.' And he replied: 'If you hate yourself as much as this knight who is seated here, get in with him, if it suits you, and I will take you in search of her.'

Gawain's abrupt words betray his self-imprisonment within courtly and knightly convention. He sees the cart and the world with the outward eye of surface illusion. He is not directed by Love. He cannot see beyond present self-interest. To harm his knightly self-esteem and reputation is unthinkable. The two knights, and their two ways of life, are in direct contrast. Folly for Lancelot lay in hesitating to obey the dwarf; folly for Gawain lies in heeding his words at all:

Quant mes sire Gauvains l'öi,
Si le tint a mout grant folie,
Et dit qu'il n'i montera mie,
Car trop vilain change feroit
Se charrete a cheval chanjoit.
(392–6)

This, when my lord Gawain had heard it, he considered to be very great folly. He says he will not get in. A horse for a cart would be too base an exchange.

Gawain offers a feeble compromise:

'Mes va, quel part que tu voldras
Et j'irai la ou tu iras.'
(397–8)

'But go, in whichever direction
you wish, and there where you
go will I go too.'

Lancelot's decision to step into the death-cart will determine his future as lover and rescuer of Guenevere, and as a human being. With one step he becomes *Le Chevalier de la Charrette*, and isolates himself from the conventional society typified by Gawain. Only by so doing will Lancelot be able to give the necessary proofs of his single-minded *Fin'Amors* for the Queen, and the revelation of himself as a person guided by a higher purpose and virtues than those of Arthur's court. He enters the world of the cart which is that of human weakness, sin and shame, of traitors and murderers who ride in it to their execution,[14] and he enters mysteriously into the aura of the Other World and of death. The dwarf was a traditional guide to the Other World,[15] and the death-cart was superstitiously associated with Evil and even with the devil. 'Men used to say', says Chrétien, 'when you see or come across a cart, cross yourself and remember God so that evil may not come upon you' (343–6). Lancelot is rejecting the world of courtly pretence, of *cortez'ufana* in troubadour terms, for that of churlish truth, or *vertat vilana*. And the cart becomes a part of his personality, a sign of humility, of self-knowledge apart from courtly society, of acceptance of social ostracism. Conversely, it is also the symbol of the momentary vainglory which made him hesitate before destroying his social reputation or *prix*. Lancelot's ride in the death-cart, like Yvain's madness, is a formal cleansing process which frees his mind from the fetters of Arthur's world and sets him apart as the Elect who alone will succeed in the quest for Guenevere, and the liberation of the prisoners in the land of Gorre.

Lancelot's shame is complete when the three travellers enter a town, and the people, great and small, old and young, condemn him without reflection. They do not conceal their feelings towards this stranger:

Ainz le huient petit et grant
Et li veillart et li anfant
Par les rues a mout grant hui,

On the contrary, the small and
the great, and old men and
young, shout taunts at him in a

S'ot li chevaliers mout de lui
Vilenies et despiz dire.
Tuit demandent: 'A quel martire
Sera cil chevaliers randuz?
Iert il escorchiez ou panduz,
Noiiez ou ars an feu d'espines?
Di, nains, di tu qui le träines,
A quel forfet fu il trovez?
Est il de larrecin provez?
Est il murtriers ou chanp chëuz?'
(409–21)

great outcry through the streets. And the knight hears about himself many a churlish and scornful remark. All ask: 'To what torture will this knight be delivered? Will he be flayed or hanged, killed by drowning or burnt on a fire of thorn twigs? Speak, dwarf, you who are driving him, tell us in what crime he was discovered? Is he guilty of robbery? Is he a murderer or defeated in trial by combat?'

In a neighbouring castle where the dwarf, still silent, stops the cart, Lancelot finds further humiliation. The damsel, who is the chatelaine, observes the clear, precise code of Arthur's world, and understands Lancelot's plight as little as do the crowd in the streets. Like the Greek court in *Cliges*, they reject unexpected truth. Gawain, in her eyes the superior knight, sits beside her at dinner. When she shows them to their beds, Lancelot asks why, as she has said, they are not fit to claim a third and more splendid bed, with sable furs and gold embroidered stars on covers of yellow samite. Her reply is brutally direct:

'A vos', fet ele, 'ne tient rien
Del demander ne de l'anquerre.
Honiz est chevaliers an terre
Puis qu'il a esté an charrete,
Si n'est pas droiz qu'il s'antremete
De ce don vos m'avez requise,
Antesmes ce que il i jise;
Qu'il le porroit tost conparer.'
(488–95)

'It is no concern of yours', she says, 'to ask or enquire about that. A knight who has been in a cart is shamed anywhere on earth, and he has no right to be interested in what you have asked me about, and even less right to lie on this bed, for he could soon atone dearly for this.'

A flaming lance crashes through the rafters and touches Lancelot, as he sleeps in the fine bed, without wounding him. He puts out the fire in the bed, tests the lance for balance, and sleeps again as soundly as before. In Celtic tradition the Flaming Lance is a token of sovereignty and power. It may only be handled with impunity by a great hero or king and will return to his hand after striking his enemies.[16] The Perilous Bed, like the Perilous Seat at the round table which Galahad eventually fills, is one of the tests in Celtic tradition designed to find the Elect, the hero who is fitted to the high Quest which he undertakes.[17]

Lancelot is such an elect hero, and on the next morning, after mass, as, deep in thought, he is gazing from the castle windows, Guenevere appears far below in a procession. Gawain and the chatelaine are conversing nearby:

Qu'aval les prez lez la riviere	For down, through the meadows
An virent porter une biere,	beside the river, they saw a bier
S'avoit dedanz un chevalier,	being carried, and on this there
Et delez duel mout grant et fier	was a knight, and beside it three
Que trois dameiseles feisoient.	damsels lamented loudly and
Aprés la biere venir voient	fiercely. Behind the bier they saw
Une rote, et devant venoit	a crowd approach, and in front
Uns granz chevaliers, qui menoit	there came a tall knight leading
Une bele dame a senestre.	a fair lady on his left. The knight
Li chevaliers de la fenestre	at the window knew this was the
Conut que c'estoit le rëine;	Queen. He does not turn his
De l'esgarder onques ne fine	eyes from gazing on her with
Mout antantis et mout li plot	rapt attention and great pleasure
Au plus longuemant que il pot.	for as long as he possibly can.

(555–68)

Once the Queen is lost to view, life has no meaning for Lancelot, and Chrétien, with gentle humour, describes the reality of the troubadour theme of 'dying for love'. Lancelot, impelled by the folie of Love, heedless of the consequences, is already out of the window in pursuit of the Queen, when Gawain hauls him in again: 'For mercy, my lord! Be at peace! For the sake of God think no more of committing such an act of madness. You do great wrong in hating your life' (575–8). Gawain does not love, and cannot understand the true motive behind Lancelot's irrational act.[18]

In this fine scene which alternates between courtly uncertainty and the other-worldly atmosphere of the procession across the meadows, the damsel also sees Lancelot's behaviour as an attempt at suicide but, sure of her values, she contradicts Gawain: 'He was right not to want people to know of his wretchedness. After riding in the cart, he must long to be killed, for he would be better dead than living' (579–84).

'Sa vie est des or mes honteuse	'His life henceforth is full of
Et despite et malëureuse.'	shame, despicable and wretched.'

(585–6)

But her courtly certainty embraces good manners. The knights arm themselves for departure:

Et lors corteisie et proesce	And then the damsel acted with
Fist la dameisele et largesce;	courtesy, excellent manners and
Que quant ele ot assez gabé	generosity, for, though she had
Le chevalier et ranponé,	greatly mocked and scorned this
Si li dona cheval et lance	knight, she gave him a horse
Par amor et par acordance.	and lance, as a token of kindness
(589–94)	and good will.

Lancelot is now the Knight of the Cart. Erec suffered slander when passionate love for his wife overcame his sense of knightly duty. Lancelot is ostracised by Arthur's world for allowing love for Guenevere to demean his knightly pride. But, unlike Erec, he knowingly commits his sin against the knightly code, and accepts the consequences, giving proof of the humility which overcomes self-love.

Humiliated by society, but equipped once more with lance and horse, he rides out with Gawain, and at a crossroads, meets the Second Damsel of his quest. She tells them the way to the land of Gorre, where Guenevere has been taken. She belongs to a traditional line of damsels who guide travellers to the Other World, and, in the context of the other damsels whom Lancelot will meet, she can also be seen as a guide to Fin'Amors. Her use of droit chemin in her opening words already hints at the troubadour dreita via 'the right path to Love' and the dreita carrau, with its connotation of moral strength, which Marcabru contrasts with the tort sentier or 'crooked path'.[19]

Cele respont come senee	She replies with a wise look:
Et dist: 'Bien vos savroie metre,	'If you would promise me
Tant me porriiez vos prometre,	enough, I could put you on the
El droit chemin et an la voie,	right road and on the way, and
Et la terre vos nomeroie	would give you the name of the
Et le chevalier qui l'an mainne;	land and of the knight who is
Mes mout i covandroit grant painne,	abducting her from here.
Qui an la terre antrer voldroit;	But great effort would be needed
Qu'ainz qu'il i fust mout se	of anyone who wished to enter
doldroit.'	that land, for he would suffer
(616–24)	great pain before he arrived there.'

Gawain claims precedence in offering his pledge:

'Dameisele, se Deus m'äit,
Je vos an promet a devise
Que je mete an vostre servise,
Quant vos pleira, tot mon pooir,
Mes que vos me diiez le voir.'
(626–30)

'Damsel, as God may help me, I promise to place all my strength and power, without reserve, in your service whenever it will please you, provided you tell me the truth.'

There is a certain arrogance in this pledge. Gawain is fully aware of his *pooir*, which can refer both to a man's personal strength and his external wealth and influence, and is ready to bestow it as a boon on the damsel, as, at the end of the story, he is prepared to fight Meleagant if Lancelot fails to return. If the damsel is seen as an allegorical guide to Love and its trials, Gawain, in this self-confident mood, is destined for the *tort sentier*.

Lancelot speaks with more humility, more sense of adventure and daring. For Gawain *pooir* is a fixed asset, a stable mass of capital, which can be lent or withheld. Lancelot has no sense of his own importance, and for him *pooir* 'the power and richness of the inner self' depends on Love which, as it puts him to trial, holds the balance between sorrow and joy, failure (*faillite*) and success (*pooir*).

Et cil qui fu sor la charrete
Ne dist pas que il li promete
Tot son pooir, einçois afiche
Come cil cui amors fet riche
Et puissant et hardi par tot,
Que sanz arest et sanz redot
Quanquë ele viaut li promet
Et tot an son voloir se met.
(631–8)

And he who was on the cart does not say that he will promise her his whole power and strength, but swears, as a man whom Love makes rich and powerful, and bold beyond all other men, that without pause and without fear, he promises her whatever she desires and gives himself over entirely to her will.

When the damsel has told them of the two perilous entrances to the land of Gorre, she reminds them of their pledges:

Si dit: 'Chascuns de vos me doit
Un guerredon a mon gre randre,
Quel ore que jel voldrai prandre.
Gardez, ne l'oblïez vos mie!'
(708–11)

And she says, 'Each one of you must give me a reward which will please me, whenever I wish to take it. Take heed, and do not forget this, under any circumstances!'

If we accept that Lancelot's trials on the way to the land of Gorre are an allegorical initiation into Fin'Amors, this Second Damsel may well be an emissary of Amors, which declares itself ready at any moment to demand repayment of a pledge which Lancelot has given knowingly, and Gawain has made unwittingly. When, during his long fight with the knight at the river ford, Lancelot feels shame at his slow progress, it becomes evident that his repayment of the debt he owes the damsel lies in the speed with which he obeys Fin'Amors and seeks Guenevere on this initiatory road to the land of Gorre to which the damsel has directed him:

Qu'an son cuer an a mout grant honte
Li chevaliers de la charrete,
Et dit que mal randra la dete
De la voie qu'il a anprise.
(876–9)

For in his heart the Knight of the Cart feels great shame, and says that [with such delays] he will ill repay the debt he has incurred in the matter of this road.

Lancelot's bargain with the Second Damsel at the cross-roads is balanced by his rescue from the tower when the Fifth Damsel, who is Meleagant's sister and the bitter adversary of the evil or Mauvestié which he represents, demands and is granted Lancelot's complete devotion. The Second Damsel, the emissary of Love, may be intended, in her aid to Lancelot and the pledge she demands, as a forerunner of the Fifth Damsel, Meleagant's sister, an emissary of Good against Evil. Such a balancing of characters, the minor foreshadowing the major, is a frequent structural device in Lancelot, and is a more likely explanation of these two Damsels than the possibility that they are one and the same person – a possibility, however, which cannot be excluded.

The Second Damsel names the Queen's abductor as Meleagant, son of Bademagu, king of the land of Gorre:

'Et si l'a el reaume mise,
Don nus estranges ne retorne;
Mes par force el päis sejorne
An servitume et an essil.'
(644–7)

'And he has placed her in this kingdom from which no stranger returns, being forced to remain in that land in servitude and wretched exile.'

There are two entrances to his land. One is Li Ponz Evages, the Water Bridge, one and a half feet wide and deep, and with as much water below as above it. The other, more perilous path is Le Pont de l'Espee, the Sword Bridge, which has never been crossed. Lancelot takes the lead, as in the adventure of the Perilous Bed, and offers the first choice to Gawain who takes the slower, less dangerous road to the Water Bridge.

This dual quest, and the two paths which it follows, the tort sentier and the dreita carrau of Marcabru, is almost certainly an allegory of two separate approaches to love and life. Gawain's choice is conventional, brave within its limits, but without the upsurge of enthusiasm which stakes all on a high cause. The road which is Lancelot's destiny will demand supreme courage, self-sacrifice, and devotion to a high ideal. And this duality will be sharpened in the land of Gorre, with its connotations of the Celtic supernatural and the Other World of Death.[20] Here Lancelot's perfect love, Fin'Amors, will triumph over Meleagant's base love, and, at the same time, the conflict between Bademagu's Goodness and Meleagant's Evil will be taken over and resolved by Lancelot whose role as the Elect, indicated in the adventure of the Flaming Lance, will be confirmed during his journey to the Sword Bridge.

Once he has parted from Gawain, Lancelot begins the series of trials which test his quality as a true lover (fin'amant) of the Queen and as the Elect who will free the prisoners in the land of Gorre. His encounter with the Third Damsel, which Chrétien recounts with good-humoured irony, is a 'multiple adventure'. It contains a rich mixture of Fin'Amors or amor de lonh carried to excess, of Celtic tradition, knightly combat and the sexual temptation of Fals'Amors which may lead Lancelot from the droit chemin.

Lancelot, defenceless against Amors, day-dreams about the Queen:

Et ses pansers est de tel guise	And he meditates in such a way
Que lui mëismes an oblie,	that he loses awareness of himself.
Ne set s'il est ou s'il n'est mie,	He does not know if he is or if
Ne ne li manbre de son non,	he is not, does not remember his
Ne set s'il est armez ou non,	name, does not know if he is
Ne set ou va, ne set don vient;	armed or not. He knows not
De rien nule ne li sovient	where he goes, knows not whence
Fors d'une sole, et por celi	he comes. No thought comes to
A mis les autres an obli.	his mind, save of one person
A cele sole panse tant	alone, and for her he has placed
Que il ne voit ne il n'antant.	the others into oblivion, so that
(718–28)	he can neither see nor hear.

Lancelot's single-minded love for Guenevere will resist the sexual enticements which await him, but Chrétien's intention is also humorous, as in the wedding-night scene between Fenice and Alis. He mocks the concept of nothingness, and the lover who in troubadour poetry loses all sense of his identity in thoughts of the beloved. In his *Farai un vers de dreyt nien* (IV)[21] Guilhem IX existed neither physically nor socially when he thought of his imaginary beloved. His mind was removed from its physical shell and he knew neither when he was asleep, or awake, unless he was told. In his *Quan lo rossinhols* (I)[22] Jaufre Rudel dreamt of the wondrous joy he enjoyed with his lady. And Bernart de Ventadorn in his *Can vei la lauzeta mover* (XLIII) felt his heart melt with desire as he saw the lark forget itself in joy and let itself fall for the sweetness that came to its heart, as he, too, lost control of his senses and felt removed from himself and the world around him. The love-struck Lancelot, unaware of his surroundings and the challenge of a knight on the far bank, is carried into a river by his horse, who drinks thirstily. Knocked from his horse into the cold water, Lancelot, roused from his trance, tussles with the mounted knight in the river. They agree to fight like knights, but when Lancelot has won, he is so enraged at the delay to his quest and his disturbed meditation of the beloved (887)[23] that he refuses to spare his adversary's life, despite a plea from the knight's damsel. He shows mercy only because the knight asks for this in the name of God. 'But first you will pledge me to make yourself my prisoner there where I wish, when I summon you' (918–20). And when the knight pledges this, the damsel, who is the Third Damsel of the quest, again pleads with Lancelot:

'. . . Chevaliers, par ta franchise,
Des que il t'a merci requise
Et tu otroiiee li as,
S'onques nul prison deslias,
Deslie moi cestui prison!
Claimme moi quite sa prison,
Par covant que quant leus sera
Tel guerredon con toi pleira
T'an randrai selonc ma puissance.'
Et lors i ot cil conoissance
Par la parole qu'ele ot dite,

'Sir knight, of your noble generosity, since he has asked you for mercy and you have granted it to him, if ever you freed any prisoner, free this prisoner for me. Release him from his imprisonment for my sake, on condition that when the occasion offers, I will render to you in exchange, as far as lies in my power, such a reward as

Si li rant le chevalier quite.
Et cele an a honte et angoisse,
Qu'ele cuide qu'il la conoisse;
Car ele ne le vossist pas.
Et cil s'an part eneslepas:
Et cil et cele le comandent
A Deu, et congié li demandent.
(923–40)

will please you.' And then, because of what she had said, he came to his senses about this situation and gave her the knight's freedom. And she feels shame and anguish because she imagines that he may take her sexually, for she would not have desired that at all. And he departs forthwith, and the knight and the damsel commend him to God and take leave of him.

The interpretation of this passage depends on *conoissance* (932) and *conoisse* (936). *Conoissance* here is almost certainly the equivalent of the Provençal *conoissensa*, the essential courtly quality of discriminating between the false and the true, the good and the bad. Lancelot in his anger at the delay and the interruption of his love meditation, comes to his senses when he realises that, although his mission is to free Guenevere and the prisoners in the land of Gorre, he is nevertheless threatening a knight with this same punishment and is maltreating the damsel who is ready to accept humiliation (935–7) and to sacrifice herself for her love. *Conoisse* here is not 'to recognise' but 'to have sexual knowledge of',[24] as when Fenice tells Cliges about Alis:

'Onques ancor ne me conut
Si come Adanz conut sa fame.'
(5238–9)

'He never knew me as Adam knew his wife.'

and this is the absolute *guerredon* which the damsel offers for her knight's freedom.

This fast-moving scene begins lightly with the knight who forgets his duty in amorous day-dreams. It continues with the rough-and-tumble in the river, with its overtones of the Celtic river guardian, and ends with the theme of the woman as a prize of combat. When Lancelot rides on, and leaves the knight and his damsel who is ready to suffer complete humiliation for love, he rejects, without being consciously aware of it, the first and most uncourtly stage of sexual temptation to which he will be exposed.

Towards evening, he greets a damsel, *mout tres bele et avenant*, who approaches him. This is the Fourth Damsel, who will tempt him with sexual love, the promiscuous *Fals'Amors* of Marcabru. 'My lord', she says, 'my dwelling is prepared for you if you are minded to accept it, but you shall lodge with me only if you share my bed. On these terms do I make this offer and gift to you' (950–4). Chrétien enjoys Lancelot's qualms, and his guileless, courteous reply:

Plusor sont qui de cest presant
Li randissent cinc çanz merciz,
Et cil an est trestoz nerciz,
Si li a respondu tot el:
'Dameisele, de vostre ostel
Vos merci gié, si l'ai mout chier,
Mes, s'il vos pleisoit, del couchier
Me soferroie je mout bien.'
'Je n'an feroie autremant rien',
Fet la pucele, 'par mes iauz!'
(956–65)

There are many who would have thanked her five hundred-fold for this offer, and yet he, completely cast down, answered her quite differently: 'Damsel, I thank you for your offer of shelter, and I value it greatly, but if it please you, I would willingly dispense with going to bed with you.' 'By the sight of my eyes', says the damsel, 'I would not do anything for you on any other condition.'

There being no other bed in sight, Lancelot, with heavy heart, agrees. He has no fear for himself, but for the distress the damsel will suffer unless she loves in the mind:

De l'otroiier li cuers li diaut:
Quant ce tant solemant le blesce,
Mout avra au couchier destresce;
Mout i avra travail et painne
La dameisele qui l'an mainne.
Espoir tant le puet ele amer,
Ne l'an voldra quite clamer.
(968–74)

His heart grieves him when he agrees to this. If the mere thought of this upsets him now, he is going to suffer great distress when they lie together. And the damsel who is leading him away will suffer much torment and pain. Perhaps she will love him so much she will not let him go

The damsel takes Lancelot into her castle 'surrounded by a high wall and a deep moat, a finer castle than any from here to Thessaly. And inside this castle there was no man except the one she brought there' (977–82). In the hall, empty of servants, there is an abundance of food and wine, goblets and basins of warm water. To Lancelot's relief, the damsel dismounts before he can offer her help, robes him in a splendid cloak of scarlet, and invites him to dine. Behind this damsel who entertains a lone knight, who offers him food and sexual pleasure and 'might keep him in thrall' (974), Chrétien's audience would undoubtedly see the theme of the Celtic fairy mistress which appears in a different form and with wider meaning in the episode of the Wall of Air in *Erec et Enide* and in the figure of Laudine in *Yvain*. Lancelot here is playing the opposite role to that of Lanval, who, in the lay of Marie de France, is also isolated from Arthur's court, but accepts the food and love offered by his fairy mistress and spurns Guenevere's adulterous advances. In the later *Queste del saint Graal*, Perceval will also be tempted into the bed of an enchanting damsel, with disastrous and sulphurous results when he makes the sign of the cross, and, from among the wreckage around him, spies the Devil dancing angrily on a ship out at sea.[25] The supernatural overtones of this opening scene in what will prove to be a long 'multiple incident' may help to explain the next episode of Feigned Rape, which, for all its hallucinatory qualities, is a major test of Lancelot's constancy in *Fin'Amors*.

After the meal, the damsel requires Lancelot to keep his side of the agreement. 'My lord, give me time to prepare for bed and then, if you wish to keep your promise, come to me' (1045–52). When Lancelot returns to the hall, it is empty. Should he not find the damsel, he will be forsworn. He follows a cry for help, and, through an open door, sees the damsel being raped by a knight:

Cele qui cuidoit estre certe
Que il li venist an äie,
Crioit an haut: 'Äie, äie,
Chevaliers, tu qui ies mes ostes!
Se de sor moi cestui ne m'ostes,
Ne troverai qui le m'an ost;
Et se tu ne me secors tost,
Il me honira devant toi.
Ja te doiz tu couchier o moi
Si con tu le m'as creanté:
Fera donc cist sa volanté
De moi, veant tes iauz, a force?
Jantis chevaliers, car t'efforce,
Si me secor isnelemant!'
                    (1078–91)

She who thought she could be sure that he would come to her aid, was shouting in a loud voice: 'Help! Help! Sir knight, who are my guest, if you do not get this man off me, I shall never find anyone to remove him. And if you do not help me soon, he will shame me in your presence. Remember that you have to lie with me, as you pledged. Shall this man then force his will on me, before your very eyes? Gentle knight, stir yourself, and help me at once.'

Lancelot is being tempted to feel jealousy, and injured pride, at the sight of 'his' mistress, naked to the navel, being sexually assaulted. He is being tempted to win by conquest a sexual love which is already promised to him. This 'rape'

127

scene is the acting-out of the amoral sexual love which Marcabru had attacked:

Denan mei n'i passon trei al passador,
Non sai mot tro·l quarz la fot e·l
    quinz lai cor.
Enaissi torn' a decli l'amors e
    torn' en negror.
            (XXIV, 19–21)

Before my eyes, three rush past in the passage. I do not know what is happening until the fourth does her, and the fifth runs there. So does love turn to degradation and blackness.

It is the extreme form of the sexual licence which Lancelot had been offered in return for hospitality. He feels no jealousy or injured self-pride at the damsel's plight. Two knights and four men-at-arms guard the entrance to the room, and Lancelot analyses and laments his situation:

'. . . Deus, que porrai je feire?
Mëuz sui por si grant afeire
Con por la rëine Guenievre.
Ne doi mie avoir cuer de lievre
Quant por li sui an ceste queste.
Se mauvestiez son cuer me preste
Et je son comandemant faz,
N'ateindrai pas la ou je chaz.
Honiz sui se je ci remaing:
Mout me vient ore a grant desdaing
Quant j'ai parlé del remenoir.
Mout an ai le cuer triste et noir.'
            (1109–20)

'Oh God! What can I do? I have set out on no less an affair than to find Queen Guenevere. I must not have the heart of a hare, since I am engaged in this quest for her. If moral cowardice lends me its heart and I do its bidding, I shall never reach that place which I seek. I am shamed if I stay here. I now find it repulsive that I spoke of staying, and my heart is sad and darkened.'

Despite its humorous side, this is a crucial test for Lancelot, comparable to that of the cart. In that case, self-pride was crushed by Fin'Amors for the Queen, and the outward forms of reputation and honour were yielded up to Love when Lancelot rode in the cart. Here, Lancelot's complicated situation would have intrigued the court of Champagne. Fin'Amors excludes all contact with Mauvestié, 'recreancy and lack of moral principles' and the Fals'Amors with which Lancelot, through self-indulgent lack of savoir and the wish for a bed for the night, has become carelessly, and now, as he faces the extreme of Fals'Amors, unwillingly involved. He cannot know the exalted state of Fin'Amors until he has seen and recognised its opposite. Once he has argued the case to himself, he is made to realise that honour in the sense of moral courage is essential to Fin'Amors. And moral courage, which should have kept him from entering this castle, now demands that he should keep his pledge to the damsel. Though she has tempted him, honour demands that he should rescue her: 'Now is my shame and grief so great that I would willingly die for having stayed here so long. And may God have no mercy on me if I speak from self-pride when I say that I would much rather die with honour than live with shame. If these men gave me leave to pass through unchallenged, what honour should I have then? In that case, in very truth, the most despicable man alive could pass through there. And I hear this unhappy girl crying for help, urging me to keep my promise, reproaching me basely' (1121–37).

The fight is fast and furious, and with the abrupt change of mood characteristic of Chrétien ends on the cool note of comedy and burlesque which was inherent in the damsel's first cries for help. Lancelot, at bay between the bed and the wall, bids defiance to the enemy:

'Or ça trestuit a moi!	'Now, all of you, come at me!
Se vos estiiez trante et set,	If there were thirty-seven of you,
Des que je ai tant de recet,	now that my back is so well
Si avroiz vos bataille assez;	protected, you would have much
Ja par vos n'an serai lassez.'	fighting to do. You will never
(1188–92)	begin to tire me down.'

And the damsel speaks: 'By the sight of my eyes, you need have no worry about that henceforward in any place where I am' (1194–5). She dismisses the knights and men-at-arms who are her retainers, chides her 'rescuer' for disrupting her household, and leads the disconsolate Lancelot to her bed.

Lancelot's temptation in the damsel's bed may correspond to a form of courtly testing (assaiars) which occurs in Provençal poetry. In this, the lover, by resisting sexual fulfilment, proves his mental and spiritual love for his lady.[26] But Chrétien also appears to be satirising Tristan's wedding night, when the desire which burns in the mind for the distant Yseut the Fair (desir) stills concupiscence (vouloir) for his bride Yseut of the White Hands.[27] Lancelot, like Tristan, reluctantly prepares to lie beside the damsel:

Et cil a mout grant painne mise	And he with great trouble began
Au deschaucier, au desnoer.	to remove his hose and to untie
D'angoisse le covint süer:	the knots. Anguish brought him
Totes voies parmi l'angoisse	out in a sweat. All the time in

Covanz le vaint et si le froisse.
Donc est ce force? – Autant se vaut.
Par force covient que il s'aut
Couchier avuec la dameisele.
(1216–23)

the centre of this anguish his promise controls him and breaks him. Is this promise then compulsion? It has the same effect. Through its constraint he must go and lie with the damsel.

Tristan resisted the impulse of carnal desire for his wife and the wish to revenge himself on Yseut the Fair who had returned to live with Mark. But Tristan does not get into the nuptial bed. Honour for an ignoble promise, lightly given, forces Lancelot, on the other hand, to get into the bed which may shame his love, as love had forced him to get into the death-cart. Chrétien's audience would appreciate this paradox, as well as the power of true love for one person alone which keeps Lancelot from touching, looking at, or speaking to the enchanting damsel on the bed beside him:

Ainz s'an esloingne et gist anvers,
Ne ne dit mot ne qu'uns convers
Cui li parlers est deffanduz,
Quant an son lit gist estanduz.
(1229–32)

On the contrary, he moves far away from her and lies on his back like a novice monk who is forbidden to speak when he lies stretched out in his bed.

Like Bernart de Ventadorn:

'et eu, las! no·n sai que dire,
c'ades es us mos talans.
ades es us e no·s muda,
c'una·n volh e·n ai volguda,
don anc non aic jauzimen.'
(xxx, 3–7)

'and I, alas, know not what to say, for my desire is always one. It is always one desire, and does not change, for with it I desire and have desired one woman from whom I never had enjoyment.'

Lancelot has but one desire. He is also the Elect of *Amors*:

Li chevaliers n'a cuer que un,
Et cil n'est mie ancor a lui,[28]
Ainz est comandez a autrui
Si qu'il nel puet aillors prester.
Tot le fet an un leu ester
Amors qui toz les cuers justise.
Toz? – Non fet, fors ceus qu'ele
  prise.
Et cil se redoit plus prisier
Que Amors daingne justisier.
Amors le cuer celui prisoit
Tant que sor toz le justisoit,

The knight has but one heart, which is no longer his own. It is completely entrusted to some one else, so that he cannot place it elsewhere. Love which rules all hearts makes this heart remain in one place alone. Rules all hearts? No, it does not, only those which it prizes. And that man, whom Love deigns to rule, must prize himself more highly. Love so prized the heart of this

Si li don oit si grant orguel[29]
Que de rien blasmer ne le vuel
S'il let ce qu'amors li deffant
Et la ou ele viaut antant.
(1240–54)

man that it ruled and constrained it more than any other,
and made him value this love
so much that I will not blame
him in any way if he leaves
what Love forbids and aspires to
that which it desires.

These apparently artless comments on love are important. The lines 1252–4 'I will not blame him in any way if he leaves what love forbids and aspires to that which it desires', appear to be a neat parody and inversion of Bernart de Ventadorn's attack on Marcabru's ideal of Fin'Amors as love governed by reason and mesura:

e cel es be fols naturaus
que de so que vol, la repren
e·lh lauza so que no·lh es gen.
(edn Appel xv, 33–5)

And that man is indeed a fool
by his very nature [or a fool
towards his own nature] who
blames it [Amors, sensual love]
for what it desires and advises
it to do what is displeasing to it.

Amors in the quotation from Lancelot (1240–54) is clearly the Fin'Amors of the lover who loves with his senses, his mind and spirit. In his D'Amors qui m'a tolu a moi (see p. 68), Chrétien had rejected Tristan-type passion in favour of a love directed by fins cuers e bone volantez 'a true heart and a whole desire'. In this further riposte to Bernart de Ventadorn, Chrétien appears to be commenting on a controversy which had involved Marcabru, Bernart and Peire d'Alvernhe, the disciple and defender of Marcabru. This controversy was concerned primarily with the different views of love and natura held by the leading metaphysical and courtly trouba-dours (see also p. 165).[30] If the tentative suggestion is correct that orguelh (1251) may also imply an ironical criticism of over-rationalised Fin'Amors (see p. 330, n. 29), it is possible that Chrétien was taking a middle path in the dispute.

Lancelot and the damsel lie chastely in state, providing, in their shifts, a courtly reply to the fortuitous chastity of Tristan and Yseut in the forest of Morois. The damsel breaks the impasse. She takes leave of Lancelot: 'You have kept your promise to me so well that I have no right to ask you for any single thing more. Now I will commend you to God and go away' (1269–73). In her room, she is aware of Lancelot's excellence and his high mission (1282–90):

'Il viaut a si grant chose antandre	'He wishes to aspire to some-
Qu'ains chevaliers n'osa anprandre	thing so great, so grievous and
Si perilleuse ne si grief;	perilous as no knight ever dared
Et Deus doint qu'il an vaingne a	undertake before. And may God
chief.'	grant him success.'

(1287–90)

With these words Chrétien prepares the way for this Fourth Damsel to accompany Lancelot on the next stage of his quest. In structure and mood this is a reversal of the incident of Feigned Rape. In that episode, a Celtic framework of the fairy mistress and her knightly lover enclosed a scene in which Lancelot's love and honour were tested in courtly fashion. Lancelot's anguish about the results of his foolhardy promise was lightened by Chrétien's sense of burlesque and paradox. The 'rape' scene is also a literary jape which would appeal to courtly taste, like the story of Peire Vidal, who, impelled by the folly of love for Loba de Pennautier, disguised himself as a wolf,[31] or like the tale of the magic monsters which Renart, a fully fledged pupil of master Henry, the necromancer of Toledo, will parade before a wedding banquet.[32] Or this 'rape' may even be seen on a remote level as an allegory of fol cuidar or 'foolish' fantasising. In the next incident, Chrétien uses a courtly framework to heighten Lancelot's isolation from the courtly world and to reveal again, as in the adventure of the Flaming Lance, the supernatural quality of his mission. In this scene, the Fourth Damsel who has failed with her Feigned Rape to induce feelings of hurt pride and possessive lust in Lancelot, will choose to ride with him, and so, according to the ancient 'custom' of the land of Logres (1311–13) expose herself and her knight to attack from marauding knights. Lancelot, as we saw, is the Elect among true lovers. In the scene which now begins, he is so clearly the Elect among knights, so superior to all others, that he fulfils this protective role with scarcely a second thought, and without needing to fight. By this we may measure the quality of his mission compared to that of Erec.

The damsel, who personifies the folie of obedience to feeling and impulse, now leads Lancelot astray from the straight path of Fin'Amors (li droiz chemins, 1357), as she had tried to do previously with her invitation to bed, and the device of Feigned Rape. For the troubadour Marcabru, self-will, which is the sign of limited 'fragmented' thinking, shows a man the bent path (lo tort sentier) in life and leads him thereby to mistake illusion for reality. Ladies and knights who follow such a way of thinking 'go off along the crooked path, whistling at the gadfly as if it were a hawk, and they abandon the straight road (la dreita carrau)' (XIX, 64–6). A courtly audience would appreciate the significance of the Fourth Damsel's wavering from the true path. Chrétien also offers a literal explanation. The damsel has noticed an ivory comb with golden hair in it, which has been left on the true path on a mounting stone in a meadow. Lancelot, immersed in thoughts of the Queen as Love reopens its wound in him (1344–9), does not at first notice the comb. But when the damsel, to prevent him from seeing it, leads him from the true path, he wakes from his reverie, insists on returning, and learns from the damsel that the comb and hair belong to the Queen. Grief-stricken, bereft of speech and colour, he almost falls in a swoon from his horse. He is helped up by the damsel, who in a fright dismounts and rushes to his aid. Alexander's joy at the gold thread of Soredamors' hair pales beside Lancelot's ecstasy before the hair of the Queen. 'This hair is so beautiful that a knight at the mart of St Denis would not wish to have all the riches there displayed except he had found these tresses, so bright that gold refined a hundred thousand times and melted down again as many, would be darker than night, compared to the fairest summer's day of this whole year, if the gold and the hair were set beside each other' (1494–1506).

Ja mes oel d'ome ne verront
Nule chose tant enorer,
Qu'il les comance a aorer;
Et bien çant mile foiz les toche
Et a ses iauz et a sa boche
Et a son front et a sa face:
N'est nule joie qu'il n'an face.
Mout s'an fet lié, mout s'an fet
  riche:
An son sain pres del cuer les fiche
Antre sa chemise et sa char.
           (1472–81)

Never will mortal eyes see anything honoured so greatly, for he begins to show his adoration of her hair. A hundred thousand times and more does he touch it with his eyes and his mouth, his brow and his face. There is no joy which he does not feel. His happiness is great, and so is his treasure. He places it against his breast near his heart between his shirt and his flesh.

From *Fin'Amors* the action reverts to low love, to lust by conquest. The damsel reveals her affection for Lancelot when she conceals her reason for rushing to his side when he swooned. She spares his pride and his secret, but, riding ahead, spies an unwelcome, passionate suitor, and asks Lancelot to protect her, the 'custom' of the land entitling this newcomer to fight for her, and if victorious, to take her. She would die rather than let this happen. The arrogant Young Knight, scorning Lancelot's presence, seizes her bridle and attempts to lead her away. Lancelot remains cool:

. . . de rien ne s'äire	. . . in no way does he show
De tot l'orguel qu'il li ot dire,	anger at all the arrogant things
Mes sanz ranposne et sanz vantance	he hears the other say, but
A chalangier la li comance,	without mockery or boastful
Et dist: 'Sire, ne vos hastez,	words he begins to challenge
Ne voz paroles ne gastez,	him for her. And he said: 'Sir
Mes parlez un po a mesure.'	knight, do not be hasty. Do not
(1605–11)	say ill-chosen words, but try to
	speak more fittingly.'

And, at Lancelot's suggestion, they ride on to find an open space for combat.

This Young Knight epitomises the egoism of a love which, though rejected, seeks possession of the beloved by force. Ruled by self-will, he signals Chrétien's return to the theme of *Mauvestié*, which will lead from this prototype of the vice to the Arrogant Knight and so once more to Meleagant.

The trio enter a meadow of delight in which girls and knights and damsels disport at chess and dice, dance and song (1647–60). When Lancelot appears, the Joy of the Court ceases:

Tantost con li troi lor sorvienent,	As soon as the three come upon
Tuit de joie feire se tienent,	them, they all cease their
Et crïent tuit parmi les prez:	pursuit of joy and shout
'Veez le chevalier, veez,	throughout the meadows: 'See
Qui fu menez sor la charrete!	that knight, see the man who
N'i et mes nul qui s'antremete	was driven in the cart! Let no
De joer tant com il i iert.'	one indulge in sport as long as
(1675–81)	he is here.'

The Young Knight, impelled by the *convoitise* of selfish love, claims the damsel: 'God has granted me what I have always most desired. He could not have granted me so much if he had made me a crowned king, nor would I have thanked him so much' (1691–5). But his white-haired father, the lord of that land and forerunner of Bademagu, recognises Lancelot as a knight set apart by his quality and his mission. He refuses to let his son fight, has him seized and bound. He knows Lancelot is beyond his understanding; with his son he will follow and observe him. The crowd of courtiers who greeted Lancelot with derision are amazed when he rides away with impunity, taking with him the damsel who is coveted by their lord's son. They return to their sport, indifferent to this issue. Lancelot is isolated from the courtly world but his role as the pariah, the Knight of the Cart, is now in doubt. Those with the wisdom to see, like the Fourth Damsel and the Young Knight's father, divine in him the quality of the Elect which will now be made clear.

Lancelot prays in a church, and is led by a monk into a graveyard of splendid tombs, enclosed by a wall. He reads the inscriptions: 'Here will lie Gawain, and here Louis (ms. A Lionel[33]) and here Yvain' together with the best knights of this and other lands. One tomb excels in its rich decoration; seven men could scarcely raise the tombstone which covers it. On it there is an inscription: 'the man who by his own efforts will raise this stone, will free the prisoners, men and women, in the land which no one, serf or nobleman, may leave, unless he was born in that place or in the land around it. From there, no one has yet returned' (1911–18).

Lancelot raises the tombstone with ease, as his son, Galahad, in the *Queste del saint Graal* will pull the sword from the stone.[34] But he refuses to give his name to the monk. 'Who will lie in this tomb?' he asks:

'Sire, cil qui deliverra   'My lord, he who will deliver
Toz ces qui sont pris a la trape all those who are trapped in the
El reaume don nus n'eschape.'   kingdom whence none escapes.'
              (1946–8)

The monk speaks of Lancelot to the Young Knight and his father: 'He has worked great miracles. Alone and without effort he has raised the tombstone which covers the great marble tomb.' And the monk prophesies: 'He goes to rescue the Queen. He will rescue her for sure, together with all the other people' (1980–6):

'Onques voir d'ome ne de fame
Ne nasqui n'an sele ne sist
Chevaliers qui cestui vaussist.'
(1990–2)

'Never, in truth, was there knight
born of man and woman who
might sit a horse and conquer
this man.'

In this complex major episode of the Fourth Damsel, Chrétien entwines the thematic threads of the romance with a fine sense of paradox and *conjointure*. The other-worldly atmosphere of the castle is used as the setting for courtly tests of *Fin'Amors* and knightly honour, and, in the forest, the courtly themes of the love 'token', the comb and hair of the Queen, and the Joy of the Court which accepts the Young Knight and rejects the Knight of the Cart, lead back again to the other-worldly, and, this time, the Christian setting of the cemetery, the empty tombs of great heroes and the monk who sees Lancelot as the Elect who is destined for the highest quest.

Seriousness also goes with jocularity in this multiple adventure which amplifies the episode of the Third Damsel. In the incident of Guenevere's strand of hair, Lancelot once again lapses into his dream world, and, in this case, is saved from a fall. But reason and moral truth return at once when he encounters the Young Knight. In the earlier scene of Feigned Rape *folie* led him into a situation where, like Alis and the Greek court, he was deceived by magic into accepting illusion as reality. Yet reason and moral truth asserted themselves, passed cool judgement on the illusory scene, restrained him from its snare. In these episodes of Feigned Rape and Guenevere's hair Lancelot indulges his fantasy, and is trapped by deceit, but *savoir*, the reasoned reflection on which *Fin'Amors* depends, controls his *folie*, the illusory deceitfulness of the senses. Amidst much good humour and gentle mockery of the love-sick knight, this important adventure epitomises the conflict in love between reason and feeling, reality and illusion, moral truth and self-interest.

Lancelot's quest moves to a higher plane once the Christian eyes of the monk have recognised him as the Elect among mortals. Yet, refusing his name to the Fourth Damsel who now leaves him, he remains *Le Chevalier de la Charrette*, a knight whose identity will be concealed until he has expiated his momentary sin of self-pride. So will Yvain remain *Le Chevalier* au Lion after rescuing Lunete (edn Reid, 4606–20), though Laudine asks him his name. Lancelot's major trials, like Yvain's, lie ahead. Lancelot has now survived the tests of Love, and the tests of his knightly destiny, the Flaming Lance and the raising of the tombstone. He enters the land of Gorre as a knight of proven virtue and excellence, destined for a high quest which he alone can accomplish.

His journey to the Sword Bridge now passes through a sort of Middle Land which surrounds the city of Bade. Here there are imprisoned the prisoners from Logres, or Britain, men and women trapped, without hope of escape, in servitude and exile, as if enclosed by an invisible wall or isolated on some plane of the supernatural. Lancelot's mission enters a new phase when he is welcomed as a saviour into the homes of these oppressed people. His fight against the evil of Meleagant has begun, and this evil soon manifests itself when at the forcing of the Stone Passage Lancelot is insulted for having ridden in the cart (2224–31).

Lancelot's fame as the invincible saviour inspires the men of Logres to rise against their captors, but Lancelot is held back from the fight in an incident which shows traces of the original story, and, at the same time, accentuates the atmosphere of magic and Celtic mystery now woven around him and the land of Gorre. Together with his followers, the two sons of a vavasour, he is trapped in a castle. Fearing enchantment, he gazes on a ring which breaks spells, and calls for help to the fairy who gave it to him:

'Dame, dame, se Deus m'äit, 'My lady, lady, as God may help
Or avroie je grant mestier me, I now have great need of
Que vos me venissiez eidier!' any aid which you may bring
Cele dame une fee estoit, me.' This lady was a fairy who
Qui l'anel doné li avoit, had given him the ring and had
Et si le norri an s'anfance. brought him up in his youth.[35]
(2354–9)

There is no spell, and, battling his way out of the tower, the invincible Lancelot helps the men of Logres to victory.

Lancelot, the outcast of the Arthurian world, is now overwhelmed by offers of Christian welcome from the people of Logres to whom he has brought joy (2440).

'Bien veignanz soiiez vos, biaus sire!' 'Be welcome, fair lord!' And
Et dist chascuns: 'Sire, par foi, each one says, 'My lord, by my

Vos vos herbergeroiz o moi!'
'Sire, por Deu et por son non,
Ne herbergiez se o moi non!'
(2456–60)

faith you shall lodge with me' –
'My lord, for the sake of God
and by his name, do not lodge
with anyone but me.'

'If you had all' replies Lancelot 'done me as great honour as could be done to any one man, by all the saints at Rome, I could not be more grateful for the goodness I might receive than I am for the good intention. This good intention pleases me as much as if each of you had already done me great honour and kindness' (2495–501). Yet all do him honour and service until he retires for the night.

Only the adventure of the Arrogant Knight now separates Lancelot from the Sword Bridge. With his two followers, he is given warm welcome by a *buene dame*:

A chiere mout riant et liee
Les salue et dit: 'Bien veingniez!
Mon ostel vuel que vos preigniez:
Herbergiez estes, desçandez!'
(2530–3)

With smiling, joyful face she greets them: 'Welcome! I want you to accept the lodging I offer. You have found shelter for the night. Get off your horse!'

As at the vavasour's, Lancelot is made at home in the bustle of a large family, where 'nothing was burdensome or grievous' (2578–9), and where Chrétien lingers happily over his description of order and contentment.

As they sit at table and the first course is served, a knight appears at the door, more arrogant than a bull, armed from head to foot, with one leg cocked jauntily over the neck of his warhorse (2584–9). He is not noticed until he comes close, and asks abruptly:

'Li queus est ce, savoir le vuel,
Qui tant a folie et orguel
Et de cervel la teste vuide,
Qu'an cest päis vient et si cuide
Au pont de l'espee passer?'
(2593–7)

'Who is the man, and this I will know, who has such folly and pride and a head so brainless that he comes to this land and thinks he can pass over the Sword Bridge?'

And Lancelot:

Et cil qui ne fu esperduz
Mout sëuremant li respont:
'Je sui qui vuel passer au pont.'
'Tu Tu? Comant l'osas panser?
Ainz te dëusses apanser
Que tu anprëisses tel chose,

And he, not at all disconcerted, replies with great assurance: 'I am the one who wishes to pass over the bridge.' 'You? You? How did you dare think of this? Before such an adventure you

A quel fin et a quel parclose
Tu an porroies parvenir,
Si te dëust ressovenir
De la charrete ou tu montas.
Ce ne sai je se tu honte as
De ce que tu i fus menez;
Mes ja nus qui fust bien senez
N'ëust si grant afeire anpris
Se de ceste blasme fust repris.'
(2600–14)

should have considered the end
and conclusion to which you
could attain. You should have
borne in mind the cart on to
which you climbed. I know not
whether you feel shame for
having been driven in that, but
no man who was in his right
mind would have undertaken
such high adventure if he were
open to blame for doing that.'

The implication of this passage is that the cart, the dwarf, and the choice between recreancy to Love or to the forms of knighthood, were set in Lancelot's path as an obstacle to his Quest. If he rides in the cart, he cannot be the Elect who will save the Queen and the prisoners, at least in the eyes of the Arthurian world of courtliness, and of the powers of Evil and of self-seeking knighthood represented by the Arrogant Knight, and especially by Meleagant. So, in this light, the trial of the cart takes its place with the tests offered by the four anonymous damsels in the land of Logres as a temptation which will reveal his weakness, and, if he fails, prove him unfit as the fin'amant of the Queen and the saviour of the oppressed in the land of Gorre.

Lancelot makes no reply, but the lord of the house and his family are stricken with wonder. They curse the cart: 'Why was he put in a cart, for what sin, for what crime?' (2626–7). Unlike Arthur's world, they show sympathy: 'Were he free of this reproach, no knight in the whole width of the world could be found equal in experience and prowess, or approach his likeness in worth. No knight so fair and noble is to be found anywhere, and this is truth' (2629–36). The family, with their Christian compassion, have the same values as the monk at the cemetery. They know that Lancelot is the Chosen One.

The Arrogant Knight resumes in words which hint at the Celtic supernatural, at the exchange of a life for a service, and also at the Styx, the Classical river of the Underworld: 'Knight, hear this, you who are going to the Sword Bridge. If you wish, you can cross the water easily and smoothly. I will have you ferried swiftly across, but, when I have you on the other side, I shall make you pay a toll, and, if I wish, will take your head for it, or, if not, you will be held in my power' (2640–9).

Lancelot remains cool. He does not seek trouble. He would not think of risking his head for such a crossing. And to this peremptory challenge he answers: 'If I could refuse this, I would willingly forego this combat. But in truth I would rather fight than be constrained to do what is evil' (2660–3).[36]

Lancelot remains seated, and sends for his arms and his warhorse. He grants the defeated knight mercy, provided only that he rides on the cart:

'Ja Deu ne place que j'i mont!'
'Non?' fet cil, 'et vos i morroiz.'
'Sire, bien feire le porroiz,
Mes por Deu vos quier et demant
Merci fors que tant solemant
An charrete monter ne doive.
Nus plez n'est que je n'an reçoive
Fors cestui, tant soit griés ne forz.
Miauz voldroie estre çant fois morz
Que fet ëusse tel meschief.'
(2780–9)

'May it never please God that I should mount on it.' 'No? then you shall die here.' 'My lord, you are indeed in a position to do this, but, in the name of God, I seek and ask for mercy, save only that I should not have to mount on the cart. Apart from that condition, there is no other which I would not accept, however grievous or rigorous it might be. I would rather be slain a hundred times than have done anything so disgraceful.'

As Lancelot hesitates, a damsel, with dress undone and dishevelled, gallops up in mad haste. In this Fifth Damsel there is a hint of the Celtic supernatural[37] as she whips her mule to outrun any horse. From Lancelot she begs a boon and promises one in return:

'. . . de loing
Sui ça venue a grant besoing
A toi, por demander un don
An merite et an guerredon
Si grant con je te porrai feire;
Et tu avras ancor a feire
De m'äie si con je croi.'
(2811–17)

'From afar have I come to you', she says, 'in great urgency, to ask for a gift as great in value and reward as any I shall be able to make you, and you will yet have need of my help. This I truly believe.'

The knight must die:

'. . . et voir, ains ne trovas
Si felon ni si desleal.[38]
Ja ne feras pechié ne mal,

'and, in truth, you never found one who is so treacherous, so unnatural and untrue. You will

140

Einçois sera aumosne et biens,
Que c'est la plus desleaus riens
Qui onques fust ne ja mes soit.'
                              (2824–9)

not be committing any sin or
wrong. This will be an act of
charity and goodness, for this
man is the most unnatural person
who exists or who might ever
exist.'

The Knight pleads in the name of God, the Father, the Son, and the Virgin Mary, and the damsel demands his head. Lancelot reflects:

Largesce et pitiez li comandent
Que lor buens face a anbedeus.
                              (2852–3)

Generosity and pity order him
to requite them both.

Once more, he will fight the Arrogant Knight, and, if he wins, he will take his life. In a harrowing scene in which the knight again pleads for life and the damsel again demands his death, Lancelot hews off his head, and hands it by the hair to the damsel, who rejoices: 'May your heart have the joy of what it most desires, as great as that which my heart now has from what it most desired. Nothing grieved me so much as that he has lived for so long. A reward awaits you and will come to you from me in your dire need' (2942–9). She commends him to God and departs.

What is the meaning of this scene which looks back to the previous one and the Fourth Damsel's hatred and rejection of the Young Knight driven by convoitise and self-will, and looks ahead to Lancelot's encounter with Meleagant? Why does the Arrogant Knight refuse at all costs to get in the death-cart? Why is he desleaus and what does the damsel represent? There can be little doubt that this 'expository' scene has an allegorical level of meaning. The Arrogant Knight takes his place in an ascending order of Evil which starts in the land of Gorre with the Knight at the Stone Passage, passes through the Young Knight and culminates in Meleagant. The Arrogant Knight may be seen, like the dwarf on the cart, as a henchman sent by Meleagant to uphold his master's view of knighthood and stop Lancelot's Quest, and he bars Lancelot's passage to the Sword Bridge because, by his standard of values, Lancelot is fitted only to be ferried across the river. The Knight would suffer death, or any disgrace, rather than ride in the cart, perhaps because, like Gawain, but in a more extreme form, he cannot forego the external values of knightly pride. If we leave aside the level of the Celtic tradition, which, with Christian overtones, colours all events in the land of Gorre, and which would lend an aura of the Other World to the Arrogant Knight, to Meleagant and the Fifth Damsel, we may see an allegorical meaning in this incident. If the Knight would die rather than ride in the cart, the values which he personifies must be the antithesis of those symbolised by such an act. These values are humility, lack of self-regard, and devotion to a higher cause inspired by a love which can include compassion and *caritas* and which can be expressed in the noblest deeds of chivalry and the highest mission which a knight, who is the Elect, can accomplish. It is evident that the Arrogant Knight, who pleads for mercy in the name of God, embodies merciless, destructive violence, arrogance, and the 'wooden heart' of Meleagant for whom he is the prototype. In short, he represents the selfish knighthood and the ritual lust for combat which Chrétien mocks in *Erec* and attacks in *Perceval*. Meleagant and the Arrogant Knight are the absolute Evil which is born of blind adherence to convention. They are also the ultimate expression of the narrow, conventional ethic of Arthur's court which ostracised Lancelot. Already with Meleagant and the Arrogant Knight there is a muffled roll of thunder for the end of the Arthurian world in the *Mort Artu*.

The damsel who demands the Knight's extinction, and his head, which in the Celtic tradition holds within it the essence of the person slain, hates him specifically because he is *desleaus*. This may just mean 'treacherous' or 'disloyal' but, as we see elsewhere (p. 168), *leals* may refer to *lei* in the sense of the 'natural law', the 'essence of a person', and, if this is the case, it is possible that *desleaus* may have here the added meaning of 'inhuman'. The Fifth Damsel, who, as we shall see, is Meleagant's sister and, just possibly, may also be the Second Damsel who directed Lancelot and Gawain to the land of Gorre, is intent on defeating Meleagant's plans and the values he represents. She may personify the generous nobility of mind which is *Franchise*, and the wider human virtue of *Leauté* in allegorical conflict with the *Desleauté* and destructive arrogance of the knight. In this incident, Lancelot is the complete parfait, gentil knight, the servant of *Franchise*, who will later repay her debt when Lancelot is deserted by those who lack her virtue.

The treacherous waters crash beneath the Sword Bridge:

Roide et bruiant, noire et espesse,	swift and roaring, black and
Si leide et si espoantable	opaque, as ugly and terrifying
Con se fust li fluns au deable.	as if it were the Devil's river.
(3024–6)	

Sharp and gleaming, the sword extends for the length of two lances, and Lancelot's companions, seeing two lions on the far bank, entreat him to give up. Lancelot replies with good humour and faith:

'Seignor, merciz et grez aiiez	'My noble friends, accept my
Quant por moi si vos esmaiiez:	thanks and gratitude for your
D'amor vos vient et de franchise.	dismay on my behalf which
Bien sai que vos an nule guise	comes from your love and your
Ne voldriiez ma mescheance;	generous minds. I know well
Mes j'ai tel foi et tel creance	that you would not wish any
An Deu qu'il me garra par tot.'	mischance to befall me, in any
(3093–9)	way. But I have such faith and
	trust in God, that He will
	protect me without fail.'

He would die rather than turn back (3104) and, while his two companions weep for pity, Lancelot removes the armour from feet and hands, accepting the certainty of dire wounds in the hope of clinging to the bridge without falling. With great suffering, with hands, feet and knees bleeding, he crosses, and proves with his magic ring that the lions he had seen were part of a spell, and are now without substance.[39]

In this supreme test of devotion to Love, Chrétien uses the imagery of the bleeding hands and feet (3115–20), not to show Lancelot as a Christ figure, but to make his audience reach down into their profound religious experience and feel, by comparison with the Crucifixion, the extremity of suffering which Lancelot endures. The same intention is at work when Chrétien hints at an analogy between the terrifying roar and blackness of the river and the terrors wrought by the Devil in Hell (3024–6), indicating, at the same time, that the crossing of this water will lead to the Other World. It has been suggested that Chrétien, in this crossing of the Sword Bridge, had in mind the testing bridge of Hell as described in the Vision of St Paul, St Patrick's Purgatory,[40] which

Marie de France translated, and other pious legends. This Christian parallel is sustained when Bademagu offers Lancelot the 'ointment of the three Marys' (3374) who in Mark 16.1 buy unguents for Jesus after Joseph of Arimathea has laid him in the tomb.[41]

Once Lancelot is over the Sword Bridge, Chrétien's style becomes expository, less allusive. The underlying conflict of moral qualities which has been hinted at enigmatically, in the juxtaposition and contrast of words, deeds and characters, is brought clearly into the open. The land of Gorre, which is given to plain speaking, is a battle-ground between Good and Evil. King Bademagu is the epitome of the *Leauté* which may be defined as 'loyalty, uprightness, and all the good and noble qualities of the human and knightly condition'. These are the qualities above all else which he wants to preserve and put into effect in life:

> Et leauté sor tote rien
> Voloit par tot garder et feire.   (3160–1)

Meleagant, his son, who watches with him as Lancelot struggles across the Bridge, denies in all his deeds the *leauté* of his father:

. . . qui tot le contreire	he always did the opposite of
A son pooir toz jorz feisoit,	this whenever he could, for
(Car desleautez li pleisoit,	inhuman, unchivalrous deeds
N'onques de feire vilenie	were pleasing to him, and he
Et träison et felenie	was never too wearied or
Ne fu lassez ne enuiiez).	reluctant to commit churlish,
(3162–7)	treacherous and felonious acts.

Chrétien sums up Meleagant in the image of the Arrogant Knight:

Nus ne fust miaudre chevaliers,	No man would have made a
Se fel et desleaus ne fust;	better knight, had he only not
Mes il avoit un cuer de fust	been treacherous and inhuman.
Tot sanz douçor et sanz pitié.	But his heart was made of wood,
(3178–81)	void entirely of gentleness and
	pity.

Chrétien, resorting to moral black and white, expounds Lancelot's virtues, and the battle between Good and Evil in life, which Evil can win too easily:

Li rois certainnemant savoit
Que cil qui iert au pont passez
Estoit miaudre que nus assez;
Que ja nus passer n'i osast,
An cui dormist et reposast
Mauvestiez qui fet honte as suens
Plus que proesce enor as buens.
Donc ne puet mie tant proesce
Con fet mauvestiez et peresce:
Voirs est, n'an dotez ja de rien,
Qu'an puet plus feire mal que bien.
De cez deus choses vos dëisse
Mout, se demore n'i fëisse.

(3184–96)

The king knew with certainty that he who had crossed the bridge was far better than any other man. For no man would have dared to cross it in whom there dwelt any trace of that Evil which shames its followers even more than excellence in virtue brings honour to good men. For this reason Prowess cannot be as active as Evil and sloth are. It is true, and have no doubt whatsoever about this, that people can do more evil than good. About these two qualities would I say much more, did I not thereby delay my story.

Chrétien here presents the argument which, until now, he has hinted at. The temptation to Evil is stronger than the impulse to Goodness, and so must be resisted with heroic virtue and self-sacrifice. He illustrates this theme with the conflict between Bademagu and Lancelot on the one side and Meleagant on the other, and with the contrast between Lancelot and Gawain. These characters, without being in any way abstract allegories, personify in word and deed the enduring battle between Good and Evil, between Leauté and Desleauté, Proesce and Mauvestié. Bademagu, the repository of goodness and generosity of mind, which Arthur is not, is torn as a father between love and scorn for his brave but evil son. Lancelot, the epitome of chivalry, of humility and self-sacrifice for Love, is set against the selfish courage and cruelty of Meleagant. And Lancelot, the Elect who overcomes self-pride and resists the temptation of self-interest in devotion to Fin'Amors for the Queen, rises thereby to a higher concept of Love and virtue than can be achieved through the correct, courtly attitudes of Gawain. Lancelot, who can do the unthinkable, can ride in the cart, has the driving inner courage through which Evil, more prevalent, as Chrétien says, than Goodness, can be defeated. Gawain is correctly virtuous and brave. He will cross the Water Bridge, will escort Guenevere back to Logres, and he will offer to fight Meleagant in Lancelot's place. But he will not get in the death-cart, and because he cannot break with convention and the honour which is self-pride, he and the knighthood he represents can fight Evil but never defeat it. On the plane of moral allegory, this is why Arthur's knights are impotent to resist Meleagant. With the character of Lancelot, Chrétien is passing beyond the formal, courtly limitations of Arthur's world, and, possibly, of his audience. Knightly bravery, seeking Adventure for its own sake, is not adequate to the highest tasks. These need inner virtue, honour and a moral courage which disregards the values of the world, the Leauté which alone can conquer Mauvestié.

Bademagu sees Lancelot's superiority. Like the father of the Young Knight, he counsels his son: 'We have witnessed the greatest and most courageous deed ever accomplished, even in thought. If you fight, you will suffer hurt, and win no advantage. Make the people believe that you are wise. Honour him by granting him what he seeks, before he can request it' (3205–19). 'If this knight is alone in your land you should bear him company':

'Que prodom doit prodome atreire
Et enorer et losangier,
Nel doit pas de lui estrangier.
Qui fet enor, l'enors est soe.'
(3226–9)

'for a knight of excellent virtue should attract a knight of equal virtue, and honour and praise him with kind words, and should not turn him away from his presence. If a man does honour to others, this honour is his also.'

'Know well', he adds, 'the honour will be yours if you give honour and service to this man who is clearly the best knight in the world' (3230–3). 'May God destroy me', replies Meleagant, 'if there is no knight as good as, or better than him' (3234–5). – And Chrétien in a cool aside: It was a pity he did not mention himself, for his opinion of himself is no less than this, that he is the best knight in the world. – 'Perhaps', says Meleagant, 'you wish me to do homage to him, with hands clasped and feet together, and hold land from him? As God keep me, I would rather be liege man to him that surrender the Queen!' (3238–43). Honour for Bademagu lies in the generous mind which honours the deeds of others. For Meleagant, honour comes from strife and power, and the prestige and submission which the

strong, in feudal ritual, exact from the weak. Love demands
the abduction and possession of the object which is loved.
But Leauté must recognise and help its kind. Bademagu, innocent of any act of desleauté (3272), declares his support for
Lancelot, and Meleagant sees the abyss between himself and
his father:

'... po m'est de quanque vos dites:	'I care little for your words.
Je ne sui mie si hermites,	I am not so much a hermit
Si piteus ne si charitables,	[as you] or so compassionate
Ne tant ne vuel estre enorables	or given to caritas, nor do I
Que la rien que plus aim li	want to be so honourable as to
doingne.'	give him the person I most love.'

(3291-5)

Let his father recognise this opposition between them; let
him agree to live in peace:

'Tant con vos plest, soiiez pius hon,	'Be a man as full of mercy as
Et moi leissiez estre crüel.'	you please, and let me be cruel.'

(3310-11)

In this dramatic scene which exposes, even over-exposes,
the conflict between the two different attitudes to life,
Lancelot's role in society has been reversed. In Arthur's
world he was the outsider, rejected for his ride in the death-
cart. In the land of Gorre, his excellence is recognised by the
prisoners and the King, both in the Middle Land and in the
city of Bade which he has now reached. Meleagant, like the
Arrogant Knight, the enemy of order, peace, piety and caritas,
is the outsider in this land, ruled by a King whose values
and positive attitude to life exceed Arthur's as Lancelot's
exceed those of Gawain.

The King goes to the Sword Bridge with words of welcome,
and Lancelot, who is trying to staunch his wounds, rises
and, without sign of pain, demands immediate battle with
Meleagant. The King grants this reluctantly, but fixes the
fight for the following day. Once more, Meleagant rejects his
father's plea for peace. Meleagant must fight to keep his
prestige. The excellence, the virtue and the noble cause of his
adversary affect him only in as much as they will increase his
own fame, if he should win. Meleagant suffers no moral
doubts. Like the Arrogant Knight, he could not envisage the
possibility of mounting the death-cart. Prestige depends on

147

keeping the Queen as a possession. Honour and fame lie in the outward eye of surface appearance. They are tangible ambitions, and their realisation, measured by a material scale, is to be achieved through conflict, or threat of conflict. 'Were I to believe you', he tells his father, 'I should deserve to be torn apart by horses' (3470–1). He cannot imagine that Lancelot may have a different view of honour and fame: 'He seeks his honour, and I seek mine. He seeks his fame, and I seek mine. If he desires battle, I desire it a hundred times more.' 'You aspire to sin [madness] (folie)', says Bademagu, 'and you will find it' (3472–7).

On the next day, when Lancelot falters, weakened by his wounds from the Sword Bridge, a damsel, watching with the Queen from a tower, knows intuitively that he is not fighting for the prisoners who are present in abundance, after fasting and praying for his success, but for Love, which alone can inspire him to victory. She obtains his name Lanceloz del Lac from the Queen – the first time we hear it in the romance – and shouts it aloud so that Lancelot hears. He turns obediently to the tower, sees 'that person whom he most desired to see in all the world', reverts to reverie and, unable to tear his eyes away, fights with backward strokes against Meleagant, and gazes on the Queen. This extreme form of the world upside-down for love, which is touched with Chrétien's gentle irony, ceases when the damsel orders him to fight the right way round and keep the Queen and the tower in front of him. Lancelot so harries his opponent that the King, in pity for his son, intercedes with the Queen. At her words, 'Vuel je mout bien que il se taingne' (3812), Lancelot stops fighting. Fame has no value. Honour obeys Love. Meleagant, maddened by shame, furiously attacks him, but is bundled away by his father's men. He agrees to let the Queen return to Arthur, provided that, at the end of a year, Lancelot will accept his challenge to fight. If Lancelot fails to appear for this match, or is defeated, the Queen and the prisoners must return finally to the land of Gorre.

Lancelot's mission is ended. Knightly courage devoted to Fin'Amors has also brought joy and freedom to the oppressed who throng forward to touch their saviour. But the service of Fin'Amors knows no end. Lancelot must face the Queen, who to Bademagu's guileless surprise, greets him with hauteur, then retires to her room (3960–87). The reasons for this are not unclear. On the level of structural necessity, the Queen's rebuff motivates the scenes of frustrated and consummated love which will follow. On the level of courtly behaviour, Lancelot is the Queen's suitor, and only the damsel who shouted his name appears to have realised this. The Queen's status as Arthur's wife demands that she should preserve this secret, especially in the presence of Bademagu. Her role as *domna* also requires her to treat her suitor with reserve and to test him with suffering and delay before granting him any token of favour. For Chrétien's audience, the Queen's behaviour, which she later refers to as a *gas* or 'jest', would accord with the role of the lady as defined in the *De amore* of Andreas Capellanus: 'a noblewoman or a woman of the higher nobility is found to be very ready and bold in censuring the deeds or the words of a man of the higher nobility, and she is very glad if she has a good opportunity to say something to ridicule him' (I, 8th dialogue).[42] Bernart de Ventadorn had said:

No·n fatz mas gabar[43] e rire,	You do nothing but jest and
domna, can eu re·us deman.	laugh about it, my lady, when
(IV, 57–8)	I ask anything of you.

The Queen must also assert her power, since Lancelot has 'won' her in combat, as Meleagant had done, and as Erec, in a different situation, won Enide. Since pride is the enemy of love,[44] Guenevere, by rebuffing Lancelot, tests his humility and his ability to keep their secret.

Kay, as Lancelot discovers, has been the battle-ground for Meleagant's evil and Bademagu's goodness, the one ordering toxic ointments for his wounds, and the other healing remedies. But the Queen, says Kay, has been fully guarded by Bademagu, and is the mistress of her own decisions:

Et li rois mout plus l'an prisa	And the king esteemed her even
Por la leauté qu'an li vit.	more for the moral ways he saw
(4082–3)	in her.

Leauté here may refer to her loyalty to Arthur, but probably means that she thinks and acts in the manner (*lei*) which belongs to a Queen.

Lancelot, riding in search of Gawain, is made prisoner, and a false report of his death is brought to the Queen.

There now begins a double play on the theme of mutual death through love which Chrétien uses in all his Arthurian romances. The distraught Queen laments her cruelty, tries to strangle herself, renounces this as mortal sin. Would that she had given herself to him! 'To appear cruel was, I thought, a jest – to make mock of him' (gas) (4223); 'but he took it otherwise and has not forgiven me. I, alone, dealt him this mortal blow when, expecting to be received with joy, he came to me with smiles' (4223–31). Guenevere laments:

'Deus! avrai je ja reançon
De cest murtre, de cest pechié?
Nenil voir, ainz seront sechié
Tuit li fleuve et la mers tarie!
Ha! lasse, con fusse garie,
Et come fust granz reconforz
Se une foiz ainz qu'il fust morz
L'ëusse antre mes braz tenu.
Comant? Certes, tot nu a nu,
Por ce que plus an fusse a eise.
Quant il est morz, mout sui mauveise,
Que je ne faz tant que je muire.'
(4238–49)

'God! Will I then ever be released from this murder, from this sin? No, in very truth! Sooner will all the rivers and the sea dry up! Alas! What healing I should find, and what great comfort, if, before he died, I had held him once in my arms. In what manner? For sure, completely naked together, to give me greater joy. Since he is dead, I am guilty if I do not prepare to die.'

Death would be release. She chooses to suffer by living with her guilt:

'Miauz vuel vivre et sofrir les cos
Que morir por avoir repos.'
(4261–2)

'I prefer to live and suffer these blows than to die and find rest.'

Guenevere's speech (4215–62) brings her to the forefront of the action and prepares the way for her acceptance of Lancelot as her lover. She fasts for two days. A rumour reaches Lancelot that she is dead. In despair he tries to kill himself. He fastens a belt round his neck, attaches it to his saddle so that he will be dragged along by his horse. He is impatient to die:

'Ha! morz, con m'as or agueitié,
Que tot sain me fes desheitié!
Desheitiez sui, et mal ne sant
Fors de duel qu'au cuer me desçant.
Cist diaus est maus, voire morteus.
Ce vuel je bien que il soit teus,

'Ah! Death, how you have laid a trap for me. How you desolate me now when I am whole and well! I am desolate and feel no ill, except for the grief which weighs down my heart. This

Et se Deu plest, je an morrai.'
(4281–7)

grief is a sickness, indeed a
mortal one. And I desire it
should be so, and if it please
God, I shall die of it.'

Lancelot is cut free from the saddle, and guarded. He curses
Death for its delays:

'. . . Ha! vis morz deputeire,
Morz! por Deu, don n'avoies tu
Tant de pooir ne de vertu
Qu'ainz que ma dame m'ocëisses!'
(4336–9)

'Ah! vile, stinking Death!
In God's name, why were you
not strong and powerful enough
to kill me before you killed my
lady?'

'Je ne sai li queus plus me het,
Ou la vie qui me desirre
Ou morz qui ne me viaut ocirre.
Einsi l'une et l'autre m'ocit.'
(4348–51)

'I know not which hates me most,
life which desires me or death
which does not wish to kill me.
So, each of them gives me a
living death.'

Folie subsides, and savoir returns to Lancelot, as it had to
Guenevere. Chrétien makes him expound the courtly significance of the episode of the cart, and of Guenevere's rebuff:
'I should have killed myself when my lady the Queen showed
me her hatred in a look [sanblant de haïne, 4356]. She must
have had a reason, though I know not what. Had I known,
before her soul went to God's presence, I would have made
her such rich amends as would have pleased her . . . Perhaps
she knew that I mounted the cart. I know no blame she could
lay on me other than this. This has betrayed me. If she hated
me for this, God, why did this crime do me harm? Any one
who used this to reproach me, never knew love . . . she
should call me her true lover, since I thought it honourable
to do whatever Love desires, even to mount a cart. This she
should count as love. This is clear proof that Love tests its
followers in this way . . . But this service did not please my
lady. I knew this from her look. And yet her lover did something for which many have cast on him shame and reproach
and blame, and they made my sweetness bitter' (4354–401):

'Par foi, que teus est la costume
A ces qui d'amor rien ne sevent,
Que nes enor an honte levent:[45]
Mes qui enor an honte moille
Ne la leve pas, ainz la soille.
Or sont cil d'amor non sachant

'In faith, for such is the custom
of those who, ignorant of love,
raise up honour from the font
and in the likeness of shame,
but anyone who baptises honour
as shame, does not enhance it.

Qui einsi la vont desachant,
Et mout an sus de li se bote,
Qui son comandemant ne dote.
Car sanz faille mout an amande
Qui fet ce qu'amors li comande,
Et tot est pardonable chose;
S'est failliz qui feire ne l'ose.'

(4402–14)

On the contrary, he sullies it.
Now those know nothing of
Love who keep dragging it
down, and anyone who does not
respect its commands, exalts
himself far higher than Love.
For, without fail, anyone who
does Love's bidding receives a
great reward, and everything he
does can be forgiven. And that
man is a proven sinner who
does not dare do this.'

These two scenes of rumour and of death through Love are related to the theme of *La fausse morte* and are both as artificially contrived for courtly entertainment as the Cariado episode in the *Tristan* of Thomas.[46] But, like Thomas, Chrétien allows human feeling to break through. He leads Guenevere and Lancelot from their courtly stance of lady and suitor to a declaration of overwhelming, self-sacrificing passion comparable in its intensity to that of Tristan and Yseut or of Dido for Eneas, and to recognition of a love, which, if unrequited through the loss of one lover, demands the physical death of the other. For Lancelot and Guenevere the mental tension and subtleties of distant love or *amor de lonh* are removed by direct desire and the fire which burns in the marrow.[47] The Queen's confession of lust sets the stage for the night of passion which is the highpoint of the narrative structure.

Lancelot's reaction to Guenevere's *sanblant de haïne* (4356) is not unlike that of Bernart de Ventadorn, who saw his death in his lady's indifference:

e car ela no sospira,
sai qu'en lei ma mortz se mira,
can sa gran beutat remir.

(IX, 38–40)

and because she does not sigh,
I know that my death is mirrored
in her, when I behold her great
beauty.

And in another poem, Bernart has lines which are very close to the setting for Lancelot's attempted suicide:

mort m'a, e per mort li respon,
e vau m'en, pus ilh no·m rete,
chaitius, en issilh, no sai on.

(XLIII, 54–6)

she has slain me, and I reply to
her through death, and go away,
since she does not keep me in
her service, a wretched captive,
into exile, I know not where.

For Bernart, who like Lancelot loves with a single, un-
changing desire (xxx, 1–7), death can be exile from the
lady, from joy, song, and the life of the court. It can also
mean physical death such as that of Tristan whose suffering
he compares to his own, as sorrow cuts his heart because he
is dying and wishes to die (xl, 75–6). 'Alas! how dark I
feel, scorned and ill-used! I cannot endure the pain which
makes me faint with such grief because she denies me her
love . . . What can I do? No one can teach me! May death
come to the man who blames me for not loving her when
I am dead and buried.'

Such declarations would clearly find courtly favour, but
Chrétien appears to cast a cool eye on the 'disloyalty' of the
amant martyr who prefers death to suffering, when Guenevere,
like Enide, chooses, with greater savoir, to suffer stoically
rather than find her rest in death:[48]

> Miauz vuel vivre et sofrir les cos
> Que morir por avoir repos.　　　　　(4261–2)

Lancelot and Guenevere share the equal desire which
Bernart demanded from true lovers:

> En agradar et en voler　　　In giving pleasure and in desiring
> es l'amors de dos fis amans.　does the love of two true lovers
> nula res no i pot pro tener,　consist. Nothing can avail in
> si·lh voluntatz non es egaus.　love, if the desire to love is not
> 　　　(xv, 29–32)　　　equal.

But they observe the courtly rules. The Queen greets Lancelot's
return with joy, and they speak of love. 'Why rebuff me?
With your silence you brought me to death' (4490–4).
The Queen replies:

> 'Comant? Don n'eüstes vos honte　'What? Did you not feel shame
> De la charrete et si dotastes?　about the cart, and fear? You
> Mout a grant anviz i montastes　were very reluctant to climb
> Quant vos demorastes deus pas.'[49]　into it when you delayed for
> 　　　(4502–5)　　　two whole paces.'

Lancelot asks and is granted pardon. He would speak with
her again, 'more at leisure'. The Queen covertly glances at a
window, invites him there that night. Like Pyramus and
Thisbe, or the lovers in Laustic, they will remain apart. 'You
may not enter. Our bodies may not be joined. Kay sleeps in

the room, and the door is guarded' (4526–43). In courtly terms, Guenevere is offering Lancelot the test or *assaiars*[50] of restraint, to touch, to kiss, to feel, but nothing more. This in the *De amore* of Andreas Capellanus is the chaste delight of *amor purus* in contrast to that of *amor mixtus*. Of pure love he says: 'it consists in the contemplation of the mind and the affection of the heart; it goes as far as the kiss and the embrace and the modest contact with the nude lover . . . This love is distinguished by being of such virtue that from it arises all excellence of character, and no injury comes from it, and God sees very little offence in it. No maiden can ever be corrupted by such a love, nor can a widow or a wife receive any harm or suffer any injury to her reputation.'[51]

In their case, passion defeats restraint. Lancelot had feigned tiredness and retired early. 'You who have done likewise', adds Chrétien, 'can understand this.' He waits, stifling a sneeze. In the blackness of night, the Queen appears at the window, in a chemise of startling whiteness and a short fur-trimmed cloak of scarlet. Nearness overwhelms them (4606–7). Guenevere lets him enter; retires to her bed in case they are discovered. Silently, Lancelot bends and removes the bars, not knowing he has cut his hand. He approaches her bed with the adoration of the true lover:

Si l'aore et si li ancline;
Car an nul cors saint ne croit tant.
Et la rëine li estant
Ses braz ancontre, si l'anbrace,
Estroit pres de son piz le lace,
Si l'a lez li an son lit tret.

(4670–5)

He adores her and bows low before her, believing no holy relic more fit for his faith. And the Queen extends her arms towards him, embraces him, binds him close to her breast, and draws him into her bed beside her.

And if she feels great love for him, he feels one hundred thousand times as much for her. Now Lancelot has all he desires,

Quant il la tient antre ses braz
Et ele lui antre les suens.
Tant li est ses jeus douz et buens
Et del beisier et del santir,
Que il lor avint sanz mantir
Une joie et une mervoille
Tel qu'onques ancor sa paroille
Ne fu öie ne sëue;

when he holds her in his arms and she holds him in hers. His love-play in kisses and caresses is so pleasing to her, and gentle and good, that in truth they experienced a joy and a wonder such as was never yet known or heard of. But by me it will

Mes toz jorz iert par moi tëue,	remain for ever unspoken, for
Qu'an conte ne doit estre dite.	it is not to be told in a tale.
(4690–9)	

When Chrétien adds:

Des joies fu la plus eslite	The most precious and delightful
Et la plus delitable cele	of these joys is the one which
Que li contes nos test et cele.	the story conceals and keeps
Mout ot de joie et de deduit	silent about. Lancelot had much
Lanceloz tote cele nuit.	joy and delight all that night.
(4700–4)	

this is the only hint that the lovers have gone beyond the naked caresses allowed by *amor purus* and *Fin'Amors*, to the complete sexual act.

With the dawn, Lancelot achieves the martyrdom of leaving the beloved (4707–9). His body goes, his heart remains (4715). Exalted, as if in religious adoration,[52] he makes supplication as he would before an altar, replaces the bars of the window, and, with sighs and tears, departs (4716–39).

Chrétien immediately reverses the mood. He moves into an ironical, burlesque episode, a coda to the joys and sufferings of passionate love. Humorously he creates a situation which parodies the bedroom scene with the drops of blood on the floor in the Tristan story.[53] Lancelot's damaged hand has left blood in the Queen's bed. Kay's wounds have bled, inopportunely, during the night. Meleagant, in the early morning, enters, sees the blood on the beds of both Kay and the Queen, and accuses the astonished seneschal of adultery and disloyalty to Arthur.

With this accusation of adultery against Guenevere, Meleagant is telling the truth to a world which does not want to hear it. Like the physicians from Salerno in *Cliges* and Froncin the dwarf in Beroul's *Tristran*, he must be proved wrong. The ensuing farce is heightened by the abject plight of the seneschal, who in many courtly romances is a devious, mischievous figure, a *losengier* who disturbs true love. A courtly audience would revel in Kay's misfortune. Lancelot comes forward as champion of Guenevere and the seneschal, and swears a ritual oath before trial by combat which is as cynical as Yseut's oath to Mark. Meleagant has sworn that Kay the seneschal lay with the Queen in her bed and had all his pleasure with her. Lancelot, kneeling likewise, swears on the holy relics: 'You lie. And I swear, for my part, that he neither lay with her nor felt her. And may God, if it please Him, take vengeance upon the man who has lied' (4987–95). Bademagu again intercedes to have the fight stopped, and Meleagant again continues to strike Lancelot when he has desisted in obedience to the Queen.

The narrative is now on the second leg of the horseshoe which will lead back to the dénouement at Arthur's court. Chrétien still has to return the Queen and the prisoners to Arthur and bring about the final combat between Lancelot and Meleagant in a year's time. How shall he fill this year of delay, and sustain interest in his story? First, he develops the contrast between Lancelot and Gawain. Gawain is dragged, water-filled and speechless, from the river crossing at the Water Bridge. He has successfully encountered many perils, but he fails his next test, as he failed to mount the cart, and as he will fail to rescue Lancelot from the tower. The cart was a test of self-sacrifice to Fin'Amors. This next test, and the test of the tower, which it foreshadows, are trials of love within the knightly brotherhood of arms. Like the cart, they demand the rejection of self-interest and of a static sense of honour, in favour of the courageous quest of the difficult and the apparently impossible. Gawain recovers his senses. He learns that Lancelot has saved the Queen, but that on the way to find Gawain, he has vanished, led away by a treacherous dwarf. Gawain has the right response: 'When we leave this bridge, we will go in search of Lancelot' (5188–9), but he lacks the persistence of true moral courage. He hears those around him: 'Go first to Guenevere and make the King find Lancelot whom Meleagant has imprisoned' (5190–8). Supinely he agrees. They return to Bademagu's castle, where all, except Meleagant, are given over to a Grief of the Court.[54] Grief turns to Joy when a false letter announces that Lancelot is safe and well at Arthur's court, and the Queen returns there with Gawain and Kay. Illusion turns to reality, joy to grief, at the news that Lancelot has indeed vanished. Lancelot's disappearance and imprisonment will enable Chrétien, as we have seen, to test Gawain's knighthood. It also avoids the difficulty of allowing Lancelot to return Guenevere to Arthur, as Tristan handed Yseut back to the credulous Mark. Such ceremonious disloyalty by Lancelot would contravene Chrétien's thematic structure, as would any formal recognition that this love affair might continue at the court of a cuckolded Arthur. The planes of Fin'Amors and marriage are kept quite separate. The ending of the love theme must be indeterminate and enigmatic.

This central episode, from the crossing of the Sword Bridge to the return of Guenevere to Arthur, has clarified almost all the main themes of the romance: the humility and self-sacrifice demanded by Love and the good effects of this; the conflict between the vainglory which masquerades as Love and honour, and the true honour which resides within the mind; and the contest between loyalty and disloyalty to the knightly and human condition, between Leauté and Desleauté. And behind these clashes of temporal values there is the ceaseless battle between Good and the Evil, which, as Chrétien says, so readily wins disciples.

Chrétien threads these themes together in a more subtle conjointure than the contrived craftmanship of Erec et Enide. In the dialogues of Meleagant and his father, and Lancelot and Guenevere, he binds the exposition of theme more closely than before to the dramatic situation and the human feelings of his characters. Conversely, he skilfully moves backwards and forwards from the central love theme of Lancelot and the Queen, to the conflict of wider values between Meleagant and Bademagu. As in the episode of the Fourth Damsel, he also varies the dramatic mood of his narrative from the courtly rebuff by the Queen, to the death wish of frustrated love, the emergence of savoir, the passion of fulfilled love, the burlesque of the drops of blood on the sheets, Lancelot's disappearance at the moment of triumph, and the return from Gorre to Arthur's world.

The tourney at Noauz is organised on Midsummer Day by the ladies and damsels at Arthur's court who are looking for a husband, and Guenevere, in an ironical situation which Chrétien would appreciate, accepts their invitation to preside over their marriage rite. This tourney symbolises the two opposing attitudes to honour and love which dominate the romance; on the one hand, the belief in the appearance of prestige which is vaine gloire, and, on the other, the selfless aspiration to a prowess inspired by humility and devotion to an ideal. The conflict between these two attitudes began

with the death-cart and was clarified in Lancelot's lament at
the 'death' of Guenevere (see p. 151). The Lancelot who
now faces this final trial is a man quite different from the
hesitant knight in the scene of the death-cart. He has been
tested by Fin'Amors, by his conscience and by the Queen, and,
when he has affirmed his devotion to Love, he will be ready
to conclude the wider struggle between Good and Evil.

Lancelot is freed on parole by the susceptible wife of his
gaoler, who is Meleagant's seneschal. Anonymously he
irrupts into the tourney as a scarlet knight and defeats all
comers, fulfilling the prophecy of a herald – who has recognised him but is sworn to secrecy – that he will take the
measure (5637)[55] of the other combatants. The Queen seeks
to know his identity, and, if he is Lancelot, to discover
whether he still loves her with complete Fin'Amors. At this
moment, she does not know whether Lancelot has deserted
her. She instructs him to fight badly, and he obeys, offering
no reply to the blows and scorn he endures. When, on the
second day, she sends him another message and he again
agrees to fight badly, the Queen is sure of his identity, and
rejoices in his safety:

Por ce qu'or set ele sanz dote
Que ce est cil cui ele est tote
Et il toz suens sanz nule faille.
(5893–5)

because she knows now beyond
any doubt that this is he to
whom she belongs entirely and
that he is entirely, indisputably
hers.

This is the state of love which Erec and Enide arrived at
through the shared trials of love within marriage, and which
Cliges and Fenice discovered through the perils of the battlefield. Guenevere and Lancelot find it when Lancelot has
given final proof of his quality as a fin amant. His resistance
to transitory and self-interested desire, his devotion to the
Queen even, were not enough without proof of fidelity after
receiving her favours. This mutual certainty in love, which
transcends the passion of the bedroom scene, is now assured
through Lancelot's constancy, his renewed humility and
obedience at Noauz. Lancelot's test on the return journey
to Arthur's court is the structural and thematic counterpart
to the incident of the cart. That episode came after Meleagant's visit to the court, this one comes before. At the test

of the cart, self-pride impaired Lancelot's devotion to love. In the tourney at Noauz, his willingness to sacrifice the forms of pride and honour which are esteemed by other knights and by society, is complete. The theme of Fin'Amors, on the plane of Lancelot's love for Guenevere, is bound up.[56]

Lancelot's reappearance at the tourney is greeted with scorn and derision by the squires and men-at-arms (5881–7), but when he is ordered to fight as best he can, he replies to the damsel who brings the Queen's message, with words which might have come from a courtly love song:

. . . 'Or li diroiz
Qu'il n'est riens nule qui me griet
A feire des que il li siet;
Car quanque li plest m'atalante'. . . .
(5910–13)

'Tell her now that there is no deed at all which I find displeasing to do as soon as I know it to be her will, for whatever pleases her is my delight.'

Lancelot is the victor of the field, the best beloved of ladies and damsels; 'by St John,[57] they will not marry this year, unless they can have Lancelot whom they love' (6071–5). Chrétien with wry humour returns him to prison:

Et Lanceloz pas ne sejorne,
Mes tost an sa prison retorne.   (6077–8)

Chrétien is equally cool about the pleasure aroused by Lancelot's valour:[58]

Que granz deporz est de veoir
Com il fet tumber et cheoir
Chevaus et chevaliers ansanble.
(5997–9)

For great delight is it to see how he makes horses and knights fall and collapse in one piece.

The externals of prowess are empty. The purpose behind the prowess, in this case, Fin'Amors, gives merit to Lancelot's triumph.

Meleagant, knowing he has immured Lancelot in a tower, issues his challenge at Arthur's court, and accepts Gawain as his adversary, if at the end of a year, Lancelot, whom he denigrates for his absence, has not returned. His boasting at his father's court: 'I am feared by Arthur's knights, Lancelot has fled' (6276–309), leads to a monologue in which Bademagu sums up the theme of Good and Evil:

'Fiz', fet li peres, 'or a droit
Te fes ici tenir por sot.
Or set tes qui devant nel sot
Par toi mëismes ta folie.
Voirs est que buens cuers s'umilie,
Mes li fos et li sorcuidiez
N'iert ja de folie vuidiez.
Fiz, por toi le di, que tes teches
Par sont si dures et si seches
Qu'il n'i a douçor n'amistié.
Li tuens cuers est toz sanz pitié:
Trop par ies de folie espris.
C'est ce por quoi je te mespris,
C'est ce qui mout t'abeissera.
Se tu es preuz, assez sera
Qui le bien an tesmoignera
A l'ore qu'il besoignera.
N'estuet pas prodome loer
Son cuer por son fet aloer;
Que li fez mëismes se loe'. . .
(6324–43)

'My son', the father says, 'now do you rightly make yourself thought of as a fool. Now anyone who did not know it before knows of your folly through your own words. It is the truth that a good heart humbles itself and that the fool and the man given to vain imaginings will never be empty of folly. My son, it is of your case that I speak, for your character is so very hard and withered that it has no sweetness or friendship within it. Your heart is completely without pity, so greatly are you enamoured of folly. This is why I despise you. This is what will cast you down to the depths. If you excel in virtue and prowess, there are many who, in the hour of need, will bear witness to this goodness. A virtuous man has no need to praise what lies in his heart in order to exalt his deed, for the deed itself speaks its own praise'. . . .

Bademagu despairs of his son: 'Words have little value for the fool. To persuade him from folly is vain' (6348–50). To moralise is vain. Words are writ in water:

'Et biens qu'an ansaingne et
    descuevre
Ne vaut rien s'an nel met a oevre,
Ainz est lués alé et perdu.'
(6351–3)

'And goodness which is taught and revealed has no value unless it is put into deeds. It passes swiftly away and is lost'. . . .

This theme of the words which wither in sterile soil will recur in the opening lines of Yvain and Perceval. It sends Meleagant into a transport of fury and disbelief. He has no mesure, his world is upside-down, his self-contained imaginings are reality, and biens 'goodness of heart' is beyond his reach. His folly touches tragedy:

'Est ce songes ou vos resvez,
Qui dites que je sui desvez
Por ce se je vos cont mon estre?'
(6363–5)

'Is this a trance in which you dream when you say I am mad because I tell you of my very being?'

Meleagant's sister, the Fifth Damsel of Lancelot's quest, hears her father mock the notion that Lancelot has fled. 'He must be imprisoned without escape' (6383–5). She will now bring her brother to his death, like the Arrogant Knight, his prototype, whose head she demanded. Her values are those of her father, Bademagu: Biens 'goodness', Franchise 'nobility of mind and spirit' and Leauté 'obedience to the true condition of nobility'. When she brings these knights to destruction, she destroys allegorically the evil which they personify. After unremitting search, as if driven by a geis or spell, she is brought by her mule to an empty landscape with a tower by the sea. She hears Lancelot's voice, weak, low, hoarse, lamenting the twists of Fortune's wheel, asking for death. Nevertheless his words are expository. As Bademagu had described the vices of Meleagant's knighthood, so Lancelot now sums up the weaknesses of Gawain:

'Ha, sainte Croiz, sainz Esperiz,
Con sui perduz, con sui periz!
Con sui del tot an tot alez!
Ha, Gauvains, vos qui tant valez,
Qui de bontez n'avez paroil,
Certes, duremant me mervoil
Por quoi vos ne me secorez!
Certes, trop i par demorez,
Si ne feites pas corteisie.
Bien dëust avoir vostre äie
Cil cui tant soliiez amer!
Certes, de ça ne de la mer,
Ce puis je bien dire sanz faille,
N'ëust destor ne repostaille,
Ou je ne vos ëusse quis
A tot le mains set anz ou dis,
Se je an prison vos sëusse,
Ainz que trové ne vos ëusse.'
(6501–18)

'Ah holy Cross, holy Spirit. How I am lost and destroyed! How I have passed away from all I hold dear. Ah, Gawain, you who have such worth, who have no equal in good deeds, I wonder greatly why you bring me no help. Indeed, you do delay too much, and courtesy is lacking in you. He, whom you were wont to love so greatly, ought indeed to receive your help. I can say for sure, in all truth, there would be no isolated place or hidden spot, on this shore or across the sea, where I would not have searched for you, at the very least for seven years, or ten, if I had known you were in prison, until I had found you'. . . .

Lancelot swears service and fealty to Meleagant's sister:

'Se fors de ci me poez metre,
Por voir vos puis dire et promettre
Que je toz jorz mes serai vostre,
Si m'äit sainz Pos li apostre!
Et se je Deu voie an la face,

'If you can free me from here, in truth I can say and promise you that I will be yours for ever, as Saint Paul the apostle may help me. And, as I hope to

Ja mes n'iert jorz que je ne face
Quanque vos pleira comander.
Ne ja ne savroiz demander
Chose nule, por que je l'aie,
Que vos ne l'aiiez sanz delaie'. . . .
(6607–16)

see God's face, there will never be a day when I do not do whatever it will please you to command. Nor will you ever be able to ask for any possession of mine without receiving it forthwith.'

Once freed, he reaffirms this loyalty:

'Par vos sui de prison estors,
Por ce poez mon cuer, mon cors,
Et mon servise et mon avoir,
Quant vos pleira, prandre et avoir.
Tant m'avez fet que vostre sui.'
(6705–9)

'Through you have I escaped from prison, and for this, whenever it pleases you, you can take and possess my heart, my body, my service and my possessions. You have done so much for me that I am yours.'

This declaration of submission lacks all the restraints and conditions of Lancelot's vow to the Second Damsel and to the gaoler's wife when they rendered him a great service. Has Lancelot switched his allegiance from Guenevere to Bademagu's daughter, and is this why he is silent about Guenevere in the last thousand lines of the romance?[59] This explanation is possible, but unlikely. The service he offers is feudal. The damsel can take his complete self, his possessions and his capacity for heroic deeds and keep them in her service, and she in her turn offers him all her possessions. But Lancelot addresses her as 'pucele' (6602) and he does not offer love. He speaks of *amors* only when he seeks leave to depart from the castle where she has restored him to health:

'Or, douce amie deboneire,
Par amors si vos prieroie
Congié d'aler, et j'i iroie,
S'il vos pleisoit, mout volantiers.'
(6714–17)

'Now, sweet, kind friend, affectionately I would seek your leave to go, and I would depart, if it pleased you, very willingly.'

And she replies,

'Lanceloz, biaus douz amis chiers',
Fet la pucele, 'jel vuel bien;
Que vostre enor et vostre bien
Vuel je par tot et ci et la.'
(6718–21)

'Lancelot, fair, dear, gentle, friend', says the damsel, 'I am happy about this, for I desire your honour and well-being everywhere, both here and yonder.'

She gives him a 'wondrous horse, the best that was ever seen by any man', and he rides off as they commend each other to God.

In sheltering and caring for Lancelot, feeding him and offering him all her possessions before sending him on his way, yonder to the other world of Arthur's court, the Fifth Damsel is acting a role which was undoubtedly associated, as we saw in the case of the Fourth Damsel, with that of the Celtic fairy mistress.[60] In addition, as has been suggested above, she appears to personify the virtues of goodness in life, of *Franchise* and *Leauté*, and in this case Lancelot's pledge to her of lasting allegiance and her desire to see his honour and *bien* 'goodness and well-being' everywhere, 'in this world and that one', are understandable. The Fifth Damsel, Bademagu's daughter, is part of the conflict between Good and Evil which, since the rounding-off of the love theme at Noauz, now engages the narrative.

The aura of the Celtic supernatural, which attends Lancelot's departure from Gorre on the wondrous horse, is suggested again in his startling appearance before Gawain, who is armed to fight Meleagant:

Et ja voloit son escu prandre
Quand il vit devant lui desçandre
Lancelot don ne se gardoit.
A grant mervoille l'esgardoit
Por ce que si soudainncmant
Est venuz; et se je ne mant,
Mervoilles li sont avenues
Aussi granz con s'il fust des nues
Devant lui chëuz maintenant.
(6807–15)

And he was just about to take up his shield when he saw Lancelot dismount unexpectedly in front of him. He looked at him and marvelled greatly because he had arrived so abruptly. And I do not lie when I say that it seemed that a miracle had happened as great as if Lancelot had fallen forthwith out of the clouds in front of him.

The double meaning of *desçandre* (6808) 'dismount' and 'descend' is unlikely to be other than intentional. It reinforces the supernatural overtones of Lancelot's departure from Bademagu's daughter and his arrival at Arthur's court. Behind the plane of the narrative there is the implication that he has been imprisoned in the land of Gorre in a dimension in which Meleagant and his sister move naturally, but which no mortal from Arthur's world could discover, let alone penetrate, in order to rescue Lancelot. This dimension might be the Other World, or Hades or an allegorical plane of heroism, virtue and love, or it might embrace all these possibilities at the same time.

The Grief of the Court turns to Joy (6833–41) and Guenevere fights to control her passion and keep the secret of their love: 'she is so close to him that her body almost follows her heart, which is kissing and welcoming Lancelot' (6849–53). 'And if reason had not taken her foolish thoughts and raging desire from her, people would have seen all that was in her heart ... she has pulled herself together, she will wait until she sees an opportunity for them to be together in greater privacy' (6864–75).

It is not chance that puts the next lines in juxtaposition with the Queen's lust:

Li rois Lancelot mout enore,
Et quant assez l'ot conjöi,
Si li dist: 'Amis, je n'öi
Certes de nul home noveles,
Piece a, qui si me fussent beles,
Con de vos. ...'

(6876–81)

The King does Lancelot great honour and when he has offered him a warm welcome, he tells him: 'My friend, for sure for a long time past, I have not heard news of any man which could please me as much as the reports which reached us of you. ...'

From the courtly viewpoint, the friendship which the guileless Arthur shows to his wife's lover would be amusing as a victory for Fin'Amors over the indifference of a husband who had maltreated his wife earlier in the romance. But from a wider viewpoint, Arthur, like the later Archambaut when he welcomes Flamenca's lover, Guillem de Nevers, is a pathetic figure, reduced in the context of the Queen's deceit to a passive, ignoble role, as in *Yvain*, *Perceval* and the thirteenth-century *Queste del saint Graal*.

Nature is full of promise as Arthur takes his place for the fight in which Lancelot will defeat and behead Meleagant. It is a splendid setting beside a spring as beautiful and bright as silver, flowing through a channel of pure gold to a valley between the woods, emerging beneath a great and handsome sycamore, surrounded by a border of thick, fresh, fine grass, newly green at all seasons. Arthur takes his seat beneath this tree, planted at the time of Abel, and nothing displeasing meets his eye. The triumph of Good over Evil is accompanied by the eternal flowering of nature in its summer kingdom. The prisoners have returned, the waste land of grief is over.

Arthur symbolises fruitful sov[...]
the perpetual threat which Mel[...]
like Abel, is deceived by those who[...]
like Enide's cousin in the garden of fe[...]
wall of air, he sits beneath the sycamore,[...]
which will collapse on the battlefield of t[...]

    Lancelot is a masterpiece, a combination o[...]
and sources of inspiration. It has a dual setting
of Gorre and Logres which are bridged by Guenever[...]
tion and rescue. Within this span of two worlds, [...]
develops a love story which, in dramatised form, is a[...]
of *Fin'Amors*, remarkable for the completeness of its intention
and achievement. If we consider for a moment the dual
nature of *Fin'Amors* in the poetry of the early troubadours,
we may see more clearly the rounded and composite quality
of this Art of *Fin'Amors* which Chrétien portrays in *Lancelot*.
On the one level, we have the ardent self-sacrificing devotion
of the lover to the lady. On another level we have Lancelot
as the epitome and champion of Goodness against Evil.
Chrétien's depiction of Lancelot as the *fis amaire* of Guenevere
may be closely related, as has been suggested earlier in this
chapter, to the poetry of Bernart de Ventadorn. Yet a question
remains about the source from which Lancelot draws the
virtues and moral courage which oppose and defeat the
forces of *Mauvestié*. Does this source lie in his religious faith?
Despite the Christian overtones in the romance, this seems
highly unlikely. It is far more probable that Lancelot's
virtues and strength stem from *Fin'Amors*.

    To consider this problem, let us look at the poetry of the
twelfth-century troubadours.[61] In this poetry four separate
patterns of thought are interwoven and the division in these
patterns corresponds broadly, but not entirely, to the stylistic
division between the reflective or metaphysical poetry in the
'closed' style and the courtly and this-worldly poetry in the
'clear' style.[62] In general terms these patterns of thought are
the philosophising or moralising, which is concerned largely
with the concept of *natura* and *universitas*, the Christian pattern,
the courtly pattern and the pattern of feudal knighthood.
The 'philosophical' and Christian patterns, which may over-
lap, are found most frequently in metaphysical and allusive
poets such as Marcabru and Peire d'Alvernhe. The courtly

...terns, which may also intermingle, are found ... such as Bernart de Ventadorn, Raimon de Miraval ...d Bertran de Born, and these poets may also be influenced to a lesser degree by the 'philosophical' and Christian patterns. All four patterns are conjoined in the poetry of Marcabru. They are also conjoined in the *Lancelot* of Chrétien de Troyes.

The troubadours who compose within these different patterns, whether using them separately or in combination, view the subject of love, happiness, honour and morality from different standpoints, and the meanings given by them to words such as *Jois, Fin'Amors, Mesura* and *Natura*[63] vary accordingly. This variation in meaning is especially evident in words which are concerned with morality and immorality, with virtue and wrongdoing. If the framework changes from the philosophical to the courtly, to the Christian or the feudal, the applied sense of the word must alter according to its context, however constant the fundamental and absolute meaning may remain.

What then is the meaning of these words *Mauvestié, Proesce, Leauté, Desleauté*, which occur so frequently in the *Lancelot* of Chrétien de Troyes? The basic meaning of *Mauvestié* appears to be recreancy or rebellion against a law or *lei*, whether this is the natural law of a living creature or organism, the law of a religious or professional calling, or an accepted law of social behaviour. *Proesce*, on the other hand, means excellence of virtue either as an absolute virtue or within any of these separate ethical frameworks. The conflict between *Malvestatz* and *Proeza* in troubadour poetry is treated in mocking style by the very first troubadour Guilhem IX of Aquitaine, who may be parodying methods of scholarly debate, and especially moral and philosophical precepts which, perhaps under Chartrian influence, may have been current in the courtly society of Poitiers.[64] In his sophisticated but ribald poem of the *cons gardatz*, he also parodies the philosophical notion of the *leis* which is the natural law according to which every organic creature lives and develops.[65]

It is in Marcabru (c. 1130–1150) that *Malvestatz* rides violently and positively into troubadour poetry. Mounted on the crupper of *Avoleza* 'the condition of all that is mean and base in the world' (xii[bis], 24–5), it will never retire from its fight with Proeza. The rich and the mighty clamour to join its ranks, it is never idle in the task of seducing all classes of society to its cause. It fractures its main enemy Proeza, the sum of all noble, courtly and Christian virtues (IX, 21–2). It fights Jovens 'youthful generosity of spirit', and, intent on wealth, it ignores honour and innate worth (honor e valor) and destroys vergonh'e mesura 'a proper sense of shame and an awareness of what is right and fitting' (IX, 13–20).

The armies of Proeza shrink before its onslaught: 'among a thousand people whom Malvestatz fractures and tears apart, I do not find forty whom Proeza loves' (XI, 9–13). Malvestatz threatens the last bastion of Proeza: 'The castle and hall are taken. In the keep Jois and Jovens are condemned to dire suffering. A hundred catapults pour in their shot as the armies of Malvestatz press in for the kill. For each man shouts: "Fire and flame! Let us get in and take the tower! Let us slit the throats of Jois and Jovens, and let Proeza be put to death." '66

In this bitter struggle, Malvestatz for Marcabru is the force which fractures the rational, ordered way of life. It destroys faith and uprightness. It encourages the self-delusion of the hypocrite, and the self-indulgence of the layabout and the social and amorous predator. It destroys mesura and vergonha, and summons unbridled desire to its dance. It is the enemy of the ideal of universitas which conditions Marcabru's belief in cuidars entiers, the 'wholeness' in the mind, the spirit and social behaviour of man, who, at one with his natura, can find order and happiness within himself and within the wider context of the natural order. And this idea of wholeness applies in Marcabru as it does in Chrétien de Troyes not only to the philosophical plane of 'natural' thinking, the plane of the essential human condition, but also to the courtly, the Christian and the feudal planes.

These four patterns of thinking and the basic 'law' of orderliness which is common to them, rely on virtues of which the most common is mesura. This virtue allows the individual to recognise the 'law' as it pertains to any of these patterns, and to behave according to Proeza which is the sum of all the virtues required in each ethical pattern. Proeza, in its highest degree, is thus compounded of all the virtue which is expressed equally effectively in all the patterns. It is this wide concept of whole thinking or *cuidars entiers* and the virtuous aspiration which embraces all that is noble in courtly, feudal, Christian and 'natural' philosophical thought and faith, which distinguishes Marcabru's moral philosophy, and illumines likewise the romances and especially the later romances of Chrétien de Troyes. In this concept of the whole man or woman, the cardinal virtue of untarnished *Proeza* enables the individual to find happiness through devotion to *Fin'Amors* and its attendant virtue of *cortesia*,[67] through the virtuous and unselfish fulfilment of knightly obligations, through Christian devotion, through the understanding of one's own *natura* and the achievement of harmony within the natural order. For Marcabru, and for Chrétien in *Lancelot*, the purpose of *Malvestatz* is to disrupt these patterns of ordered aspiration, to alienate the individual from *Proeza*, and to weaken and extinguish acceptance of the 'law' by which *Proeza* is expressed in virtuous behaviour and in ways of thinking which are whole and free from the fragmentation caused by self-interested vanity.

In twelfth-century troubadour poetry, *Proeza*, within set ethical patterns, 'natural', feudal, Christian or courtly, is always in retreat before the insidious, incessant warfare waged against it by *Malvestatz*. *Proeza* in this poetry is a delicate plant, an ideal of an absolute excellence which cannot improve and can only deteriorate unless zealously tended. In the hierarchy of allegorical virtues and vices in troubadour poetry, however, *Proeza* does not correspond to the active, all-pervasive *Malvestatz*, but to *Avoleza*, the static condition of absolute baseness. It is *Leautatz* which acts as the champion of *Proeza* in the fight against *Malvestatz*. It is the man who is *pros* within himself and whose conduct is *leals* who combats all that is *malvatz*, rebellious, disruptive and recreant. It is true that *leautatz* and *leals* may frequently be translated as 'loyalty' and 'loyal' in the present-day sense, but the use of these terms by the troubadours and by Chrétien de Troyes indicates the existence within them of richer overtones of meaning.

Leals can mean obedience to the innate 'law' by which a living organism behaves in accordance with its nature. It can also refer to the 'law' of a calling, a profession, or any ethical system such as *cortesia*. A monk, a knight, lady, queen or king can be *leals* through fulfilling the 'law' associated with their position.[68] To take one example among many, Arthur in *Erec et Enide*:

> 'Ce apartient a leal roi
> Que il doit maintenir la loi,
> Verité et foi et justise.
> Je ne voudroie an nule guise
> Feire desleauté ne tort.'   (1797–1801)

'For it belongs to the integrity of a genuine (*leal*) king to maintain the law, truth and faith and justice. I would not wish in any way to commit an act which does not befit my calling, or which is wrong.'

Leals can also be applied to inanimate objects. In Chrétien's *Le Conte du Graal*, Perceval, having left the castle of the Fisher King, is interrogated by his cousin. She demands to know the re ason for his fresh and rested appearance. 'A man might ride', she says, 'without finding for twenty-five leagues in a straight line in the direction which you have followed any single dwelling which would be *leaus* ['suitable for a knight'] or good and comfortable' (edn Hilka, 3469–73).

In Marcabru it is *Fin'Amors*, a deity representing the highest form of profane love, which alone can match the forces of *Malvestatz* and consign to the torments of Hell its retinue of murderers, hypocrites, magicians, usurers, liars, deceivers and promiscuous lovers (XL, 10–35). Conversely, to those whom it accepts, *Fin'Amors* grants *Jois*, *Sofrirs* and *Mesura* (XXXVII, 19–24). *Jois* for Marcabru is the serenity of a mind free from deceit, from the burden of lust and from fragmented, self-interested ways of thinking. *Sofrirs* is humility and patience. *Mesura* is the ability to direct oneself to those deeds and to a way of life which are suited to one's *natura*, talents and position in society.

If we return to *Lancelot*, we may see that Marcabru's ideas apply also to the conflict in this romance between Good and Evil, and between ways of thinking which are 'whole' and those which are 'fragmented' or narrowly 'single-minded'. In all these conflicts Lancelot, when he is being tested and proved as a *fis amaire*, epitomises the values of *Fin'Amors* which are in conflict with the narrow-mindedness of Gawain and Arthur's world. In the greater battle against the unending *Mauvestié* of Meleagant, he acts as the strong right arm of

169

Fin'*Amors*, and with the support of Bademagu and his daughter, emerges victorious. Although Lancelot, Bademagu and his daughter, and Meleagant and his henchmen are in no way abstract allegories, they personify in their words and deeds the conflict between *Proesce* and *Mauvestié*. They fight the battle which was threatened in Marcabru's *Bel m'es quan la rana chanta* when *Malvestatz* urged its minions to slit the throat of *Jois* and *Jovens* and to slaughter *Proeza*, the sum of all knightly and courtly excellence (XI, 21–4).

This conflict between *Malvestatz* and *Proeza*, hinted at by Guilhem IX and magnified by Marcabru, is waged in full dramatic fashion in *Lancelot*, with *Leauté*, the protagonist of *Proesce*, emerging as the ultimate victor in the context. The emphasis on the virtue of *Leauté* in *Lancelot* appears to have been an innovation by Chrétien de Troyes. The word *Leautatz* in its wider meaning of obedience to the law of a natural or ethical code is found in troudabour poetry, as in Arnaut Daniel's *Lancan son passat* in which *Leautatz* holds off the predatory attacks of *Fals'Amors* (IV, 9–16).[69] But it is in the *Lancelot* of Chrétien de Troyes that *Leauté* with this wider meaning of devotion to the *leis* of *Fin'Amors* comes to the fore as the adversary of *Mauvestié*. The conflict between the *Proesce* and *Leauté* of Lancelot and the *Mauvestié* and *Desleauté* of Meleagant extends to all patterns of thought, 'natural', courtly, Christian and knightly. But the major framework within which *Leauté* fights and defeats *Mauvestié* is that of *Fin'Amors*. At the trial of the Cart Lancelot is *desleaus* towards *Fin'Amors*. As soon as he achieves the integrated wholeness of *Leauté* on all four levels, he is invincible.

For Chrétien, as for Marcabru, the spread of *Mauvestié* throughout the world derives from the self-pride and self-interest which nourish it, together with the belief that its view of life alone is correct. Thus Meleagant to his father: 'I care little for your words. I am not such a hermit as you, nor so compassionate or given to *caritas* . . . Be a man as full of mercy as you like; let me be cruel' (3291–3, 3310–11).

In a milder form, this *Mauvestié* is evident in the narrow and fragmented thinking of Gawain who is adept at 'mistaking a gadfly for a hawk'.[70] Since he answers only to the demands of his knightly and courtly profession, *mesura* for him is not related to any self-recognition or awareness of his own *natura*, of himself as body, mind and spirit, a microcosmic entity which is also part of a universal, cosmic entity. It is because *mesura* for Gawain is related only to the conventions of Arthur's court that he cannot mount the cart or sleep in the Perilous Bed, that he chooses the left-hand path – in *Perceval* the path of *vaine gloire* – that leads to the Water Bridge, that he cannot rescue Guenevere because he lacks the virtues of the *fis amaire*. Gawain is brave, but like Yvain before he becomes the Knight of the Lion, he lacks moral courage. Rescued from the Water Bridge, he is soon dissuaded from the search for the abducted Lancelot. He agrees to fight Meleagant in the presence of Arthur's court, should the imprisoned Lancelot not return in time. He will not, however, stir from the court in order to find him.

Lancelot alone is the Elect who can show up the fragmented thinking of Gawain and Arthur's world, who can behead and destroy the *Mauvestié* incarnate in Meleagant and in the Arrogant Knight who accosts him in his last test before that of the Sword Bridge. To a twelfth-century audience well acquainted with the troubadour ideas of *Fin'Amors* which were born and nurtured at Poitiers, it might not appear in the least unusual that Lancelot, the ideal *fis amaire* and pattern of virtuous excellence (*proesce*), should draw his strength and daring from profane *Fin'Amors*, through which, according to Marcabru, a man must grow in virtue, and from which beneficial effects must flow. Lancelot is the warrior in the fight which *Fin'Amors* wages, as Marcabru had said, against the people of *mal cuidar*, or evil ways of thinking, the hypocrites and liars, the cruel and the treacherous. Lancelot, in his first combat with Meleagant in the land of Gorre, does not fight out of knightly or Christian duty to the prisoners who, fasting and praying, are present in abundance. He fights for love of the Queen (3653–8), and this alone, we are told, can inspire him to victory, though he is already the repository of all *bien* and of all *proesce* (3710–11). This is what the Queen's maid-in-waiting knows instinctively as she watches the battle from the tower.

A study of Marcabru's poetry reveals the possibility that the commission for *Lancelot* which Chrétien received from Marie de Champagne may have been more complete than has been thought, and that it was not only her *matiere* and *sen*

but her *paine* or efforts and her *antancion* (21–9), that went
into the work.[71] It does not seem too fanciful to consider
that Chrétien may have been given the task of composing a
love story narrated in the form of an Art of Fin'*Amors* which
would combine Bernart de Ventadorn's concept of love for
the *domna* and Marcabru's moral philosophy of Fin'*Amors*.
Such a commission would have been especially opportune
in view of the controversy which appears to have arisen at
this time following Bernart de Ventadorn's attack on
Marcabru as a *fols naturaus* 'a fool by his very nature', and
Peire d'Alvernhe's lively defence of his master's 'whole' or
entiers way of thinking.[72] Chrétien, it appears, was no stranger
to such poetic controversies, and, if this hypothesis is correct,
would undoubtedly have welcomed the task of conjoining
in a whole and rounded Art of Fin'*Amors* the contrasting
ideological traditions of troubadour poetry.[73] Alternatively,
it is possible, though less probable, that Chrétien may have
have devised for himself the wider theme of Good against
Evil in the romance. In this case, Marie de Champagne,
commissioning an Art of Fin'*Amors* limited to the love story
of Lancelot and Guenevere, may have acted as a possibly
unwitting agent in prompting him to amplify the outlined
task with a moralising approach to Fin'*Amors* akin to that of
Marcabru.

There can be little doubt that Chrétien would have welcomed the opportunity of depicting Lancelot's recovery
from self-pride and his attainment of wholeness of character
through Fin'*Amors*. Lancelot is indeed Chrétien's most rounded
creation. Invincible in deeds, patient towards the scorn of
the world, he is restrained in his behaviour to lesser and
more turbulent knights, modest and generous to those who
see him as their saviour. Obedient in love, humble and self-
sacrificing, he is driven to despair, to the heights of spiritual
exaltation and to sensual delight. Beneath an inner quiet,
there lies within him a zest and fire which dares and
achieves deeds unthinkable for those who lack his inspiration.

This rounded quality of Lancelot's character is also part
of the general richness and colour which characterises the
romance. This quality is apparent also in the character of
Guenevere which is compounded of preciosity, humility,

despair, generosity and passion, and of Bademagu, torn between compassion for his son and his sense of moral truth.
It is found in the patterns of contrasting characters, and in
the particular and universal qualities of Fin'Amors. It is evident
in the diversity of mood interwoven in the 'multiple' episodes such as those of the Fourth Damsel and the central
love episode in which the exalted blends with the trivial,
the ideal with the ironical and the burlesque. It is to be seen
in the way in which the conflict between Mauvestié and Leauté,
the champion of Proesce, spreads out from its original source,
Meleagant's abduction and imprisonment of the Queen and
the excellence of Lancelot's devotion to Fin'Amors for her, to
the wider ethical patterns. On the planes of love and knighthood, Meleagant and those infected by his evil, the predatory
lovers and the knights for whom senseless violence is the
sole purpose of knighthood, exemplify the Mauvestié which
is recreancy or Desleauté towards the knightly or courtly ethic,
and the ethic of Fin'Amors. With subtle overtones of meaning,
Chrétien also implies that Meleagant and his minions are
linked with the Devil,[74] and that Lancelot, once he has overcome the self-will and lack of humility which he shows at
the test of the Cart, is not only the Elect of Fin'Amors, in addition to being by origin a Celtic Elect,[75] but is also indirectly
an Elect of God, welcomed as such by the prisoners in the
land of Gorre.[76]

For Chrétien in Lancelot, the victory of Proesce and of Leauté,
however temporary, is complete, for in this romance it is
not only the codes of Fin'Amors, and of true cortesia and knighthood which Mauvestié and Desleauté attack. These vices contravene the 'law' of Christian compassion and caritas, and the
goodness which Chrétien sees as the positive side of the
human character. It is the leis associated with this bien, the
natural goodness of humanity, a concept of a Leauté as enduring as Mauvestié, which inspires Chrétien's work from Erec et
Enide to Perceval and which receives its clearest formal recognition in this romance of Lancelot.

Richness in Lancelot lies also in the arresting symbols, the
Cart, the Sword Bridge, the tomb in the cemetery, which
simultaneously suggest auras of Celtic and Christian meaning, and even the Other World of Classical Antiquity.
Omnipresent above the narrative there hovers the Celtic

theme of supernatural figures such as Meleagant and his sister, who visit this world, and of human figures who cannot penetrate the Other World unless they are abducted, or the Elect, or summoned. This aura of Celtic mystery is never stated, but never absent. Equally nebulous and less insistent is the atmosphere of Christian belief. And beyond these levels, dimly perceptible, there is the universal fertility myth of the summer queen abducted from the winter king.

The appeal of *Lancelot* lies in its immense power of suggestion and in its inconclusiveness. We do not know the outcome of the affair between the Queen and Lancelot, which must wait for the *Mort Artu*. We know that the personification of Evil in the shape of Meleagant has been destroyed. But Evil will persist, since men, as Chrétien says, are more inclined to Evil than to Good. What Chrétien comes to recognise in *Lancelot* is that the manifestations of evil in the world and the problems of profane love are not to be cured in the context of worldly values. There is no impregnable wholeness of the spirit, no lasting peace of mind, no absolutely pure and complete love to be found in the world of Lancelot and Guenevere. Chrétien turns to the view that such serenity and happiness must come through the quest of *caritas*. This ideal underlies *Yvain* and becomes the major theme in *Perceval*. The problems which persist in *Lancelot* can be resolved only in the symbol of the Grail.

5

Yvain

Yvain, though written at approximately the same time,[1] differs in many ways from Lancelot. Lancelot is quite clearly, from the outset, an elect warrior, a lover who swiftly remedies his lack of humility, who wins the passionate love of Guenevere, defeats the evil and violence of Meleagant and his kind, and preserves Arthur's kingdom from destruction. His quest is individual, his heroism epic amidst an onrush of events in which Good and Evil are in continuous turbulent conflict. Yvain, on the other hand, is contained in a more austere, inturned narrative structure in which the action pivots on Laudine and her Fountain.

Although one episode may be enclosed within another, as in the adventures of Harpin de la Montagne and the Château de Pesme Aventure, incidents in Yvain are sparse and simple compared to the diversity of multiple episodes, and the mingling of tragic and comic moods in Lancelot. Humour and irony are restrained, and social morality is set, clear-cut, within the bounds of marriage. Richness lies in a language which is graceful, elegant and imaginative, in excellent dialogue, lively imagery, and in the pervasive aura of mystery, the implicit sense of another world of the supernatural into which the characters, leading their lives in this world, may yet slip quite easily without disturbance to the story-line. Richness lies especially in the complexity of Yvain's character, his lacks and failure, his madness and rehabilitation with the help of the lion. Within a rigorously simple narrative, Chrétien deploys his enigmatic gifts with a subtlety so well concealed that Yvain can be taken as a plain romance of love and knighthood. But if we apply to Yvain the methods of composition, the ways of revealing the sen which are apparent in Chrétien's other works, we see that

Yvain stands out as his most 'complete' romance. It provides a *summa* of the themes of the earlier works, love, knighthood, virtue, humility and charity, and points the way to the Grail, of which Chrétien appears already to have fixed the mark and taken the height. Yvain as a character foreshadows Perceval. Man as an individual, and his quest for peace of mind, have become Chrétien's main concern. This peace Yvain will find through a *Fin'Amors* which leads to *caritas* in its lower form of compassion and charity towards his fellow beings. Perceval will find a wider peace through the Christian revelation of a sublime *caritas* which offers union with God.

Chrétien's methods of revealing his *sen* also undergo a shift of emphasis. Analogy and contrast, which were visible features of the linear method in *Erec et Enide* and *Lancelot*, are now used with restraint. The expository, lateral method is scarcely present at all. The *sen* of *Yvain* touches the soul. It is not to be stated, and the lion which links Yvain's personal failure and triumph to the universal qualities which he also embodies, represents, with the Grail, the high point of Chrétien's allusive method, unveiling his meaning in the measure of the perception and understanding of his audience. Chrétien indicates this, obliquely, through Calogrenant: 'for the word, once heard, is lost, unless understood by the heart. Some there are, who without understanding it, praise what they hear; they have no more than their hearing, since their heart understands nothing in this. The word falls on the ear like the wind which blows, neither staying its course nor dwelling within, but departing with all haste, if the heart is not so spiritually awake that it is ready to catch it. Such a heart can take it in its flight and enclose it within and keep it for itself' (151–64).[2]

In *Yvain* two ways of life are in conflict. Folly is set against wisdom, self-will against *caritas*, self-indulgence against duty, counterfeit joy against true joy – in short, the fragmented against the whole way of life, on the levels of knighthood, social duty and love. These two ways of life are represented by two neighbouring but different worlds. One is courageous yet self-absorbed, parochial, frivolous, quarrelsome, impotent to meet the demands of extra feeling, judging and acting by conventional standards. This is Illusion, the world of Arthur's court. The other world is based on knowledge of self, the duty to detect and remedy one's human weaknesses. Strengthened by self-knowledge, recognising and obeying, through mesure, the call of self-sacrifice, this world can aspire to the highest forms of love, courage and knighthood which are directed not to the ends of vainglory and the joust, but to the service of others. This is Reality, the world of the lion, the way of life in which the new Yvain, cleansed through madness of his former self, moves towards caritas and the peace of mind, which Perceval, also purged in the wilderness, must discover through the meaning of the Lance and Grail. In Erec et Enide wholeness was expressed in terms of temporal order, social happiness and the promise of good government which radiate from the wholeness of love achieved in marriage by Erec and Enide. In Yvain the wholeness of mind and spirit which transcends, then opposes, temporal values, is an ideal which Yvain as an individual, an isolated pilgrim, the Knight of the Lion, finally attains. In Erec et Enide the dichotomy between Erec's world and that of Arthur is hinted at, but is not made explicit. In Lancelot, the 'whole' view of life of Bademagu and Lancelot is set against the fragmented view of life of Arthur and Gawain, and, both their views of life are set in opposition to the evil of Meleagant, the ultimate expression of the self-willed, fragmented life. In Yvain, the sense of order, duty and responsibility, is represented by Laudine's view of life, love and marriage. But Laudine, who like Bademagu, springs from a fundamentally Celtic tradition, shows little compassion or feeling which is not self-centred. She is essential to the narrative as the courtly lady, feudal ruler, and Celtic fairy mistress, who by her beauty inspires Yvain to advantageous and sensual love, and then later to perfect and whole Fin'Amors, but on the level of the allegorical morality of the romance her values are finally surpassed by those of Yvain as the Knight of the Lion.

Love in Yvain is not so concerned, as in Lancelot, with the loving of the beloved, but with the virtues which sustain this love and, which, proceeding from Fin'Amors, extend into compassion and caritas, allowing Yvain to discover the serene, complete view of life, which Lancelot may never attain. These virtues, says Chrétien in his opening lines, are now abased:

Car cil, qui soloient amer,
Se feisoient cortois clamer
Et preu et large et enorable.
Ore est amors tornee a fable
Por ce que cil, qui rien n'an
   santent,
Dïent qu'il aimment, mes il mantent,
Et cil fable et mançonge an font,
Qui s'an vantent et droit n'i ont.
                (21–8)

For those who were wont to love, deserved to be called courteous, excellent in virtue, generous in spirit, worthy of honour. Now has love turned to illusion since those who say they love feel nothing of love. They lie, and when they boast of love and have no right to do so, they make of love an illusion and a lie.

These lines contain no commonplace of the golden days that are past. They give us the essence of *Yvain*, the self-induced *fable* and *mançonge* of Arthur's world which has the pretence of being *cortois*, *preu*, *large et enorable*, but lacks the reality of these virtues, especially if we take *large* in its wider meaning of 'free from self-interest'.[3] In this respect, Yvain's lack of moral courage at the beginning of the romance reflects the disorder which rules Arthur's court, for although Chrétien has praised the prowess of the king which 'teaches us to excel in knightly and courtly virtue', Arthur comes on to the stage as a courtly layabout, amidst querulous courtiers, void of manners and *mesure*.

The court has been disturbed by Calogrenant's tale of defeat at the Magic Fountain (581–676). Its vainglory has been provoked by his honest words: 'he was bigger and stronger, and so was his horse'. Yvain attacks Calogrenant, his kinsman (581–9), Kay blames Yvain (590), and, seeing what is clearly in his mind, forbids him to leave the court without permission (608–9). The Queen, detained in her bedchamber by the King, signals her return to court by an attack on Kay for his words of hatred (612–29). Yvain's mind is made up. He will not 'bristle and snarl with the other mastiffs'. He stands aside from the fight, and from the delight of the court when Arthur, restored by slumber, swears by the soul of Uterpandragon, his father, he will visit the Fountain after two weeks, on St John's Day. Yvain's ignoble exit, as he steals away to the adventure which he sees as revenge for his kinsman's shame, may be seen as obedience to the call of destiny, even to a form of Celtic *geis*, but it marks his first failure in moral courage, and also the first example of the self-will and the alienation from the court which will bring him to madness. Paradoxically it is this assertion of his individuality as an outsider at court which will enable him to find his higher self as the Knight of the Lion.

Yvain's adventure is crowned with success. He slays the Knight of the Fountain, Esclados lo Ros, and, hidden by the ring of invisibility given him by the maid, Lunete, is beset by *amor de lonh* for the widow Laudine as he sees her stricken by grief. He recognises the folly of desiring what he will never possess (1428–9), of desiring peace[4] with Laudine. Yet there may be hope; women have more than a thousand ways of thinking (1431–6). But Love, says Chrétien, is fierce and cruel, and Laudine avenges the death of her lord by inflicting the wounds of love from which Yvain will never be free:

> Cele plaic a mes sire Yvains,
> Dont il ne sera ja mes sains.   (1375–6)

At this stage, Yvain is essentially a simple soul, ruled by the *folie* of impulse, like a leaf blown after the wind. Yet already Love fights with vainglory, for Yvain would dearly like to escape and give proof of his exploit to Arthur's court, and the doubting, contemptuous Kay (1531–5). Love wins the battle which it will later lose. Yvain stays and Chrétien with an oblique reference to Yvain's future madness, mocks the *folie* of love's impulse: 'No man, I believe, who is held in a prison like Yvain's and who fears to lose his head, could love so madly that he makes no entreaty in love, or has no one to do this for him' (1509–15). Lunete pleads his cause with her mistress. Love is born from Prowess. To the victor, the spoils. 'Yvain will defend your fountain more successfully than your husband whom he conquered.' Laudine is ignited like the smoking bush (1778), the Ovidian and troubadour symbol of long lasting love.[5] 'Yvain', says Lunete, 'desires to have her heart and body within his keeping' (1922–4). Assured of his noble lineage, Laudine desires this too, grows impatient at thought of the 'delay' before he can 'arrive' at court. Finally, Yvain, timid, tongue-tied, offers homage to his lady with hands clasped, on his knees in feudal and courtly fashion, and submits to her mercy and command, even though she demand his life. 'I fear to accomplish no deed at your bidding. Could I make amends for this death – in which matter I have done no crime – I would willingly do so' (1990–4). Submission comes from his heart, and to the heart from his eyes, to the eyes from his lady's beauty which makes him love (2015–22). With words which Marcabru would have called 'false and gilded'[6] he protests a love from which he will be recreant.

The path to disaster is prepared as Yvain declares his love:

'Amer? Et cui?' – 'Vos, dame chiere.'
'Moi?' – 'Voire.' – 'Voir? an quel meniere?'
'An tel, que graindre estre ne puet,
An tel, que de vos ne se muet
Mes cuers, n'onques aillors nel truis,
An tel, qu'aillors panser ne puis,
An tel, que toz a vos m'otroi,
An tel, que plus vos aim que moi,
An tel, s'il vos plest, a delivre,
Que por vos vuel morir ou vivre.'
(2023–32)

'You love? who is it then?' – 'You, my lady dear.' – 'Me?' – 'Indeed.' – 'Truly? In what way?' – 'In such a way that I cannot love with greater love: in such a way that my heart is with you always, can never be found elsewhere: in such a way that to you do I give myself entirely; in such a way that I love you more than myself; in such a way, so completely, that if it please you, for you do I wish to die or to live.'

In this avowal of love there is sympathy for the youthful folly of the young lover who aspires to love in a way which is beyond his reach, and humour in his promise of a devotion which will yield to recreancy. Yvain is not speaking the *falso razo daurada* of the practised suitors who deceive with their honeyed words. He is naive, untutored in love, *nice*. He lives in a state of illusion about himself and love and other people, and his words, in Chrétien's phrase, are like the wind that blows (158), for as yet they have no place in his heart. They are the words of naive sudden love, and, at the same time, the correct courtly gloss on a feudal marriage of mutual self-interest and attraction. Yvain loves Laudine for her beauty. She accepts him for his lineage, his bearing and prowess: 'And would you dare to defend my fountain?' 'Indeed, my lady, against all men.' 'Then we are agreed' (2033–6). Laudine has no other choice. She must find protection for her land and her fountain against the challenge from Arthur's knights which no baron in her castle will accept.

This scene of courtly love, in which the widow accepts the knight who has slain her husband, would have much attraction for Chrétien's audience, not least for its rapid flow of dialogue, for Laudine's changing moods, for the coolness with which she examines Yvain's feelings, and the irony with which Chrétien presents Yvain's protestations of love which for the moment are beyond the reach of his heart and mind. He has attained a summit of happiness. On the courtly plane he is Laudine's successful suitor, on the feudal plane he is the lord and protector of her castle, on the Celtic plane he is the mortal who defends the magic fountain of his fairy mistress.

Mes ore est mes sire Yvains sire,	But now is my lord Yvain the
Et li morz est toz obliëz.	master, and the dead man quite
Cil, qui l'ocist, est mariëz	forgotten. The man who killed
An sa fame, et ansanble gisent,	him is married to his wife, and
Et les janz aimment plus et prisent	they lie together. And the people
Le vif, qu'onques le mort ne firent.	love and esteem their living lord
(2164–9)	more than they did the dead one.

The scene of the wedding, and the Joy of the Court which follows, round off the *premier vers* of the romance. This opening sequence, though fashioned in more temperate style than in *Lancelot* – there are no flaming spears crashing through roofs into beds – offers a surprising variety of mood and incident. From the surliness of Arthur's court we move to the brashness of Yvain, the Celtic magic of the Fountain and the tempest aroused by the water on the Stone, Yvain's comical game of invisible hide and seek, the wooing of Laudine, the unhorsing of the obnoxious Kay, Yvain's joy at feasting the King, and Chrétien's subtle and pervasive irony about words that belong to the lips and not the heart: 'And the lady does such honour to them all, to each one as a person and to them all together, that there are fools there who think that the kindnesses and looks she gives them are inspired by love. Those people can be rated as untutored (*nices* 2459) who believe that a lady wants to love them when she is courteous enough to speak to some unfortunate man, and bring him joy and embrace him. A fool is made happy by fair words. He is easily deluded' (2454–65).

Yvain is *nice* once again, when Arthur and his court invite his company. He has no *mesure* so he cannot choose and follow the path of true living, of his reality. He has no *savoir* so he cannot reason with himself. He follows impulse and accedes to Gawain's blandishments:

'Comant? Seroiz vos or de çaus',
Ce disoit mes sire Gauvains,
'Qui por lor fames valent mains?
Honiz soit de sainte Marie,
Qui por anpirier se marie!
Amander doit de bele dame,
Qui l'a a amie ou a fame,
Ne n'est puis droiz, que ele l'aint,
Que ses pris et ses los remaint.'
(2484–92)

'What? Will you be one of those', said my lord Gawain, 'whose fame is less on account of the women they marry? Let that man be shamed by Holy Mary who marries in order to become degenerate; for a fair lady, whether mistress or wife, should inspire a man to better deeds, and it is not right she should love him when his fame and renown are lost'. . . .

'Break the bridle and halter. You and I will go to the tourneys, so no one may call you jealous' (2500–2). Reputation lies in jousting and submission to courtly convention. This is the form of reputation which Lancelot rejected for love. Yvain lacks moral courage, and drifts with Gawain, who admits he would not himself leave such a fair mistress:

Mien esciant fos an seroie.
Mes tes consoille bien autrui,
Qui ne savroit conseillier lui,
Aussi con li preecheor,
Qui sont desleal tricheor:
Ansaingnent et dïent le bien,
Dont il ne vuelent feire rien.'
(2532–8)

'I would indeed think myself a fool, were I to do so. But a man who could not advise himself, can give good counsel to others, just as the preachers, who are hypocrites and cheats, teach and speak of the goodness which they will not practise.'

The conflict is not between love and knighthood, but between the values of Laudine's and Arthur's world, the acceptance of duty or the life of self-indulgence. Yvain is anything but generous in seeking leave of Laudine for he uses the device of the 'gift given under constraint':[7] 'My dearest lady, my heart, my soul . . . grant me one thing for your honour and mine.' And Laudien, unaware of her fate, grants it in all generosity and trust (2549–57).

 Laudine is precise in her decision: 'I grant you leave to depart for a fixed time. But the love I have for you will become hatred, be quite sure of this, if you outstay the limit

of time I will tell you. Know full well I will not lie about
this. Though you may lie, I will speak the truth. If you wish
to have my love, and if, in any way, you hold me dear, remember you must return within at least a year, eight days
after the feast of St John' (2562–74). Midst tears and sighs,
Yvain, like Eneas leaving Dido, protests his love in words
as devoted as his first vows. But Chrétien's sympathy is now
less, his irony sharper: 'My lord Yvain weeps and sighs, can
scarcely speak: "My lady, this is too long a time for me to
be absent. Were I a dove, I would be with you so very often,
whenever I wished. I pray God He may not please to keep
me from you so long"' (2579–86). Yvain's protestations
are sincere in the sense that for the moment he believes in
what he says. In the light of future events, Chrétien is invest-
ing him with the ironical halo of the Crusading knight who
takes leave of his beloved. Laudine, who at this stage of the
romance is as generous, forthright and clear-sighted as
Yvain is self-indulgent, plays the part of chatelaine, courtly
dame and fairy mistress, presenting him with a ring which
will preserve him from imprisonment, wounds or hurt.

Yvain delights in the tourneys from which Gawain will
not release him (2668–71). Yvain wins fame at the jousts.
The first year passes. The two companions hold court on
their own account, so that Arthur himself leaves his court
nearby in order to join them (2672–93).

In this extreme of self-pride, Yvain comes to his senses,
in a scene of great poignancy. With Arthur seated among
them, Yvain suddenly thinks of his lady, knows the time
limit is passed, knows he has lied. Shame alone holds back
his tears. He is so sunk in thought that he sees a damsel
straight ahead riding towards him at speed on a black palfrey:

> Tant pansa, que il vit venir
> Une dameisele a droiture,
> Et venoit mout grant anbleüre
> Sor un palefroi noir bauçant. (2704–7)

What follows may be taken at its face value. On this level
the damsel has been sent by Laudine to dismiss Yvain from
her service, her marriage and her land. On another level,
this may also be seen as a supernatural happening in which

a messenger is sent from the Celtic Other World to a mortal in despair. Such 'visions', which may correspond to the mental state or dream wish of a character, occur in Marie de France, in *Lanval* and *Yonec*. In these cases they offer comfort and relief. The visitation which appears to Yvain offers neither. It merely gives temporal reality to the isolation of mind and imagination which has struck him a moment before. The damsel may be a real person, may be a supernatural being, and may be as well the creation of Yvain's distressed mind which is now at breaking point.

The damsel dismounts and no one helps her, or goes to take her horse. In the fashion of a Celtic fairy spirit, she drops her cloak[8] when she sees the King. She gives greeting to all except Yvain. For him her words are bitter:

'Le desleal, le traïtor,
Le mançongier, le jeingleor.'
(2719–20)

'Recreant, traitor,
liar, deceiver.'

'My lady has seen the deceit of this man who pretended to be a true lover . . . This thief has betrayed my lady . . . she never thought he would steal her heart and keep it: those who love do not steal hearts' (2722–9).

'Et cil sont larron ipocrite
Et traïtor, qui metent luite
As cuers anbler, dont aus ne chaut;
Mes li amis, quel part qu'il aut,
Le tient chier et si le raporte.
Mes Yvains a ma dame morte;
Qu'ele cuidoit, qu'il li gardast
Son cuer et si li raportast.'
(2737–44)

'And those men are thieving hypocrites and traitors who strive to steal hearts for which they have no care. But the lover, wherever he may go, holds dear his lady's heart and brings it back to her. Yvain has slain my lady for she thought he would guard her heart and return it to her.'

She denounces Yvain:

Yvains! n'a mes cure de toi
Ma dame, ainz te mande par moi,
Que ja mes vers li ne revaingnes
Ne son anel plus ne detaingnes.
Par moi, que ci an presant vois,
Te mande, que tu li anvois.
Rant li! car randre le t'estuet.'
(2767–73)

'Yvain, my lady has now no love for you, but orders you, through me, never to return to her or to keep her ring any longer in your possession. She orders you to send it to her by me whom you see present before you. Give it back to her, for you are in duty bound so to do.'

Yvain is stunned into silence. The damsel leaps forward, takes the ring from his finger, excluding him from his wife, his courtly lady, his Celtic mistress, the castle and lands where he had received the King. Yvain, like Perceval, is brought low at the moment of illusory triumph.

It is as if a magic curtain were lowered over his mind. He feels disgust at himself, and at those in whose presence he stands. His grief hisses with the repetition of 's', 'i' and 'u':

Et ses enuiz tot adés croist:
Quanquë il ot, tot li ancroist,
Et quanque il voit, tot li enuie.
Mis se voldroit estre a la fuie
Toz seus an si sauvage terre,
Que l'an ne le seüst, ou querre,
N'ome ne fame n'i eüst,
Ne nus de lui rient ne seüst
Ne plus, que s'il fust an abisme.
Ne het tant rien con lui meïsme,
Ne ne set, a cui se confort
De lui, qu'il meïsmes a mort.
(2781–92)

And his grief grows and grows within him. All that he hears makes him despair, all that he sees causes him grief. His only wish is to take flight, to be quite solitary in a forest so wild that no one might know where to seek him, where no man or woman would live, where no one would know anything about him, any more than if he were plunged into an abyss. He hates no one and nothing as much as himself. He knows not with whom he may find comfort for the person within him whom he himself has slain.

He feels the madness grow upon him (2793–5). His despair increases with increasing solitude:

D'antre les barons se remue;
Qu'il crient antre aus issir del san.
Et de ce ne se gardoit l'an,
Si l'an leissierent seul aler.
Bien sevent, que de lor parler
Ne de lor siecle n'a il soing.
(2796–801)

He moves away from among the knights, for he fears he may go out of his mind in their presence. And no one took any heed of this, and they let him go off alone. They know well he has no desire for their words or their world.

Seized and harried by madness, Yvain rushes blindly into the countryside:

Lors li monta uns torbeillons
El chief si granz, que il forsane,
Lors se descire et se depane
Et fuit par chans et par arees
Et leisse ses janz esgarees,
Qui se mervoillent, ou puet estre.
(2804–9)

Then a whirlwind mounted in his head, so strong that he goes right out of his mind; he tears at himself, tears his clothes to shreds, flees across fields and ploughed land, leaving his men bewildered, wondering where he can be.

Lack of *mesure* and true feeling have brought disaster. Honour and reputation are lost, as surely as they were when Lancelot mounted the cart. The court which has fêted him remains as still as the knights and damsels when Lancelot entered their meadow (p. 134). They cannot help, and as Yvain, with the whirlwind in his head, tears at himself and his clothes, he casts away their values, and his former self. This terrible scene puts an indelible mark on the romance. Its earlier nonchalant air of taking life as it comes changes to a sterner mood. Yvain touches the depths of agony, and from this moment the interest and meaning of the work is concentrated in his character in a way that is unique in Chrétien's romances. In terms of Fin'*Amors*, Yvain is in the condition of the lover, who, with the world turned upside-down for love, has lost his heart and sense of identity to a lady who now represents his castle of reassurance against the uncertainty and evil of the court. Such themes are found in the poetry of contemporary troubadours such as Raimbaut d'Aurenga, Peire d'Alvernhe and the later Arnaut Daniel. But Yvain's madness is more important than this. It is also an allegory of man's isolation, his sudden awareness of this and the need of a rock to which to cling. It is comparable to Arnaut Daniel's realisation that, come what may, he must try to gather the wind, must chase the hare with the ox and swim against the incoming tide. It is possible that Chrétien, like Arnaut Daniel in his poem *En cest sonet*,[9] went through a grave mental crisis and that this is reflected in a distressed view of the world which is apparent in *Lancelot*, is central to this scene in *Yvain*, and is ameliorated in the Hermit Episode in *Perceval*. Yvain's sickness in the waste land of his mind will cleanse him of his former self, his self-interest, his lack of true feeling and of the moral courage which comes from *mesure*, as Perceval's years of mindless wandering will prepare him for his new self. So as Yvain, naked and mad, hunts with the bow, with no human contact save that of the hermit who *par charité* (2839) puts out dry bread and water for him, as for a wild animal, he is purged of the *folie*, the yielding to irresolute impulse, which Lunete has already detected in him (1323–8).

His final cure is effected in a scene of Celtic magic, true feeling and light-hearted humour. Two damsels, accompan-

ied by a lady, find him asleep in the forest. One of the
damsels dismounts, inspects the symbolically naked man.
Without his attire he would not be recognised, but for a
scar on his face. The damsel is overcome by amazement,
pity, inexpressible grief: 'My lady, I have found Yvain, the
most distinguished and valiant knight in the world' (2921–
3). They return to the town where the lady produces an
ointment, a cure for sickness of the mind, given her by
Morgan the Wise: 'Be sparing with it. Rub the temples and
the forehead, for there is no need to put it elsewhere'
(2966–9). She provides clothes for Yvain, a robe of shimmering fur, a coat and cloak of scarlet silk. The damsel
takes with her a fine palfrey, and, from her own possessions,
a shirt, breeches of fine cloth, and new, well-shaped hose.
Yvain will be welcomed with good feeling and love as
Lancelot was received by the prisoners in the land of Gorre.
The damsel industriously 'rubs his temples and brow, and
all his body right to his toe . . . Had she had five sesters of
the balm, she would have done the same' (3000–9). To
spare him, she places the garments beside him, and hides
behind an oak. Yvain, freed of his madness and melancholy,
wakes, is shamed to see he is naked as ivory, cannot walk
for weakness, dresses, is approached by the damsel looking
aimlessly about her. He calls, 'Pray lend me your palfrey.'
'Gladly sir, but you must go where I go.' 'Where?' 'To a
castle, beyond the forest' (3071–7). Then, spontaneously
Yvain begins his cure and senses the troubles of another:

'Dameisele! or me dites donc,　　'Damsel, tell me then. Are you
Se vos avez mestier de moi?'　　in need of my help?'
　　　　　(3078–9)

Help, though not asked for, is needed by the damsel and
her mistress, the Lady of Noroison, to thwart Count Alier
who is attacking and ravaging their town. Yvain, cared for
and restored to health, rallies the townsmen, and, like the
falcon with the teal, forces the enemy to submit. He no
longer jousts. His cause is good. His new reputation is won
in battle. Those within the town are amazed by his prowess:
'Roland with Durendal never made such a slaughter of
Saracens at Roncesvals or in Spain' (3235–7). 'Fortunate the
woman to whom his love were given, for in arms he is as

mighty and distinguished as a taper among candles, as the moon among the stars, and the sun above the moon' (3243–49). The Lady of Noroison accepts the Count's pledge of peace and recompense for her losses and her buildings destroyed. To Yvain she offers herself as mistress, or as wife. Like Laudine she needs a knight to defend her; but, unlike Laudine, she is rapacious in her role of feudal chatelaine with overtones of Celtic fairy mistress. She entreats Yvain, offers land and wealth beyond desiring. The old Yvain would have listened, as he did to Gawain. The new Yvain has no doubts:

Mes il n'i vost onques antandre	He had no wish to hear any
Parole d'ome ne de fame.	further word spoken there by
(3336–7)	man or woman.

Impelled to his quest, as if by a *geis*, he rejects this society, as he had rejected Arthur's world. Abruptly, alone, he leaves the lady and her knights to their sorrow.

Immediately after this first assertion of moral courage, the major symbolical event of the work occurs. Sunk in thought, he hears in a deep forest a cry of pain. A serpent has gripped a lion's tail in its jaws and is burning its hindquarters with its flame:

> . . . et si li ardoit
> Trestoz les rains de flame ardant. (3351–2)

Once more Yvain is put to the test. He must decide. Which shall he aid? He chooses the lion:

'Qu'a venimeus et a felon	'for a creature full of poison and
Ne doit an feire se mal non.'	treachery merits nothing but
(3357–8)	harm.'

'Pity summons and entreats him to succour and help the noble and honourable beast' (3373–5). He braves the flames and slays the serpent. His decision to fight, and his choice of the side of nobility and honour, were disinterested. To his surprise, the lion, whom he had expected to attack him, now makes its submission.

What does the battle between the lion and serpent represent – or, more precisely, the attack by the serpent on the lion's rear? On the literal level, as we have seen, the battle lies between a beast which is noble and honourable and one which is treacherous, and so, by allegorical extension, between nobility of mind and perfidy. In an age in which the conflict of lion and dragon is a common device of church decoration, the fight would suggest inevitably the battle between Good and Evil, between Christ and Christianity and the powers of darkness – and in the later *Queste del saint Graal* it even comes to be interpreted as the conflict between the New and the Old Testaments. In its wide implications of meaning, the Lion takes its place between the Cart and the Grail in a progression of allusive imagery to which Chrétien gives an increasingly spiritual and Christian significance. Yet, for the troubadours Marcabru and Arnaut Daniel the fire which burns the flanks refers directly to carnal lust,[10] and on a profane level, the defeat of the serpent may be seen additionally as symbolising Yvain's understanding and rejection of his self-interested love for Laudine, and of the casual sexual love he was offered by the Lady of Noroison. In this case, the rescue of the lion represents Yvain's conversion to a *Fin'Amors* which will equal and transcend that of Lancelot.

At this point, we may ask whether the lion has any importance for the meaning of the romance, or whether he is merely part of a work which from beginning to end has been termed a *leichtbeschwingte Komödie*?[11] It is true that the lion is depicted as a real lion who acquires human characteristics which lead him into human situations, and that Chrétien uses him for lightly humorous effects as well as the creation of pathos. But this use of the lion as a means of entertaining an audience and enlisting their sympathy is secondary to the lion's distinctive quality, which is the nobility of his character. If we look back to the Cart in *Lancelot* and forward to the Grail in *Perceval*, we see that the Lion fulfils a function similar to that of these two other major symbols which also form part of the title of the romance in which they figure. The lion is central to the *sen* of *Yvain*. He represents the virtue which Yvain lacks and which he must possess in order to be regenerate. He symbolises the idea of the moral courage which Yvain must develop, and, above all, the completeness of effort, the knightly zest of Lancelot, the discipline of *savoir* and *mesure*, the self-abnegation for a cause, through which Yvain will match Laudine's ideal of love and knighthood. The lion is the measure of the difference between the old Yvain and the Knight of the Lion, as the new Enide set the distance between the old and the new Eric. The belief that man can take lessons in moral and social behaviour from the natural world is commonplace among the philosophers of Antiquity and of Chrétien's day. It is central to the thought of Seneca, who was widely read in the twelfth century, and plays an important part in the work of Bernardus Silvestris. In profane poetry in the vernacular this belief had been advanced by the great troubadour Marcabru,[12] a generation before Chrétien.

The lion plays a major part in the narrative itself, and on this level he is the stalwart companion of Yvain who is the knight with the lion. He introduces a Shakespearean note of novelty, humour, comedy and the courtly virtue of *simplece*, or immediacy of feeling. But he also symbolises the virtues which Yvain lacks and must gain if he is to develop from a fragmented to a whole person. And in this process of development the lion becomes a form of moral and psychological allegory, at one with the better side of Yvain's thought and behaviour as he acquires the universal qualities which turn him from the knight with the lion into the Knight of the Lion, a human person and also an ideal of knighthood and love. In Yvain's quest to prove to himself that he is worthy of Laudine's love, the lion, as physical being and allegorical form, plays an essential part in the development of the narrative, and of its psychological, moral and spiritual meaning. When Yvain is 'whole within himself' and ready to end his quest and find his peace with Laudine, the lion ceases to help him, but he will not depart, says Chrétien, from Yvain's presence.

The lion's major significance proceeds from the completeness of its love. Chrétien highlights this by comparing the lion's love for Yvain with that of Yvain for Laudine. The lion offers him submission, as Yvain had done to his lady:

Et ses piez joinz li estandoit	It extended to him its paws
Et vers terre ancline sa chiere,	which were joined together, and
S'estut sor les deus piez deriere;	its head to the ground. It raised
Et puis si se ragenoilloit	itself up on its two hind legs,

Et tote sa face moilloit	and then knelt down again, and
De lermes par humilité.	its face was covered with the
(3396–401)	tears it wept for humility.

To humility, the lion adds devotion. It will never leave Yvain:

Et li lions lez lui costoie;	And the lion walks beside him,
Que ja mes ne s'an partira,	never more will it depart from
Toz jorz mes avuec lui ira;	him. For all his days it will go
Que servir et garder le viaut.	with him, for it wishes to serve
(3412–15)	and protect him.

The lion scents food. Hunger and nature urge him to the prey (3420–2). Nature wills him to this, but only with Yvain's assent does it seize a deer, and, without eating it, brings it back to Yvain:

Qui puis an grant chierté le tint	who then held him very dear,
Et a lui a pris conpaignie	and has taken company with
A trestoz les jorz de sa vie	him for all the days of his life,
Por la grant amor, qu'an lui ot.	for the great love which he
(3452–5)	found in him.

Yvain went jousting with Gawain for reputation and vainglory. He goes with the lion for the great love he finds in him, and which, now that he sees this in the lion, he will also find in himself.

The analogy between the lion's devotion to Yvain, and Yvain's desertion of Laudine is self-evident. The lion loves Yvain, as Yvain should have loved Laudine,[13] not in a 'fragmented' way, but as part of a wider, 'whole' awareness of love in life. In love the lion demonstrates the qualities which Yvain lacks: generosity, care for others and the rejection of self-indulgence. So the lion denies his hunger, offers Yvain food (3471–5), and, like Enide, stands guard over his horse.

Et li lions ot tant de sans,	And the lion was so intelligent
Qu'il veilla et fu an espans	that of its own accord it stayed
Del cheval garder . . .	awake and took great heed to
(3481–3)	guard the horse.

The lion is the moving 'pivot' of the story, a symbol of the motive force which impels Yvain to rehabilitate himself, to regain what he has lost and surpass it. The fountain, which is also a part of Laudine's being, the static and continuing symbol of her power and her way of life, is the other pivot. On the narrative level the fountain is the test by which Laudine and her wealth can be won. It offers the joy after violence which is symbolised by nature's storm and subsequent joy when the water is poured on the stone (802–10). But such joy is dependent on the loyalty, the service and lack of self-regard of the knight who seeks her love. Yvain wins the test of violence. He fails the test of love. The fountain becomes for him the symbol of the joy he has lost, and of joy which may be regained. It provides a test for which he must re-equip himself, and a new ideal of knighthood which he must discover within himself.

Yvain's first return to the fountain shocks him into a state of near madness. Stricken with sorrow at lost happiness, he falls, unconscious, his sword piercing his neck. As the blood flows beneath the bright mail, the lion is demented with grief, believes his lord dead, tries to kill himself. The lion 'like the wild boar heedless of wounds' is rushing blindly on to the same sword, when Yvain awakes, and in a tragic monologue laments his wasted years:

. . . 'Que fet, que ne se tue
Cist las, qui joie s'est tolue?
Que faz je, las! que ne m'oci?
Comant puis je demorer ci
Et veoir les choses ma dame?
An mon cors por qu'areste l'ame?
Que fet ame an si dolant cors?
S'ele s'an iere alee fors,
Ne seroit pas an tel martire.
Haïr et blasmer et despire
Me doi voir mout et je si faz.
Qui pert la joie et le solaz
Par son mesfet et par son tort,
Mout se doit bien haïr de mort.
Haïr et ocirre se doit.
Et gié, tant con nus ne me voit,
Por quoi m'esparng? que ne me tu?
Don n'ai je cest lion veü,
Qui por moi a si grant duel fet,
Qu'il se vost m'espee antreset
Parmi le piz el cors boter?
Et je doi la mort redoter,
Qui a duel ai joie changiee?
De moi s'est la joie estrangiee –

'Why does this wretch that I am, bereft of joy, not kill himself? What am I doing, alas! Why do I not kill myself? How can I stay here and see the things that belong to my lady? Why does my soul still bide in my body? What is a soul doing in a body so stricken by grief? Had it departed from the body, it would not be in such martyrdom. In truth I deserve to hate and blame and despise myself greatly; so I do. Any man who through his misdeed and wrong-doing, loses joy and the delight of his lady's company, ought indeed to hate himself with mortal hatred. He should hate himself and take his life. And I, while no one can see me, why do I spare my life? Why do I not kill myself? Have I not seen this lion so full of grief for me

Joie? La ques? N'an dirai plus. . . .'
(3531–55)

that he wanted just now to thrust my sword through his chest? And should I, who have changed joy into sorrow, fear to die? Joy has estranged itself from me – Joy? What joy is that? I will say no more about it. . . .'

For Chrétien, to desire death when the beloved is 'dead' is absolute love. Such love belongs to Enide, Cliges, Guenevere, Lancelot, and to the lion. For Yvain, the wish for death is the moment of self-recognition, the acknowledgement of sin and folly. Exiled from the beloved, and so, in courtly language, 'dead', deprived of love and joy, and, as he thinks, of his identity, why not choose to die? Yvain's moral courage is about to die, and on the lateral plane of exposition he is now acting out what the lion, the allegorical form of this moral strength, has already indicated with his own desire for death.

At this nadir of existence, Yvain begins his recovery. He forgets self-pity in the plight of another. Through a crack in the chapel wall he hears a damsel lamenting her fate. Lunete has been charged with treason for offering Laudine a recreant husband. Defiantly she has pledged that within forty days a champion will defend her cause against her three accusers. In vain. Only Gawain or Yvain could face such odds. At Arthur's court she has found no comfort or counsel. Gawain was absent, searching, less than heroically as we know, for the abducted Guenevere. Yvain has disappeared, none knows where. Yvain, after the moment of self-recognition, will now begin his quest by righting a wrong caused by his niceté, his unthinking disregard of others. In this he is the model for Perceval who after leaving the castle of the Fisher King and being brought to a degree of self-recognition and awareness of his name, redresses the wrong he did to the Damsel in the Tent.

Yvain's shame is great. He has been thinking of escape in death at a time when Lunete, who saved him and gave him joy with Laudine, faces death at the stake. Lunete, out of caritas, begs him not to risk his life in a bataille si tres felenesse (3739):

'Mes trestoz quites an soiiez!
Car miauz est, que je sole muire,
Que je les veïsse deduire
De vostre mort, et de la moie.
Ja por ce n'an eschaperoie,
Quant il vos avroient ocis;
S'est miauz, que vos remeigniez vis,
Que nos i fussiens mort andui.'
(3742-9)

'Consider yourself now released
from this duty! It is better that
I alone should die than that I
should see them delighting in
your death, and in mine. If they
were to slay you, as they will,
I would never escape death.
It is better for you to remain
alive than that we should both
be dead.'

Yvain is gentle but adamant:

'Mout m'avez or dit grant enui',
Fet mes sire Yvains, 'douce amie!'
. . .
'Que vos avez tant fet por moi,
Certes, que faillir ne vos doi
A nul besoing, que vos aiiez.
Bien sai, que mout vos esmaiiez,
Mes, se De plest, an cui je croi,
Il an seront honi tuit troi.'
(3750-2, 3757-62)

'Sweet friend, what you have
just said causes me great
distress', says my lord Yvain,
. . . 'for you have done so much
for me that I must not fail you
in any need which you may
have. I well know how great is
your fear, but if it please God
in whom I believe, all three of
them shall be brought to
shame.'

Yvain must find a place to rest. He is welcomed into a
castle, but he will not enter without the lion: 'Either we shall
both find shelter, or I will remain here outside, for I love him
as much as my own being' (3795-8). The momentary joy
of Yvain's arrival is replaced by grief, lamentation and
weeping. The court tear at their clothes and themselves.
They cannot pretend to a joy in order to please their guest:
the lord of the castle will not sadden him with their tale.
Yvain has true feeling for their distress, a compassion void
of self-interest. He must share their sorrow:

'Ce ne porroit estre a nul fuer,
Que je duel feire vos veïsse
Et je a mon cuer n'an meïsse;
Ainz le desir mout a savoir,
Quel duel que je an doie avoir.'
(3846-50)

'In no way could it happen that
I should see the sorrow you feel
and not place it within my own
heart. I wish very much to
know this, whatever grief I may
suffer thereby.'[14]

The lord of the castle tells his story. A giant has taken his
six sons who were knights. Two are dead, the other four will
die tomorrow, unless a champion can be found for them or
unless his daughter is surrendered to the giant, who has
already destroyed and plundered and burnt his town. From

194

Arthur's court no help can be expected. Gawain, his wife's brother, would have come with speed, were he not searching for the Queen, abducted through the folly of the King and Kay (3851–939). Yvain once more agrees to stand in for Gawain, absent, as Chrétien's audience would realise, in an inglorious quest for the Queen.[15] For pity, he pledges himself as champion against the giant, provided only that the monster arrives early enough for him to defend Lunete at mid-day.

Yvain is faced with his earlier failures, his callous breach of faith towards Laudine concerning the appointed time limit for his absence. Now he must fight for two separate damsels, and must so judge his time that Lunete will not die. He cannot drift. On his power of decision depends the life and death of Lunete, and of himself, since he cannot in honour live if she should die. The lord of the castle in gratitude bids his wife and daughter throw themselves at the feet of Yvain, 'the virtuous knight sent to them by God and good fortune'. Yvain speaks with humility: 'May God defend me from ever allowing such pride within me that I should see them at my feet' (3983–5).[16] He shows them kindness but will not reassure them completely. He may have to depart before the giant arrives. He will not break his vow to Lunete. God must consent to aid them by sending the giant in good time. But they continue to hope, and place their trust in the prowess of a knight who, they think, must be of great virtue since they see him in the company of a lion who lies beside him as gentle as a lamb (3979–4015).

On the morrow, after mass, Yvain is pushed to the limits of anguish. At the hour of prime, the giant has still not come. Yvain must depart. He is untouched by a bribe of lands and wealth, but yields to the damsel, Gawain's niece, who entreats him:

Come destroite et angoisseuse	As one distraught and torn by
Por la reïne glorïeuse	anguish she entreats him by the
Del ciel et des anges li prie	glorious Queen of Heaven,[17]
Et por De, qu'il ne s'an aut mie.	by the angels, and by God, that
(4063–6)	he should not go away.

Moved by compassion, Yvain puts Lunete's life and his own honour and life at stake.

The giant arrives, in his arrogance (4137) and *vilenie*,

threatening to give the girl to his menials to rape. He is the extreme evil against which Lancelot had fought in Meleagant. He is the devil (*li maufez, li anemis*, 4173) and Yvain goes forth to fight, commended to God by the prayers of all present. Nevertheless it is the lion who wins the combat, leaping forward when Yvain is hard pressed to the point of defeat.

Again Yvain refuses to stay, asking only that news of his victory be conveyed to Gawain. Like Erec, when he fought the giants on his quest for rehabilitation, Yvain is proud of this first adventure since leaving the fountain. 'Tell him', he says, 'I was called the Knight of the Lion':

'Et avuec ce priier vos doi,	'And, in addition, tell him from
Que vos li dites de par moi,	me, I beg you, he knows me
Qu'il me conoist bien et je lui,	and I him, and yet he does not
Et si ne set, que je me sui.'	know who I am.'
(4293–6)	

In form this is a riddle, of the type favoured by courtly society.[18] In essence it is Yvain's declaration of the new Yvain, whose aims and principles diverge from those of Gawain and will be tested against him in the adventure of the Noire Espine.

Yvain, with the aid of the lion, has defeated the very embodiment of evil, violence and the works of the devil. Now, as he defends Lunete, he must fight their human manifestation in the three barons who seek her death. The race is close. Lunete, naked in her shift, like Yseut, is about to be hurled on the flames. Unlike Yseut, she is reconciled to her fate, confessing her sins to God on her knees and asking for pardon (4390–3). God and right and the lion are Yvain's companions in this fight against odds, and his trust lies in them (4333–6). He thrusts his way through the throng; 'Let the damsel alone, let her alone, you evil people' (4338–9). Once more, he is moved to great pity (4357) by the ladies weeping for Lunete and praising her virtues. Lunete sees him as sent by God. Yvain answers the scorn of the seneschal and his brothers:

'Qui peor avra, si s'an fuie!	'Let the coward flee! I do not
Ne criem pas tant voz trois escuz,	so fear your three shields that I
Que sanz cop m'an aille veincuz.'	should depart defeated without
(4424–6)	a fight'. . . .

'Ja tant, con je sains et vis soie,
Ne m'an fuirai por tes menaces.
Mes je te consoil, que tu faces
La dameisele clamer quite,
Que tu as a grant tort sordite;
Qu'ele le dit et je l'an croi,
Si m'an a plevie sa foi
Et dit sor le peril de s'ame,
Qu'onques traïson vers sa dame
Ne fist ne dist ne ne pansa.
Bien croi ce, qu'ele dit m'an a,
Si la deffandrai, se je puis;
Que son droit an m'aïe truis.'

(4430–42)

'Never, as long as I am alive and able, will I flee from your threats. But I advise you to ask forgiveness from the damsel whom you have so unjustly accused. For she tells me this, and I believe her, and she has pledged to me by her faith and on the peril of her soul that never by deed or word or thought did she commit treason against her lady. I believe her words about this, and I shall defend her, as I am able. For in the rightness of her cause do I find my help.'

Yvain, since his madness, has discovered great humility within himself. He is more doubting than Lancelot, more aware of his limitations, and of the help he needs in order to overcome the odds which he faces. He is cast in the mould of Vivien rather than Roland: 'God and right are one, and they being on my side, I have in them a better company than yours, and better aid' (4445–8). Later in the romance, in the adventure of the Noire Espine, Yvain's chivalry, fighting for right, and thus for God, and for pity and feeling, will be in conflict also with the knighthood of Gawain. But the new Yvain, the Knight of the Lion, to atone for his sins, must first defeat the forces of Evil.

The lion intervenes as Yvain once more faces disaster in the fight for Lunete. Though sorely wounded, it helps to destroy the slanderers as it had slain the giant Harpin de la Montagne. It makes the mail fly like straw from the hauberk of the seneschal whom it tears to pieces (4523–32). Yvain, spurred to fury by the sight of the lion's wounds, forces the two survivors to surrender.

The shock of battle is followed by a moment of truth for Yvain. Lunete is now reunited with Laudine. Yvain must decide whether to reveal his identity and accept shelter for himself and the lion, and care for their wounds or whether to pursue his quest. His resolve is the same as Erec's when he and Enide, after their first adventures, were tempted to remain at Arthur's court (p. 33). Yvain's quest is unfinished. He will find completeness within himself only

when he needs no overt help from the lion. 'Lady', he replies
to Laudine's invitation, 'it is not possible for me to remain
here in this place today, until my lady forgets her anger and
hatred of me. Then will all my toil be ended.' 'This truly
causes me great sorrow', Laudine replies, 'I do not hold that
lady for courteous who bears ill will against you and refuses
her door to a knight of your quality, unless your sin against
her is very great.' 'My lady, though my grief is great, all
that seems right to her is pleasing to me' (4588–600). With
humility, Yvain conceals his identity:

. . . 'Et vostre non	'And your name?
Seviaus, biaus sire! car nos dites!	At least, fair lord, tell this to us.
Puis si vos an iroiz toz quites'.	Then you can depart quite
'Toz quites, dame? Non feroie.	freely'. . . . 'Quite freely, my
Plus doi, que randre ne porroie.	lady? That I could not do. I owe
Neporquant ne vos doi celer,	more than I could pay. Yet I
Comant je me faz apeler.	must not hide from you the
Ja del Chevalier au Lion	name which I give myself. You
N'orroiz parler se de moi non'.	will hear nothing spoken about
(4606–14)	the Knight of the Lion unless it
	be about me.'

'In the name of God, fair lord, how does it happen that
we never saw you before, or heard your name?'

'Dame! par ce savoir poez,	'My lady, by this you may know
Que ne sui gueires renomez.'	that I am not at all famous.'
(4619–20)	

Yvain has rejected Yvain, and his fame. As the Knight of the
Lion, he has no human friends, except Lunete who alone
knows him for what he is. He is isolated. He has no reputation as the Knight of the Lion, who must fight without self-
interest and for a just cause. This role and disguise are his
path to regeneration. Had he remained Yvain, his former
reputation and reaching for *vaine gloire* would have been insuperable obstacles. The measure of his new self and his new
way of life lies in acting out of *caritas* and rejecting self-
indulgence, in using *savoir* and rejecting folly, in loving with
humility and completeness, and in recognising his weakness,
his earlier sins, and in remedying them. Laudine grants him
leave: 'Then go with God, fair sir! And may He, if it please
Him, turn your grief and sorrow to joy' – a moment of irony
to delight a courtly audience.

As the Knight of the Lion, Yvain will now be recognised as the symbol of prowess, courage and justice, the avenger of the weak, and especially of women. This atonement for his earlier neglect of Laudine is emphasised in the dire adventure of the castle of Pesme Aventure, in which a multitude of damsels are rescued. This episode is set within the framework of the adventure of the Noire Espine, in which Yvain secures justice for one individual maiden.

The younger daughter of the lord of the Noire Espine has been dispossessed of her inheritance. Her sister, not unlike the old Yvain when he slipped from the court to claim the adventure of the Magic Fountain, has already arrived at Arthur's court and enlisted Gawain as her champion. The younger sister pleads her just cause in vain. Gawain, recently returned from the land of Gorre, behaves in less than honourable fashion towards her. He has made the elder sister swear to keep his championship of her cause a secret (4733–6). He evasively tells the younger sister that he has *anpris un autre afeire* (4770). His knighthood and courtesy has no *savoir* or discretion, *conoissensa*, as the troubadours would say. Gawain accepts the unjust cause, without acknowledging his championship of it, and blandly brushes aside the just petitioner. Gawain is a courtly mechanism, as he was when he failed to rescue Lancelot. He has no extra quality of *Franchise*, no acute feeling for justice extra to the responses of courtly convention. To swear the elder sister to silence is a narrative necessity, since Yvain and he must fight each other anonymously, but it also suggests that Gawain has doubts about her cause. Had his interest been revealed, Arthur, who had perceived the rights of the younger sister, would have put pressure on him to think again. Forty days remain to the younger sister in which to find a champion. There being no help from 'Arthur's court, she must find the 'outsider', the Knight of the Lion, for whom a search is now instituted and continued by a damsel who, devoid of self-interest and enduring great hardship, acts entirely out of *caritas* for the younger sister. And Yvain will respond with equal generosity.

The younger sister falls ill, and her quest is taken up by another damsel (4832–4), who rides through storm, rain, and a darkness so black she cannot see the horse she is riding (4853–4). With constant prayer to God, to His mother, and all the saints, she is guided by a horn, blown three times, to a cross by the road, and to news of the Knight of the Lion from the castle where he slew the giant. Then to the Magic Fountain where Lunete offers comfort and help, and would offer more positive aid but for the risk of arousing Laudine's anger (5006–7).[19] The damsel gallops on with her palfrey, and spies the knight with the lion behind him. In a moment Yvain has understood her distress: 'May God keep you, fair damsel! and take from you your care and grief!' 'And may he keep you, my lord, who, as I hope, will be able to take these from me' (5054–7). Yvain accepts the task. He is being brought back into society not by Arthur, by Kay, Gawain or Laudine, but by this younger sister, her just cause, and her selfless friend, as he was by Lunete and her righteous cause. So Perceval, brought back to Arthur's court by Gawain in the episode of the Three Drops of Blood on the Snow, will then depart in a quest of self-discovery until he too is brought back to himself by the pilgrims on Good Friday, and by the hermit. Justice and *droiture* determine the deeds of the Knight of the Lion, who has progressed from knightly pastimes to selfless chivalry. 'Would you dare to take up this cause', asks the damsel, 'or would you prefer to rest?' And Yvain:

'Nenil', fet il; 'de reposer
Ne se puet nus hon aloser,
Ne je ne reposerai mie,
Ainz vos siurai, ma douce amie!
Volantiers la, ou vos pleira.'
(5095–9)

'No', he says, 'No man can win repute by resting, and I will not rest. Instead, I will follow you, sweet friend, willingly, wherever it may please you to go.'

Yet before he fights for this just cause, he must defeat the powers of darkness, of cruelty and oppression, in the shape of two sons of the devil, born of a woman and a demon (5271–3). These tyrants are nominally the 'men' of the lord of the castle of Pesme Aventure,[20] but their demoniac violence and magic arts have made them its rulers. They exact a yearly tribute of thirty maidens from the King of the Isle of Damsels, and these they set to work in appalling conditions in a compound of large and pointed stakes. The hunger, privation and tears of the damsels, sewing ceaselessly with gold thread and silk, move Yvain to pity: 'I know not the reason for your grief, but may it please God to take it from your heart and turn it to joy' (5247–9). Significantly, these words are almost identical to the last words which Laudine had addressed to Yvain (4628–9). Yvain prays to God for help:

'Et Des, li voirs esperitables',   'And may God, the true spiritual
Fet mes sire Yvains, 'm'an deffande   being, protect me from the
Et vos enor et joie rande,   devils, and may He restore
Se il a volanté li vient!'   honour and joy to you, if that
            (5338–41)   should be His will.'

The next morning, after Mass, Yvain prepares to fight. He does not choose to do so, being intent on his mission to Arthur's court, but he must submit to his destiny in the shape of the 'devilish institution' which the lord of the castle upholds. He must obey the custom and fight the devils. And if he achieves the impossible and slays them, he must marry the daughter of the lord of the castle, and become its ruler. Troubles press hard upon Yvain. This is the very last thing he desires: 'Your daughter is so fair and accomplished that the Emperor of Germany would rejoice in her. May God not grant me that which I do not seek' (5479–84). He receives a harsh, unfeeling reply: 'Cowardice makes you refuse her, but in no way will you find an excuse to escape this battle' (5494–5501). Behind the supernatural overtones of this castle, with its devils, its compulsions and cruelty, we see the lord of the castle completely under the sway of the evil generated by the demons, without feeling or good intention towards the slave damsels in his castle yard. His people are equally self-centred and compliant in the face of wickedness. They, like Meleagant, are the extreme form of the degenerate human spirit which Yvain has escaped and must now fight as the Knight of the Lion.

The lion is the implacable enemy of the demons. When battle is joined, he burrows a way out from under the door which imprisons him, and leaps to the attack with raging ferocity, symbolising Yvain's own hatred of the devil's brood, against whom he has sought God's protection:

Car au lion triues ne pes   for no truce or peace will they
N'avront il tant con vis les sache.   find with the lion as long as he
            (5632–3)   knows they are alive.

The demons are destroyed. The three hundred damsels, commending Yvain to God, return to their lands, and Yvain escaping an unwelcome marriage to the daughter, sets out with the younger sister to Arthur's court. The castle of Pesme Aventure presented Yvain with his most difficult test. The evil he conquered was the extreme form of his earlier malaise, the personification of the evil against which he will now fight once more. With selfless motives, and with the zest and ferocity of the lion, and God's protection, he has done penance for his cruelty to Laudine by restoring the three hundred damsels to honour and joy.

The duel between Yvain and Gawain has elements of grotesque humour, of the epic theme of father and son fighting as strangers, and of moral satire, for the elder sister insists against all advice, including Arthur's, that the knights shall risk death for the inheritance which she wrongly holds. She epitomises the self-interest, the brashness and lack of true feeling which characterised the inhabitants of the castle of Pesme Aventure. In opposing her cause, Yvain is opposing and defeating the image of his former self, as Erec did in the adventure of the Joy of the Court. Yvain cannot fight the elder sister directly as Erec fought Mabonagrain, but the similarity between the final adventures in these two romances can scarcely be fortuitous, and the elder sister, in her neglect of the rights of others and her self-seeking methods of defeating competition, is cast in a similar mould to that of the mistress of Mabonagrain.

Although Arthur sees the injustice of her cause, he and his court are entrapped in their ritual of trial by combat. Lives are risked for the obstinacy of a self-willed person. And Chrétien implies as much when Arthur refuses to accede to the pleas of the Queen, and of the knights and ladies and citizens. He will not stop the fight and grant a portion of the inheritance to the younger sister. He complies with custom, however unjust, in the same way, though without the supernatural overtones, as the lord of the castle of Pesme Aventure. He drifts in indecision, until Yvain and Gawain reveal their identity to each other, and in knightly modesty vie with each other to concede defeat in a pleasantly ironical situation. Arthur decides he will declare Gawain the loser unless the elder sister relents. She does so, and peace and justice are restored. The lion, whom Yvain left behind at his last resting place, now arrives. He will never be separate from Yvain:

'Qu'il est a moi et je a lui,
Si somes conpaignon andui.'
(6467–8)

'He is mine, and I am his, and
so we both go in companionship
together.'

That Yvain should fight Gawain on equal terms is a mark of
his knightly prowess and of his acceptability in Arthur's
world. The lion is the measure of the extra moral and
physical courage, the resolution, zest and self-sacrifice of a
Lancelot, which are required to fight the evil in the world
and the powers of darkness. Yvain's victories over these
forces have raised him to a view of the world beyond that
of Gawain. The fruits of this prowess, which is inspired and
guided by moral courage, are pity and *caritas*, and these are
made apparent in the rescue of the three hundred damsels
from Pesme Aventure, as they were, in different degree, when
Lancelot overcame Meleagant and freed the captives from the
land of Gorre. Lancelot's success and Yvain's progress are
evidence of the good results which flow from knighthood
dedicated to *Fin'Amors*. From the *Fin'Amors* or distant love
which Yvain had for Laudine, whom he has loved and then
left, then loved again in mind, memory and spirit, Yvain has
gained the completeness which comes from true feeling for
others, in fact the essence of *caritas*. Yvain's progress from
Fin'Amors to *caritas* may be the model for the declaration by
Guillem de Nevers, the hero of the thirteenth-century romance *Flamenca*. Through his suffering in love Guillem realises
that to feel mercy is to understand the pain of others: 'Pity
is the root of Mercy; if it speaks to me, it is the flower of
Mercy; if it acts, instantly and disinterestedly, it is the fruit
of Mercy; it brings with it *caritas* which crowns all good
things. Never have I felt so much pity or suffered so much
for the grief of others. Love has produced this change in me.
May my lady see my suffering and feel kindly towards me'
(edn Lavaud and Nelli, 4625–66).

The theme of reciprocal kindness runs through the
romance of Yvain. This is more than a relic of the Celtic
tradition of one good turn, or, as in *Sir Gawain and the Green
Knight*, of one good blow deserving another. It helps to
distinguish the good, positive characters in the romance,
Yvain, the lion, Lunete, and the damsel who seeks Yvain in
the storm, from the conventional figures such as Gawain and
Kay, who fail or are absent at the decisive moment. This

reciprocity between Yvain and the lion, and Yvain and Lunete, is based on mutual love in the sense of that *amicitia,* the *benevolentia* of Cicero,[21] which desires the well-being of the person loved, and is distinct from the comradeship in arms and the pursuit of fame which had bound Yvain and Gawain in friendship. This higher form of loving affection is not to be found at Arthur's court. To rediscover it, Yvain must now return to the Magic Fountain. Should his lady have no pity on him, he knows he must die.

Once more, Yvain steals secretly away from the court, but this time the lion goes with him. Once more he pours the water on the stone, and produces a tempest so great 'that no one could tell the tenth part of it. The lady fears that her castle and town will collapse in ruins. The walls shake and the tower rocks and almost falls' (6536–43). Lunete seizes her chance. 'You must find a knight who can defend the fountain', she tells Laudine, 'else we shall live in perpetual torment. The Knight of the Lion would do, yet he dies of grief for his lady.' Laudine promises on oath to do all in her power to help the Knight of the Lion to recover his lady's love. When Yvain appears, she fears she is trapped: 'I would rather endure these winds and tempests all my life, than love someone who neither loves nor respects me' (6762–7). But she relents, keeps her vow, accepts Yvain's plea:

. . . 'Dame! misericorde	'My lady! A sinner deserves to
Doit an de pecheor avoir.	be shown mercy. I have atoned
Conparé ai mon fol savoir,	for my folly and I have had to
Et je le dui bien conparer.	atone for it dearly. Folly made
Folie me fist demorer,	me stay away and I confess my
Si m'an rant coupable et forfet.	guilt and my sin. And in daring
Et mout grant hardemant ai fet,	to approach your presence I
Quant devant vos osai venir;	have acted with great presump-
Mes s'or me volez retenir,	tion; but if you will keep me
Ja mes ne vos mesferai rien.'	in your service, never more will
(6780–89)	I do anything which may harm you.'

Now my lord Yvain, giving thanks to God and the Holy Spirit, has his peace (6795–9); feudal, courtly and conjugal peace with Laudine, and peace in his mind.

Chrétien's three later romances all have inconclusive endings. This may be because they are concerned with the irreconcilable conflict of Good and Evil, and the human dilemma in which his main characters are involved. The quest for *Fin'Amors* is a quest for the unattainable. It has no ending, and suits the genre of lyric poetry better than that of the romance. At the end of *Lancelot*, the courtly and adulterous triangle persists, transferred from the land of Gorre, its 'forest of Morois', to the court of Arthur the husband, as a hundred years later, in *Flamenca*, it will be transferred to the court of Archambaut. Chrétien and the poet of *Flamenca* accept that there is no solution to the quest for *Fin'Amors*. The answer which Tristan and Yseut find in death is predetermined by the accident, or the symbolical *geis*, of the love potion, and their passion, lacking *mesure* and the conflict of desire in the mind and the body, is not *Fin'Amors*. The ending of *Yvain* is unconvincing, and Chrétien's commonplace references to the mutual joy and peace without end of Yvain and Laudine, leave some doubt whether he did not see in this conclusion the patching together of a story which on its higher level of meaning had transcended its narrative framework. It is impossible to know whether this happened as a part of Chrétien's original intention, whether it occurred naturally as he became more involved with the story and its *sen*, or whether he was influenced in this matter by his wide treatment in *Lancelot* of the universal conflict between Good and Evil. Certainly, in the character of Yvain, and especially in the description of his madness, Chrétien depicts more intensely than in any other of his romances, the human reaction to sin, suffering, guilt, remorse and the quest for rehabilitation. Yvain's journey towards moral courage and the awakening within him of responsibility, compassion and *caritas* towards others, are indicated by Chrétien with a sensitivity that is more finely tuned. His habitual distance from his chief character lessens from the moment of Yvain's madness and utter desolation. Chrétien wishes to associate himself with Yvain, and to invite his audience to do likewise.

The narrative cycle of the romance is complete when Yvain returns to the Magic Fountain and is accepted once more by Laudine as her husband and lover. But the Magic Fountain and the manner of life it symbolises for Yvain are essentially static, however often peace and joy may be transformed into tempest and grief and back again. The true completeness of the romance lies in Yvain's transformation from a feckless and self-interested adventurer into a man who is whole and integrated in every aspect of his life, whether religious, knightly, courtly or human. To achieve this wholeness Yvain suffers more deeply than any other of Chrétien's Arthurian characters. Yet can the Lion, and the Knight of the Lion, and the dynamic virtues they represent, really retire from the fray? The problems of individual morality and spiritual peace which arise from the sequence of Yvain's sin, his madness, self-rehabilitation and quest, and the symbolical deeds of the Lion, are of the widest significance, and in their solution lies a truth which Chrétien will not find within the framework of the Magic Fountain, of Laudine and *Fin'Amors*. Its discovery must come about through a symbol which will transcend any temporal or Celtic framework.

6

Perceval or Le conte du Graal[1]

As the Fisher King and his guest converse before eating, a procession[2] passes to and fro in the hall of the castle, bearing aloft a white lance which bleeds from the tip of its blade, candles in holders of pure gold, a grail or serving dish resplendent with light, and a silver carving board. Perceval fails to see his moment of trial. Self-absorbed, earth-bound (3210–11),[3] he stifles an impulse to ask: 'Why does the lance bleed? To whom will the grail be served?' Had he spoken, the King who is mehaigné 'maimed', ill and half paralysed, would have been healed, his lands restored to fertility. Because Perceval stays silent, evil days must follow: ladies will lose husbands, lands will be laid waste, maidens will be orphaned, and knights must die. All this Perceval learns from a damsel, his cousin, when early the next morning he has barely escaped from the castle.

With this intensely memorable scene in the castle of the Fisher King Chrétien has created the theme of the Grail and has presented us with its main elements:

1   The King who is wounded and impotent.
2   The Waste Land surrounding his castle which is a prey to misfortune associated with the King's infirmity.
3   The Castle which is seen only by Perceval and which disappears when he departs from it.
4   The Lance which bleeds from the tip of its blade.
5   A Grail, which is a flat, hollow dish for the service of food.
6   Perceval's role as an Elect, who, if he asks the right question, can heal the Fisher King and restore happiness and fertility to his land.
7   The disasters which must follow his failure to do this.

In this framework we have the basic Grail theme of

devastation followed by rebirth, of sterility and fecundity, a theme as old as the first sentient man who saw winter turn to spring. The antecedents of this theme, in religious and folk beliefs, are many and ancient. It inspired the cult of Mithras, the Persian god of light and fecundity, who, slaying a sacrificial bull, caused the blood from its side to give life and fecundity to the earth. It inspired the fertility myths of Middle Eastern Antiquity, such as the cults of Osiris and Adonis which were based on the seasonal withering and re-appearance of vegetable life, on devastation and grief followed by resurrection. It also occurs in Celtic tradition, and this may well have provided Chrétien with one of his sources of inspiration.

This Celtic tradition, as we have seen (see p. 15), accepted a close and continuous relationship between this earthly world of human beings and the Other World. Journeys both ways are frequent. Gods can visit this world, in different incarnations. Men can be summoned by a fairy mistress, or by a king of the Other World who needs help. They may cross the water to Avalon, island of eternal youth. They may visit the Tuatha de Danann who dwell in a subterranean world of haunted hills. The Tuatha, earlier inhabitants of Ireland, are the custodians of Talismans or Magic Objects which endow their owner, who must be an Elect warrior or a god, with powers of sovereignty and abundance. An earthly hero, if he is victorious in his quest to this Other World, may return with such Talismans.

What were these objects? Are they similar to those in Chrétien's Grail story? In fact, they are. A magic cup or vase, which is associated with the idea of sovereignty, does occur in Irish tales.[4] In one of these, Conn, the king of Tara, visits Lug, god of the Tuatha de Danann, and is served with meat by a crowned maiden who asks Lug: 'For whom shall the cup be poured?' 'Pour it for Conn', answers Lug, and the damsel pours from the cup as many times as Conn will have descendants at Tara. Then the god Lug and the damsel disappear, and Conn finds himself back at Tara with the cup.[5] The Magic Lance is also found in both Irish and Welsh stories. Flaming with fire or dripping blood, it is linked with the power and fame of a king, and with the fertility of his land. It can strike nine men, of whom one will be a king, and return to the hand of the thrower. It belongs to the house of Lug, and its power to harm can be appeased only in a cauldron, or a bowl of boiling water, or of blood mixed with poison. The lance destroys, the bowl of blood cures. The Treacherous Blow or *Coup Felon*, which destroys the virility of a king and lays waste his land, is also found in Celtic tradition, and likewise the magic castle in which a knight may be tested, so that, if successful, he may rescue the enchanted country from its devastation. The Fisher King may be identified with the Celtic Bran, the hospitable king of the Other World,[6] or with Nuadu, the Fisher King of the Tuatha de Danaan.[7] And both Bran and Nuadu own cauldrons of abundance and personify fecundity.

Chrétien was almost certainly aware of this background of Celtic tradition, and it is even possible that he may have found it in the source book to which he refers in line 67 of the romance. Some indication of Celtic traditions associated with Chrétien's romance is provided by the so-called *Elucidation*, a poem of 484 octosyllabic lines composed by an early thirteenth-century writer as one of two prologues added to Chrétien's *Conte du Graal* in the manuscript of Mons.[8] In this story the springs near the court of the Fisher King are guarded by fairy maidens. Whenever a traveller passed, we are told: 'there came from the spring a damsel who could not be more beautiful, holding a gold cup or *coupe* with meats and bread. Another damsel brought a dish of gold and silver with the food for which the traveller had asked.' This happy abundance is destroyed by King Amangon, possibly the Celtic demi-god Amargen, and his vassals, who rape the maidens and steal the gold cup. The damsels and the castle of the Fisher King vanish, the land falls waste and the springs dry up. But Fortune changes. Arthur and his knights defeat the knights born of the ravished fairy maidens, and rescue the land. Perceval and Gawain each find the Grail Castle, and the Grail, circulating among the tables, provides an abundance of food. A miracle is foretold, the springs gush forth, the meadows grow green and the trees are covered with leaves.

Before we consider the possible Christian significance of the objects in Chrétien's Grail Procession, it is important not to forget that the poet of the *Elucidation*, writing shortly after

Chrétien, chose to describe a Grail story in terms of a Celtic nature myth, of fecundity, of destructive violence, the loss of a cup of abundance, of sterility, rescue, and then the return of fecundity.

It is highly probable that when Chrétien came to write *Perceval*, his audience would have been so accustomed to the framework of Celtic tradition in the lays and romances of the *matière de Bretagne*, that, like the poet of the *Elucidation*, they would have recognised, on this level, the Celtic antecedents of the objects in the Grail Procession, and of the disappearing castle of the Fisher King.[9] But, although Chrétien talks of *a* grail, and although his Grail Procession carefully avoids all overt Christian references, there can be little doubt of the impression which the Grail and Lance in association would have made on his audience. Chrétien could be as enigmatic as he wished, for, with such imagery at his disposal, the Grail, in association with the Bleeding Lance, would be seen immediately as a symbol of the vessel of the Last Supper and of the vessel in which Joseph of Arimathea gathered the blood of Christ. The Lance which Bleeds would be linked with the lance with which a Roman soldier pierced the side of Jesus: 'but one of the soldiers with a spear pierced His side and forthwith came there out blood and water' (John 19.34). The name Longinus, which may derive from the Greek word for lance, *longkhê*, appears in the *Acta* or *Gesta Pilati*, a part of the gospel of Nicodemus. This tells the story of the blind centurion, Longinus, an enemy of Jesus, who is guided to Golgotha and plunges his lance into the side of Christ. The blood flows along the lance to his hand, and Longinus, brushing his eyes with his blood-stained hand, recovers his sight, is baptised, becomes a fervent Christian and dies a martyr.

Antonius Placentinus reports about A.D. 570 that the Holy Lance and the Chalice of the Last Supper were displayed at that time in Jerusalem, the Lance being in the Church of Sion and the Chalice in the basilica on the site of the Holy Sepulchre. An earlier source of A.D. 530 describes the Lance as being in the same basilica as the Chalice. When the Arabs destroyed Jerusalem, these relics were lost, though the 'Holy Lance' was displayed at Constantinople, and was adored in the middle of the tenth century by the Emperor and his retinue who had gone to the Church of St Irene for this purpose. The dish of the Last Supper, the famous *paropsis* of St Matthew (26.23) is also reputed to have been among the treasures of Constantine at the Church of St Sophia. The vision of the Holy Lance provided the knights of the First Crusade with a symbol of Christian and chivalrous achievement, and great was the rejoicing when the Lance was 'found' again at Antioch in 1098.[10] Nothing could be more natural than that the minds of Christian knights should also turn to thoughts of finding the Chalice, which, preserving the blood of Christ, possessed even higher intrinsic value.

Chrétien praises Count Philip of Flanders who gave him the book which contained *li contes del Graal* (66–8). Philip was closely associated by family ties with the Holy Land and the holy relics. His ancestor had been a leader of the First Crusade, and his mother Sybil of Anjou was the daughter of Foulques IV of Anjou, King of Jerusalem, who died in 1143 and was succeeded by his two sons. Flanders was also a centre for the cult of the Holy Blood, which had been 'brought' there in a phial.[11] These associations with the Holy Land must be kept in mind when we consider the likely reactions of Chrétien's audience, and of his patron Count Philip of Flanders, to the outwardly profane procession of a bleeding lance and a dish or grail in the castle of the Fisher King.

This procession, it may be added, also has an indirect affinity with the liturgy of the Greek Church which is an allegory of Christ's suffering. In the office of Mass the priest strikes the bread, which is the communion Host, with a small triangular knife called a lance, *hagia longhkê*. He places the Host on the *diskos*, a wide and deep vessel supported on a base, and the Introit into the Church begins. Lighted candles are borne aloft, followed by the chalice with wine and water, the *diskos*, comparable to Chrétien's grail, with the host, then the lance, the sponge, gospels and relics.[12]

The Lance and the Chalice had immense Christian symbolical value at the time when Chrétien was writing. The Lance was associated with the idea of the destructive blow and the healing flow of blood which turns blindness into sight, so that Christian truth may be revealed and understood, as it was for Longinus. The Chalice in which the blood from the wound is gathered is the receptacle of the divine inspiration passing from Christ to the Church, and the source of man's salvation.[13]

For his *Conte du Graal* Chrétien conjoined three threads: the Celtic theme of material devastation and rebirth, the Christian theme of spiritual sterility and redemption, and the story of Perceval.[14] But this *conjointure* of mood, *sen* and narrative incident is looser, more volatile and suggestive, than in any other romance by Chrétien. Compared to *Perceval*, *Erec et Enide* seems to have been riveted together in its symmetrical conjoining of incident and meaning. This looseness in the *conjointure* of *Perceval* may be a sign of its unfinished state. More probably, it is a part of Chrétien's creative intention. No longer is he interested in fashioning an ideal of temporal order. On the contrary, he appears in *Perceval* to despair of such a possibility, and to be searching in the sands of human confusion for enduring truth and the hope of redemption.

In order to reveal his *sen*, Chrétien uses the oblique, indirect and allusive methods which are usually associated with lyric poetry. If we accept that this was his intention, we may see the vanity of any attempt to pinpoint the significance of the Grail Procession, of the castle of the Fisher King, of the size and shape of the Grail. Suggestion is all, and Chrétien uses all manner of levels of association to convey his meaning to his audience, and, through a dark glass, to us. This allusive method, which reaches its perfection in *Perceval*, is used also, as we have seen, in his earlier works. There is in *Erec et Enide* the poignant image of the Wall of Air, and in *Lancelot*, the crossing of the Sword Bridge with its subtle suggestion of Celtic, courtly, chivalrous and Christian associations, and its quality of universal human devotion, suffering and achievement. Chrétien's genius lies in his ability to suggest different and parallel levels of meaning through a character, a situation, incident or image. Laudine's acceptance and dismissal of Yvain, the incident of the Cart, Erec's Coronation cloak, the Lion, must all be seen in the round. They are all permeated by associations of wider significance and are never the expression of one level of meaning. So, in *Perceval* we have Chrétien's recognition of the almost identical symbols of waste land and rebirth in Celtic mythology and Christian belief, and his ability to conjoin them and present them to us in the story of Perceval. The Grail, the Lance, the Fisher King may be given a Celtic or a Christian interpretation, or both, depending on the eye and imagination of the beholder or listener. It does not matter what the Grail is, but what we, and Chrétien's audience in their turn, believe it to be.

In this respect the symbols of the Grail Procession are displayed to our view, and to that of Chrétien's audience, through the eyes of Perceval. When in their self-interest his eyes see the outside world as surface, material substance, the Grail Procession can be understood as a profane, though enigmatic ritual, and the contents of the grail as of no more spiritual significance than the feast which Perceval enjoys as the Procession passes to and fro in front of him. In such a view, the Celtic material overtones of a vessel of abundance, of a lance of destruction, of a Fisher King and a castle which disappears, are paramount. But beyond this, the eye of inner vision must see the Christian implications of the Procession, and wonder at this blending of the Celtic supernatural with the Christian belief in life, death and rebirth, and with comparable though different truths in the religions of Antiquity, of Rome, Greece, Egypt, and Persia.

Paradoxically, we, and Chrétien's audience, may see the wider implications of the Procession, the Grail and the Lance, which escape the mind of the noble but ignorant Perceval. Chrétien prepares our mind for the revelation of a meaning which he will unmask through the character of Perceval, who, before he awakes from ignorance, combines the qualities of the buffoon and the Elect. Of all Chrétien's heroes, it is Perceval who, until he meets the hermit, is most enclosed within the desert of his solitude. Only when he sheds his complacency and is made aware of his guilt will he, and we through him, be allowed to recognise the Christian significance of the Grail which Chrétien has already put into our minds. In broad medieval philosophical terms Perceval progresses from a nominalist view of material things to realism, the belief in the reality of the spiritual values which underlie surface appearances. It is Chrétien's faith in the realist view of life, and the intricate, unobtrusive and subtle art with which he interweaves this into his three late romances which distinguish him from the other romance-writers of his age, and assure his position as one of the most original and creative writers of the Middle Ages.

In *Perceval*, Chrétien uses his three methods, linear, lateral and allusive, both to obscure and then to disclose and reveal the inner meaning of his work. The gradual linear revelation of meaning progresses with the evolution of Perceval's character from ignorant churl and youthful warrior, to courtly knight and knight of the Grail quest. It is made clear in the contrast of his final quest with that of Gawain. The lateral exposition of the *sen* is suggested in the Prologue, where it is shrouded in praise of his patron, and is then made explicit in the scene with the Hermit. The allusive style, buttressed with comedy in the incidents of Perceval's youth, is most apparent in the scenes of the Grail Procession and the Drops of Blood on the Snow.

The richness of meaning associated with Chrétien's basic theme of sterility and fecundity has led to interpretations of the Grail Procession which Chrétien can scarcely have intended. The Cathar, Oriental, Persian and Hermetic views of the Grail[15] are concerned essentially with the universal and perennial theme of the waste land and its regeneration. They are not supported, other than episodically, by the text of Chrétien's *Perceval*. If we consider this surviving text as a whole, and Chrétien's dialectical, expository and allusive methods of revealing his meaning, we may see the emergence of a coherent *sen*, despite the unfinished state of the work itself.

There are scholars who deny any Christian meaning to the *Conte du Graal*. They see the Grail Procession as profane and void of Christian overtones, the Hermit episode as unauthentic,[16] the Prologue as a rhetorical device without significance for the *sen*.[17] A prologue which flattered a patron and gained the goodwill of an audience was certainly a commonplace usage in the Ciceronian rhetoric which was taken over by medieval writers and was clearly known to Chrétien. This does not mean, however, that the Prologue, or more accurately the first sixty-eight lines, of Chrétien's *Perceval* was not also intended to be an oblique introductory exposition of the inner meaning of the romance, and an integral part of its *sen*:

Perceval

Qui petit seme petit quiaut,	He who sows little, reaps little.
Et qui auques recoillir viaut,	And let the man who desires a
An tel leu sa semance espande	good harvest, sow his seed in a
Que fruit a çant dobles li rande;	place which will give him back
Car an terre qui rien ne vaut,	fruit two hundredfold, for in
Bone semance i seche et faut.	soil which has no virtue good
Crestiiens seme et fet semance	seed withers and fails. Chrétien
D'un romanz que il ancomance,	sows and uses as seed a romance
Et si le seme an si bon leu	which he now begins. And he
Qu'il ne puet estre sanz grant preu,	sows it in such a good place
Qu'il le fet por le plus prodome	that it cannot fail to bring forth
Qui soit an l'anpire de Rome:	great profit, for he composes it
C'est li cuens Phelipes de Flandres,	for the most excellent man in the
Qui miauz vaut ne fist Alixandres,	Empire of Rome. This is no other
Cil que l'an dit qui tant fu buens;	than Count Philip of Flanders
Mes je proverai que li cuens	whose virtue is greater than
Vaut miauz que cil ne fist assez;	that of Alexander, who they say
Car il ot an lui amassez	was so good. But I will show
Toz les vices et toz les maus	that the Count's virtue is much
Don li cuens est mondes et saus.	greater than his, for he had
(1–20)	gathered within himself all the
	vices and all the evils from
	which the Count is free and
	safe.

Immediately we are concerned with fertility and waste land, with sowing and reaping, with the fertile soil of the mind and spirit which will nourish the seed and bring forth a harvest a hundredfold, as in Luke 8.8: *Et aliud cecidit in terram bonam, et ortum fecit fructum centuplum*, and the spiritual waste land, the stony soil, in which the seed withers and dies. This theme of fruitfulness and sterility is basic to the conflict of Good and Evil in this romance, in which mind and spirit must be rescued from their condition of waste land, and made fruitful through *caritas*.

Count Philip is an *exemplum* of this:

Li cuens aimme droite justise	The Count loves righteousness
Et leauté et sainte iglise	and justice, loyalty to one's
Et tote vilenie het,	estate, and holy Church. Hating
S'est plus larges que l'an ne set,	all baseness, he is more generous
Qu'il done selonc l'evangile,	than anyone knows, for, free of
Sanz ypocrisie et sanz guile,	hypocrisy and deceit, he gives
Qui dit: 'Ne sache ta senestre	according to the gospel which
Le bien quant le fera ta destre.'	says: 'Let your left hand not
(25–32)	know of the good deed which
	your right hand will do.'

For God sees and knows all the secrets and recesses of men's hearts and their very being (34–6).

Chrétien enlarges on the theme of the right and left hand, as in Matthew 6.3–4: *Te autem faciente eleemosynam, nesciat sinistra tua, quid faciat dextera tua, ut sit eleemosyna in abscondito, et Pater tuus qui videt in absconso, reddet tibi.*

L'evangile por quoi dit ele:	Why does the gospel say: 'Hide
'Tes biens a ta senestre cele'?	your good deeds from your left
La senestre, selonc l'estoire,	hand'? The left hand, according
Senefie la vainne gloire,	to the Scripture, signifies vain-
Qui vient de fausse ypocrisie;	glory which comes from false
Et la destre que senefie?	hypocrisy. And what does the
Charité, qui de sa bone oevre	right hand signify? *Caritas* which
Pas ne se vante, einçois se cuevre	does not boast of its good work,
Si que nus nel set se cil non	but rather conceals itself so that
Qui Deus et charitez a non:	no man may know of it save
Deus est charitez, et qui vit	only Him who is called God
An charité, selonc l'escrit,	and *Caritas*. God is *Caritas* and if
Sainz Pos le dit et je le lui	a man dwells in *caritas*, according
Il maint an Deu, et Deus an lui.	to the Scripture, Saint Paul says,
(37–50)	and I say it to him, that that
	man dwells in God, and God in
	him.

This distinction between the left and right hands is common to medieval homilies. Thus Rabanus Maurus in his *Allegoriae in sacram scripturam*: 'dextra = bona actio, ut in Psalmis: dextra eorum repleta est muneribus (Psalms 25.10) = vita aeterna' (PL, CXII, 909); 'Sinistra est vita praesens . . . Sinistra delectatio laudis humanae' (PL, CXII, 1055).[18] Do not, says Chrétien, allow the good things in life, such as generosity, to be dealt with in terms of the left hand of *vaine gloire*. This is the life of false hypocrisy, the acting-out, on the stage of the world, of an illusory way of life which ignores the true values of good and evil. Alexander, 'who they say was so good' (15), lived by the secular standards of this world. His generosity, however munificent, was self-interest, attracting worldly praise and reward. Generosity, like the exercise of all virtue, must be a part of life in God, free from self-love and the search for worldly advantage. It must not be the largess of the *vita praesens, gloria vitae praesentis* but the manifestation, concealed from the world, of the *caritas* which is the presence of God within the soul. 'God is *caritas* and he who dwells in *caritas* dwells in God and God in him' says Chrétien, transcribing John, Ep. I, 4.16: *Deus caritas est, et qui manet in caritate, in Deo manet, et Deus in eo.* This is quite clearly the *sen* of the Prologue into which Chrétien skilfully binds his praise of a patron. Philip and Alexander, and the contrasting quality of their generosity, are *exempla* of two conflicting ways of life, the right hand of *caritas* and the left hand of *vaine gloire*. Without *caritas* and the way of life and thought of which it is part, deeds which appear to be good are inadequate because they are rooted in the values of this world and the acting out of a false way of life which is *fausse hypocrisie*.

The divergent and irreconcilable paths of *caritas* and *vaine gloire*, of the fecund soul and the soul which wanders in its waste land, also provide the *sen* of the *Conte du Graal* itself. In this respect it may be helpful to look at the ideas of St Bernard, who became abbot of Clairvaux in 1115 and made of it one of the great spiritual centres of Europe. Man, says St Bernard, is made noble in the likeness of God.[19] Original sin which disfigures him causes him to remove himself from the land of likeness to God to that of unlikeness to God. Nevertheless, the Image of God, which resides in man's free will, can never be lost, but the likeness to God can be lost because man is capable of choosing evil. So the soul can lose its uprightness (*rectitudo*), its love for eternal things, and can become bent (*curva*). But man can regain the lost likeness to God, and the quest to regain this lost likeness forms the basis of Cistercian thinking.

Man has two contrasting ways of thinking and acting: *voluntas communis* and *voluntas propria*. *Voluntas communis* is *caritas* which is eager to share with others the good things it enjoys. *Voluntas propria* is self-will, which refuses to share, and wills nothing save for itself. Associated with this is *cupiditas*, the quest for pleasure which traps a man in a 'circle of the impious', wearying of what he has and hankering for what he has not. So self-will makes the exercise of its activity an end in itself. God is *caritas*. So a man directed by self-will, which turns back on itself, becomes alienated from God's will. More serious, says St Bernard, is *consilium proprium*, the ability to judge and believe that our selfish ends are right. This *sensum proprium*, the opinion of self for self, is self-adoration and revolt against God, and the source of all evil.

The reconstitution of the human soul to its divine likeness demands the extinction of *voluntas propria*, of *consilium proprium* and *sensum proprium*. Reason, which has been choosing blindly, must be cured and illuminated by faith.

This renunciation of self applies to learning. To learn in order to know is base curiosity (*turpis curiositas*), the self-indulgence of a mind making an end in itself of its own activity. To learn in order to gain money from learning is cupidity. The sole purpose of learning is to acquire *caritas*. This is prudence, the rest is curiosity. This distinction should be borne in mind in relation to Perceval's selective acquisition of knowledge of life.

It is only through the life of *caritas* that man may regain the divine likeness which he has lost, and aspire to final unity with God. He must overcome the immoderate love of the body and keep it alive within the limits imposed by necessity. He must follow the cardinal rule of 'know thyself' and so recognise the sin which obscures the divine likeness in himself, and thereby follow the apprenticeship of humility. To know oneself is to know others and to have compassion which is expressed in alms giving, in good deeds which will bring social justice to others. This is the first active stage of *caritas* in which the will passes from oneself to one's neighbour. In this renunciation of self and elimination of *consilium proprium*, a man unites himself in will with God's will to justice. So man's will can be made to pass from his neighbour to God on an initial, human plane of devotion to God who was made man, and was crucified, and then on a spiritual plane leading through many stages of mystical experience to the final exaltation of spiritual oneness with God. Like knows like, and the possibility of the soul's knowledge of God lies in its likeness to God when it has been changed, purified and restored to the likeness of its Creator. The soul, loving thus, loves God *caste*, *sancte* and *ardenter*, without self-interest, without concupiscence, absorbing all other affections into this great love: 'As a small drop of water mingled in much wine seems to be wholly lost and to take on the colour and taste of the wine; as a kindled and glowing iron becomes most like to fire, having put off its former and natural form; and as the air, when flooded with the light of the sun, is transformed into the very brightness of light, so that it seems to be not so much illumined as to be the light itself, so it must needs be that all human affection in the Saints will then, in some ineffable way, melt from itself, and be entirely poured over into the will of God' (PL, CLXXXII, 991).[21] This is the achievement of Galahad when, in the thirteenth-century *Queste del saint Graal*, he beholds in the Grail the mysteries of God.

Perceval's progress from untutored lad, to tutored and courtly knight and then to knight of the Grail Quest can be viewed against this Cistercian background of the two ways of life which are governed by the right hand of *caritas* and the search for oneness with God, and the left hand of *voluntas propria* which seeks the *vaine gloire* of this world.

In the Hermit scene, the Christian interpretation of the *Perceval*, which has been suggested obliquely in the Prologue and the Grail Procession, becomes explicit. Let us leave the detailed discussion of this episode for the moment, and look at the question of its authenticity and its setting in Chrétien's unfinished romance. The problems that arise about it concern its position in the romance and discrepancies in the sequence of time. After Perceval has been denounced by the Hideous Damsel, he and Gawain and the other knights set out from Arthur's court. The narrative then gives 1,500 lines to Gawain's adventures, switches abruptly for 500 lines to the hermit episode, and then back to Gawain's adventures for the remaining 2,000 lines of what ms.A, in the last line of the fragment, calls *Perccvaus le viel*. The injury to the time sequence occurs because Perceval and Gawain leave Arthur's court together, yet, at the point in the story when the Hermit episode begins, Gawain is only in the third day of his adventures, though Perceval has been wandering for five years, and Chrétien refers to this long lapse of time on six occasions in seventeen lines. Three main solutions to this problem have been suggested, with variations. The 'orthodox' one is that the 9,234 lines of Hilka's edition, which is concluded by an *explicit* in two mss., contain Chrétien's romance as it remained unfinished at his death. The second solution sees these lines not as a unified fragment but as two separate romances, a *Perceval* and a *Gauvain*, both by Chrétien, which have been clumsily bound together by a writer who composed linking passages.[20] The third view is that only that part of the text which concerns Perceval is by Chrétien, and that the Gawain episodes are the work of a continuator. The question has arisen about the authorship of the Hermit episode which occurs so abruptly in the long sequence – over 4,000 lines – of Gawain adventures. The majority of critics see the Hermit episode as genuine, but D. D. R. Owen, who says: 'without the [Hermit] episode there is no hint in the romance that the Grail has any Christian connotations', takes the view that the *Conte du Graal* is an incomplete *Perceval* which is linked to an incomplete *Gauvain*, both by Chrétien, and that the agent who fused these unfinished works together did not know of the Hermit episode.[22] It is, he considers, an addition by a pious interpolator who also wrote the interpolated passage about the Grail which occurs in the *First Continuation*. For the purpose of discussing the *Perceval*, I shall take the view that the whole of the Perceval story in Hilka's edition is by Chrétien, that the Gauvain story is by him and formed part of the original unfinished romance, and that the Hermit episode is by Chrétien and is probably, as will be argued later, in the right place in the romance. It is, however, just possible that the Hermit scene was originally intended to follow the probable conclusion of Gawain's adventures in the meeting of Arthur's court presaged in the closing lines of the extant romance. This view presupposes that Chrétien intended to follow Gawain's quest for the lance, with its connotations of knighthood bent on the search for *vaine gloire*, with a Perceval quest of spiritual knighthood which would discover why the Lance was bleeding, and to whom and why the Grail was served. It is also possible, though this is mere hypothesis, that Chrétien, finding that time was going before his desire, inserted the Hermit episode, possibly in a draft summary form, in the body of his romance rather than leave it adrift as an isolated fragment without any contextual setting.

Thematically the story of Perceval's progress appears to fall into three main divisions, of which the third is unfinished. All three sections begin with instructions in knightly and courtly behaviour and in love of God, from his mother, from Gornemant and from the hermit. Perceval understands these instructions, or fails to understand them, according to the degree of spiritual waste land within him. In the first section (IA in the table which follows), his worldly and spiritual ignorance leads him into situations which, though a burlesque of knighthood, produce tragic results. The second section concerns his knightly progress to worldly fame and to profane love. This section divides into two balanced parts. The first half, which covers his search for his mother, begins with Gornemant's instructions and ends with a worldly triumph at Belrepeire. This is turned into spiritual defeat when his cousin attacks him for his failure in the Grail Castle. In the second half of this section, Perceval, who has discovered his name, redresses by worldly means the wrong he did to the Damsel in the Tent, and, in the incident of the Three Drops of Blood on the Snow, has higher thoughts of distant love for Blancheflor. But, once more, after a worldly triumph, this time at Arthur's court, he suffers spiritual defeat and worldly shame through the castigation of the Hideous Damsel.

Immediately there begins the first of three Gawain episodes. In the version which we have of the *Conte du Graal*, the first Gawain episode is followed by the Hermit episode of the Perceval story. This is then followed by two major Gawain episodes, of which the second is unfinished. This was very probably Chrétien's original intention, but, as we have seen (p. 220) there is a possibility that the Hermit episode is misplaced and should come after the Gawain story. This would lessen the chronological discrepancy of Perceval's five years of wandering and of Gawain's three days of adventures. In this case the Hermit's instructions to Perceval would introduce the third section of the Perceval story, and might also form the beginning of a hypothetical third main section of the romance which would recount Perceval's spiritual progress as a knight of the Grail. There is, however, little doubt that such a neat and logical construction would have been out of keeping with the persistent underlying note of temporal dissonance and disorder in the romance. It is probable that Chrétien would have cared little, at this stage in his composition, about the discrepancy between the lapse of 'temporal' time in the Gawain adventures and that of the 'spiritual' time of Perceval's wandering in the wilderness. He may well have inserted the Hermit episode in its present position as an interruption in the expanse of Gawain's 'social' episodes and an indication of Perceval's redemption and conversion to his new and higher self, a preparation for the final part of his quest. Although Perceval does promise to return to Blancheflor (2960), there is no certainty whatsoever that Chrétien intended that he should return to the Castle of the Fisher King. Indeed, such an ending might have seemed to Chrétien to be out of keeping with his oblique and enigmatic methods of allowing his *sen* to permeate the minds of his audience. All we can postulate as an ending to the romance is a further Perceval adventure or adventures at or after the meeting of Arthur's court at the Castle of the Two Queens. This would give us the thematic alternation ABABA, where A is the Perceval theme and B the Gawain theme. This would bring the structure of *Perceval*, in this respect, into line with that of *Lancelot*, and the Hermit episode into direct comparison with the tourney at Noauz (see pp. 225, 272, 338, n.46.[23]

The thematic structure of the romance might then be shown as:

I PERCEVAL'S WORLDLY PROGRESS

A   *Worldly and spiritual ignorance. Complete self-will.*
  1. Instructions from mother.
     a. Perceval meets knights in the Waste Forest – *vaine gloire* theme.
     b. His mother's fear of the knights as agents of destruction. Her instructions. His failure to understand her. His departure, her collapse.
  2. 'Love' theme.
     Damsel in the Tent. Applied self-will and *niceté* lead to her suffering and the death of knights.
  3. 'Prowess' theme.
     Perceval visits Arthur's court, believes he is knighted, defeats Red Knight.

B   a   *Complete self-will in knighthood: 'guilt' about mother's collapse.*
     1. Instructions from Gornemant.
        Knighted by Gornemant. Intent on quest to find his mother.
     2. Love and Prowess.
        Belrepeire. Waste City. Love of Blancheflor. Worldly triumph in saving city. Ignores its religious life.

3   *Worldly prowess: spiritual defeat.*
    Castle of Fisher King. Worldly prowess (granting
    of the sword to him). Failure to see significance
    of Lance and Grail. Restrained by values of
    Gornemant, and lack of *caritas*. Spiritual defeat.
    Cousin's admonition. Discovers name. Failure of
    quest for mother.

b   *Self-will, but growing awareness of self.*
4   *'Love' and Prowess.*
    Defeats Orguelleus de la Lande, frees Damsel of
    the Tent and avenges slain knights.

5   Love.
    Three Drops of Blood on Snow. Fin'Amors for
    Blancheflor.

6   *Prowess.*
    Worldly triumphs at Arthur's court. Friendship
    of Gawain.

7   *Spiritual defeat.*
    Castigation by Hideous Damsel. Accepts quest
    for *explanation* of Lance that Bleeds and purpose of
    the Grail. Believes the answers can be discovered
    by deeds of knightly prowess [goes 'out of mind'
    and forgets God].

II GAWAIN ADVENTURES

A   Gawain's previous knightly sin and its retribution.
    Insulted at Tintagel. Attacked by townsfolk at Escavalon.
    Freed by promise of quest to find the Lance that will destroy
    Logres.
    [The Hermit episode of the Perceval theme.]

B   Gawain's humiliations. World upside-down. Burlesque
    of knighthood. Damsel desires to inspire him to shame-
    ful deeds. Gawain's knightly fortitude.

C   Gawain's worldly triumph at the Castle of the Two
    Queens. Supreme Joy of the Court. Sorrow at his
    'imprisonment'. Revenge on Gawain sought by Guirome-
    lant for previous injury. Arthur's court summoned to
    the forest for the combat. Arthur and Gawain will both
    meet their mothers at this court.

III PERCEVAL'S SPIRITUAL PROGRESS

A   The Hermit *episode* (occurs in the text after the first Gawain
episode, Section II A above).

  1   *Instructions* from pilgrims and hermit. Good Friday
meeting with pilgrims a replica in reverse of his
meeting with the five knights in the Waste Forest
(Section I A1 (*a*) above). Spiritual redemption
through repentance. Perceval celebrates communion
of Mass : finds inner joy and peace of mind. Receives
from the Hermit the answer to the question 'To
whom is the Grail served?'

  [2   Quest for the answer to the question: 'Why does the
Lance bleed?' Apprenticeship in humility and
caritas? Reunion with Blancheflor? Answer to the
question about the Lance — theme of knightly
violence displaced by that of the Lance that bleeds
and restores sight?]

In its unfinished state, the text of *Perceval* gives undue weight
to the adventures of Gawain. This imbalance would appear
less evident, if the *Perceval* was planned on a larger scale than
Chrétien's other romances. If we see Perceval's worldly progress up to his humiliation by the Hideous Damsel and his
lapse into 'madness' as a *premier vers* which in Chrétien's other
romances, except *Lancelot*, amounts to one third of the total
work, the intended length of *Perceval* may possibly have been
about 12,000 lines, with a closing section of some additional
4,000 lines. Although Gawain's adventures, at first sight,
feature so prominently as to unbalance the existing text,
they appear to be extremely important for the structure and
the meaning of the work, and to be a development of the
method of composition which Chrétien had used in *Lancelot*.
Perceval's disappearance from the story for so long during
Gawain's adventures may be a device to provide his audience
with an abrupt change from the exalted and mysterious
nature of the Grail theme in the Perceval story. On the other
hand, if we consider the structural similarities between
Perceval and *Lancelot*, this disappearance may have a deeper intention. Both heroes fail an initial test which leads to later
and more serious failure. Lancelot fails initially with Guene-

vere because he hesitated to mount the cart; Perceval fails at the castle of the Fisher King because he sinned against his mother. Lancelot disappeared into prison after the exalted scene of consummated love with the Queen, and, apart from his visiting performance at the tourney of Noauz, the stage was taken over by Gawain and Meleagant. This device allowed Chrétien to make explicit the vices of Meleagant and the limitations of Gawain which had been indicated earlier in the story. Evil and moral weakness are depicted in extreme form so that goodness and moral strength may be defined. The tourney at Noauz, which may appear to be a disconnected episode among the adventures of Meleagant and Gawain, has nevertheless the direct purpose of confirming Lancelot in the sense of humility and devotion demanded by his Fin'Amors for Guenevere. His position is established as chief opponent to the ways of life of Meleagant and Gawain. Similarly, Perceval disappears after his success at Arthur's court and his humiliation by the Hideous Damsel. Gawain takes the stage and Perceval reappears only briefly in the Hermit scene which makes explicit the reasons for his earlier failures, and confirms him in rejection of self-will, in submission to God, in repentance of sin and in the path of caritas. This interlude, like the tourney at Noauz, appears to be out of place, but it is not. It has the direct purpose of defining the virtues which can rescue Perceval from the wilderness of the world, and knightly violence, and guide him to spiritual peace. Conversely, the adventures of Gawain reflect the triviality of worldly fame, the quest for vaine gloire, the sin of violence which can only be 'redressed' by further violence, the topsy-turvy quality of a world which is controlled by self-interest. In Lancelot, the hero clears his character of imperfections through absolute devotion to Fin'Amors. In Perceval, the hero is tested on an altogether higher plane of spiritual development. Whereas Lancelot triumphed through rejecting the inanity of the knightly joust in favour of the immolation of the self demanded by Fin'Amors, Perceval is shown by the Hermit that his quest for an explanation of the Grail and Lance is a religious quest, in which the madness of purposeless violence has no part. If, as we have suggested, the structure of Perceval was influenced by that of Lancelot, it is possible that Perceval was intended to reappear at the tournament to be attended by Arthur at the Castle of the Two Queens, and that the explanation of the Lance that Bleeds would have been made evident in the confrontation of the new Perceval with the obsessive destructiveness of Guiromelant and the inane valour of Gawain.

Let us look at the events which lead to Perceval's failure at the Grail Castle. On a spring morning when all living things are alight with joy, the son of the widowed lady of the Waste Forest rises from his bed, and equips himself with three throwing spears:

Et pansa que veoir iroit
Herceors que sa mere avoit,
Qui ses avainnes li herçoient:
Bués doze et sis herces avoient.
(81–4)

And he thought he would go and see the harrowers who belonged to his mother and who were sowing her land for oats. They had twelve oxen and six harrows.

Immediately we return to the theme of the Prologue, the seeding of fertile soil. Impelled by the joy around him, Perceval hurls his spears in all directions, presaging the destruction of the forest idyll by five knights whose clashing weapons and armour disturb the birdsong of the new and gentle season, as they force their way through the wood:

Car sovant hurtoient as armes
Li rain des chasnes et des charmes.
Les lances as escuz hurtoient,
Et tuit li hauberc fremilloient;
Sonoit li fuz, sonoit li fers
Et des escuz et des haubers.
(105–10)

for often were their arms struck by the branches of oaks and yoke-elms. Lances crashed against shields, and the rings on their coats of mail were jingling, in constant motion. The wood resounded, and the iron of their shields and hauberks rang out.

Perceval's innate aggression and violence is kindled by this warlike uproar.[24] These must be the devils against whom his mother gave warning. He does not cross himself, as she had bade him do. His instinct is to fight. But the sight of gleaming hauberks, of bright and gleaming helmets, lances and shields, of green and scarlet shining in the sun, and the gold, azure and silver of knightly accoutrements, fills Perceval with joy. He sinned when he thought they were devils. They must be angels. His mother was right indeed to say that angels are the most beautiful beings, save only God whose beauty surpasses all (111–45). The most handsome knight must be God (146–7):

'Et si dist ma mere meïsme
Qu'an doit Deu croire et aorer
Et sozploiier et enorer:
Et je aorerai cestui
Et toz les autres avuec lui.'
(150–4)

'And my mother told me especially that we must believe in God, and worship and bend the knee to Him and honour Him. So will I worship this man and all those who are with him.'

Perceval falls to the ground repeating by rote the Creed and prayers learnt from his mother. Beneath this comic veneer of the profane and the absurd there is a serious intention to this scene which anticipates not only the comic/serious upside-down world of Gawain's adventures, but also the Good Friday episode with the pilgrims and the Hermit, which in its reversal of mood and intention is its counterpart. Beneath the folly of Perceval's innocence, the profane paradox of knights who are devils and angels, there can be discerned the theme from the Prologue, and from *Yvain*, of fruitless words which are not understood in the heart. Perceval has no spiritual being. God and the devils, angels and knights live on the same plane of material appearance and are judged by their outward beauty and splendour. In Perceval's naivety lies Chrétien's satire of courtly values, the vanity of this world. The leader or *mestre* of the knights comes forward:

. . . 'Vaslez, n'aies peor.'
'Non ai je, par le Sauveor',
Fet li vaslez, 'an cui je croi.
Estes vos Deus?' – 'Nenil, par foi.'
'Qui estes dons?' – 'Chevaliers sui.'
'Ainz mes chevalier ne conui',
Fet li vaslez, 'ne nul n'an vi
N'onques mes parler n'an oï;
Mes vos estes plus biaus que Deus.
Car fusse je ore autreteus,
Einsi luisanz et einsi fez!'
(171–81)

'Good youth, have no fear.' 'I have none, by the Lord and Saviour in whom I believe', says the youth. 'Are you God?' 'No, by my faith.' 'Who are you then?' 'I am a knight.' 'I never knew a knight before', says the youth, 'never saw one, and never heard tell of one. But you are more beautiful than God. Would that I could now be just like you, gleaming, and made in your likeness.'

'You are more beautiful than God', albeit from the lips of an innocent, is the mark of *fausse ypocrisie*, the *vaine gloire* of the brave show which sins because of its limitations and its self-interested confidence in its spiritual waste land.

Perceval is intent on asking questions about the name and purpose of the material appurtenances of knighthood, the lance which strikes others (201) and is therefore, he thinks, of less value than his hunting spears, and the shield which arrests the lance. His fresh curiosity and judgement of the information he receives is in marked contrast to the parallel scene in the Grail castle in which he fails to ask about the purpose of the lance and grail. In this first scene he is an innocent in material things, in the second he is blinded by worldly considerations to the spiritual truths which hover beyond his reach.

The knights grow restive and address their leader: 'My lord, know indeed that the Welsh by their very nature are more foolish than cattle at pasture, and this one is just such an animal' (242–5). But the *mestre* swears to tell Perceval whatever he desires to know (251–2). He will tell him of Arthur and the glory of his world, as the Hermit will speak of God.

Perceval returns to his mother with joy. He has seen beings more beautiful than God, or his angels (393–4). This is Perceval's first moment of choice, and he decides for knighthood and *vaine gloire*:

La mere antre ses braz le prant
Et dit: 'Biaus filz, a Deu te rant,
Que mout ai grant peor de toi:
Tu as veü, si con je croi,
Les anges don les janz se plaingnent,
Qui ocient quanqu'il ataingnent.'
'Non ai, voir, mere, non ai, non!
Chevalier dient qu'il ont non.'
(395–402)

His mother takes him in her arms and says: 'Fair son, turn to God, for I have such great fear for you. You have seen, I think, the angels of whom people complain, angels who kill whatever they find.' 'I have not, in truth, mother, I have not. No! They say they are called knights!'

At the word *chevalier* his mother falls in a faint, foreshadowing her imminent death. She speaks in anger:

'Ha! lasse, con sui mal baillie!
Biaus douz filz, de chevalerie
Vos cuidoie si bien garder
Que ja n'an oïssiez parler
Ne que ja nul n'an veïssiez.
Chevaliers estre deüssiez,
Biaus filz, se Damedeu pleüst
Que vostre pere vos eüst
Gardé et voz autres amis.'
(407–15)

'Alas, how wretched I am, how ill treated. Fair and gentle son, I thought I could guard you so well and keep you away from the ways of knighthood that you would never hear anyone speak of it, and never see anyone of that kind. You could have been a knight, fair son, had it pleased God that your father could have protected you, and your friends.'

There was, she tells him, no knight of higher renown than his father, nor one so feared in all the Islands of the Sea. His lineage was great, and her lineage was the greatest in the land:

'Es Isles de mer n'ot lignage
Meillor del mien an mon aage;
Mes li meillor sont decheü,
S'est bien an plusors leus seü
Que les mescheances avient
As prodomes qui se maintienent
A grant enor et an proesce.
Mauvestiez, honte ne peresce
Ne chiet pas, car ele ne puet;
Mes les bons decheoir estuet.'
(425–34)

'In all my days there has been no better lineage than mine in the Islands of the Sea. But the best in lineage have declined, and it is well known in many places that misfortunes befall men of excellent virtue who by their deeds uphold great honour and prowess. Wickedness, shameful deeds, idleness do not decline, for it is beyond their power. But those who are good are destined to decline.'[25]

Her view of life, like Chrétien's, is pessimistic. Virtue must decline, wickedness and recreancy are everywhere and it is beyond their nature to grow worse. The bold and the honourable are destined to disaster. So Perceval's father and his brothers fell victims to this wanton age, a Waste Land of violence.

'Vostre pere, si nel savez,
Fu parmi les janbes navrez
Si que il maheigna del cors.
Sa granz terre, ses granz tresors,
Que il avoit come prodon,
Ala tot a perdicion,
Si cheï an grant povreté.'
(435–41)

'Your father, and you do not know this, was wounded between his legs so that he became infirm and impotent in his body. His great land, his great treasure, which he owned as a knight of supreme virtue, was completely destroyed, and he fell into great poverty.'

Such a fate befell all the nobles of Arthur's realm after the death of Uterpandragon, Arthur's father. Everyone fled who could. Perceval's father, carried in a litter, sought refuge in his house in the Waste Forest. But destruction pursued him. Perceval's eldest brother was dubbed knight at the royal court of Escavalon, his other brother being dubbed by King Ban de Gormeret:

'An un jor andui li vaslet
Adobé et chevalier furent,
Et an un jor meïsmes murent
Por revenir a lor repeire,

'Within the space of one and the same day the young men were dubbed and made knights, within the space of one and the

Que joie me voloient feire
Et lor pere, qui puis nes vit.'
(468–73)

same day they set out to return
to their home to bring joy to me
and to their father, who never saw
them more.'

'The eyes of the eldest were picked out by crows and rooks'
(478–9):

'Del duel des filz morut li pere,
Et je ai vie mout amere
Soferte puis que il fu morz.
Vos estiiez toz li conforz
Que je avoie et toz li biens;
Car il n'i avoit plus des miens:
Rien plus ne m'avoit Deus leissiee
Don je fusse joianz et liee.'
(481–8)

'Your father died of grief for his
sons, and, since he died, I have
endured a life of bitter sorrow.
You were all my comfort, all my
good, for there was no one else
of my own left to me. God had
left me no one else in whom I
might find joy and happiness.'

In the tragic directness or *simplece* of this speech Chrétien states an essential part of his *sen*, the reverse side of knighthood, the purposeless quest for *vaine gloire*, void of virtue, the inconsequential slaughter of youths on their first day of knighthood. And he indicates the results of this violence which breeds on violence so that destruction of life and virtue and goodness are universal, lands become waste and widows are left to their misery. Although Chrétien draws here on Celtic tradition, this is for him the condition of life devoted to a self-seeking knighthood, heedless of *caritas*, upholding its honour by slaughter. This is the underlying theme of the Gawain adventures towards the end of the romance.

Perceval, driven by self-will, has no sympathy for his mother. Lacking all *caritas*, he cannot grasp her words of tragedy. This is his first test, and he fails it as he will fail with the Damsel in the tent and the Fisher King. His carnal delight in food takes hold of him:

'A mangier', fet il, 'me donez!
Ne sai de quoi m'areisonez;
Mes mout iroie volantiers
Au roi qui fet les chevaliers,
Et je irai, cui qu'il an poist.'
(491–5)

'Give me something to eat', he
says, 'I do not know what you
are talking to me about. But I
would very much like to go to
the king who makes knights.
And I will go, whether you like
it or not.'

Perceval, in his *niceté*, is impelled towards the life of *vaine gloire*, whence his destiny as an Elect, his lineage and virtue will lead him to *savoir*, and, beyond this, to *caritas*. His progress is foreshadowed in the instructions his mother gives him. They are threefold. Honour ladies and damsels and render them aid and service; this is the foundation of honour and without this honour must die:

'Et se vos aucune an proiiez,
Gardez que ne li enuiiez;
Ne feites rien qui li despleise.
De pucele a mout qui la beise;
S'ele le beisier vos consant,
Le soreplus vos an desfant,
Se leissier le volez por moi.'
(543–9)

'And if you entreat any lady or damsel, take heed not to vex her, or do anything to her displeasure. To kiss a maiden is to receive a great gift from her. If she allows your kiss, I forbid you to take anything more, and from this you will desist for my sake.'

'And if she has a ring on her finger or purse on her belt, and gives this to you as a love token or reward for your plea, I shall be pleased if you wear her ring' (550–4):

'De l'anel prandre vos doing gié
Et de l'aumosniere congié.'
(555–6)

'I grant you leave to accept [take] the ring and the purse.'

His second duty is to his fellow man. Know him as a person:

'Ja an chemin ne an ostel
N'aiiez longuemant conpeignon
Que vos ne demandiez son non;
Le non sachiez a la parsome;
Car par le non conoist l'an l'ome.'
(558–62)

'Never be the companion of a man for any length of time, either on the road or in a dwelling, without asking his name, without knowing exactly what his name is, for by the name one knows [understands] the man.'

'And seek above all the company of virtuous knights, and their counsel' (563–6).

Perceval's chief and last duty is to God: 'Go to church and pray to our Lord to grant you honour in this world and to so lead your life here that you may come to a good end' (568–72). 'Mother, what is a church (*iglise*)?' 'A place where one serves the Creator of Heaven and earth and the men and animals in it' (573–6):

'Et mostiers quoi?' – 'Filz, ce
        meïsme:
Une meison bele et saintisme

'And what is a minster?'[26] – 'Son just this. A house, beautiful and most holy, the abode of sacred

Et de cors sainz et de tresors,
S'i sacrefie l'an le cors
Jesucrist, la prophete sainte,
Cui giu firent honte mainte :
Traïz fu et jugiez a tort,
Si sofri angoisse de mort
Por les homes et por les fames ;
Qu'an anfer aloient les ames
Quant eles partoient des cors,
Et il les an gita puis fors.
. . .
Por oïr messes et matines
Et por cel Seignor aorer
Vos lo gié au mostier aler.'
　　　　　(577–88, 592–4)

relics and treasures. And a place where they sacrifice the body of Christ, God's holy prophet, on whom the Jews inflicted many shameful injuries. He was betrayed and unjustly condemned. And he suffered the anguish of death for the sake of men and women, because souls, when they left their bodies, used to go to Hell, and He, after His death, cast them out from there. . . . So that you may hear masses and matins, and worship that Lord, I give you counsel to go to church.'

Perceval in the zest of *niceté*, gives a ready promise :

'Donc irai je mout volantiers
As iglises et as mostiers',
Fet li vaslez, 'd'ore anavant :
Einsi le vos met an covant.'[27]
　　　　　(595–8)

'Then, from now on, will I go right willingly to places of worship and to churches with relics', says the young man, 'about this I now give you my word.'

This speech by Perceval's mother complements her lament for the decline of virtue and the persistence of evil.[28] It also presents us with the other, more positive side of Chrétien's *sen*. The widowed mother, escaping from human violence and this threat to her son, must live in the Waste Forest and endure her fate with patience. In this context we can see that the Waste Land may have an additional meaning beyond that of the legendary destruction of Uterpandragon's kingdom, and that of the Celtic land which is laid waste by a spell or through the maiming of the sovereign. The Waste Land is also an allegory of the human violence and destruction which are born of self-will. Isolated on her land in the Waste Forest, Perceval's mother, who is herself one of the Elect of the Grail lineage, has attained wisdom through suffering. In this life she sees no remedy for the pervasive evil which diminishes virtue, goodness and honour. Yet through her belief in salvation in Christ she has preserved for herself an island of tranquillity, and, on the material plane, of symbolical fecundity. The seed is sown, the soil is fertile, nature is joyful. On this level, the Waste Land has universal significance. It represents in society and the individual a denial of the search for salvation in God, and a devotion, as ends in themselves, to this worldly life and the self-interested pursuit of *vaine gloire* through violence. This situation and allegory will recur in the Waste City of Belrepeire, in which again the surviving few, supported by their numerous holy men and women, will overcome the threat of extermination by violence. It is implicit in the way in which the castle of the Fisher King appears to Perceval in the midst of the Waste Land and vanishes since he is not fit to see it any more. In an ironical, often burlesque way, it underlies the later adventures of Gawain.

True hope for Perceval's mother is to be found in the example of Christ destroyed in human form by the violence of evil men. But the blow which fell on Christ, unlike those which destroyed her husband and elder sons, gives hope to the world, and salvation to the souls of men and women in the Waste Land of Hell. This violence done to Christ, and his sacrifice and promise of redemption, she says (580–1), are remembered in the sacrament of Mass. Her speech represents a stage, intermediate between the Prologue and the Hermit scene, in the exposition of the Christian *sen* of the romance. She does not speak of the Resurrection of Christ or the ascent of the souls freed from Hell. This is what Perceval will learn years hence (6290–1) when, on Good Friday, he meets the pilgrims who direct him to the Hermit, to knowledge of the Grail and the repentance of his sin in the sacrament of Mass. His mother's words provide the outline of Perceval's progress. He must endure and experience the worldly life from which she has failed to protect him. Eventually, after great suffering, he is destined to recognise and accept her view of the worldly and the spiritual life, and in this acceptance the major *sen* of the romance will be bound up. The paths of *vaine gloire* and *caritas*, the left hand, the right hand, both offer visions of destruction and violence. Only on the right hand path, however, is there a remedy for the violence and evil of this world. This is the truth which Perceval unwittingly seeks when he sets out to discover why the Lance bleeds and to whom the Grail is served.

As Perceval rides off to his mother's words, 'Fair son, may

God grant you, wherever you go, more joy than remains to me', he commits his great and mortal sin of omission:[29]

Quant li vaslez fu esloigniez	When the young man was as far
Le giet d'une pierre menue,	away as one may throw a small
Si regarda et vit cheüe	stone, he looked and saw his
Sa mere au chief del pont arriere;	mother had fallen to the ground
Et jut pasmee an tel meniere	at the end of the bridge he had
Con s'ele fust cheüie morte.	crossed, and he saw her lie
(620–5)	unconscious as if, when she fell,
	she was dead.

Perceval sees his mother lying in the semblance of death. He is aware of what he has done. He is close, but he rides on, committing a mortal sin, as the Hermit will tell him. This is an important moment, for failure in this first test will lead directly to greater failure in the castle of the Fisher King. Perceval's state of mind is conveyed by sharp words, a fast narrative pace as he runs away, and mournful rhymes in ure.

Et cil ceingle de la reorte	With his switch he lashes the
Son chaceor parmi la crope;	rump of his hunter, which,
Et cil s'an va, qui pas n'açope,	without a stumble, carries him
Einz l'an porte grant aleüire	away at full speed through the
Parmi la grant forest oscure.	midst of the great, dark forest.
(626–30)	

Having met his 'Charrete' and failed the test, Perceval, unlike Lancelot, continues to fail the tests to which he is submitted. His failures have their humorous and tragic aspects, and his journey to adventure turns for a while into a vain quest to find his mother again.

Perceval, for all his likeable naivety, is entrapped by self-will. He has no care for anyone, no hint of *caritas* for women, for his companions on the road or in dwellings, or for God, and his mother's instructions which foreshadow those of Gornemant and the Hermit, provide the structural pattern for his adventures and failures. Her counsel withers in his nice mind. He looks on the surface appearance of life, of material things and gestures, especially if they offer sensual pleasure. Perceval cannot see beneath this appearance. He cannot grasp abstract ideas. His inner eye is blind, his spiritual self a waste.

This is immediately apparent in the episode of the Damsel

whom he finds in a tent, which shines scarlet, green and gold
in the sun, so that the meadows are lit by its brilliance. So
splendid, thinks Perceval, it must be God's house. He will
pray for food (655–66). He wakes the damsel who is asleep
in her bed:

Et li vaslez, qui nices fu,[30]	And the young man who was
Dist: 'Pucele, je vos salu,	raw and untutored, said:
Si con ma mere le m'aprist.'	'Damsel, I give you greeting as
(681–3)	my mother bade me do.'

He insists on kissing her, come what may, 'as my mother
instructed me to do' (695). He kisses her roughly, as she
struggles in her bed, twenty times, 'as the story says' (709),
drags an emerald[31] ring from her finger and places it on his
own:

. . . 'me dist ma mere	'My mother told me to take
Qu'an vostre doi l'anel preïsse,	[accept] the ring from your
Mes que rien plus ne vos feïsse.'	finger but to do nothing else
(712–14)	to you.'

He takes his leave: 'Now I will go, well rewarded, and you
are much better to kiss than any maid in my mother's house,
for your lips are not bitter' (723–8). The distraught damsel
pleads for her ring: 'I shall be ill-used and you will lose
your life' (731–2). Perceval's heart does not hear her words
(734–5). Dying of hunger, as indifferent to her suffering as
he had been to his mother's, he devours a venison pasty:

Por la fain qui formant l'angoisse	Driven by the pangs of hunger
Un des pastez devant lui froisse	which torment him he takes one
Et manjue par grant talant	of the pasties in front of him,
Et verse an la cope d'arjant	and breaks it and eats with
Del vin, qui n'estoit mie lez,	great zest [desire]. Into the
S'an boit sovant et a granz trez	silver cup he pours some wine,
Et dit: 'Pucele, cist pasté	more potent than milk, drinks
Ne seront hui par moi gasté.[32]	long and frequent draughts, and
Venez mangier, il sont mout buen;	says: 'Damsel, these (other)
Assez avra chascuns del suen,	pasties will not be finished off
Si an remandra uns antiers.'	by me today. Come and eat.
(745–55)	They are very good. Each of us
	will have his share, and a whole
	one will be left over.'

He eats and drinks his fill while the girl wrings her hands.
He covers the pasties which are left (756–63) and takes his
leave in courtly style: 'May God keep you, fair love. Do not

grieve for your ring: before I die I will repay you for it.'
But she, foreseeing shame and suffering, refuses to commend
him to God (767–80).

In this light and humorous scene there is a serious intention. Perceval's lack of *caritas* is displayed in burlesque
performance, but his *nice* and self-willed behaviour will lead
to disaster for the damsel, and the death of knights. He
begins to create the personal waste land which will over-
whelm him after his failure at the Grail Castle and the
denunciation of him by the Hideous Damsel. The contrast
between Perceval's carnality and the damsel's suffering foreshadows the irony of the moment when Perceval continues
to munch his food while the Lance and the Grail pass to and
fro before his eyes. In the scene with the Damsel in the Tent
there is also analogy and contrast between the description
of Perceval's meal and his celebration of Mass in the Hermit
episode. In such an allusive writer as Chrétien it is impossible to ignore the profanity which is as implicit in this
scene as it was when Perceval worshipped the five knights.
When Perceval pours the wine, and breaks the pasty and
eats it, and covers over the unused food, Chrétien burlesques
the Mass in this sacrament of the physical senses. There is
refined comedy in this profanity as there is in the burlesque
of knighthood when Perceval fights with the Scarlet Knight.
There is also a sense of down-to-earth relief after the exalted
speeches by Perceval's mother, and a premonitory definition
of Perceval's spiritual destiny. At this stage, the upside-
down travesty of a holy rite measures, in comic fashion, the
gulf which separates Perceval from *caritas*, the antithesis between this crass youth and the knight who will have traversed
the wilderness and been inducted by the Hermit into inner
peace.

The damsel's knight has the wooden heart of a Meleagant.
Whereas Perceval, through ignorance, commits sins of omission, this knight is actively vicious through the hurt pride
of *vaine gloire*. He seeks revenge against the despoiler of the
ring, and, until he finds it, will deprive the damsel of all
care and comfort. For him knighthood is a vendetta, as it
will prove to be in the Gawain adventures. He refuses to
believe the girl's innocence; her palfrey will not eat oats or
be re-shoed; if it dies, the damsel will follow on foot:

'Einz me siuroiz a pié et nue
Tant que la teste an avrai prise;[33]
Ja n'an ferai autre justise.'
(830–2)

'You shall follow me on foot,
and naked, until I have cut off
his head. I will admit no other
punishment than this, ever.'

And so Perceval comes to Arthur's castle. A charcoal-burner shows him the way. 'My fair and gentle friend, you will find King Arthur happy, and full of grief; happy because he has defeated Rion, King of the Islands, grieving because his companions have gone to their castles where they find better diversion' (844–58). Perceval, who had addressed this eloquent peasant in abrupt, discourteous fashion, gives him no thanks:

Li vaslez ne prise un denier
Les noveles au charbonier
Fors tant que an la voie antra,
Cele part ou il li mostra,
Tant que sor mer vit un chastel
Mout bien seant et fort et bel,
Et voit issir parmi la porte
Un chevalier armé, qui porte
Une cope d'or an sa main;
Sa lance tenoit et son frain
Et son escu an la senestre
Et la cope d'or an la destre,
Et ses armes bien li seoient,
Qui totes vermoilles estoient.
(859–72)

The young man does not care a cuss for the charcoal-burner's news, except that he took the path in the direction which he showed him until, beside the sea, he saw a castle well set up, both strong and handsome. And through the door he sees an armed knight come forth carrying in his hand a cup of gold. In his left hand he held his lance, his bridle and his shield, and in his right hand the cup of gold. And his arms which were entirely scarlet became him well.

The knight stops Perceval: 'Where are you going? Tell me.' 'To court to ask for these arms [of yours].' 'Young man. You do well. Go swiftly and return. And tell the evil king there that if he will not hold his land from me, he must either surrender it to me or send someone to defend it against me, for I declare it is mine' (884–93). The Scarlet Knight is playing the role of Meleagant. He claims Arthur's lands. He has removed Arthur's gold cup as a token of this sovereignty, which will be restored to Arthur by a youth who has no higher motive than lust for the arms of the Scarlet Knight.

Perceval finds the court in disarray, given to feckless talk, unconcerned about the humiliation of the King, his impotence against the Scarlet Knight, his grief for his absent comrades. Perceval's greeting finds no answer. The King remains slumped over the table in front of which the handsome youth with fire in his eyes sits waiting on his hunter:

Li rois panse et mot ne li sone.
'Par foi', dist li vaslez adonques,
'Cist rois ne fist chevalier onques.
Quant l'an n'an puet parole treire,
Comant porroit chevalier feire?'
(926–30)

The King is deep in thought and says no word. 'In faith', says the young man, 'this king never made a knight. If one cannot drag a word out of him, how could he make a knight?'

In a moment of high comedy, Perceval impatiently turns his horse, but so close to the King (*sanz nule fable*, 935) that the hunter knocks Arthur's woollen cap on to the table. Arthur raises his head, greets Perceval, apologises for his silence and tells his tale of woe: 'The Scarlet Knight not only took this gold cup from me, but poured all the wine in it over the Queen who, burning with mortal grief and anger, has gone to her room, and I may never see her alive again' (958–67).

Perceval is as little concerned with the King and the Queen as he was with his mother, the Damsel in the Tent, the charcoal-burner, or the Scarlet Knight:

Li vaslez ne prise une cive
Quanque li rois li dit et conte;
Ne de son duel ne de la honte
La reïne ne li chaut il.
(968–71)

The young man does not care a hoot about anything which the King may say to him or tell him about. He has no care for his grief or for the shame of the Queen.

After Arthur's quavering speech, Perceval's stance is epic.

'Feites moi chevalier', fet il,
'Sire rois, car aler m'an vuel.'
Cler et riant furent li oel[34]
An la teste au vaslet sauvage.
Nus qui le voit nel tient a sage;
Mes trestuit cil qui le veoient,
Por bel et por jant le tenoient.
(972–8)

'My liege and lord, make me a knight', he says, 'for I wish to be gone.' Bright and laughing were the eyes in the head of this young man from the forest. No one who sees him could think he was wise, but all who saw him thought him handsome and noble in his bearing.

Perceval spurns Arthur's invitation to dismount:

'Foi que je doi le Criator',
Fet li vaslet, 'biaus sire rois,
Ne serai chevaliers des mois,[35]
Se chevaliers vermauz ne sui.

'My fair liege and lord', says the youth, 'by the faith I owe my Creator, I will not be a knight for a long time to come,

Donez moi les armes celui	unless I am the Scarlet Knight.
Que j'ancontrai defors la porte,	Give me the arms of the man I
Qui vostre cope d'or an porte.'	met outside the gate who is
(994–1000)	carrying off your cup of gold.'

Kay mocks him in angry impotence: 'Friend you are in the right. Go and take his arms from him. You would act sensibly in so doing, since that is why you came here' (1003–7). Kay has no scruples about sending a fledgling to instant death. Arthur, murmuring Polonius-like saws, reproves Kay: 'The youth will be slain, and he could be trained. There is no virtue in a promise which cannot be granted' (1008–21).

As Perceval rides from the hall, he greets a damsel, who, not having laughed for six years, laughs and foretells he will be an Elect among knights:

'Vaslez, si tu viz par aage,	'Young man, if you live long
Je pans et croi an mon corage	enough, I think, and I believe
Qu'an trestot le monde n'avra,	in my heart, that in all the
N'il n'iert, ne l'an ne l'i savra	world there will not be, nor was
Nul meillor chevalier de toi.'	there ever any better knight
(1039–43)	than you, nor will such a one
	be known.'

Kay in anger strikes her face and knocks her down (1048–52). He kicks into the fire a fool who had prophesied that the girl would laugh only when she saw the knight who would become the flower of chivalry (1059–62).

The fool shouts his pain, the damsel weeps, as Perceval rides out of this scene of farce in which royalty has been insulted by the Scarlet Knight and by the inept Perceval, and has been scorned by uncaring, self-indulgent courtiers. This is the nadir of Arthur's court, threatened with destruction, bereft, as in Erec (6416–23), of the heroes who lend it substance. Arthur, fearing his wife, impotent to defend his sovereignty, capable of sage saws against Kay, incapable of saying 'Yes' to Perceval, is revealed in his human weakness as he mopes, woollen-capped, over his dinner table. He is the foil for the young, intent, self-interested Perceval, the child of nature void of courtly weakness, who will inadvertently save his realm.

The raw material for this scene may have come from the story which Chrétien says he is following, but his skill in blending the moods of comedy, of moralising, of grief, of epic courage, and of supernatural prophecy is all his own, comparable to similar rounded scenes in Lancelot (see p. 136). And Perceval's character becomes more complex. He is now an Elect as well as a dolt, a hero with fire in his eyes, seeking vaine gloire yet rescuing Arthur's lands and honour.

The burlesque combat which restores Arthur's sovereignty forms a fitting epilogue to the scene in the hall. The Scarlet Knight waits for 'chevalerie et avanture'. In naive tones Perceval orders him to lay down the arms which he covets:

> . . . 'Metez les jus
> Les armes, ne les portez plus;
> Que li rois Artus le vos mande.'
> (1083–5)

> 'Lay those arms down. Do not bear them any more, for Arthur the King orders you to do this.'

The Scarlet Knight, disdaining this unarmed youth, smites him across his shoulders with the haft of his lance. Perceval hurls a spear through his eye and brain, but has no idea how to remove helmet, sword and armour from the corpse. He will not exchange the tough clothes his mother gave him for those of the knight. But his companion, Yonez, lends a hand, and, armed and mounted on the warhorse, Perceval changes his role. He bestows largesse on Yonez, again with a burlesque note: 'My good friend, accept my hunter and take it with you. He is a very good horse and I give him to you, since I don't need him any more' (1193–6). 'And take this cup to the king with my greetings and tell the damsel whom Kay struck on the cheek that if I can, before I die, I will cause Kay such hurt that she will think herself avenged' (1197–203). Yonez recounts Perceval's triumph. Arthur accepts the cup, grieving that Kay's spite has driven Perceval away. The fool alone dances and rejoices, and foretells that when Perceval avenges the insult to the damsel, Kay will suffer a broken right arm – a fitting vengeance for the knight who has no caritas within him. The fool's words would have cost him his life, if Arthur had not protected him against Kay before lapsing into laments for the youth who is now lost to him. Knowing nothing of arms, such a lad must soon be slain. The world is upside-down. The prescient fool sees the nice youth as the Elect among knights; the king, concerned with the immediate present, fears the slaughtering of

the youth who could have been saved by training in knighthood: 'He will meet some knight who, to win his horse,
will not hesitate to maim (*maheignier*) him. He will quickly
kill or maim him for he will not know how to defend himself, he is so untutored and irrational' (1294–9):

> 'Que desfandre ne se savra,
> Tant est nices et bestïaus.'[36]   (1298–9)

As Perceval goes on his way, the dominant mood of the
narrative, which remains earthbound until the Procession
in the Grail castle, changes. Perceval's earliest adventures
were marked by the grief and disorder caused by impulsive
and irrational deeds. His egotism kills his mother and condemns the Damsel in the Tent to suffering, and knights to
death. Orguelleus de la Lande is a destroyer who will not
heed reason. Kay's hurt pride and violent impulses, the
seeds of his own disaster at the hands of Perceval, sow uncertainty and fear at court, and driving away the best knights,
who 'seek happier times' in their own castles, bring grief
and solitude to the King. For this Arthur blames Kay, as for
the harsh words which he believes alienated the young and
promising Perceval who does not return to court after his
triumph. But Perceval, with the clarity of the *nice*, untutored
mind had found Arthur wanting when *he would not speak* (924–
30) because of his hurt pride. In the second stage of his
education which he enters under the guidance of Gornemant,
the discord and folly of impulse which characterised his
actions and those of Arthur's court, are replaced by *savoir*, the
ability to use one's reason and to act accordingly. The principle of Gornemant's code is the search for *vaine gloire*, but
within the rational conventions of courtly and knightly
behaviour.

Gornemant, unlike Arthur, is a happy worldly man,
delighting in rich furs (1352), living in comfort in a strong
and beautiful castle beside the sea (1326–55). Perceval turns
to the left (1325) to arrive at a strong stone bridge, with the
drawbridge down, and here he finds a *prodon* or excellent
knight, carrying a swagger stick (1356–7), enjoying life
(1353) and waiting to welcome him. This is Gornemant.

In this worldly setting Perceval's conscience about his
mother comes to life, at first almost imperceptibly, then so

strongly that he leaves Gornemant in order to find her again. His mother is still in his mind as, in gauche manner, he greets the prodon on the bridge: 'My lord, my mother told me to greet people.' 'May God bless you, fair brother, whence come you?' 'From the court of King Arthur, who, may good fortune be with him, made me a knight' (1363–70). Gornemant who has recognised this youth as nice et sot 'uncourtly and foolish' (1365–6), evasively expresses doubts about this and a reproof that Perceval has not recognised Arthur's plight: 'As God may grant happiness to me, I did not think he would remember such things at this moment. I imagined the King would have other concerns than that of granting knighthood. Now tell me, gentle brother, who gave you these arms?' 'The King', says Perceval, 'gave them to me', and he tells the story of the Scarlet Knight, and his own new-found ability to ride his warhorse, like his hunter, up and down hill, and to take off and put on his arms and armour. 'What need brought you here?' 'My lord, my mother told me to go to knights of excellent virtues (prodomes) and take advice from them, for there is much gain to be had from them.' Gornemant, delighted at this, offers him lodging, provided 'you believe in the advice which your mother gave you and which I will give you' (1371–417).

Gornemant, unlike Kay, treats Perceval's innocence with courtesy. He teaches him how to use lance, shield and horse, and how, if his lance shatters in combat, he should fight with his sword, and not with his fists, as Perceval expected to do (1514–17). Having received this advice from a pro-dome, Perceval, obeying his mother's further instruction, now asks his name:

'Sire, ma mere m'anseigna	'My lord, my mother taught me
Qu'avuec home n'alasse ja	that I should never go on my
Ne conpeignie o lui n'eüsse	path with any man, nor bear
Granmant que son non ne seüsse;	him company for any length of
Et s'ele m'anseigna savoir,	time without knowing his name.
Je vuel le vostre non savoir.'	And since she taught me to
(1541–6)	know this, I wish to know your
	name.'

Yet Perceval, replete once more after a sumptuous meal, refuses Gornemant's invitation to stay for a month, or a year if he should wish. The thought of his mother lies heavily on his mind: 'My lord, I know not if I am near my mother's house, but I pray that God may lead me to her and that I may see her again, for I saw her fall unconscious in front of her door, at the end of the bridge' (1580–6). He acknowledges his blame for her collapse:

'Del duel de moi quant la leissai, 'It was for grief at my leaving
Cheï pasmee, bien le sai, her that she fell unconscious.
Et por ce ne porroit pas estre I know this well. And for this
Tant que je seüsse son estre, reason it is not possible for me
Que je feïsse lonc sejor, to make a long stay until I
Einz m'an irai demain au jor.' know how she is. Instead, I shall
  (1587–92) leave tomorrow morning.'

Gornemant does not destroy Perceval's illusion that he has already been knighted by Arthur, but makes him a knight, providing him with fresh clothes, which Perceval accepts in place of those his mother made. Young men arm him and Gornemant, doing as the Fisher King will later do, and as Arthur or Kay should have done, fixes his right spur for him and girds him with a sword:

Et li prodon l'espee a prise, And the excellent knight took a
Si li çainst et si le beisa sword and girded it around him,
Et dit que donee li a and embraced him and says that
La plus haute ordre avuec l'espee with this sword he has endowed
Que Deus et feite et comandee: him with the highest order that
C'est l'ordre de chevalerie, God has created and ordained.
Qui doit estre sanz vilenie. This is the order of chivalry
  (1632–8) which must be free from all
   baseness.

Gornemant teaches him the rules of his order. Do not knowingly kill a knight whom you have defeated. Always have mercy. Observe *mesure* in speech and silence.

Et gardez que vos ne soiiez 'And take heed that you be not
Trop parlanz ne trop noveliers:[37] too talkative, nor too inquisitive.
Nus ne puet estre trop parliers No man can talk too much
Que sovant tel chose ne die without saying many things
Qu'an li atort a vilenie, which will be turned to his
Et li sages dit et retret: discredit, and the sage says and
"Qui trop parole, pechié fet."' relates: "He sins who talks too
  (1648–54) much."'

Courtly care with words, to deprive the *losengiers* of their scandal-mongering, is balanced by its counterpart: 'Do not hold back when your advice or help are needed.' This is the affirmation of his mother's instruction to ask a companion his name.

'Por ce, biaus frere, vos chasti
De trop parler. Et si vos pri:
Se vos trovez home ne fame,
Ou soit dameisele ou soit dame,
Desconseilliez d'aucune rien,
Conseilliez les, si feroiz bien,
Se vos conseillier les savez
Et se le pooir an avez.'
                    (1655–62)

'For this reason, fair brother, I warn you not to talk too much. And yet I entreat you: should you find a man or woman, whether a damsel or a lady, who are in any way distraught, give them help and advice, and you will act well, if you know how to do this and are able to do it.'

Gornemant reinforces the mother's teaching about going to church:

'Volantiers alez au mostier
Proiier celui qui tot a fet,
Que de vostre ame merci et
Et qu'an cest siegle terriien
Vos gart come son crestiien.'
                    (1666–70)

'Go to church with a willing heart to pray to Him, the Creator of all, that He may have mercy on your soul and that He may protect you in this worldly life as He protects His Chrétien (or: His good Christian disciple).'

'Be blessed, fair sir, by all the apostles of Rome for this is just what I heard my mother tell me' (1672–4). Gornemant orders him to put away the things of a child, to never say more that his mother taught him this or that. He is now a knight and the source of his instruction in knighthood, if he is asked, is the knight who fastened his spur (1675–88). Gornemant raises his hand and salutes him as a knight, commending him to God:

Et dist: 'Biaus sire, Deus vos saut!
Alez a Deu, qui vos conduie.'
                    (1696–7)

And he said: 'Fair sir, may God grant you salvation! Go with God, that He may guide you.'

Gornemant's lessons in knightly and courtly behaviour will prove to be effective. But Gornemant fails to give the true spiritual guidance which Perceval so badly needs. He must help those in distress, must go to church with a good heart and pray for salvation. A knight may carry out these duties by rote as part of the code he lives by, or with *caritas*, a sense of the spiritual dignity within him, the need to understand and judge himself and so discover compassion towards others and unity with God. Gornemant's teaching, however well intentioned, points to the left hand path of knighthood, to Perceval's triumph at Arthur's court and his failure in the castle of the Fisher King.

Perceval, tutored and equipped, rides into the lonely forest. His quest to find his mother safe and well marks his progress from his earlier uncaring self. As a knight, he now knows he should have gone to her aid. In a Christian sense, his sin against her will oppress his spirit until it is redeemed. By analogy with his early tripartite adventures in the days of his niceté, he is led first to a damsel who lives, not in a tent but in the castle of Belrepeire, ironically 'beautiful dwelling'. And so begins the very long Blancheflor episode (1699–2932), a Gawain-type adventure in which Perceval triumphs in love and war, yet reveals the spiritual waste within him.

The contrast between Gornemant's castle and Belrepeire is grotesque in its sharpness. Belrepeire, for all its strength, is a Waste City with no easy welcome for the traveller. Outside the walls there is only sea, water and waste land (1708–9). The bridge, in contrast to Gornemant's solid construction, is so feeble that it scarcely bears his weight. The door is locked and nobody heeds his banging. At last, a damsel, thin and pale, appears at a window, and offers him hospitality, which, she fears, will be quite inadequate. The Waste City within is worse than the waste land without. The men-at-arms are wasting away through lack of food and their unceasing duties:

Et s'il ot bien defors trovee La terre gaste et escovee, Dedanz rien ne li amanda; Que par tot la ou il ala Trova anhermies les rues Et les meisons viez decheües; Qu'ome ne fame n'i avoit. <div align="center">(1749–55)</div>	And if he had found the land without the city waste and ravaged, there was nothing within to make up for this, for wherever he went he found the streets desolate and the houses old and decayed, for there was no man or woman to be seen there.

Two abbey churches, frightened nuns in the one, distraught monks in the other, lie with roofs open to the sky and their walls cracked and split. The houses are left open day and night. No mill turns, no oven cooks; in all the castle area, there was no bread or cake, or anything for sale (1756–70).

So Perceval enters this Waste Castle or *chastel gaste*, which is without bread or pasties, wine, cider or beer (1771–3).

Perceval is given a thin reception. The ritual cloak of welcome is grey and not scarlet, the stable is almost devoid of fodder. In a fine hall he is received by two knights (*prodome*) and a damsel. The two knights are white haired, yet without the afflictions of grief and sorrow they would have been in the full vigour of their age. In a startling moment of surprise and contrast, the damsel Blancheflor shines forth as she comes forward 'more graciously and splendidly attired than hawk or parrot' (1795–7). Her dress is of deep purple with stars of shimmering fur, her cloak of sable, black and white, embroidered with gold at the neck, her beauty supreme, her hair, shining like pure gold, undone, her eyes alive with laughter. Her speech is courtly and elegant, as she makes her apologies: 'Come and share what we have, and may God give you better tomorrow' (1835–45).

Perceval is struck dumb, as he is taken into a fine and large room, and is seated with this damsel on a bed with a cover of samite. 'Such looks', say the knights who are present. 'What grief if this knight is truly speechless, since he suits my lady as if God had made them for each other' (1860–74). But Perceval, in the first part of a double episode which will end in his silence in the Grail Castle, remembers Gornemant's advice and does not speak. So Blancheflor, like his cousin later in the story (3466–82), asks where he spent the night – a question more than usually important in a Waste Land. She praises Gornemant: 'May God in his majesty reward you for calling him a *prodome*':

'Et sachiez que je sui sa niece,	'And know that I am his niece,
Mes je nel vi, mout a grant piece,	but I have not seen him for a
Et, certes, puis que vos meüstes	very long time, and certainly I
De vostre ostel, ne coneüstes	know well that since you left
Plus prodome mien esciant.	your home, you have not known
Mout lié ostel et mout joiant	a knight of greater virtue. He
Vos fist, que il le sot bien feire	must have given you a pleasing
Come prodon et deboneire,	and joyful reception, for he was
Puissanz et aeisiez et riches.	well able to do this, being a
Mes ceanz n'a mes que sis miches,	knight of virtue and noble race,
Qu'uns miens oncles, qui est prïeus,	powerful, comfortable and rich.
Mout sainz hon et religïeus,	But here there are no more than

M'anvea por soper enuit,
Et un bocel plain de vin cuit.
De vitaille n'a plus ceanz
Fors un chevrel, qu'uns miens
   serjanz
Ocist hui main d'une saiete.'
     (1901–17)

six small loaves which an uncle of mine who is a prior, a very holy and religious man, sent to me for our supper this night, and a small keg full of mulled wine. We have within this castle no other food except for a young goat which one of my men shot this morning with an arrow.'

This is an important speech. The two areas of plentiful, easy living, and of Waste Land, hunger and fear, lie within a day's ride of each other, yet Gornemant, the epitome, plus prodome, of the excellent knight, is sealed in a separate world, in his comfortable castle and knightly ways. He bids Perceval name him and not his mother as his teacher, but he sends no food or help to his niece, who must depend on the alms of her other uncle, a saintly and religious man. Blancheflor's praise of Gornemant's excellence as a knight is followed immediately by her apologies for the meagre fare which she must offer Perceval. This juxtaposition is not accidental. Blancheflor does not criticise Gornemant, but Chrétien certainly does. His largess is of low degree, because self-indulgent. Like that of Alexander, it lacks caritas. Gornemant, like Gawain, is contained within the bounds of virtuous knighthood. He knows he should offer help to any man or woman in distress, but he does not go forth to find them. In this sense he is recreant, as Gawain was recreant when he failed to search for Lancelot imprisoned in the tower. Gornemant, keeping to his house, is decidedly not one of 'the gentle and the bold', as Marcabru had said, whom God desires to test in his cleansing place.

The men-at-arms and squires go on guard, and Perceval is put to bed with every comfort and delight 'save only the pleasure of a damsel if it should have pleased him, or of a lady, if there were the opportunity; but he knew nothing at all of such delight and gave it no thought at all' (1938–42). He sleeps, and Blancheflor stays awake, turning and twisting, knowing she has no defence against the army which will attack her. She covers her shift with a short cloak of scarlet silk and goes to confess her worries to her guest. Her limbs tremble and her body sweats for fear. She comes to his bed, and weeps and sighs, and bows down and kneels and weeps again, so that her tears wet his face and he wakes in amazement at seeing her kneeling as she embraces his head tightly (1945–76). Perceval acts with great kindness:

Et tant de corteisie fist	And he acted with such courtesy
Que antre ses braz la reprist	that forthwith he took her into
Maintenant et vers lui la trest.	his own arms and drew her
Si li dist: 'Bele, que vos plest?	towards him, and said to her:
Por qu'iestes vos venue ci?'	'Fair one, what is your pleasure?
(1977–81)	Why have you come here?'

Blancheflor asks him not to scorn her: 'Gentle knight, have mercy. I pray you, for the sake of God and His son, not to think ill of me for coming here. Although I am almost naked, I never intended any folly, wickedness or baseness in so doing. No one alive suffers more grief and misery than I. I will never see another night after this one, nor another day after tomorrow. I shall kill myself' (1982–98). Her castle has been besieged for a whole winter and a summer. Most of her knights are captured, her food exhausted. Tomorrow the castle must fall to Anguigneron, seneschal of Clamadeus des Isles, who lusts after her. But with a knife of pure steel she will kill herself. 'This I came to tell you. Now I will go and leave you to your rest' (2013–37).

The request for help accords so clearly with Gornemant's instructions that Perceval sees his duty. But he also acts with innate kindness:

. . . 'Amie chiere,	'Dear love. This is no time to be
Feites enuit mes bele chiere;	looking sad. Be comforted.
Confortez vos, ne plorez plus	Weep no more. Come close to
Et traiez vos vers moi ceisus,	me here, and take the tears from
S'ostez les lermes de voz iauz.	your eyes. God, if it pleases Him,
Deus, se lui plest, vos fera miauz	will give you better help
Demain que vos ne m'avez dit.	tomorrow than you have said.
Lez moi vos couchiez an cest lit;	Lie beside me in this bed for it
Qu'il est assez lez a oés nos.'	is wide enough for both of us.'
(2047–55)	

Holding her in his arms, he kisses her, and settles her under the cover gently and comfortably. And she allows herself to be kissed and finds it not unpleasant. So they lie all night beside each other, with their lips together until dawn (2058–66). Chrétien's description of love offered as comfort and companionship (solaz, 2067) leaves little doubt that

Perceval is obeying his mother's order: 'you may kiss a damsel, with her permission, but I forbid you anything more than this' (546–8).

In the morning she generously bids him farewell, but he intends to fight for her love, as Erec fought for Enide:

'Mes se je l'oci et conquier,
Vostre druërie requier
An guerredon, qu'ele soit moie;
Autres soudees n'an prandroie.'
(2103–6)

'But if I slay and conquer him, I seek as my reward to have your love as my very own. I would accept no other payments for this.'

Blancheflor is willing to grant him her love, but not in this way. He is too young in years and body to risk death from such a hardened warrior. But Perceval insists and fights for love, for Blancheflor's life, and the liberty of her imprisoned knights. Having defeated Anguigneron, who addresses him scornfully as *vaslet*, he spares his life, as Gornemant had instructed him, and orders him to Arthur's court as the prisoner of the Damsel who Laughed and evidence to reassure her that he will avenge the blow which Kay struck (2107–323).

Joy in Belrepeire is unbounded, although Perceval must excuse himself for not returning – in Celtic fashion – with the head of his adversary: 'I would have liked to kill him, but once I had the upper hand, I would not have had enough goodness within me, had I not granted him mercy' (2347–50). Perceval is no longer the youth who in animal high spirits killed the Scarlet Knight for his armour; and in love he has progressed far from his assault on the damsel in the tent. Blancheflor greets him joyfully:

Et jusqu'an ses chanbres le mainne
Por reposer et aeisier.
De l'acoler et del beisier
Ne li fet ele nul dangier:
An leu de boivre et de mangier
Joënt et beisent et acolent
Et deboneiremant parolent.
Mes Clamadeus folie panse. . . .
(2356–63)

And takes him right into her rooms for his rest and comfort. She does not spare her embraces and kisses. Instead of eating and drinking they play and kiss and embrace with soft words. But Clamadeus has evil and violent thoughts in his mind. . . .

So the second part of this war begins and Perceval defends the besieged citadel, as Gawain in comic-opera fashion will defend Escavalon. Hostile forces which enter the city are annihilated, and the opportune arrival of a food ship pro-

vides joy and abundance, as Clamadeus settles down outside
the wall.

Or se puet li vaslez deduire	Now can the young man find
Delez s'amie tot a eise :	delight without hindrance beside
Cele l'acole, et il la beise,	his love. She embraces him, he
Si fet li uns de l'autre joie,	kisses her and they find joy in
La sale ne rest mie quoie,	each other. And the hall is not
Einçois i a mout joie et bruit :	silent; it rings with the happy
Por le mangier font joie tuit . . .	sounds of the joy which the
(2574–80)	food has brought them all.

Clamadeus challenges the 'Scarlet Knight' (2596) to single
combat. Blancheflor, grieving, tries to dissuade Perceval with
entreaty and love :

Grant douçor qu'ele li feisoit ;	. . . the great gentleness which
Car a chascun mot le beisoit	she showed him, for at each
Si doucemant et si soëf	word she kissed him so sweetly
Que ele li metoit la clef	and softly that she set the key of
D'amor an la serre del cuer.	love in the lock of his heart.
(2633–7)	

Perceval triumphs. He orders the arrogant Clamadeus to
offer homage to the Damsel who Laughed, together with his
promise to avenge the insult inflicted on her by Kay.
Clamadeus must free his prisoners, and never again approach Belrepeire with an armed force.

Base violence is vanquished, the Waste City is filled with
joy, delight, dancing, and prayers of thanks :

De joie bruit tote la sale	The hall of the castle and the
Et li ostel as chevaliers ;	dwellings of the knights resound
As chapeles et as mostiers	with joy. In the chapels and
Sonent de joie tuit li sain,	churches all the bells peal their
N'il n'i a moinne ne nonain	joy. No monk or nun who fails
Qui Damedeu ne rande graces.	to give thanks to God. Through
Par les rues et par les places	the streets and squares, men and
Vont carolant totes et tuit :	women all go dancing. Now was
Ore ot el chastel grant deduit ;	there great delight in the castle
Que nus nes assaut ne guerroie.	at their freedom from attack and
(2738–47)	war.

All seems to be right with the world, as it was when Erec
defeated Mabonagrain. Belrepeire, with its full complement
of knights, turns from Grief of the Court to Joy. The Waste
City enjoys abundance and the assurance of peace.

Skilfully Chrétien digresses as he follows Clamadeus to

Arthur's Whitsun court at Dinasdaron.[38] Here the Joy of the
Court balances that at Belrepeire:

. . . la reïne sist dejoste Le roi Artu au chief d'un dois, S'i ot contes et dus et rois, Mout ot reïnes et contesses, Et fu aprés totes les messes Que venu furent del mostier Les dames et li chevalier. (2786–92)	. . . the Queen sat beside King Arthur at the head of a dais, and there were counts there, and dukes and kings, and there were many queens and countesses. And it was after all the services of mass that the ladies and knights had come from the church.

Fortune's wheel has turned. All is apparent serenity, the
world is in order, Arthur's sovereignty, so feeble when
threatened by the Scarlet Knight, is now assured. Even Kay,
a *losengier* perhaps taken from life as well as the source story
(2806–7), fair-haired, with clothes of fine silks and a belt
of pure gold, cannot still this joy with his spite. Perceval,
who had failed to see Arthur's need, as he will fail to see
that of the Fisher King, has defeated the forces of destruction,
and has restored joy to Arthur and his court, a joy now reinforced by the arrival of Clamadeus, his submission and
announcement of Perceval's *desfi* against Kay (2862–3) for
the shame he caused the Damsel who Laughed. This shame
is not the artificial shame of the world which Lancelot
accepted with humility, but the shame inflicted by unjust
violence which must be corrected if order is to persist:

Que mout est mauvés qui oblie, S'an li fet honte ne leidure; Dolors trespasse, et honte dure An home viguereus et roide, Mes el mauvés muert et refroide. (2902–6)	For that man is recreant[39] who forgets an act of shame or out- rage which is done to him. Grief passes away, and shame endures in a man of vigour and principle. But in the unprincipled man it dies and grows cold.

Skilfully Chrétien returns to Perceval. He could remain in
happiness with Blancheflor but he is impelled to continue
the Quest for his mother. To all who entreat him to stay,
he gives a clear promise:

Mes n'a mestier quanque il dient Fors qu'il lor met an covenant, S'il trueve sa mere vivant, Que avuec lui l'an amanra Et d'iluec an avant tandra	But whatever they say has no effect save that he promises them that should he find his mother alive, he will bring her with him and from then on will hold

La terre, ce sachent de fi,	and rule that land – let them be
Et se ele est morte, autresi.	sure of this in their minds, and
(2926–32)	if she is dead, he will act in the
	same way.

This promise he repeats to all the monks and all the nuns who are in the procession, worthy of Ascension Day, which accompanies his departure: 'It is no wonder that we grieve, since you brought us from exile back to our houses.' 'Weep no more. I will return, as God may guide me. To give oneself to grief is useless. Is it not right for me to go to see my mother who lived alone in the wood which is called the Waste Forest? I will return, whether she is alive or not, and in this I will not fail whatever may befall. If she is alive, I will make her a nun in your church. And if she is dead, you will offer a Mass for her soul every year so that God may place her with all pious souls in the bosom of Abraham. My lord monks, and you, fair ladies, there is no cause for your grief, for, as God may bring me back, I will offer you great benefits for her soul's sake' (2946–71).

Perceval takes leave not of Blancheflor, his profane love, but of the Church in Belrepeire, which he propitiates in order to secure peace for his mother's soul in Heaven. This is the transaction of a knight who supports the Church in exchange for benefits for his family and himself. It is no evidence that Perceval has religious convictions, that he has worshipped in church, as his mother and Gornemant bade him do, and has 'prayed to the Creator of all things to have mercy on his soul and to keep him in this earthly world as his Christian follower' (1667–70). Perceval will reach this stage of his spiritual development under the guidance of the Hermit. But the importance given to the role of the Church is significant. It comes at the end of the episode of Belrepeire which contains within itself the whole theme of material devastation and rebirth. The lust of Clamadeus des Isles and his self-willed violence have laid waste a city and the land around, turning joy to grief and desolation. In the face of such destruction, courtly knighthood, turned in on itself and stay-at-home, is impotent (Arthur) or indifferent (Gornemant and the knights who have abandoned Arthur's court). Blancheflor resists amidst desolation, as does her uncle the prior who provides her with food. With two knightly victories and the advent of the food ship, Perceval turns material disaster to prosperity and is acclaimed by populace and Church as Erec and Enide were at their coronation. But Perceval, having restored the Joy of the Court, cannot settle down like Erec to rule the lands which he is offered. Higher destiny and uneasy conscience summon him to leave Blancheflor and the joys of mutual love. He must find his mother, and it is for her sake especially that he speaks kindly to the monks and nuns, seeking her benefit and future happiness when he shall have returned with her to Belrepeire.

Perceval has reached a high point of worldly excellence. He has won Blancheflor's love, he has defeated Clamadeus, redeemed the Waste City, and restored prisoners and Joy to the land. He has been fêted by the nuns, whom he sees as 'beles dames', and by the monks from the abbeys of Belrepeire. The Waste Land, void of human life, into which he now rides, symbolises his spiritual darkness which is lightened only by concern for his mother and his prayer that he may find her alive and well, if this should be God's will (2976–84). Perceval's initial spiritual stirrings lead him to the episode of the Grail Castle which is concerned with the spiritual world of waste land and regeneration, as Belrepeire had been with the material.

Perceval is stopped by a river, and again addresses God: 'Lord and mighty God, if I could cross this water, I would, I know, find out on the other side whether my mother still lives' (2990–3). He hails a man fishing in mid-stream with hook and line. 'There is no boat large enough to take your horse', says the fisherman, 'no ferry or bridge or ford.' Symbolically Perceval cannot cross as a mounted knight. The implication is that a spiritual barrier has now to be crossed. If he climbs through a cleft rock, he will find in a valley the dwelling of the fisherman and there he may lodge for the night. Perceval sees nothing from the hill top but earth and sky. He has no faith, no inner eye, he reacts with distrust and anger, reverts to niceté:

. . . 'Que sui je venuz querre?	'What have I come here to find?
La musardie et la bricoingne.	Deceit and fraud. May God inflict
Deus li doint hui male vergoingne	grievous shame on the man who
Celui qui ça m'a anvoiié,	sent me here. He certainly gave

253

Si m'a il or bien avoiié
Que il me dist que je verroie
Meison quant ça amont seroie!'
(3040–6)

me good directions saying that
when I arrived up here, I would
see a house.'

What he has missed is the indication of the house, the tip
of a tower which appears before him in the valley, as he
curses the fisher. Now 'he praises him, no longer calls him
cheat, disloyal, lying' (3061–3). But Perceval has no regrets
for his harsh words. He is received and cared for, and brought
into the great hall, where in front of a large fire set between
four columns of bronze, a handsome *prodome*, attired in mul-
berry-black fur, reclines on his side.

This lord, as Perceval will learn from his cousin, is the
Fisher King, the fisherman who offered him lodging:

Quant li sire le vit venant,
Si le salua maintenant
Et dist: Amis, ne vos soit grief,
Se ancontre vos ne me lief;
Que je n'an sui pas aeisiez.'
(3105–9)

When the lord saw him
approaching, he greeted him
forthwith, and said: 'Friend, may
it not displease you if I do not
rise to greet you, for I am not
able to do so with any ease.'

This is Perceval's test, and he fails it as Gawain failed the test
of the cart. He shows as little feeling under his courtly
façade as he did when he cursed the Fisher King and felt no
regret for his violence.

'Por Deu, sire, or vos an teisiez',
Fet il, 'qu'il ne me grieve point,
Se Deus joie et santé me doint.'
(3110–12)

'In God's name, my lord, say no
more of this, for it displeases
me not at all, as God may grant
me happiness and health.'

The Fisher King is all that Perceval is not. He appreciates
Perceval's gauche diffidence, knows he is ill at ease and
worries about this. He feels compassion for the young
knight. Chrétien emphasises this by using *grieve* yet once
more, not in its social but its literal sense:

Li prodon tant por lui se grieve
Que tant come il puet se sozlieve,
Et dist: 'Amis, ça vos traiiez:
Ja de moi ne vos esmaiiez,
Si seez ci seüremant
Lez moi; que je le vos comant.'
(3113–18)

The wise knight makes such an
effort [is so grieved] for his
sake that he raises himself up as
much as he can: 'Friend, come
over here. Be not afraid of me,
be assured and sit here in
comfort beside me. This I bid
you do.'

'Whilst they were talking' (3130) a young man enters the hall with a sword sent by the niece of the Fisher King, a wondrous sword, to be given to a knight who will use it well (3130–57). The Fisher King presents it to Perceval:

... 'Biaus sire, ceste espee
Vos fu jugiee et destinee,
Et je vuel mout que vos l'aiiez;
Mes ceigniez la, si la traiiez.'
(3167–70)

'Fair lord, this sword was destined and intended for you. I greatly desire that it should be yours. But gird it on, and draw it.'

With this sword, the Fisher King recognises Perceval's destiny as an Elect, a member of the Grail lineage who will accomplish the highest tasks of knighthood. But Perceval will not yet live up to these expectations. Figuratively he still wears the sword of Gornemant. Repeating the phrase 'While they were talking, a young man came in', Chrétien moves into the scene which bursts on the narrative with enigmatic, unearthly brilliance:

Que qu'il parloient d'un et d'el,
Uns vaslez d'une chanbre vint,
Qui une blanche lance tint
Anpoigniee par le mileu,
Si passa par antre le feu
Et çaus qui el lit se seoient.
Et tuit cil de leanz veoient
La lance blanche et le fer blanc,
S'issoit une gote de sanc
Del fer de la lance an somet,
Et jusqu'a la main au vaslet
Coloit cele gote vermoille.
(3190–201)

Whilst they were talking of this and that, a young man came out of a room holding a white lance which he gripped in its middle, and he passed across between the fire and those who were sitting on the bed. And all those who were there saw the white lance, and its white blade, and from the very tip of the blade there came forth a drop of blood, and this scarlet drop flowed down as far as the young man's hand.

Perceval remembers Gornemant's advice not to talk too much or be inquisitive. Fearing to be thought churlish, he does not ask why the lance bleeds (3202–12). Two other young men enter with candlesticks of pure gold, worked in enamel:

An chascun chandelier ardoient
Dis chandoiles a tot le mains.
Un graal[40] antre ses deus mains
Une dameisele tenoit,
Qui avuec les vaslez venoit,
Bele et jante et bien acesmee.
(3218–23)

In each candlestick there burned ten candles at the very least. A damsel, who accompanied the young men, of fair and gracious looks and in handsome attire, was holding a grail in her two hands.

255

Brightness fills the hall:

Quant ele fu leanz antree	When she had entered there
Atot le graal qu'ele tint,	together with the grail which she
Une si granz clartez i vint	held, there came a brightness so
Qu'ausi perdirent les chandoiles	great, that the candles lost their
Lor clarté come les estoiles	brilliance as do the stars when
Quant li solauz lieve ou la lune.	the sun rises, or the moon.

(3224–9)

A silver *tailleor* or cutting-board is carried by another damsel behind the grail:

Et li vaslez les vit passer	And the young man saw them pass
Et n'osa mie demander	and did not dare to ask to whom
Del graal cui l'an an servoit.	the grail was being served.

(3243–5)

'for always he carried in his heart the words of the wise knight, and yet I fear he was wrong', says Chrétien, 'for I have heard it said that one can as easily be too silent as too talkative' (3246–51).

The meal which is now served to Perceval has great significance. A young man cuts venison on the silver carving-dish:

Et les morsiaus lor met devant	And he places the pieces of meat
Sor un gastel qui fu antiers.	before them on a platter of bread
Et li graaus andemantiers	which was unbroken. And
Par devant aus retrespassa,	meanwhile the grail, in its turn,
Et li vaslez ne demanda	passed in front of them and the
Del graal cui l'an an servoit.	young man did not ask to whom
	the grail was being served.

(3288–93)

The contents of the serving dish or grail shining with brightness could scarcely be brought into more open juxtaposition with the unbroken platters of bread with food on them. What *is* in the grail? The grail is uncovered, yet there is no ordinary substantial food in it. That the contents must then offer spiritual sustenance, is the next immediate prompting of the imagination, and in fact they are, as Perceval will learn from the Hermit, the sacramental Host of the Mass which keeps 'alive' the father of the Fisher King. With this suggested antithesis of carnal and spiritual sustenance Chrétien highlights Perceval's moment of crisis, his weakness and failure. As he did in the 'False Mass' in the tent, and earlier in the scene with his mother, Perceval busies himself with food for his body. He fails to answer the summons of the brightness and richness of the grail and its seeming emptiness, and real, immediate desire to know the name of its recipient slips away from him:

Qu'a chascun més don l'an servoit
Par devant lui trespasser voit
Le graal trestot descovert,[41]
Mes il ne set cui l'an an sert,
Et si le voldroit mout savoir.

(3299–303)

For as each course is served to him, he sees the grail, completely uncovered, passing before him; but he does not know to whom it is served, though he wants very much to know this.

For Perceval, the grail and its paucity of content is an item of curiosity which appears to belong to the feast he enjoys. He has no inkling of the allegorical dichotomy of the two meals or of the evanescent quality of the castle itself. He will put the question to one of the young men at court, in the morning, before taking his leave (3304–9). He pushes this matter away and devotes himself to the feast of food and drink fit for a king, or count or emperor (3310–33). As Chrétien says: *s'antant a boivre et a mangier* (3311) where *s'antant a* can have the additional ironical meaning of higher aspiration.

In the morning the castle is still intact but as desolate as the Waste City. All the rooms are locked. Perceval is excluded. He has no alternative but to leave through the entrance door to the hall. His horse is saddled outside, his lance and shield against a wall. That he has intruded into the plane of the supernatural never occurs to him: 'The young men of the court have gone to the forest to check their traps. I will follow and ask why the lance bleeds (3399) and to whom the grail is being carried' (3401). The drawbridge is lifted as he approaches, and only with an extraordinary leap do horse and rider escape. Perceval has failed and been rejected. He shouts his need to put the two questions, but no voice replies.

The scene of the Grail Procession, the most remarkable of any scene in Chrétien's romances, achieves mystery through the anonymity of its characters and objects. Perceval and the Fisher King have not yet been named, the lance and grail have no specific identity, and the castle, as Perceval learns from his cousin, is both there and not there. Chrétien speaks only of *li prodon, li vaslez, une espee, une pucele, une blanche lance.*

257

un *graal*. On one plane, he uses a narrative device which allows him to mystify his audience and gradually reveal the meaning of this central scene, as the story unfolds. We know, from troubadour poetry, that such a riddle-like form, concealing a hidden truth, often of universal significance, had great appeal for a courtly audience.[42] On another level, the lack of a name implies a lack of identity. Each character and object is presented as a material being or thing, but their inner significance, the deeper, 'realist' sense of their existence, is not disclosed. The reader or the audience see the Grail Procession through Perceval's self-interested outward eye, and through the devices of irony, contrast and juxtaposition are shown, according to their degree of perceptiveness, the gulf between Perceval's 'surface' values and those which are implicit in the life of the Grail Castle, the Fisher King, the Grail and the Lance. Though nothing is stated, all is suggested.

At this stage in the romance, the Grail Procession is not intended to be seen as part of a Celtic or of a Christian tradition. By introducing a supernatural happening in sharp contrast to the earthbound episode at Belrepeire, Chrétien startles and mystifies his audience. He also widens the meaning of Perceval's life and destiny. The moment has come for Perceval to transcend the worldly view of life and his clumsy efforts to accommodate himself to this. He will become increasingly aware of the universal truths which he has glimpsed and failed to recognise in the Grail Castle. His progress, as an individual, from ignorance to understanding of the world is no longer an end in itself. Nor is his *niceté*, his self-willed boorishness allied to innate kindness. The narrative is not now concerned with the qualities which he lacks but with his need to overcome this lack and to grow in virtue beyond that of the ordinary worldly knight. The Grail and the values it represents exemplify his weaknesses as the Lion exemplified those of Yvain, and, to a lesser degree, the Cart those of Lancelot. Although the Grail and its values and the Lance will become part of Perceval's imagination and being, and offer an ideal to which he must aspire, they cannot, as the lion did with Yvain, go with him and share his physical adventures. Perceval's quest is not so much a moral quest, as Yvain's was, but a spiritual quest of the highest degree.

Until his heart and mind are attuned to the higher qualities of Lance and Grail, until he moves beyond the plane of physical adventure and knightly violence, he will find no answer to his questions about their function.

The adventure in the castle of the Fisher King takes place out of time and space. For a moment it lifts Perceval out of his worldly, physical being, then returns him to stock. In so doing, it implants in him the direction of his future progress, and clarifies the dichotomy within him. He is physical being, in tune with nature, given to the *folie* of impulse, especially the desire for food, listening to higher instruction, lacking the *savoir* to understand it and apply it to his life. Paradoxically, he is also an Elect, a member of the Grail lineage, innately sympathetic to its spiritual ideas. This latent nobility of spirit is obscurely evident in his sense of guilt towards his mother. It appears again in the genuine, unforced kindness he offers to Blancheflor, and, after his departure from her, when as he crosses the waste land which is a reflection of the desolation within him, he suddenly receives the vision and the adventure of the castle of the Fisher King. He cannot adapt his manner and actions to those of the Fisher King, and to the summons of the Lance and Grail. But his recognition of the need to discover their meaning changes the direction of his life. The old Perceval gradually gives way to the new Perceval as the *voluntas propria* of his physical being gives way to the awareness of *caritas* and submission to God. The progress of this change is slow and portrayed enigmatically. Perceval's conflict between his two selves will lead him to madness, before, with the guidance of the Hermit, he enters his new self completely. It is especially in the depiction of the two selves of Perceval and his madness that the influence of *Yvain* can be detected. This process in *Perceval* is revealed in a more concealed, allusive and suggestive way even than in *Yvain*. Yet Perceval's ultimate destiny and the peace which he seeks is on a higher plane altogether than that of Yvain.

The Procession in the Grail Castle brings into focus this conflict between the physical and social constraints which imprison Perceval, and his intuitive response to a higher cause which will eventually free his spirit. Perceval fails the test of the Lance and Grail because his *niceté*, his outward eye and the *voluntas propria* and *consilium proprium* of his worldly being hold him down. He fails because, lacking *caritas*, he cannot respond to the plight of the Fisher King and succour him with the key question, which in Celtic tradition was used to break a spell, and on the Christian level will reveal the *sen* of the romance. Perceval's lack of *caritas* on the lower plane of good feeling and deeds towards others is part of his failure to know himself, and to recognise his sin towards his mother. This burden of 'mortal sin' which deprives him of grace on the Christian plane, will be removed only through repentance and absolution from the Hermit. Lacking grace he cannot, in Christian terms, be the Elect who will restore health and contentment to the Fisher King. Before him there now lies the quest for self-knowledge and humility. With these he can find the spiritual heritage of the Grail lineage, an understanding of the spiritual meaning of life and the search for union with God.

Perceval's progress is slow but perceptible in the next series of triple episodes in which he is forced to recognise his sins of omission and commission towards the Fisher King, his mother, the Damsel in the Tent and Blancheflor. The series begins and ends with the castigation of his faults, in private, from his cousin, who makes him aware of his identity, and, in public, from the Hideous Damsel who turns him from the life of worldly triumph to the desolate quest for the meaning of Lance and Grail, the values of the Fisher King, and his own salvation.

Perceval remains blithely impervious to his dismissal and exclusion from the locked and 'empty' Grail Castle. On a track, in the forest, he comes upon a damsel, holding in her arms the headless corpse of her lover:

. . . il vit par avanture	It happened that he saw beneath
Une pucele soz un chesne,	an oak a damsel crying aloud
Qui crie et plore et se desresne	and weeping in extreme
Come cheitive, dolereuse:	wretchedness and grief: 'Alas',
'Lasse!', fet el, 'maleüreuse!	she says, 'how unhappy I am!
Con de pute ore je fui nee!	In what a foul hour was I born!
L'ore que je fui anjandree	I curse the hour when I was
Soit maudite et que je nasqui.	conceived, and when I was
. . . Je ne deüsse pas tenir	born . . . Had it pleased God,
Mon ami mort, se Deu pleüst;	I should not have had to hold

Qu'assez miauz esploitié eüst,   my dead love, for God would
S'il fust vis, et je fusse morte.'   have achieved far more, if he
     (3430–7, 3440–3)   were alive and I were dead.'

For Chrétien, love which desires death in the company of
the dead beloved is true love, as in the case of Enide, Cliges,
the lion, Lancelot and Guenevere. Perceval shows no feeling,
but he asks a question: 'Who killed this knight?' The damsel
replies with even more questions: 'Where did you and your
horse, shining with food and good care, spend the night?
There is after all no proper dwelling for twenty-five leagues
in the direction from which you have come'. Perceval is
complacent:

'Par foi', fet il, 'bele, je oi   'In faith, fair one', he says,
Tant d'eise anuit con je plus poi,   'I was cared for last night as
Et s'il i pert, c'est a bon droit.'   comfortably as I could possibly
     (3483–5)   be, and if that is apparent to
     you, it is with good cause.'

In his ignorance, he adds: 'You cannot know this part of the
country well, for I was better lodged than I could be anywhere else.'

'Ha! sire, geüstes vos donques   'Ah! my lord, did you then find
Chiés le riche roi Pescheor?'   a bed in the house of the rich
'Pucele, par le Sauveor,   Fisher King?' 'Damsel, by our
Ne sai s'il est peschierre ou rois, Lord and Saviour, I know not
Mes mout est riches et cortois.' if he is a fisher or a king, but
     (3494–8)   he is very rich and courtly.'

Perceval shows no concern for the ill-health of the Fisher
King. The damsel tells him how he was injured:

'Mes il fu an une bataille   'He was wounded in a battle and
Navrez et maheigniez sanz faille totally maimed so that he can
Si que puis eidier ne se pot,   no longer lead his own life.
Qu'il fu navrez d'un javelot   He was wounded by a javelin
Parmi les hanches anbedeus,   between his two thighs, and he
S'an est ancor si angoisseus   is still in such great pain
Qu'il ne puet sor cheval monter.' that he cannot mount a horse.'
     (3509–15)

'You speak true', says Perceval, 'for he told me to sit beside
him and not to be affronted if he did not rise to greet me!'
'When you sat beside him, tell me, did you see the lance
with the point which bleeds though there is no flesh or
open wound to be seen?'

'Did I see it? Yes, in faith.'
'Did you ask why it was bleeding?'
'I never said a word about it?'
'As God help me, know that you acted very wrongly.'
Naively Perceval answers her catechism about the grail, the
candles and the carving dish (3545–67).

'Demandastes vos a la jant
Quel part il aloient einsi?'
'Onques de ma boche n'issi.'
'Si m'aït Deus, de tant vaut pis.
Comant avez vos non, amis?'
Et cil qui son non ne savoit
Devine et dit que il avoit
Percevaus Li Galois a non,
N'il ne set s'il dit voir ou non.
(3568–76)

'Did you ask the people there
where they were going in this
fashion?' 'My lips were sealed.'
'As God may help me, that is
much worse. What is your
name, good friend?' And he who
did not know his name knows
intuitively and says he was
called Perceval the Welshman –
and he knows not whether he is
speaking the truth or not.

The damsel, knowing his name, realises the enormity of his
failure. With no concern for his worldly fame, she is deeply
interested in his destiny as an Elect. In anger she attacks him:

'Tes nons est changiez, biaus amis.'
'Comant?' – 'Percevaus li cheitis!
Ha! Percevaus maleüreus,
Con fus or mesavantureus
Quant tu tot ce n'as demandé!'
(3581–5)

'Your name has changed, fair
friend?' 'How?' – 'Perceval the
wretched! Alas! Perceval the
unhappy; how ill-fated you
were just now not to have
asked all those questions!'

Had he asked, the king would have been cured, would have
ruled his lands with great goodness and benefit to all. Now
Perceval and others must suffer great sorrows:

'Por le pechié, ce saches tu,
De ta mere t'est avenu;
Qu'ele est morte de duel de toi.'
(3593–5)

'You should know that this has
happened because of your sin
against your mother, for she is
dead from the grief you caused
her.'

The damsel, his cousin, brought up with him as a child by
his mother, generously extends to Perceval the love and
grief she feels for his mother and her dead lover:

'Ne ne me poise mie mains
De ce qu'einsi t'est mescheü
Que tu n'as del graal seü
Qu'an an fet et cui an le porte
Que de ta mere qui est morte,

'I do not grieve less for the
mischance that has befallen you
in that you did not know what
is done with the grail nor to
whom it is carried, any less than

262

Perceval

Ne qu'il fet de cest chevalier
Que j'amoie et tenoie chier.'
(3602–8)

I grieve for your mother who is dead or for what has happened to this knight whom I loved and held dear.'

Perceval is direct in his questions:

'Se ce est voirs que dit m'avez,
Dites moi comant le savez.'
'Je le sai', fet la dameisele,
'Si veraiemant come cele
Qui an terre metre la vi.'
'Ore et Deus de s'ame merci',
Fet Percevaus, 'par sa bonté!'
(3613–19)

'If what you have told me is true, tell me how you know it.' 'I know it', says the damsel, 'as truly as she who saw her laid in earth.' 'Now may God in his goodness have mercy on her soul', says Perceval.

Perceval, through knowing his name, is aware of his identity as a person, but he still sees life as a flat surface. At the news of his mother's death he shows no guilt or remorse. What bothers him is the effect that her death will have on his actions. His quest to find her has ended abruptly. His future appears aimless, desolate. Instinctively, he knows he must have a higher quest than that of fighting and *vaine gloire*:

'Felon conte m'avez conté.
Et puis que ele est mise an terre,
Que iroie je avant querre?
Que por rien nule n'i aloie
Fors por li que veoir voloie.
Autre voie m'estuet tenir.'
(3620–5)

'This is a terrible tale you have told me. Since she is placed in earth, what shall I now go forward to seek? I was going onwards for no other reason than for her whom I desired to see. I must take another path.'

'Come with me', he says to his cousin, 'this man, who lies here dead, will never more be of use to you' (3626–29):

'Les morz as morz, les vis as vis.' (3630)
'Let the dead go with the dead, the live with the living.'

'It is folly for you to keep watch over this dead man. Let us follow the man who killed him. If I catch him, he will make me yield, or I will defeat him, I promise you' (3631–7).

Perceval is direct, purposeful, intent on action. He offers his cousin no word of sympathy or *caritas*. He is concerned with the next thing to be done. In the tent it was to eat a pasty and drink wine. In this case it is the spontaneous desire to seek knightly violence and revenge, a path which will confront him more closely with his former sins. Perceval

263

cannot grieve because he has not loved. His cousin on the other hand has everything he lacks: love, feeling, grief, knowledge of the Grail and the Lance, of Perceval and the Fisher King, the disasters which will befall them because the questions were not asked. She foretells that his new sword will break and betray him in battle (3660–3). She believes in her feelings: she will not go with him:

Et cele qui ne puet refraindre	And she, unable to restrain the
Le grant duel qu'ele a a[n] son cuer	great sorrow within her heart,
Li dist: 'Biaus amis, a nul fuer	said: 'Fair friend, in no way
Ansanble o vos ne m'an iroie,	could I go with you, in your
Ne de lui ne me partiroie	company, nor could I leave (my
Tant que je l'eüsse anterré.'	dead love) until I have buried
(3638–43)	him.'

The damsel cannot go with Perceval because she has reached the state to which he must aspire. She loves with true feeling, she is contemplative and what the troubadours would call 'whole' or *entiers* in her awareness of the many planes of life. Perceval, unfeeling, is 'active', surface-bound and so 'fragmented'. He spurs onwards and overtakes a thin and weary palfrey, trembling with starvation, a prey for the attendant dogs (3691–711). The catalogue of the palfrey's wretchedness is the realisation of the disaster, the *ennui* which his cousin foretold, and which Perceval has caused through his lack of feeling, his self-will and lack of *caritas*. For the damsel on the palfrey, wearing a torn dress, roughly mended, and yet not enough to conceal her breasts, is the Damsel of the Tent:

Et sa charz paroit dehachiee	And her flesh, which seemed to
Ausi con s'il fust fet de jarse;	be cut and rasped as if by a
Que ele l'ot crevee et arse	lancet, was broken and burnt by
De chaut, de halle et de gelee.	the heat, by sunburn and frost.
(3726–9)	

Her tears fall ceaselessly on her breast and knees, as she rides along. At Perceval's approach, she tries in vain to cover her naked body with the scraps of her dress. She asks God for death or deliverance from the knight who gives her no mercy, will neither kill her nor let her escape.

The girl's human desolation is directly caused by the self-pride and possessiveness of her knight, who is the extreme example of the *voluntas propria* which made the young knight in *Lancelot* lust after the Fourth Damsel. Such also was the lust of the knights who fought Erec for Enide. This violence which creates a continuous chain of destruction and vendetta, was begun in this case by the brash, wooden-hearted actions of Perceval. When Perceval defeats this knight, he will, on the allegorical plane, have defeated one aspect of his former self.

The damsel recognises Perceval, and has his measure: 'May your heart have all it would wish; yet I have no right to such things' (3783–4). Perceval, not recognising the girl, blushes for shame at this sharpness. 'I do not believe I ever saw you before, nor did you any harm' (3788–90). The damsel will not reveal her identity: 'You did, for I am so wretched and full of sorrow that no man may greet me':

'D'angoisse me covient suer   'I must sweat for terror when
Quant nus m'areste ne esgarde.'   any man stops me or looks at
    (3794–5)   me.'

'Be quiet, and flee from here', she says. 'Leave me in peace. Sin makes you stay. Flee and you will do well' (3808–11). But Perceval must know why. Orguelleus de la Lande, her knight, kills any man who addresses her or makes her pause on the road. He uses the girl as a bait for combat, as Erec used Enide. Orguelleus makes an abrupt appearance:

Li Orguelleus del bois issi,   Sir Arrogant issued forth from
Et vint ausi come une foudre   the wood and came like a bolt
Par le sablon et par la poudre   of thunder through the sand
Criant: 'Voir, mar i arestas   and the dust, shouting: 'In
Tu qui lez la pucele estas!'   truth, you there, standing by
    (3832–6)   the damsel, you made the
                                     mistake of your life in stopping
                                     there.'

Orguelleus is a misogynistic villain for whom women are sexual objects. Without feeling for the damsel, he tells the story of the Welsh lad who kissed her in the tent:

'Fame qui sa boche abandone   'A woman who yields her mouth,
Le soreplus de legier done,   will lightly grant the rest,
S'est qui a certes i antande.'   certainly, if a man is intent on
    (3863–5)   it!'

Woman enjoys being raped:

'Et bien soit qu'ele se desfande,
Si set an bien sanz nul redot
Que fame viaut vaintre par tot
Fors qu'an cele meslee sole:
Quant ele tient home a la gole
Et l'esgratine et mort et tue,
Si voldroit ele estre vaincue,
Si se desfant et si li tarde.
Tant est de l'otroiier coarde,
Einz viaut qu'an a force li face;
Puis si n'an a ne gré ne grace.
Por ce cuit je qu'il jut a li.'
          (3866–77)

'Though it may chance that she defends herself, we know well, and without doubt, that woman wants to win in everything except in this combat alone. When she holds a man by the throat and scratches him and bites and kills, she would yet wish to be overcome, and it is in this way that she defends herself and gives him delay, so cowardly is she about granting it to him. On the contrary she wants to be taken by force, and then afterwards she feels no pleasure or gratitude about it. For this reason I believe she lay with him!'

Orguelleus is superbly trivial: 'He stole from her a ring I had given her, he drank my good wine and ate three pasties.' He continues:

'Ore an a si cortois loiier
M'amie come il li apert:
Qui fet folie, sel conpert
Si qu'il se gart del rancheoir.'
          (3884–7)

'Now she has a reward as courteous as you can see from her appearance. Let anyone who commits folly, pay for it, and so take heed not to fall into error again.'

Perceval proclaims the girl's innocence – 'and I only ate one and a half pasties' (3899–910) – and they set about hitting each other in a fight which Chrétien considers a waste of time to describe (3920–9), and rightly so, since it has value only as the means by which Perceval, through violence, redeems his sin against the girl.

Perceval also delivers Orguelleus from the insanity of self-pride, possessiveness and maniacal jealousy. Sparing his life, he orders him to show mercy to the damsel, to take her to a castle and look after her health, then to go with her to Arthur's court, admit his maltreatment of her, and tell the damsel, whom Kay slapped, that she will be avenged before Perceval enters Arthur's court again. Kay, like Orguelleus, is surface-bound, cold-hearted and physically brutal. But Orguelleus has undergone a change of heart. The spell of self-pride is broken; he repents the suffering he has inflicted.

He can re-enter society. To the Queen and her damsels and the Damsel who Laughed, he tells the tale of his past cruelty. The Fool foresees Perceval's revenge against Kay who, in his disregard of others, is a force for evil in this romance, as Meleagant was in *Lancelot*. By defeating Kay, Perceval will defeat the extreme form of base self-interest and violence. In this respect, Orguelleus is the forerunner of Kay, as the Arrogant Knight was of Meleagant, though Kay in *Perceval* has a far less central role than Meleagant.

Kay's defeat is described in one of Chrétien's most memorable settings. The court, seeking to welcome the conqueror of Orguelleus, has moved out with bags and baggage, tents and pavilions, into the snow-covered forest (4141–63). On that morning, Perceval wakes with a desire for chivalrous adventure (4166–7). He still has no Quest. He rides straight into the snowy, icy meadow. But before he comes to the tents of the King, a flock of wild geese fly by, dazzled by the snow, honking for fear of a falcon which pounces on a straggler, hurls it wounded to the ground, and flies off.

Chrétien's vowel sounds convey the flurry of the chase in the winter sky and, with the final flat-sounding *abati*, the fall of the goose:

Mes einz que il venist as tantes,	But before he came to the tents,
Voloit une rote de jantes,	there flew by a flock of wild
Que la nois avoit esbloïes.	geese dazzled by the snow. He
Veües les a et oïes;	saw and heard them, for they
Qu'eles s'an aloient bruiant	went along honking noisily
Por un faucon qui vint traiant	because of a falcon which
Aprés eles de grant randon	approached them from behind
Tant qu'il an trova a bandon	with great speed until it found
Une fors de rote sevree,	one of them separated from the
Si l'a si ferue et hurtee	flock and flying along on its
Que contra terre l'abati.	own. This one it has struck,
(4171–81)	hurled out of its flight and
	thrown to the ground.

Perceval spurs up to the wild goose:

La jante fu navrce el col,	The goose was wounded in the
Si seigna trois gotes de sanc,	neck, and it bled three drops of
Qui espandirent sor le blanc,	blood which spread out on the
Si sanbla natural color.	snow of which it seemed the
(4186–9)	natural colour.

The falcon, feeling no hunger at so early an hour,[43]

disdains its prey. The wild goose recovers and flies away. Is Chrétien using this imagery to remind his audience of the Fisher King and the fate that befell his land? Are the hunt by the falcon, the crushed snow and the drops of blood from the neck of the wild goose symbolical of the momentary, wanton violence, which, for example, destroyed Perceval's father and brothers? Certainly, their effect on Perceval is profound. As Chrétien reverts to his description of lance and blood, reminiscent of the Procession in the Grail Castle, Perceval, for the first time, is liberated from his shell of self-absorption:

Quant Percevaus vit defolee
La noif sor quoi la jante jut
Et le sanc qui antor parut,
Si s'apoia desor sa lance
Por esgarder cele sanblance;
Que li sans et la nois ansanble
La fresche color li resanble
Qui ert an la face s'amie,
Si panse tant que il s'oblie.
(4194–202)

When Perceval saw the crushed snow on which the goose had lain and the blood which had appeared around it, he leant on his lance to contemplate this strange sight, for the blood and the snow in combination bring to his mind the fresh complexion of his beloved's face, and he thinks so long and deeply that he loses all sense of himself.

At this moment the new Perceval begins to stir to life. No longer the man of action, dealing in surface appearance, he now 'forgets himself' for a whole morning and falls into a reverie. The word *s'oblie* (4202) is double-edged. It is a courtly commonplace for the lover lost in thoughts of the beloved. It is also a significant moment in Perceval's life when, for the first time, he ceases to be fully aware of his own self, joining himself in thought with another person. The scene is set up in a way which is highly reminiscent of the adventure in the castle of the infirm Fisher King: the wild goose is damaged and drops of blood issue from its wounds. Perceval leans on his lance with its tip among the blood on the snow. This parallel symbolism, self-evident to Chrétien's audience, may have been intended to lead Perceval's burgeoning imagination back to the problem of the white and bleeding Lance and the Grail, and the test he failed when he neglected their challenge. This problem is still beyond his understanding and he will only be able to face it with the help of the Hermit. But his awakening imagination now transmutes lived experience to a higher level of sensibility, and of concern for others. Perceval progresses to Fin'Amors, to self-forgetfulness in the vision of the beloved, to amor de lonh. He day-dreams about Blancheflor as Lancelot mused about the Queen:

Li ert avis, tant li pleisoit,	It seemed to him, so much did
Qu'il veïst la color novele	it please him, that he was
De la face s'amie bele.	beholding the fresh complexion
Percevaus sor les gotes muse,	of the face of his fair love.
Tote la matinee i use . . .	Perceval day-dreams about the
(4208–12)	drops [of blood]; he spends all
	the morning in this way . . .

With the word muse and the jingle of rhymes in -use, an ironical note enters as it did in the case of the lovelorn Lancelot. This mood of gentle mockery persists when the squires from the tents believe they see a knight asleep on horseback:

Tant que fors des tantes issirent	Until the squires came out of
Escuiier, qui muser le virent,	the tents and, seeing him day-
Si cuidierent qu'il someillast.	dreaming, thought he slumbered.
(4213–15)	

They proclaim this to Sagremor:

'. . . fors de cest ost	'Beyond the outposts of the army
Avons veü un chevalier	we have seen a knight
Qui somoille sor son destrier.'	slumbering on a horse.'
(4224–6)	

This may be an humorous reference to the famous poem Farai un vers de dreyt nien which the first troubadour Guilhem d'Aquitaine composed while 'slumbering on a horse', a sex-symbol, in his poetry, for a woman:

Qu'enans fo trobatz en durmen
Sobre chevau.   (edn Jeanroy, IV, 5–6)

Since Guilhem IX, for thoughts of imaginary love, also loses all sense of his corporeal identity, it is not improbable that Chrétien has this poem in mind, and treats it with ironical good humour in describing Perceval's rapt communion with the image of his distant amigua. Sagremor wakes the King: 'Sire', he says, 'there is a knight asleep out there on the plain' (4232–3). Arthur, who is holding court mout

priveemant since only three thousand famous knights are present (4005–7), entreats him: 'Don't let him go. Bring him
in' (4236).

Sagremor is abrupt towards Perceval and unsuccessful. He
is mocked by Kay, who is equally discourteous in disturbing
Perceval from his day-dream of love. Kay cannot resist
Perceval's lance. He falls with a broken right arm, as the
Fool foretold. Chrétien indulges his sense of the ridiculous
by describing the grief of the court at Kay's supposed death,
whilst Perceval thinks on:

Et Percevaus sor les trois gotes Se rapoia desor sa lance. <div align=center>(4328–9)</div>	And Perceval once more leant on his lance above the three drops [of blood].

The blood has almost disappeared in the warmth of the sun
when Gawain greets him in courteous and sensitive fashion.
The joy of their meeting accuses the arrogance of the earlier
knights who sought combat merely to dominate Perceval and
force him to court.

Perceval has achieved the highest worldly success. He is
welcomed by Arthur, who will never willingly let him
depart (4565), by Guenevere and the Damsel who Laughed.
At this moment public disgrace falls on him as abruptly as
on Yvain. A damsel arrives on a *fauve mule*, carrying a riding
crop. Her hideousness is remarkable, certainly beyond that
of the drover in *Yvain*:[44] 'And if the book speaks the truth,
she was uglier than any creature outside of Hell. Her neck
and hands are as black as iron, her eyes like two holes, as
small as rat's eyes, her teeth the colour of egg yolk . . . She
was bearded like a billy goat, with a boss in the centre of her
chest, hunchbacked . . . with legs knotted like wickerwork.
Bien fu feite por mener dance' (4610–37).

The Hideous Damsel curses Perceval, and repeats the
admonition of his cousin. She lists the results of his failure
in the Grail Castle. The King is wounded. He will never be
healed. His land falls waste. Ladies and damsels will suffer.
Knights will die (4670–82). The Hideous Damsel must leave
for Chastel Orguelleus. There, she says, are to be found fine
ladies, joust, combat, knighthood, and there the fame of
this world, *le pris de tot le mont* (4701–2), can be achieved by
the rescue of a damsel besieged on a hill below Montes-

cleire. The Hideous Damsel departs. The knights offer themselves for adventure; Gawain will rescue the damsel, Girflet
will go to Chastel Orguelleus, Kahedin will climb Mont
Dolereus (4715–26).[45]

Such knightly tests are not for Perceval. His quest will be
to 'discover to whom the grail is served, to find the lance
and the proven truth about why it bleeds. This he will not
forego for any pain he may suffer'.

Et Percevaus redit tot el:	And for his part Perceval speaks
Qu'il ne girra an un ostel	quite otherwise. He will not lie
Deus nuiz an trestot son aage,	in a house two nights as long
Ne n'orra d'estrange passage	as he lives, nor will he hear
Noveles que passer n'i aille	news of any strange pass without
Ne de chevalier qui miauz vaille	going to pass through it, nor of
Qu'autres chevaliers ne que dui	any knight of greater valour than
Qu'il ne s'aille conbatre a lui	any single knight, or than any
Tant que il del graal savra	two knights, without going to
Cui l'an an sert, et qu'il avra	fight with him, until he knows
La lance qui sainne trovee	to whom the grail is served, and
Et que la veritez provee	until he finds the lance that
Li iert dite por qu'ele sainne;	bleeds and has been told the
Ja nel leira por nule painne.	very truth about why it bleeds.
(4727–40)	From this he will not desist for
	any suffering.

This is a further step in Perceval's development. He ignores
the knightly tests for worldly fame, and the chance that the
opportunity to ask the fateful questions may not recur
(4662–9). Free will is added to his predestination as a
knight of the Grail lineage. Perceval reflects and chooses.
His days of drifting, carefree *avanture* are behind him. But the
alien methods he chooses for his quest will lead to madness
and ceaseless wandering. His destiny and imagination direct
him to seek for the meaning of Lance and Grail. To achieve
this quest requires, he believes, supreme excellence in knightly prowess. He will fight, and force his adversaries to give
him the answers he demands, as he forced Orguelleus to
care for the damsel, and so freed himself of his own guilt
towards her. Perceval chooses to use the methods of *vaine
gloire* to find the answer of *caritas*. His aims are exalted, related
to the happiness of the land, but his methods are those of
Gawain, to whom the story now turns. If we accept the
romance in the form in which it has survived in ms. *A*,

where it is called *Percevaus le viel*, this is a turning-point in the story as significant as the disappearance into imprisonment of Lancelot. The stage is left free for the way of life which is antithetical to that of the hero. If we look back to *Lancelot*, we see a thematic structure based on the sequence ABABA where A represents the parts of the romance in which Lancelot's quest for Guenevere and humility are in the ascendant, and B represents the major passages in the work when the characters antithetical to Lancelot, Gawain and, in larger degree, Meleagant, hold the stage. It is not at all improbable that Chrétien intended a similar sequence for *Perceval* where A would represent Perceval's search for his identity and spiritual being and B would signify the antithetical Gawain-theme of prowess as an end in itself, of *vaine gloire* and conventional courtliness in all its limited Arthurian excellence. If this interpretation is accepted, the positioning of the Hermit episode in *Perceval* is as critically important as that of the tourney at Noauz in *Lancelot*, and the Gawain adventures in *Perceval* have a profound significance for the meaning of the romance.[46]

For Chrétien, knighthood takes its quality from the purpose to which it is directed. Gawain has the attributes of the perfect worldly knight,[47] but his gifts are misapplied by a world in utter confusion. He sustains his knightly courage and bearing, but his adventures are ephemeral and he has no real quest, either for worldly or for spiritual ends. He harvests the violence he has sown in earlier mortal combat. In these adventures, human society in castle and town resorts to violence for the resolution of its most trivial problems. Chrétien mocks this attitude with gentle irony, and, in extreme cases, parodies it with the device of the 'world upside-down' which he had already used in *Cliges*.

Gawain rides out from Arthur's court into the waste land of destructive knighthood in which combat leads to revenge and violence. He stands accused of treachery in the killing of the lord of Guinganbresil and is under oath to defend his honour within forty days at Escavalon. He enters a land reft by spitefulness, hatred and violence, void of all order and *mesure*. His first adventure takes place at Tintagel where the lord of the castle, Tiebaut, is challenged and threatened by a youth, Melianz de Liz, whom he has nurtured and knighted.

The quarrel has been instigated by Tiebaut's elder daughter, beloved of Melianz. She and the courtly ladies scorn Gawain who, mindful of his oath to fight at Escavalon, remains aloof from the fighting. They send a squire to take his horses from him, believing that 'he will not defend them'. The elder sister sends her father to Gawain's lodgings to denounce him as a merchant masquerading as a knight. Finally, the long-suffering Gawain champions and carries to victory the cause of the younger daughter who has been buffeted by her elder sister. Given to mockery, mischief, false values and physical violence, this elder sister is the female counterpart of the wretched Kay, an intensified version of the wicked sister in Yvain.

Escavalon is a city of bustling prosperity, the antithesis of the Waste City, Belrepeire. Within, however, it is a waste land of hatred directed against Gawain who slew its lord. Fortunately, Gawain is not immediately recognised. He is entertained in the castle by the sister of the lord of Escavalon, and to her he addresses complete and sudden love:

Mes sire Gauvains la requiert	My lord Gawain woos her in love,
D'amors et prie et dit qu'il iert	and entreats her and says he will
Ses chevaliers tote sa vie.	be her knight for as long as he
Et ele n'an refuse mie,	lives. And she has no thought of
Einz li otroie volantiers.	refusing him, but grants him
(5827–31)	this with a willing heart.

Suddenly Gawain is recognised, and denounced as a murderer. The lord of Escavalon is out hunting. His sister will defend her new love, and the castle:

. . . 'Ha! or somes nos mort!	. . . 'Alas! Now we shall die!
Por vos morrai ancui a tort,	For your sake will I today suffer
Et vos, mien esciant, por moi.'	an unjust death, and you, I know
(5875–7)	well, will die for me.'

The parody implicit in this mock heroism, of dying in order to love, like Yseut, is strengthened when Gawain, having girded on his sword Excalibur, is given a chessboard by his beloved to use as a shield. Uproar breaks out in the town:

Une assanblee de voisins,	Men from the locality rallied
Le maior et les eschevins	together, the mayor, the sheriffs
Et d'autres borjois a foison,	and an abundance of other worthy
Qui pas n'avoient pris poison,	citizens who had not been
Qu'il estoient et gros et gras.	eating poison, being both plump
(5907–11)	and fat.

The preparations for battle are depicted in a burlesque style like that of the *Roman de Renart*[48] or of Beroul's *Tristran* when Governal fights the lepers;[49] such a style will become a commonplace for the later poets of Arras:[50]

Tantost s'est li maire levez
Et tuit li eschevin aprés.
Lors veïssiez vilains angrés,
Qui pranent haches et jusarmes;
Cil prant un escu sanz anarmes,
Et cil un huis et cil un van.
Li crïere crie le ban,
Et trestoz li pueples aüne.
Sone li sainz de la comune
Por ce que nus n'an i remaingne.
(5934–43)

Soon the mayor got up, and all the sheriffs after him. Then you would have seen wretched churls taking up axes and billhooks. One takes a shield without holding-straps, another takes a door, and another a wicker basket. The town crier cries the summons and all the people assemble. The bell of the commune rings out, so that none may remain behind.

Chrétien continues in the style of *Le Jugement de Renart*:

Ez vos mon seignor Gauvain mort,
Se Damedeus ne le consoille!
(5950–1)

Now you will see my lord Gawain slain, if God the Almighty does not succour him.

The noble maiden shouts her defiance:

'Hu, hu!', fet ele, 'vilenaille,
Chien anragié, pute servaille,
Quel deable vos ont mandez?
Que querez vos, que demandez?'
(5955–8)

'Avaunt! You pack from the gutter, you rabid curs, smelly servants. What devils have got into you? What are you looking for? What do you want?'

Gawain's defence of the door to the tower is a burlesque counterpart of Perceval's defence of the door at Belrepeire against the invading army of Clamadeus. The assailants shrink from Gawain's sword. With a touch of Alice in Wonderland, the enraged damsel hurls giant chessmen at the mob:

La dameisele les eschas
Qui jurent sor le pavemant,
Lor rue mout irieemant,
Si s'est estrainte et escorciee
Et jure come correciee
Qu'ele les fera toz destruire,
S'ele onques puet, ainz qu'ele
  muire.
(6000–6)

The damsel picks up the chessmen lying on the paving stones, and hurls them in full fury at them. So she has pushed herself to the limit, worn herself to the bone, and, mad with rage, swears she will cause them all to be destroyed, if she is ever able to do so, before she dies.

The damsel, like Nicolette, takes charge of the action. But beneath the atmosphere of Tore Lore and the fighting with chessmen, the sense is clear. Escavalon, which appears to house a well fed and worthy community, nurtures within itself a capacity for hatred and violence which will destroy anything in its way. The townsmen prepare to undermine the tower. Amidst the bedlam, the King arrives and order is restored.

The lord of Escavalon is torn between hatred for his father's murderer and the laws of hospitality. A vavasour suggests that Gawain's duel should be postponed for a year. He lays down the terms for his release:

'. . . et il s'an aille
Querre la lance don li fers
Saingne toz jors, ja n'iert si ters
Qu'une gote de sanc n'i pande:
Ou il cele lance vos rande,
Ou il se remete an merci
An tel prison come il est ci.'
(6112–18)

'Let him go to seek the lance with the blade which always bleeds and which will never be so clean that a drop of blood may not hang from it. Let him surrender that lance to you or let him submit to your mercy as a prisoner such as he is here at this moment.'

Gawain refuses the form of oath imposed on him: 'that he will surrender, within a year and no more, the lance of which the point weeps tears of bright blood, and of which it is written that it will one day destroy the whole realm of Logres, which formerly was the land of ogres' (6164–71). Gawain would die rather than be forsworn for an oath he cannot fulfil, and which, if it were fulfilled, would incidentally destroy Arthur's kingdom.[51] The vavasour compromises: 'You will swear to do all in your power on the quest for the lance. If you do not bring the lance, return to this tower and you will be absolved of your oath' (6187–91).

Gawain does not seek to know why the lance bleeds. He must actually find the finite lance of destruction and bring it to Escavalon, a city rich in material wealth, anger and violence. Already in this Lance which causes havoc and sheds tears of bright blood (6166–7) we may discern not only the Celtic Lance of Destruction,[52] but a symbol of the worldly pride and knightly violence which have brought disaster to Arthur's knights and lands.

275

In the adventure at Escavalon, Chrétien defines the 'madness' of a society without spiritual guidance, the absurdity of an 'upside-down' life based on a vendetta code of violence which is symbolised by a Lance that weeps tears of blood. At this moment of Gawain's misfortunes and of the definition of a quest which, in its allegorical form, will make him and his like into the destroyers of Arthur's realm, Chrétien returns to Perceval. This juncture in the narrative corresponds, as has been suggested earlier (p. 225), to the tournament at Noauz, when Lancelot, temporarily freed from imprisonment, discovers within himself the full self-abnegation, humility and scorn of *vaine gloire* which he had lacked in the test of the Cart. Perceval now emerges from the waste land in which he has been imprisoned because, though in his imagination he glimpsed the high quality of his quest, his inner spiritual self was too uninformed to understand its true nature. Perceval, still burdened by his sin against his mother, has continued to lead a life of worldly knighthood: 'He has gone out of his mind[53] so that he no longer thinks of God. April passed five times and more, five whole years it was before he entered a church or adored God and his cross. For five years he dwelt in this condition, but did not renounce the search for knightly adventure . . . Within these five years he despatched sixty knights of great renown to the court of King Arthur. In this way he used up the five years, and so never thought of God' (6218–21, 6233–7). Perceval, in fact, has never truly thought of God, or, as far as we know, entered a church since his first visit as an unfledged youth to Arthur's court. In this case, the repetition of the phrase 'five years' may also be intended to lend perspective to his whole career as a worldly knight.

Symbolically, he rides, fully armed, through a desert:

Au chief des cinc anz li avint	At the end of the five years it
Que il par un desert aloit	befell that he was going across
Cheminant, si come il soloit,	a waste land, following a path,
De totes ses armes armez.	fully arrayed with all his arms,
(6238–41)	as was his custom.

On the path there are three knights and seven ladies, hooded, barefoot, in ragged clothes:

Que por sauvemant de lor ames	For the salvation of their souls
Lor penitance a pié feisoient	they were making a pilgrimage
Por les pechiez que fez avoient.	on foot as penitence for the sins
(6250–2)	they had committed.

One of the knights stops him: 'My lord, do you not believe in Jesus Christ? . . . It is neither right nor proper to bear arms on the day when Jesus Christ was slain' (6254–60). Perceval is as direct to the pilgrims as he was as an untried youth to the leader of the knights in the forest. Now however the roles are reversed. He is the knight in the panoply of armour and steel. This was the course which Perceval was then impelled to choose, the path of worldly knighthood. Now, when he cannot rid himself of the burden of sin through knightly prowess, he is led to repentance, humility and submission to God. 'What day is it then today?' The knightly pilgrim speaks of Christ 'who, in truth, on a day such as this was put on the cross, and drew out of Hell all those who love him. Most holy was that death which to the living gave salvation and to the dead, resurrection in life eternal' (6264–91). He curses the Jews who should be killed like dogs (6292–3). 'Today should all believers repent, and no man who believes in God should bear arms' (6297–300). 'Whence come you?' asks Perceval. 'From a good man, a saintly hermit who dwells in this forest. So holy is this man that he saw nothing save the glory of Heaven' (6301–6).

This is the first positive help Perceval has received in his quest for knowledge of the Lance and Grail. He will not fail this test through silence:

'Por Deu, seignor, la que feïstes?	'In the name of God, my lords,
Que demandastes, que queïstes?'	what did you do there? What
'Quoi, sire?' fet une des dames,	did you ask? What did you
'De noz pechiez i demandames	seek?' 'What did we seek, my
Consoil et confesse i preïmes.'	lord?' says one of the ladies, 'we
(6307–11)	asked for help with our sins, and
	we made our confession there.'

Perceval goes to the hermitage 'sighing deeply from his heart because he felt he had sinned before God, and repented greatly of this' (6334–6). He dismounts, disarms himself and enters a small chapel where the hermit is beginning the service of Mass:

. . . le servise
Le plus haut qui an sainte eglise
Puisse estre diz et li pluz douz.
(6345–7)

the highest and most comforting
service which can be said in
holy Church.

Perceval, freed from knightly trappings, has regained his youthful innocence:

Percevaus se met a genouz
Tantost come antre an la chapele;
Et li buens hon a lui l'apele,
Qui mout le vit sinple et plorant;
Que jusques au manton colant
L'eve des iauz li degotoit.
(6348–53)

As soon as he enters the chapel,
Perceval falls on his knees. And
the good man, seeing he was
innocent and weeping so much
that the tear drops flowed down
to his chin, calls on him to
come to him.

Perceval, fearing greatly he has sinned against God, grasps the Hermit's foot and begs for advice. The priest orders him to confess:

'Sire', fet il, 'bien a cinc anz
Que je ne soi ou je me fui,[54]
Ne Deu n'amai ne Deu ne crui,
N'onques puis ne fis se mal non.'
(6364–7)

'Good sir', he says, 'for a full
five years I have not known
where I was. I neither loved God,
nor believed in God, and never
since then have my deeds been
other than wicked.'

He confesses his sin of omission in the castle of the Fisher King. For this he suffered, and forgot God and the need to ask Him for mercy. The Hermit, hearing his name, knows his sin:

Et dit: 'Frere, mout t'a neü
Uns pechiez don tu ne sez mot.'
(6392–3)

And he says: 'My brother, a sin
of which you know nothing,
has done you great harm.'

'Your sin was that you caused your mother such grief that she died. It was this sin within you which held you back from asking about the Lance or the Grail' (6394–401). 'You were preserved from death and imprisonment, because your mother commended you to God. It was sin which cut off your tongue' (6402–9).

Without being asked, he tells Perceval what he wants to know about the Grail:

'Cil cui l'an an sert, est mes frere;
Ma suer et soe fu ta mere,
Et del riche Pescheor croi

'The man to whom it is served
is my brother. Your mother was
his sister and mine. And I

Que il est filz a celui roi	believe that the rich Fisher is the
Qui del graal servir se fet.'	son of that king who causes the
(6415-19)	grail to be served to him.'

This is no ordinary grail, he tells his nephew, no dish for the service of victuals. Intuitively, he realises Perceval's amazement at having seen an apparently empty dish, *trestot descovert*,[55] being carried in procession, for service to an unknown recipient. The dish did not contain, as he would undoubtedly have thought, the catch of the Fisher who from his boat had directed him to his castle:

'Mes ne cuidiez pas que il et	'Do not think there was any
Luz ne lamproies ne saumon:	pike or lamprey or salmon in it.
D'une sole oiste li sainz hon,	With one solitary host which is
Que l'an an cest graal li porte,	borne to him in this grail does
Sa vie sostient et conforte;	the holy man sustain and nourish
Tant sainte chose est li graaus,	his life. So holy a thing is the
Et il est si esperitaus	grail[56] and so spiritual is he that
Qu'a sa vie plus ne covient	nothing else is necessary to his
Que l'oiste qui el graal vient.'	life save only the host which
(6420-8)	comes in the grail.'

Perceval warms with good feeling towards his uncle (6434-8) when he offers him the chance to repent of his sins: 'Go to church, the first thing every day. If the Mass has begun, stay there and listen until the priest has sung and said the service. So will your soul find great advancement' (6442-51). 'Seek the greater honour which comes from love of God and from humility':

'Se ce te vient a volanté,	'And if it pleases you to do so,
Ancor porras monter an pris,	you can grow yet more in virtue,
S'avras enor et paradis.	and you will gain honour
Deu croi, Deu aimme, Deu aore,	and paradise. Believe in God,
Buen home et buene fame enore,	love God, worship God. Honour
Contre le provoire te lieve;	the good man and the good
C'est uns servises qui po grieve,	woman. Stand up in the presence
Et Deus l'aimme por verité	of the priest. This is a form of
Por ce qu'il vient d'umilité.'	service which is not arduous,
(6456-64)	and which is in truth beloved
	by God because it proceeds from
	humility.'

'Do not fail to give aid to damsels, widows, orphans. And I ask you to stay two whole days with me and share such food as I eat' (6465-79). Perceval learns the prayer of the many names of God, to be used only in moments of mortal fear. He hears the service, repents and finds joy and peace of mind:

Einsi remest et si oï	So he stayed and heard the
Le servise et mout s'esjoï.	service and rejoiced greatly.
Après le servise aora	After the service he adored the
La croiz et ses pechiez plora	cross and wept for his sins, and
Et se repanti duremant,	in grievous state made his
Et fu einsi tot coiemant.	repentance, and thus found
(6493–8)	absolute quiet.

And so the Hermit episode ends: 'In this way Perceval recognised that God was slain on Good Friday and crucified, and with the true sacraments he received the Easter Communion.' The story, says Chrétien, speaks no more at this time of Perceval. 'On the contrary, you will hear a great deal about Gawain before you hear me say anything more about him' (6509–18).

From spiritual certainty and joy the story switches back to the upside-down world in which Gawain seeks the Lance of Destruction. This is now a land of violence, malevolence and anarchy in which evil struggles with the knightly values which Gawain upholds. The comedy of situation, which will recur in *Aucassin et Nicolette*, now acquires overtones of nightmarish fantasy and menace, deriving from Chrétien's use of magical themes and of the Celtic supernatural tradition. As Gawain pursues his quest, he encounters increasing violence, hostility and humiliation.

Gawain, freed from the tower of Escavalon, finds a damsel seated beneath an oak, grieving over a wounded knight. This situation is analogous to Perceval's meeting with his cousin, but in this case the forces of destruction have been supernatural. 'He could die from the least of his wounds' says the damsel (6566). But Gawain has little patience with the knight's condition:

Et il li dist: 'Ma douce amie,	And he said to her, 'My sweet
Esveilliez le, ne vos poist mie;	love, wake him up, if you will,
Que noveles li vuel anquerre	for I want to find out what is
Des afeires de cest terre.'	going on in this land.'
(6567–70)	

The damsel refuses. Gawain wakes him with the butt of his lance. 'Go no further', says the knight:

'Que c'est la bosne de Galvoie.
Einz chevaliers n'i puet passer
Qui ja mes puisse retorner,
N'ancor n'an est nus retornez
Fors moi qui si sui atornez,
Si malemant que jusqu' anuit
Ne vivrai pas. . . .'
(6602–8)

'for this is the borne of Galway.
Never can any knight pass
beyond with any hope of
returning. No man has returned
thence save me alone, and in
such wretched plight that I shall
not live till nightfall.'

Gawain insists he must go on. 'You must go, I know', says the knight, 'to increase your renown. But if you return, pass this way, and, if I am dead, look after this damsel' (6625–42).

In a splendid castle beside sea and river, Gawain finds a damsel alone, beneath an elm in a meadow. Her face and throat are whiter than snow, a coronet of gold on her head. He spurs towards her:

Et ele lie crie: 'Mesure,
Mesure, sire, or belemant,
Que vous venez mout folemant!'
(6684–6)

And she cries out to him: 'More
gently, more gently, my lord,
approach now in seemly fashion,
for you ride like a madman.'

The damsel affects the *dame* who demands *mesure* and rejects the impulse of *folie*. And she adds:

'Fos est qui por neant s'esploite.'
(6689)

'Only the fool strives after
nothingness.'

an aphorism which in a wider sense sums up the vanity of Gawain's quest. 'Why did you shout "mesure"?' asks Gawain (6692–5). 'Because I know what you are thinking. You wish to ride off with me . . . (6697–6700). I am not one of those simple (Breton) girls with whom some knights find pleasure, carrying them off on their horses when they seek knightly adventure' (6706–9).[57] The damsel is as clear-headed as Marcabru's shepherdess,[58] as dominating as any lady, or fairy mistress. 'If you were to fetch my palfrey from that garden, I would go with you':

'Je iroie tant avuec toi
Que male avanture et pesance
Et diaus et honte et mescheance
T'avenist an ma conpeignie.'
(6716–19)

'I would go with you so that
misadventure and sorrow, and
grief and shame and mischance
might befall you in my
company.'

On the far side of a plank bridge, a crowd curse her: 'May

a hundred devils burn you, damsel, for having worked so much evil' (6752–3), 'for never having esteemed a worthy man, and for causing so many to have their heads cut off. Sir knight, you know not the ills which await you if you touch the palfrey' (6755–61).[59] Fear of shame impels Gawain onwards, though a tall knight foretells disaster. 'If I were to give up', says Gawain,

'Je seroie honiz an terre
Come recreanz et failliz.'
(6800–1)

'I should be shamed in the whole world as a recreant and failure.'

He brings the palfrey to the damsel who has let her cloak and wimple fall, uncovering her face and body, a characteristic action of the Celtic fairy mistress. 'You may not touch me in any way', she says as Gawain offers to help her mount the palfrey. 'I will travel with you until I have brought you disaster and death' (6860–8). She reproaches him for trying to tidy her cloak: 'May God keep me from accepting your service' (6880–94). The damsel uses the formulae of the *dame*, but, by courtly standards, her world is upside-down:

'Et je vos siurai tote voie
Tant que por moi honir vos voie.'
(6899–900)

'And I will follow you along every path until I see you suffering shame because of me.'[60]

Behind this caustic attitude there lies more than a burlesque of the *dame* who, as in *Milun*, is over-exigent. There is malevolence, possibly against Gawain as a seducer of damsels, or, on a wider plane, against the pride which in *Lancelot* kept him back from mounting the cart. And, beyond this, there is the hint of disaster from some supernatural spell.

To reinforce this impression of forces beyond Gawain's ken, an Ugly Squire appears, like the herdsman in *Yvain* and the Hideous Damsel who denounced Perceval. This squire, with his wide forked beard, appears when Gawain, with a special herb, has restored life to the stricken knight under the tree. At the squire's insult, Gawain knocks him from the saddle of his ugly nag, a blow, the squire says, which will bring retribution to Gawain: 'you will lose the hand and arm with which you hit me and the blow will never be forgiven' (7038–40). Gawain, who at Tintagel answered slander with disdain, is now as impulsive and *fols* as Kay was in the Perceval story. The wounded knight desires, so he says, to go to confession. He asks Gawain for the squire's nag, and, when Gawain is preoccupied, gallops off on his warhorse, with cries of hatred: 'I would like to hold your heart in my hands, torn out of your body. You shamed me, Gawain. Do you not remember the knight who for a month, with hands bound, had to eat with the dogs' (7096–117). The knight is Greoreas who had raped a damsel. 'I punished you fittingly *por leal justise*' (7129), replies Gawain. But in vain. He reaps the harvest of his former self as he had done at Escavalon. The Male Pucele laughs (7145) at seeing him left with the Ugly Nag which is described in detail (7161–77). The shame of the Cart is now heaped on him a hundred-fold. His misadventures which began at Tintagel and Escavalon are intensified with the threat of a supernatural violence against which he has little defence. The Male Pucele mocks him:

'Or serai je liee et joieuse
D'aler quel part vos voldroiz!
. . . .
Ore estes vos bien a hernois!
Or seez vos sor buen destrier,
Or sanblez vos bien chevalier.'
(7180–1, 7186–8)

'Now shall I find delight and joy in going wherever you wish. . . . Now you are indeed finely arrayed. Now you are horsed on a fine warhorse. Now do you indeed have the semblance of a knight.'

Behind such irony, it is impossible not to see criticism of knighthood's martial array, as in the scene of the five knights in the forest, and of Perceval on Good Friday. And also there are discernible undertones of sexual mockery of his un-distinguished mount.[61] When Lancelot was 'shamed', we saw the situation from his point of view, and were asked to sympathise. Now, we see Gawain's shame from the shamer's point of view, and our sympathy is muted. By the standards of courtesy and worldly knighthood, Gawain is mocked unjustly, but by Chrétien's standards, deservedly. It was in-human to degrade the knight Greoreas to the status of an animal, and, though Gawain healed him, he did this without compassion, or thought of giving him his own warhorse. So he is shamed, as Lancelot was when he rode in the cart. But Lancelot chose his shame, Gawain has it thrust upon him in a world of ugliness.

So he rides through the waste land on the Ugly Nag, in great discomfort, until he comes upon a wondrous castle:

Par forez gastes et soutainnes	Through waste, remote forests,
Tant que il vint a terres plainnes	until he came to fertile lands
Sor une riviere parfonde.	beside a deep river.
(7225–7)	

On the other side, on a cliff, stands a castle, strong and splendid, with a palace of dark grey marble. Ladies and damsels look out of five hundred windows. The Male Pucele (Qui felon cuer avoit el vantre, 7270) dismounts, leads her palfrey on to a boat, bids Gawain raise the anchor:

'Que ja anterroiz an mal an,	'For you will enter a year of
Se tost ceste eve ne passez	disaster if you do not swiftly
Ou se tost foïr ne poëz.'	cross this water, or if you cannot
(7278–80)	flee without delay.'

'Why?' 'Do you not see what I see?' (7281–2). 'This knight following you on your horse is the nephew of Greoreas. His uncle has ordered him to follow you, and bring back your head' (7283–7308).

At this moment of supernatural magic, when the crossing of the water offers escape from the probability of knightly defeat, Gawain, mounted on his Ugly Nag, stands firm. Honour overcomes fear of shame:

'Certes, ja ne fuirai por lui,	'For sure, I will never flee from
Dameisele, eniçois l'atandrai.'	him, but will stay and await
(7312–13)	him.'

'Right', says the Male Pucele, 'I shall enjoy watching your defeat.' In her mockery there are once more undertones of a wider criticism of knighthood engaged in purposeless violence:

'Mout sanblez or bien chevalier	'You now have, indeed, the very
Qui a autre doie joster.'	semblance of a knight who must
(7324–5)	joust with another.'

Gawain is steadfast. He longs to recover his horse (7329–30). The Ugly Nag refuses to move, let alone charge. The knight rushes down on him, but Gawain unseats him, seizes his horse, and leaps into the saddle. 'He was never happier about any adventure in his whole life' (7360–3). The Male Pucele and her ship have now disappeared, as if Gawain, by his victory, had broken her spell.

This magical disappearance concludes the testing of Gawain in circumstances of nightmarish adversity. The comparison with Perceval's trials in the Grail Castle, which is 'there and not there', does not need to be stressed. If we look back to *Lancelot*, however, we may see that Gawain, unlike Perceval, is undergoing a test of worldly knighthood in which *Leauté* overcomes and atones for the *Mauvestié* of his former self. Gawain's weaknesses, his failure to control impulsive violence, his lack of true concern for others, and especially his pride, meet with retribution. His knighthood is humbled when he loses his horse, as Lancelot lost his when he began the quest for Guenevere. Having been forced into humility in supernatural scenes which have some resemblance to the case of False Rape in *Lancelot*, and may just possibly be intended to reflect his own traumatic doubts, Gawain is now ready for the castle which is full of ladies and damsels who send greetings and a boat to bring him to them across the river.

Once more, he is deprived of his horse. The ferryman demands it as payment for the crossing. But Gawain refuses. The ferryman must keep it and return it to him. Already Gawain is resisting the 'threat' of courtly imprisonment within the castle. Unlike Lancelot he affirms his knighthood and his right to ride away. Significantly it is at this moment that he asks the ferryman about the Male Pucele: 'Where has she gone?'

. . . 'Sire, ne vos chaille	'My lord, do not concern your-
De la pucele, ou que ele aille;	self with that damsel, or her
Que pucele n'est ele pas,	whereabouts, for she is no girl.
Einz est pire que Sathenas,	She is worse than Satan for she
Car a cest port a fet tranchier	has caused the heads of many
Maintes testes a chevalier.'	knights to be cut off at this
(7453–8)	river crossing.'

'Stay with me, in my house. Do not stay on this bank of the river':

'Que c'est une terre sauvage,	'For this is a strange, wild land,
Tote plainne de granz mervoilles.'	full of great marvels.'
(7464–5)	

The ferryman's house is splendid enough to house a count. Plovers, pheasants, partridges and venison are served for supper, with strong clear wine. At dawn Gawain looks from the battlements at the fertile lands around the castle. 'Who is lord of this land and castle?' he asks. 'I know not . . .', replies the ferryman, 'there is a queen who came here with her treasure, and brought with her another lady whom she loves so much that she calls her queen and daughter; and she, in her turn, has a daughter who is the fairest in the land. The hall of this castle is guarded by magic devices. A clerk, wise in astronomy, was brought here by the queen and has set up such wondrous objects that no knight can enter there with safety if he is guilty of covetousness, deceitful flattery or greed (*coveitise, losange, avarice*)' (7480–558).

Uncourtly vices cannot endure in this castle:

'Coarz ne traître n'i dure
Ne foimantie ne parjure :
Cil i muerent si a delivre
Qu'il n'i pueent durer ne vivre.'
(7559–62)

'Neither coward nor traitor can last in it, nor the man who is forsworn or perjured. Such men perish here so readily, for they cannot endure here or stay alive.'

Yet this city devoid of knights is as isolated, and, in its way, as devastated as Belrepeire. Its dwellings are intact, and food is abundant, but it is a castle of women whose lives have been ravaged by deeds of violent knighthood, by lack of compassion and *caritas*. The prophecy of Perceval's cousin is realised in this Castle of the Two Queens in which women without husbands, lords or possessions are defended by five hundred unfledged young men:

'Et s'i a dames anciienes
Qui n'ont ne mariz ne seignors,
Einz sont de terres et d'enors
Desheritees a grant tort.'
(7574–7)

'And there are here ladies who have lost their high positions, who have no husbands or lords, and who have been disinherited most unjustly of their lands and possessions.'

All the people spend their time coming and going in the city, hoping for what the ferryman calls 'a great foolishness' (*une grant folie*, 7583), namely that a knight should rescue them from their desolate condition. The ferryman is cynical:

'Mes ainz iert mers tote de glace
Que l'an un tel chevalier truisse
Qui el palés demorer puisse;
Qu'il le covandroit a devise
Sage et large, sanz coveitise,
Bel et franc, hardi et leal,

'But all the seas will be covered by ice before we find such a knight who could dwell in this city. For he would need absolute wisdom and generosity free from all covetousness, good

Sanz vilenie et sanz nul mal.'

(7590–6)

looks, a noble spirit, boldness, and promptness to the call of duty, freedom from baseness and from all evil.'

'Such a knight', says the ferryman, 'would restore lands to the ladies, would bring these many wars to an end, would give the damsels in marriage, would dub the young men knights' (7599–7602).

'Et osteroit sanz nul relés
Les anchantemanz del palés.'

(7603–4)

'And he would totally remove the magic arts from the castle.'

He would by his *Leauté* and power of sovereignty restore the city to happiness. Order would reign as in *Erec et Enide* after the Coronation scene.

Of material wealth the castle enjoys a Byzantine abundance. Gawain and his host, on their way up to the palace, pass a cripple with a silver leg, inlaid with gold, encrusted with precious stones.[62] If the ferryman's house was splendid, the palace itself is a miracle of richness. One gate is of sculpted ivory, the other of ebony illuminated with gold and jewels. The hinges are of gold, the paving of many hues, worked and polished. In the centre of the palace stands a bed entirely of gold, with a cover of samite. Each of its feet encloses a carbuncle as bright as four large candles. The bed rests on four little sculpted dogs with their cheeks puffed out, and moves lightly on its wheels at the touch of a finger. At its head, bright windows provide a view of anyone entering the palace (7648–724).

This bed of light and brightness and gold and jewels has a sinister side. Gawain rejects the warning words of the ferryman. 'I will sit on this bed for a while, and rest. I never saw a bed of such rich splendour' (7744–6). The ferryman foresees his death, pleads in vain, leaves him to his fate. 'Whatever may befall, I will not fail to sit on the bed, and see the damsels whom I saw yesterday in the evening, leaning out of these windows' (7770–4). The ferryman prepares to flee: 'You will not see them. You will die. You will leave your head here as an irredeemable pledge. May God have mercy on your soul. My heart cannot endure to see you die' (7776–816). Such warning before an adventure is a commonplace in Chrétien's work. Here, in an amplified form, it creates tension for the tests which await Gawain, and emphasises the power of the magic barrier which seals off the damsels, the ladies and the two queens, within their world of glass. Only the Elect can break this self-imposed magic. Other knights must die.

The testing of Gawain differs absolutely from that of Perceval in the castle of the Fisher King. Gawain takes his seat, fully armed, on the bed.[63] The bells attached to the silver bed cords ring and jangle to stupefy the hearer. All the windows fly open, the magic begins. Arrows and bolts fly through the windows. Five hundred strike Gawain's shield. Yet no one could see whence the arrows came, or who fired them. The windows close again. Gawain, bleeding from his wounds, picking the arrows from his shield, is attacked by a fierce and wondrous lion. It sticks its claws in his shield, as if it were wax, and forces him to his knees. Gawain leaps up, and cuts off its head and paws, which are left dangling from his shield.

Gawain has passed his trial of physical courage. 'Lay aside all your armour', says the ferryman, hastening to his side, 'you have removed the magic spells from this palace for ever, and you will be served and honoured by young and old, for which all glory be to God' (7878–84). Waves of young men offer service, on their knees, to this man 'whom we have greatly longed for and desired' (7885–91).

In a passage which in its phrasing bears some likeness to the opening lines of the Grail Procession:

Et que que il se desarmoit,	And while he was being disarmed
Une pucele antra leanz,	a damsel entered therein, beautiful
Qui mout ert bele et avenanz,	and pleasing in her person, with
Sor son chief un cercelet d'or	a chaplet of gold encircling her
Don li chevol estoient sor	hair which was as yellow as gold
Autant come li ors ou plus.	or even more so.
(7898–903)	

The Queen, she says, has ordered all the damsels to accept him as lord and do him homage. For Gawain this is the limit of joy:

Auques por ce que beles sont	partly because they are beautiful,
Et plus por ce que eles font	and, more so, because they make
De lui lor prince et lor seignor.	him their lord and prince. His

288

Joie a, qu'onques mes n'ot greignor, joy at the honour which God has
De l'enor que Deus li a feite.   done him is greater than any he
        (7945–9)   ever had before.

Gawain, attired in an ermine robe sent by the Queen, goes
to the tower with his host, the ferryman, to view the fertile
lands and rivers and forests, full of wildlife, which surround
the castle. 'I shall be very happy to stay here and go hunting
in these forests' (8009–11). The ferryman replies, 'My lord,
you can keep very quiet about that. I have often heard it
said that anyone so beloved of God as to be acknowledged
as master and lord here, would never go forth from this
place, for any reason whether right or wrong. You must not
talk of hunting. Your place is here, and you will never depart
from here' (8012–24). Gawain reproves him: 'Be silent. You
will drive me mad if I listen to you any more. As God may
help me, I could not live here for seven days . . . without
going out whenever I wished' (8025–32).

At this point in the development of the Gawain adventures
we begin to see a background thematic structure not unlike
that in the *Lancelot*. Though Gawain and Lancelot represent
different gradations of knighthood, they both suffer knightly
humiliation and their adventures are cast within the same
framework of conflict between the forces of Good and Evil,
of order and disorder. By defeating Meleagant and the Arrogant Knight, Lancelot checked the forces of evil and senseless
destruction. He also stood apart from the world of Arthur
which judged according to outward show and skill at arms.
His only help in this fight was the daughter of Bademagu,
Meleagant's sister, who demanded the head of the Arrogant
Knight and, in recompense, rescued him from the tower. In
the land of Gorre, sealed off from the world by the Sword
Bridge and the Water Bridge, a civilised society is ruled by
Bademagu, whose aims, devoted to peace, harmony and understanding, represent a different and probably higher ideal
of knighthood than that of Arthur. In the Gawain adventures
of the *Perceval* we find a Waste Land peopled by knights and
townsmen who are ruled by hatred and destructive violence,
especially in the form of a vendetta against Gawain for his
previous slaughter of knights in this land. On the edge of
this Waste Land, in a fertile area, the Queen, who, as we shall
discover, is Arthur's mother, has established an 'island' of

tranquillity in her castle on a rock protected by the river crossing. Lacking a knightly company, she has established magic devices to protect her palace, and her ladies and damsels, from the incursion of unworthy knights who might have survived the violence of the Waste Land outside. Her standards of knightly *leauté* are met by Gawain who has survived the degradation and the traps laid for him by the Male Pucele who seeks to destroy him and all other knights.

Gawain cannot, however, stagnate in the Castle of the Two Queens. The challenge to knightly adventure offered by the Male Pucele and her desire to destroy him cannot be ignored. After a sumptuous feast and dancing, he sleeps in the Wondrous Bed and is wakened next morning by Clarissant, the virtuous, the excellent, the gracious, wise and eloquent damsel (8269–71) who had addressed him on the previous evening and who will prove to be his sister. He spies the Male Pucele on the far bank accompanied by an armed knight. Gawain cannot resist the challenge: he demands permission to leave the castle, and this is given by the Two Queens, provided that he returns by nightfall. He crosses the water, defeats the knight who charges at him on sight, *sanz desfiance*, and gives him as prisoner to the ferryman. The Male Pucele rebuffs his invitation to come back with him across the water. She regrets and belittles his victory. His opponent, her friend, was suffering from former wounds. Gawain, she says, can prove his worth only by crossing the Perilous Ford, the Guez Perilleus (8479–97), and 'may it never please God that I may see you return from there' (8446–7). The damsels and ladies in the palace tear at themselves and lament his certain death. Gawain remembers the story that anyone who crosses the Ford over the deep water will have the highest renown in the world (*Q'il avroit tot le pris del monde*, 8510). Gawain's horse fails to leap the chasm, and they struggle out of the stream and up the far bank, where he finds an explanation of the mysteries he has encountered.

In a meadow he comes upon a knight, supremely handsome, hunting with a sparrow hawk. This is Guiromelant who had tried in vain to force his love on the Male Pucele after killing the knight she loved. She had left him and taken as her lover the knight whom Gawain has just defeated. Because you dared to fight him, you have won "Le pris dell mont et le los" ' (8586). The Male Pucele is called L'Orguelleuse de Logres, where she was born, and her knight, whom Gawain killed, was L'Orguelleus de la Roche a l'Estroite Voie. The castle, to which Gawain must return, was built by Yguerne, Arthur's mother, who came to this land after her husband, Uterpandragon, Arthur's father, was buried. The second queen, whom she brought with her, was the wife of King Lot and the mother of Gawain and of Clarissant. Guiromelant loves Clarissant with desperate love, and hates Gawain. He will kill him on sight, since he slew his cousins' knight (8618–785). 'Take this ring to my love in the castle', says Guiromelant, 'and give it to her . . . and tell her that I so trust in her love that I believe she would rather her brother Gawain were slain in bitter death than that I should suffer harm to the smallest toe on my foot' (8788–96). The name of the castle is La Roche de Chanpguin (8817).[64] In return for his information he asks and learns Gawain's name.

Though Guiromelant and the Hermit both reveal the identity of characters in the romance, and help to elucidate its meaning, their functions are in absolute contrast. The Hermit gives spiritual peace and joy to Perceval, Guiromelant offers combat to Gawain and a continuation of the chain of violence which has caused misery to countless ladies and damsels. The mothers of Arthur and Gawain will be spectators at the fight, and so will Arthur and his court who are now summoned by Gawain. Should Gawain be slain, the Two Queens will suffer. Yet his victory will apparently bring sorrow to his sister. Gawain and Guiromelant, intent on the fight and the spectacle it will make, are as heedless of the women and their grief as Perceval was of his mother and the Damsel in the Tent, and as Kay was of the Damsel who Laughed, or Guiromelant of the Male Pucele. Only the latter had reacted in fury against violent knights, and sought to lead them to destruction. It was, she says, grief for her first love which first led her to insult knights so that they would slay her. She asks Gawain to execute her as an example to any damsel who might try to shame a knight (8947–63). Gawain refuses, and, back at the castle, she is welcomed into the Joy of the Court by the ladies and damsels and the Two Queens. Here, in a moment of light comedy, the Two Queens, not recognising Gawain, make plans for his marriage to Clarissant 'for they will love each other like sister and brother'. Clarissant rejects the claim by Guiromelant to be her lover: he loves her only 'from afar'. She would die sooner than hear of hurt to her long-lost brother. Gawain knights the five hundred youths, and the narrative ends as the invitation to the joust at Chanpguin reaches Guenevere at Orcanie.

Ms. B signals the end of the romance: *Explicit li romanz de Perceval*. Ms. A adds after l.9234 *Explycyt Percevax le viel*, and then carries on with the *Premiere Continuation* of the story. Mss. ELMPQRSTUV go straight on with the continuation, and, apart from L, in the same hand. Mss. C and H finish the story at l.9228, and F at l.8608.[65]

The Gawain adventures exemplify the anarchy of knightly violence which drove Perceval's mother to the Waste Forest and the mothers of Arthur and Gawain to Chanpguin. This is the violence suggested by the five knights in the forest and typified by Kay and by the Scarlet Knight who made Arthur quail. It is the violence from which Perceval could have rescued the lands of the Fisher King if he had sought to know the functions of the Grail and the Lance that Bleeds. And it is the vendetta of this violence which Gawain had called down upon himself when he acted from *consilium proprium* and the belief that his values were right, and killed and degraded his knightly adversaries. Gawain lacks the lineage of the Elect, the imagination of the spirit which might allow him to glimpse the castle of the Fisher King. Though he has more *savoir* and less *folie* than in his days of youthful knighthood, he is bound by his limitations to the path of *vaine gloire* and *fausse hypocrisie* on which Perceval entered when he fought the Scarlet Knight, and from which he was gradually released after his visit to the Grail Castle. We are not told whether Gawain fought in the past for any useful or charitable purpose, but only that by killing other knights he sowed a harvest of hatred. In the adventures which test the *leauté* of his knighthood, he is forced to fight against opponents who are unjust and full of hatred, and he conducts himself nobly when he is cheated, humiliated and attacked. At Tintagel he defends the Younger Sister who has the just cause, and at Chanpguin he frees the castle and its Queen from the isolation of its self-imposed defences and brings it joy and the promise of a wider life by inviting Arthur and his court to watch the fight with Guiromelant. If Guiromelant, the ravisher of damsels and the love-struck knight, may be seen as the other side of Gawain, then Gawain, by defeating him and leading him to the Joy of the Court at the tourney where the two Queens and their sons will be reunited, would be facing and overcoming his former self. But this is no more than speculation, and there is no evidence that Gawain, like Erec, was destined to restore the full Joy of the Court to Arthur, Guenevere and the Two Queens.

Gawain's four major adventures are divided into two parts by the Hermit episode, and this arrangement does not appear to be fortuitous, for the first two adventures are enacted in a setting of worldly reality at Tintagel and Escavalon, and the second two, the meeting with the Male Pucele and the episodes in and around Chanpguin, take place in an eerie, incomprehensible, frightening world dominated by evil, unexpected violence and danger. It is noteworthy that in these four adventures the mood of violence and fear increases progressively. At Tintagel we are at the level of injustice, self-will and false values symbolised by the Elder Sister in the adventures of Noire Espine in *Yvain*. In this case, the Elder Sister at Tintagel, foreshadowing the Male Pucele, tries to humiliate Gawain for his refusal to join in the tourney. Her values are as superficial as those of the society which condemned Lancelot for riding in the cart, and Gawain, under duress from her spitefulness, acquits himself honourably. At Escavalon, he is faced with the hatred, anger and lust for destruction of knights and burghers alike, and is hard pressed when he defends his life and that of the damsel with whom he has fallen in love. The mob which tries to destroy their tower is afflicted by a 'madness' which Chrétien, as Peire Cardenal was to do in his *Una ciutatz fo*,[66] lightens with the deft Alice in Wonderland touch of the world upside-down.

After the Hermit episode, the mood of Gawain's adventures changes. Violence and hatred brood over the largely waste land in which he moves. Insuperable evils seem omnipresent, and such humour as exists, as in Gawain's jousting on the Ugly Nag, is black, with supernatural overtones. In this world of chaos, against which the Two Queens and their followers have sealed themselves in their castle, there is no goodness, no love, no control. Damsels are raped, and fought for in combat. Knights fight to kill, on sight. This is the world of Meleagant, of Mauvestié, of the wooden-hearted search for renown, of a courage which is no more than an instantaneous reflex action of violence. It is the realm of the Lance of Destruction. Lacking mercy and courtesy, it contrasts with the world of Arthur and Gornemant, in which erring knights are restored to society. Yet Arthur's world is tainted by this violence in the deeds of Kay, and, possibly, of the younger Gawain, to judge by the killings for which he must atone. And it is for the merciless killing of knights that Gawain will be finally excluded from the fellowship of the Grail in the thirteenth-century Queste del saint Graal.[67]

Perceval, more than any other romance by Chrétien, is based on a series of dialectical contrasts of mood, situation, character, adventure and aspiration. Behind this juxtaposition of opposites there lies the fundamental conflict of Good against Evil, of the moral and spiritual side of man against the physical, of caritas against voluntas propria, of a true and whole view of life against the self-interested blindness of consilium proprium. Chrétien stirs the imagination of his audience with the allusive use of images and characters such as the Lance, Grail and Fisher King, but it is through this device of sustained, and, at times, enigmatic contrasts, that he reveals the sen and purpose of the romance. His methods of suggesting meaning are far more advanced than the clear-cut contrasts, comparisons and juxtapositions, in fact the bele conjointure, of Erec et Enide. His ways are more poetical, shadowy and subtle, offering an oblique suggestion, a fragmentary disclosure of meaning which an audience or reader, aware of his methods, will fit together with the overtones of meaning in the Prologue and the expository speeches of Perceval's mother and cousin, and the Hermit. No single explanation of the romance can be valid, as Chrétien must have realised when he failed to return to the story of Perceval and the reason why the Lance bleeds.

If we look back at the scene in the castle of the Fisher King, we see that the Grail Procession and the functions of the Lance and Grail in this procession are central to the meaning of the romance. These functions are indicated by the key questions: 'Why does the lance bleed?' 'To whom is the grail being served?' Perceval is spiritually awake to the extent that he can see the Grail Castle and feel the need to ask these questions but he is not awake enough to grasp their importance.

In this scene in the castle of the Fisher King, Chrétien juxtaposes the service of two contrasting meals, one of which, as sumptuous as the later meal at Chanpguin, is served to Perceval, and the other of which, void of material foods, passes before him as each new course of the carnal feast appears. The juxtaposition of the physical and non-physical is not fortuitous:

Li premiers més fu d'une hanche	The first course was a haunch of
De cerf de greisse au poivre chaut.	venison in pepper sauce. There
Vins clers ne raspez ne lor faut	was no shortage of wine, clear
A cope d'or soëf a boivre.	or sharp, for them to drink
De la hanche de cerf au poivre	smoothly in a gold cup. A
Uns vaslez devant aus trancha,	young man, in their presence,
Qui a soi treite la hanche a	cut pieces from the haunch of
Atot le tailleor d'arjant,	peppered venison, having drawn
Et les morsiaus lor met devant	the haunch towards himself,
Sor un gastel qui fu antiers.	together with the silver cutting-
(3280–9)	board. And he places the pieces
	of meat in front of them on a
	platter of bread which was whole

The description of the silver *tailleor* as a form of butcher's block, with the rough and jerky rhythm of ll.3285–7, is contrasted immediately with the gliding smoothness of the Grail Procession:

Et li graaus andemantiers	And the grail meanwhile passed
Par devant aus retrespassa,	again in front of them, and the
Et li vaslez ne demanda	young man did not ask who was
Del graal cui l'an an servoit.	being served from the grail.
(3290–3)	

This is no passing curiosity. He would dearly like to know the answer:

Qu'a chascun més don l'an servoit	For as each course was served
Par devant lui trespasser voit	to him, he sees the grail, entirely
Le graal trestot descovert,	uncovered, pass across the hall
Mes il ne set cui l'an an sert,	in front of him. But he does not
Et si le voldroit mout savoir.	know who is being served from
(3299–303)	it. Yet he would very much like
	to know this.

It is difficult not to see in this juxtaposed service of meals the suggestion of two contrasting ways of life. On the one hand, the hot, cooked meal with rich and spiced sauces, the meat carved before Perceval's eyes, are intended to sate an appetite for food indulged beyond the limits of *necessitas*, and to stir carnality and *cupiditas*. In contrast to this busy feast, splendid in victuals, the service of the other meal, resplendent in light, is apparently devoid of physical sustenance. Nothing can be seen over the edge of the flat serving dish, which, having no cover, can be seen to contain no hot food, nor any food at all.

Even if there were no Prologue in Chrétien's *Perceval*, no Christian teaching from his mother, no meeting with his cousin, or Hermit episode, the juxtaposition of these two meals in the mysterious castle of the maimed and impotent *prodon* would suggest, especially to a twelfth-century audience, the dichotomy of man's flesh and the spirit, and the sustenance which each of these requires. When we learn that the *prodon* is the Fisher King (3495), whose castle is 'there and not there' (3468–95) and that, fishing from a small boat, he appears as an earthly figure, and then, almost simultaneously, as a supernatural being in the vision of the Grail Castle, and when we learn further that a host from the Grail sustains the father of the Fisher King, who is also a Fisher King, we may see that the image of the son, maimed in the flesh by the *coup felon*, and of the father whose being is spirit, sustained by the food of the spirit, could scarcely fail to suggest God as the Father and Holy Spirit, the source of *caritas*, and God as the Son 'destroyed' in the flesh. This is not to say that the Fisher King is a Christ-figure, or that he has lost his clearly Celtic associations, or his human role as a *prodon* who presents a sword to the young Perceval. Chrétien is accepting all these levels of meaning, and so can his audience, but it is unlikely that a twelfth-century audience would fail to see the significance of the two services of meals, of the two Fisher Kings and of the two aspects of the Lance that Bleeds, and the significance of the wafer in the Grail as symbol of the Holy Spirit and the hope of man's union with God.

The Lance contains within itself the suggestion of destruction and of spiritual revelation and enlightenment. The lance of the leader of the five knights is the first weapon about which Perceval asks questions. Like the lance which Gawain must seek, the lance which will destroy the kingdom of Britain, it kills and ruins. Should Gawain succeed in finding this lance, he must return with it to the King of Escavalon, a land of maniacal violence where Perceval's elder brother was knighted and slain on the same day (463–70). But the lance in the Grail Procession, which, by dialectical contrast with the feasting at table, is concerned almost certainly with spiritual matters, suggests undeniably the Lance which damaged the body of Christ and which enlightened Longinus and brought him through martyrdom to Christian salvation. It is not too fanciful to suggest that the Lance that Bleeds heads the Grail Procession because, in the image of the Lance of Longinus, it brings enlightenment and the revelation of the Christian message; and that Perceval, whose dormant spiritual self has nevertheless stirred him to remorse about his mother, feels obscurely the summons of the Lance and Grail, and that had he asked the questions, the final answers might have been: 'The Lance bleeds to reveal the hope of salvation' and 'In the contents of the Grail which come to you from God the Father and are served to all Christian folk, lies the source of *caritas*, redemption of sin, and the granting of salvation.' In these hypothetical conditions, happiness would be restored to mankind, and the physical and spiritual waste land of human life become fertile. Such an ending to the romance is pure speculation, but not impossible. We infer from the Hideous Damsel that there will be no further opportunity for Perceval to ask the questions (4662–77), and that therefore he will find his answers only through experience and suffering. Though Perceval has promised (2960–71) to revisit Belrepeire and find Blancheflor again, possibly after a Joy of the Spirit, when he has found the answers he seeks, it is not improbable that the work was near its end, when it was abandoned by Chrétien.[68] In this case, he may have intended that the real hero, as in *Lancelot*, should supplant Gawain at the final reunion of Arthur's court, and, in an episode centred on the meaning of the Lance that Bleeds, restore to the world the hope of spiritual peace through *caritas*. It would scarcely be part of Chrétien's enigmatic and allusive methods to allow

Perceval to find the Grail Castle again. The sight of the Grail Procession was a moment of revelation, a source of inspiration towards self-knowledge. Perceval is made to discover the message of the Grail Procession in the adventure of life, and, it is probable that, having found this truth, he would be left, at the end of the romance, to use it for the general good. Although we are told by the author of a Grail Continuation, Gerbert de Montreuil, that death interrupted Chrétien's work, it is noteworthy that neither *Lancelot* nor *Yvain* have a clear-cut, harmonious ending, such as we find in *Erec et Enide*. It is possible that Chrétien, aware, as he says in *Lancelot*, of the unending struggle of Good and Evil in the world, may have hesitated to offer a solution to the enigma of Lance and Grail. He had partially disclosed his *sen* by his linear, expository and allusive methods. He was clearly aware of the disorder in human affairs, and in the human personality, which he must have seen as universal, and he may have shrunk from dogmatic utterance, the facile, contrived solution to the universal and continuing riddle of the human condition. If this were the case, he would have been reflecting the views of contemporary thinkers who saw in the divinely created diversity of natural life the source of cosmic unity and harmony. Thus Arnold of Bonneval near Chartres and a friend of St Bernard: 'This whole fabric of the world, made of such dissimilar parts and yet uniform, composed of such diverse things and yet one, of such opposite elements and yet tranquil, pursues its lawful and ordered course, without any fearful likelihood of ruin' (*De operibus sex dierum*, PL, CLXXXIX, 1516).

Though *Perceval* ends on an indeterminate, melancholy note, it is in its entirety a romance of hope and positive belief. In the Gawain adventures the whole world may appear to fall apart, yet the centre holds. The evils of violence, the *folie* of destructive knighthood will persist, since vainglory and false hypocrisy will not die. Yet the world of Arthur, still struggling for survival, offers an ideal of *savoir*, of rational conduct and temporal order buttressed by virtues which, being of this world alone and so tarnished, limit and constrain it. Such virtues are the belief in courage, chivalry, knightly renown, and the Joy of the Court, and they are unknown to Gawain's adversaries who are driven by the *folie* of a vindictiveness which he himself has sown in earlier days. *Perceval* contains an amalgam of themes and *motifs* from the earlier romances. From *Cliges* it takes irony and the two-fold observation of life, the acceptance of the real and the illusory, the device of the world upside-down; from *Lancelot*, it uses the structure of the journey to and from a castle, where the central episode occurs, and the conflict between Good and invincible Evil; and from *Yvain* it borrows and develops the theme of the inadequate, self-caring knight who is reborn after moral weakness and madness into a life associated with deeds of *caritas*. To search for the whole is to define and explore its component parts. This Chrétien has done in his earlier romances. In *Perceval* he transcends these works with his implicit belief that wholeness must embrace and move beyond the temporal to the eternal. True whole-ness comes to Perceval from the peace and harmony in mind and spirit which are free from *voluntas propria* and are guided by *caritas*. In this way, *Perceval*, unfinished yet possibly as complete in its meaning as Chrétien might have wished to see it, binds up the sequence of romances which began with *Erec et Enide*. *Folie* has been ousted by *savoir*, and *savoir* in its worldly sense has been superseded by a search for spiri-tual knowledge, for knowledge of God and human redemp-tion. The quest for temporal order and happiness which inspired *Erec et Enide* persists in *Perceval*. It is still an essential part of human endeavour, but in the wider perspective offered by the contrast between the values of Arthur and those of the Grail lineage, Perceval's mother, the Fisher King and the Hermit, it is revealed as the minor part of life.

Chrétien has not resolved the dichotomy of worldly and spiritual knighthood, the quests of Gawain and Perceval. He may well have intended not to do so. This dichotomy will be determined separately in the slaughter of Arthur's worldly knights in the *Mort Artu* and in the revelation of the divine mysteries of the Grail to Galahad, son of Lancelot, in the *Queste del saint Graal*.[69] In Chrétien's *Perceval* the world and the spirit are still conjoined. They coexist in the image of the Lance which can destroy fruitfulness, order and happiness, and, which, in another manifestation, can sow enlighten-ment, faith and the hope of redemption. They are together in the image of the Grail, which can furnish food to the flesh, or to the spirit. They may lie together in the symbolism of the Three Drops of Blood on the Snow. The falcon must drop its earthly prey and soar aloft. The stricken bird must resume its flight, and snow and the soil absorb the blood. The cycle of nature, of devastation and resurgence, must continue. But, at the same time, Perceval's quest for a meaning and an order which will explain this process, is all. The falcon must escape his earthly falconer.

7
The Legacy

W HEN we consider Chrétien's five romances in the round, we can see a sharp division in style and intention between the first two, *Erec et Enide* and *Cliges*, and the last three. This division corresponds in many ways to the distinction in contemporary troubadour poetry between the *trobar leus* or clear style, which was concerned with courtly reality, and the *clus* or allusive, metaphysical style. In *Erec et Enide* and *Cliges* Chrétien is involved with the affairs of this world, with love which leads to dynastic marriage, with the issues of personal and social order and disorder, with the conflict between wisdom and folly, between the reality and the illusion of earthly living. In the interval between *Cliges* and the first part of *Yvain*, which in its beginnings almost certainly preceded *Lancelot*, a major change occurs. The rational and benevolent optimism which had inspired *Erec et Enide*, and, also, though tinged with a sharper irony, *Cliges*, has diminished. The naive belief in the divine *ordo* of life, in which knowledge, experience and reason offer guidance to an idealised and general concept of joy, gives way to a closer and more realistic view of life as a conflict which is not to be resolved in a facile or comforting manner. Hints of such uncertainty are apparent in *Cliges*. They play a major part in *Lancelot*, *Yvain* and *Perceval*.

In these later romances there is a constant dramatic tension which defines the characters, illuminates the action and gives infinite range to Chrétien's meaning. This tension arises from a conflict between two contrasting views of life. On the one hand, there is the *simplece* of the personality which is a whole within itself, and which, because it is aware of itself and its identity, can respond with intuitive generosity to the demands of life and so achieve a wider wholeness with its surroundings. In such an ideal personality natural virtue and happiness abound, untouched by the tarnish of self-interest. In contrast, there is the personality which adheres to the patterns of virtue and morality formulated by courtly society and, in so doing, surrenders its pristine purity. Such a personality, lacking true *Franchise* or nobility of mind and spirit, constrained by its environment, tainted in varying degree by self-interest and the assumptions of *vaine gloire*, is fragmented.

It is in terms of this conflict that Chrétien becomes increasingly concerned with a theme which he had adumbrated in *Erec et Enide*. This is the struggle of an individual who allows conventional moral values to disguise his true self, and who, wakened from this complacency to a crisis of self-doubt and even madness, regains peace of mind in a sense of identity and oneness with life. In *Lancelot* and *Perceval* Chrétien expands this individual struggle into an allegorical conflict between the Good of this world and the Evil which he admits can never be suppressed. To allow for a wide development of this struggle between the powers of Good and Evil, Chrétien changes the thematic form of these romances from a bipartite to a tripartite construction.[1] His language in *Yvain*, as well as in *Lancelot* and *Perceval*, sheds the unadorned simplicity of *Erec et Enide*, and in its imagery of the Cart, the Lion, the Grail and Lance, reaches out to moral and spiritual values which place Chrétien in the forefront of European literature. Chrétien's mind has abandoned the certainties of *Erec et Enide* and the happiness to be attained through temporal order. In *Perceval*, or *Percevax le viel* in ms. B, he progresses to a 'whole' view of life which can embrace secular anarchy and the persistence of Evil and yet find the *summum bonum* of spiritual order.

The allusive reaching out to seize the imagination of the audience according to its level of perception and experience can be related to the art of the metaphysical troubadours such as Marcabru, Peire d'Alvernhe and Arnaut Daniel. These poets in the *clus* and *ric* styles interwove in their works extra levels of meaning, often with Christian moralising or philosophical significance, and used words as entities in their own right, with their own particular smooth or harsh sounds and rich overtones of meaning. In the years around 1170 this creative poetry was in retreat before the spreading waves of courtly poetry in the clear style. It is not improbable that Chrétien was aware of the controversy about this issue among the troubadours of his day.[2] It is clear, however, that his romances move from what the troubadours would have called the 'clear' style of the romance genre, typified by the *Eneas*, and by *Erec et Enide* and *Cliges*, towards a mature 'close', 'rich' style which gives us Chrétien's most memorable scenes, such as the Sword Bridge, the Grail Procession or the Three Drops of Blood on the Snow. The symbolical description of sceptre and cloak in the Coronation scene in *Erec et Enide* has been transformed into an imaginative art in which the narrative genre of the romance becomes a form of three-dimensional poetry.

This art is apparent also in the concealed and enigmatic combinations of themes, myths and beliefs which have a separate and parallel existence within their own individual frameworks. The Grail Procession may evoke thoughts of Christian or of Celtic traditions, or of the religions of ancient Rome and Egypt. This profusion of different auras, of patterns of thought and mythology, lends richness to the texture of both *Lancelot* and *Perceval*. It also helps us to understand Chrétien's purpose in avoiding the definable in order to prompt the imagination of his audience to move outwards in an expanding universe of the spirit. In the allusive method all is implicit, nothing is earthbound or static. Yet there is intellectual control in the imaginative pattern which Chrétien presents to his audience. Each separate aura, mythology or level of meaning, whether Christian, Celtic, courtly or knightly, preserves its particular virtue which may then be added to and so may enrich the quality of the others. This process has been discussed in the chapter on *Perceval* in connection with the dual function of the Lance in which Celtic and Christian traditions may be conjoined and yet preserve their separate identities.

In the later romances, Chrétien sees life as a cosmic unity of conflicting influences, divine and profane, spiritual and material, good and evil. Though he sees the conflict with clarity, he defines it in oblique and enigmatic fashion through deeds and words which reveal the unspoken thoughts and feelings in his characters. It is through the opposing qualities of Lancelot and Meleagant, of Perceval, Gawain and Guiromelant that he establishes a sense of his disgust at the destructiveness of evil, of his mistrust of the narrowly rationalistic and codified view of life, and his faith in the visionary experience.

As Chrétien progresses from the symbolism of the sceptre to that of the Grail, from a belief in the virtues of knowledge and sovereignty, and the temporal order they offer, to the certainties of the spiritual life, his treatment of the themes of love and knighthood deepens and matures. This evolution in Chrétien's view of life is independent of, and, as in the case of Lancelot, may conflict with and so enrich his narrative material. Yet the basic, unifying sen in his work remains unchanged. It stems from the conviction that deeds and words take their quality from the quality of the intention which motivates them. The more selfless their intention, the greater the possibility of happiness and peace of mind for the doer. The more self-interested the purpose, the more inevitable the spiral of social and personal misery.

In Chrétien's view of life the concept of bien and Leauté is of primary importance. The quality of bien has been discussed in the chapter on Erec et Enide, and that of Leauté in connection with Lancelot. Briefly stated, bien in this context appears to be the goodness associated with the intuitive or 'natural' virtue of the person who is endowed with simplece, or the immediacy of true and virtuous human feeling, with humility, self-abnegation and caritas. Allied to Leauté, it confronts the common enemy Mauvestié. Leauté is the quality of fidelity to a lei or law. It may vary from obedience to a courtly, feudal or knightly law, to submission to the lei which is the basis, the very essence of natural virtue. Such Leauté, which has connotations of Christian goodness, pity and caritas, is akin to the natural lex divinely bestowed on man. It transcends the conventional courtly and knightly virtues epitomised by Gawain. It alone can check the forces of evil, whether these appear as the courtly Desleauté of Kay, the anti-social violence of Yder, Mabonagrain or Guiromelant, or the irredeemable wickedness of Meleagant and his henchmen. This ideal of a 'natural' bien and Leauté which are innate in man and woman, and so both individual and universal, and the human aspiration towards their rediscovery, is the essential *sen* of Chrétien's romances. In this lies his right to be called a poet of *universitas*. It is this quality, apparent also in the *simplece* of his style, the tonality of his language, his evocation of atmosphere, drama and comedy,[3] which assures the lasting influence of his work.

In what was one of the most important centuries in the history of European civilisation, Chrétien's achievement was unique. His sequence of great Arthurian romances established the romance as the major literary genre for the depiction of the weaknesses and triumphs, baseness and idealism of individual man faced with the problems of the human condition. Chrétien's work inspires and influences the great medieval German romances such as the *Erec* and *Iwein* of Hartman von Aue, the *Parzival* of Wolfram von Eschenbach. And his influence reaches out in reverse direction to the traditional Celtic stories of Erec, Yvain and Perceval contained in the *Gereint, Owein* and *Peredur* of the later Welsh *Mabinogion*.[4] It spreads to the south, to Spain, Italy, Provence, to the troubadours, and more particularly to the thirteenth-century poet of *Flamenca* who not only follows Chrétien's linear, expository and allusive methods of indicating meaning but approves and mocks his idealism.[5] Chrétien's real triumph, however, lies in his failure to finish the *Perceval*. The consequence of this was that the Grail theme, together with the equally 'unfinished' story of Lancelot and Guenevere, inspired within fifty years a sequence of French Arthurian romances which, through the genius of Sir Thomas Malory and other writers, immeasurably enriched English, European and world literature.

The temptation offered by the unfinished Grail story prompted numerous *Perceval Continuations*[6] which probably used a source or sources related to those followed by Chrétien. The anonymous *First Continuation* or pseudo-Wauchier (*c.* 1200) continued the Gawain adventures; the *Second Continuation* (*c.* 1200), by an unknown writer working under Wauchier de Denain, continued the Perceval adventures; the *Third Continuation* (*c.* 1233–7) by Manessier was intended as a completion of Chrétien's work and established Perceval, the nephew of the Fisher King, as his successor in the Grail Castle; and the *Fourth Continuation* (*c.* 1233) by a Gerbert, probably Gerbert de Montreuil, author of the *Roman de la*

Violette, concluded in 17,000 lines the adventure of Perceval's broken sword.

Shortly after 1200, Robert de Boron gave a fresh direction to the development of the Grail theme. He also wrote a *Merlin*, which was intended to link the stories of Joseph and Arthur and of which five hundred lines have survived, and a *Perceval* which exists in a prose version known as the *Didot-Perceval*, but the work which concerns us here is his *Roman de l'Estoire dou Graal*.[7] This work, composed in a flat and clinical style, is a milestone in the evolution of the Grail tradition. Whereas Chrétien had suggested the Celtic and Christian associations evoked by the Grail, and had emphasised the function of the Grail and its contents, rather than the importance of the Grail as an object in its own right, Robert de Boron defined it with thirteenth-century precision as the Chalice in which the Holy Blood, gathered by Joseph of Arimathea, was transported to Britain as a symbol of the power which would convert the country to Christianity. The idea of the Grail as an aid to Christian conversion occurs also in the early thirteenth-century prose romance of *Perlesvaus*.[8] But the culminating work of the Grail theme and of the whole Arthurian tradition is undoubtedly the *Prose Lancelot*[9] or Vulgate Version which was probably written in Champagne between 1220 and 1230 by several hands under a central direction.[10] It had five branches: Robert de Boron's 'history' of the origins of the Grail and its journey to Britain; the story of Merlin, also from Robert de Boron; the story of Lancelot; the *Queste del saint Graal*; and the *Mort Artu*. The *Queste*,[11] under clear Cistercian influence, makes explicit what was implicit in Chrétien de Troyes. Arthur's knights are tested and divided into a worldly and a spiritual knighthood. The three Elect among the spiritual knights, Galahad, Perceval and Bohort, are entrusted with the mission, which they accomplish, of returning the Holy Grail to Jerusalem. In the *Mort Artu*,[12] the worldly knighthood of Arthur, Gawain and his court is torn apart by the adulterous love of Guenevere and Lancelot, and when finally betrayed by Mordred, destroys itself on the battlefield of Salisbury Plain. Excalibur is hurled into the lake. Arthur dies.

The unique quality of Chrétien's achievement shines more brightly beside such spiritual and worldly conclusiveness.

His poetic intention in the later romances becomes clearer. He is not a man who accepts absolutes such as the immaculate Galahad, nor even a Holy Grail in which the most secret mysteries of God are revealed. Chrétien allows himself only to give us intimations of our mortality and immortality, and of the almost ungraspable wholeness of a human condition which embraces cruelty and *caritas*. Such poetic intimations are the true legacy given to us by Chrétien, together with an image of the ideal which 'slips through and evades us', but which, when present, we cannot fail to recognise.

Appendix 1

Chronological table

c. 500	The British defeat the Saxons at the battle of Badon Hill (*Mons Badonicus*).
540	Gildas in the *De Excidio et Conquestu Britanniae* mentions the battle of Badon Hill, but not Arthur.
c. 600	The Welsh poem the *Gododdin* has a reference to Arthur.
c. 800	Nennius in his *Historia Brittonum* records the victories of Arthur, *dux bellorum*, over the Anglo-Saxons.
814	The name Arthur attested in a historical document in France.
c. 955	*Annales Cambriae* record, under the years 516 and 537, the victory of Arthur at Badon and his death with Medraut at the battle of Camlann.
10th century	Welsh poem *The Spoils of Annwn* includes mention of Arthur as a figure of legend and pagan folklore.
10th/11th cent.	*Black Book of Camarthen* gives a list of Arthur's warriors which includes Key and Bedwyr.
	Vita Gildae of the Welsh monk Caradoc of Llancarvan relates the abduction of Guenevere by Melvas.
993–1030	Guilhem the Great, III Count of Poitou, V Duke of Aquitaine.
994–1040	Odilon, Abbot of Cluny.
1006–28	Fulbert, Bishop of Chartres.
1019	Marriage of Guilhem the Great, III Count of Poitou, to Agnes of Burgundy.
1019–c. 1100	References to Arthur in: a life of Saint Goeznovius (c. 1019); the *Vita Cadoci* (c. 1075); the *Vita Carantoci* (c. 1100); the *Vita Iltuli* (c. 1100); and the *Vita Paterni* (c. 1100+).
1043	Marriage of Ala (Agnes), daughter of Agnes of Burgundy, to the Emperor Henry III.
1066	William the Conqueror wins the battle of Hastings and becomes King of England.
1070–1140	Bledri ap Cadivor, *Latinarius*, 'interpreter', Welsh nobleman, allied to the Normans.
1080–1145	William of Conches, pupil of St Bernard and tutor to Henry of Anjou, later Henry II of England.

Appendix I

1086–1127	Guilhem IX Duke of Aquitaine, VII Count of Poitou, the first troubadour (b. 1071).
1098	Foundation of the Cistercian Order by Robert of Molesme.
1099	The Crusaders establish the kingdom of Jerusalem.
c. 1100	The Welsh prose love-story *Kulhwch and Olwen* exemplifies the power of Arthur's name.
1100	Coronation charter of Henry I of England.
1108–37	Louis VI, King of France.
1110	The name Gawain attested in historical document in France.
1113	The name Tristan attested in historical document in France.
1115–53	St Bernard (b. 1091), first Abbot of Clairvaux.
1125	William of Malmesbury writes his *Historia Regum Anglorum*.
c. 1130–c. 1150	Marcabru fl.
1135–8	Geoffrey dedicates his *Historia Regum Britanniae* to various royal and noble personages.
1137	Eleanor, grand-daughter of Guilhem IX of Aquitaine, becomes Duchess of Aquitaine, Countess of Poitou, is married to Prince Louis of France, who within a month of the marriage becomes King Louis VII of France.
c. 1139	Geffrei Gaimar writes *L'Estoire des Engleis*, in Hampshire and in Lincolnshire.
1144	Rebuilding of Chartres Cathedral, dedicated to the Virgin, begins.
c. 1145–80	Bernart de Ventadorn fl.
c. 1147	Jaufre Rudel fl.
1147–8	The Second Crusade.
1148	Death of William of Saint-Thierry.
1150–6	The *Roman de Thèbes* composed.
1150–80	Peire d'Alvernhe fl.
1152	Eleanor of Aquitaine marries Henry of Anjou.
1154–89	Henry II (formerly Henry of Anjou), King of England with Eleanor as his Queen.
1154–73	Benoit de Sainte-Maure composes his *Roman de Troie* which he dedicates to Eleanor of Aquitaine between 1160 and 1170.
1155	Wace dedicates his *Roman de Brut* to Eleanor of Aquitaine.
c. 1156	The *Roman d'Eneas* is written.
1160–70	Beroul composes the first half of the extant fragment of the *Roman de Tristran*.
1160–70	Thomas composes his *Roman de Tristan*.
c. 1160–90	Marie de France fl.
1162	Becket Archbishop of Canterbury.

Appendix I

1164–74	Wace works on the *Roman de Rou*, which he leaves unfinished.
c. 1165–c.1200	Guiraut de Bornelh fl.
1170	Henry the Young King, eldest surviving son of Henry II, crowned in Westminster Abbey by the Archbishop of York and other prelates.
	Thomas Becket killed in Canterbury Cathedral on 29 December.
c. 1170	Chrétien composes *Erec et Enide*.
1172	Henry the Young King and Margaret of France, daughter of Louis VII, crowned at Winchester.
1173	Death of Raimbaut d'Aurenga, Count of Orange (b. c. 1146).
	A *Christianus canonicus sancti Lupi* signs a document now in the archives of the episcopal palace at Troyes.
	Henry II suppresses an armed revolt led by his sons and their mother Queen Eleanor.
1173–89	Queen Eleanor 'imprisoned' in England by Henry II.
1175–80	Andreas Capellanus fl.
c. 1176	Chrétien de Troyes writes *Cliges*.
1177–81	Chrétien de Troyes writes *Yvain* and *Lancelot*.
c. 1178–80	Alanus de Insulis writes his *De Planctu Naturae*.
1180–2	Philip of Alsace, Count of Flanders from 1168, acts as *de facto* regent of France during minority of Philip Augustus.
c. 1180–c. 1200	Arnaut Daniel fl.
1180–1223	Philip II Augustus, King of France.
1181–91	Chrétien de Troyes writes *Perceval*.
1181–97	Bertran de Born fl.
1183	Henry the Young King dies.
1189–99	Richard I, King of England.
1189	Eleanor of Aquitaine (d. 1204) released from imprisonment by Richard I of England.
1189–92	The Third Crusade.
1191	Philip of Flanders dies at Acre on the Third Crusade.
1190–1210	Hartmann von Aue, author of *Erec* and *Iwein* fl.
c. 1200	Robert de Boron writes his *Roman de l'Estoire dou Graal*.
	Perlesvaus written.
	The *Elucidation*, Prologue to the *Perceval*, written.
	The *First Perceval Continuation* composed.
	The *Second Perceval Continuation* composed.
c. 1200–1220	Wolfram von Eschenbach fl.
c. 1233–37	The *Third Perceval Continuation* composed by Manessier.
1220–30	The *Prose-Lancelot* written (including *La Queste del saint Graal* and the *Mort Artu*).
c. 1233	The *Fourth Perceval Continuation* composed by a Gerbert, probably Gerbert de Montreuil.
c. 1270	The romance of *Flamenca* written by an anonymous author.

311

Appendix I

1300–25   The *White Book of Rhydderch* and the later *Red Book of Hergest* (1375–1425), two Welsh collections containing the earlier stories known as the *Mabinogion*, including the prose tales of *Gereint, Owain* and *Peredur.*

1469–70   Sir Thomas Malory (d. 1471) concludes his *Tale of the Death of King Arthur.*

Appendix 2

A short glossary of poetic, courtly and feudal terms

The meanings offered in this glossary are related to the context in which these words are used in the text of this book. For a fuller range of meanings for these terms, reference should be made to the major dictionaries of Old French, such as the *Altfranzösisches Wörterbuch* of A. Tobler and E. Lommatzsch, and in the case of Old Provençal, to the *Provenzalisches Supplement-Wörterbuch* of E. Levy (Leipzig, 1894–1924) or the *Petit Dictionnaire Provençal–Français* by the same scholar.

Antancion. The intention behind the composition of a literary work; the direction or purpose given to such a work; the attempt to reveal this direction or purpose and the underlying meaning or meanings of a work to an audience or a reader.

Assaiars (Provençal). The courtly testing by a lady of a suitor's patience and sexual forbearance.

Bel Acueil. Fair Welcome. The kind response expected of a lady towards an aspirant suitor or a knight at her court or castle.

Bien. Goodness; innocence of all vice; individual and communal well-being and happiness.

Chanson (Provençal, *canso*). The courtly love song of the troubadours and their counterparts, the Northern French *trouvères*.

Chansons de geste. Epic poems in Northern France composed largely between the late eleventh and the early fourteenth centuries. Their true inspiration was the heroic age of Charlemagne, and his wars in Spain, Italy and Germany. The most famous of these works, which in their early days were chanted by minstrels (*jongleurs*) to a simple musical accompaniment, was the *Chanson de Roland*.

Chansons de toile (sewing songs). Sometimes called *chansons d'histoire*. Short Northern French love songs, usually in assonance. Popular in origin, they are influenced by courtly terms and motifs. The characters, usually noblewomen, long for the return of their absent or disdainful lovers.

Conjointure. The arranging and joining together of the component parts of a narrative; the formal method by which a poet effected a smooth transition from one adventure or situation to another; the organised arrangement of incident, monologue, dialogue and allusive imagery so that the *sen* or inner meaning of the romance, in both major and minor themes, might be revealed to the percipient audience or reader.

Conoissensa (Provençal). The power of discrimination, especially the ability to distinguish the good from the bad, the true from the false, the real from the illusory.

Conoistre. To know; to discriminate; to have sexual knowledge of a person.

Conte. A short narrative story, frequently involving a single sequence of events proceeding to or from a major incident or *avanture*.

Convoitise. Greed, covetousness, the desire to capture and possess the object of love.

Cortesia (Provençal). The sum of all the courtly virtues and their expression in social behaviour.

Cuidier (Provençal, *cuidar*). To think, to believe, sometimes with the connotation of believing erroneously, of imagining or fantasising; a way of thinking, a belief.

Desfi. The ritual pronouncement of a knight who takes back his feudal pledge of loyalty from his overlord or his comrade-in-arms.

Desir. The desire of the senses and of the mind for one particular person. See also *Vouloir*.

Estoire. A story which may imply, or may be credited with the implication that it possesses, 'historical' authenticity or importance as an authoritative source of material for future narrative writings.

'*Fausse Morte, La*'. The theme of the heroine who feigns death and is rescued from her coffin by her lover with whom she is then reunited in a secret love.

Fin'Amors (Provençal). True love; loyal love; perfect love; love which unites the desire of the mind, the senses and the spirit; love which is free from self-interest and which is devoted to the beloved; a reciprocal love of this quality.

Folie (Provençal, *foudatz*). Folly; mockery of convention and of conventional views; submission to the demands of impulse and feeling and the consequent rejection of *mesure*. See also *mesure*.

Franchise. Nobility of character; generosity of mind and spirit; the good manners which epitomise these qualities.

Geis. In the Celtic tradition a spell laid on a mortal by an inhabitant of the Celtic Other World. A *geis* may take the form of a veto or taboo, or it may compel a human to undertake a course of action, for example, to set off on a quest, or to fall irrevocably in love.

Jois (Provençal). The quest for individual and/or communal happiness; the attainment of this joy; a positive attitude to the cultivation of, and the search for happiness in life; behaviour epitomised by this.

Jongleurs (Provençal, *Joglars*). The minstrels who performed the poetic works composed by the *trouvères* and the troubadours, the mostly anonymous *chansons de geste* and lays. Their repertoire was immense. A *jongleur* could rise to the status of *trouvère* or troubadour and compose his own works. He might also earn a living as an acrobat or juggler, like the Roman *joculator*.

Jovens (Provençal). Youthfulness and generosity of spirit; behaviour epitomised by these qualities.

Appendix II

Largesce. Generosity; a generous gift; a width and adventurous generosity of the mind and spirit which are free from self-interest.

Leauté (Provençal, *Leautatz*). Loyalty: The rejection of self-will and pride and the acceptance of one's duty to obey and uphold the *lei* or 'law' of a profession or calling, whether courtly, knightly or Christian, or the natural *lei* which is innate in every created being. See also *Lei*.

Lei. The natural, innate 'law' which should determine the behaviour of every created being; the 'law' or code of a profession, calling or system of belief, whether courtly, knightly, feudal or Christian.

Los. Praise and reputation accorded to a knight for his exploits, especially for jousting at tournaments.

Losengier. A flatterer or slanderer at court; a gossip; the adversary of all true lovers.

Mauvestié (Provençal, *Malvestatz*). The vice of self-willed recreancy and the rejection through *Desleauté* of the 'laws' which provide the basis of moral, social and religious order; the purposeless violence which epitomises this rejection of order in the life of the individual and society.

Mehaigné, mahaing. Maimed, wounded, with the frequent connotation of impaired virility.

Mesure (Provençal, *Mesura*). The rational faculty of being able to follow the course of action most suited to the demands of social, courtly and knightly convention and to the talents, aspiration and quality of the individual (as revealed through *conoissensa*); moderation, the mean between too much and too little.

Miels, Lo (Provençal). Ultimate happiness; the furthest limit of *Jois*.

Nature (Provençal, *Natura*). The essence of each individual being as it exists within the natural order of created things; the sexual impulse in mankind.

Niceté. The condition of being ignorant of and untutored in the ways of the world, especially in courtly and knightly matters; the naivety, stupidity, boorishness, and childish simplicity which, depending on the situation, results from this.

Orguel. Arrogance; the sin of pride.

Pastourelle (Provençal, *Pastorela*). A poem in which the poet or knight attempts the seduction of a shepherdess by flattery, gifts, promises. The genre provided light relief to the courtly *chanson* and flourished in the North and South of France in the twelfth and thirteenth centuries. In a different form, especially at Arras, the poet describes the joys and tribulations of rustic lovers, or the merrymaking of shepherds and shepherdesses, or of artisans on a picnic.

Peintura (Provençal). The painted image; the illusory appearance of reality.

Peors (Provençal). Fear; reticence and timidity in matters of love.

Planh (Provençal). A laudatory poem composed on the death of a ruler, a poet or a person of consequence.

Prix (Provençal, *Pretz*). The reputation given to an individual by society, especially in a courtly or knightly context.

Proesce (Provençal, *Proeza*). Absolute excellence of virtue in a courtly, knightly, feudal or Christian context.

Romanz. Speech in the vernacular language; a narrative work translated into the vernacular; a narrative work composed in the vernacular; a narrative amplification of a story or *conte* in which a new arrangement of incident and dialogue (*conjointure*) may have been effected in order to suggest an underlying meaning or *sen*. See also *Conjointure*.

Savoir. The capacity for reasoned thought and for the ordering of one's personal and social behaviour; the mental control to which self-indulgence must submit; the resulting wisdom of heart and mind.

Sciance. The knowledge and wisdom that is acquired through experience and trials.

Sen. Good sense; intelligence; the inner meaning of a literary work.

Simplece. Direct, virtuous feeling, innocent of guile; the manifestation of this quality.

Sirventes (Provençal). A troubadour poem, usually of blame, or a poem concerned with impending war or deeds of war, or incidents of everyday life.

Sofrirs (Provençal). Humility; patience; endurance.

Tenso (Provençal). A troubadour poem in the form of a debate, frequently on a topic of love casuistry.

Trobar clus (Provençal). The 'closed' style. A term applied to troubadour poetry which contained different levels of meaning, allusive words and imagery, and variations of tonal quality which evoked extra nuances of meaning.

Trobar leu (Provençal). The 'clear, easy style' of composition which was generally used by the troubadours for their courtly love-songs. From 1170 onwards, songs in this clear style increasingly supplanted the more metaphysical troubadour poetry in the *trobar clus*.

Troubadours. Poets from all stations of life who, composing in Provençal, created the first cultivated vernacular lyric poetry in Europe. Their best work, always set to music, was composed between 1100 and the onset of the Albigensian Crusade in 1209. The work of the major troubadours reflected their views of the courtly tastes and the metaphysical interests of the courts in the South of France. Their reputation was such that Provençal came to be recognised in the early thirteenth century as the pre-eminent language for the composition of love lyrics in Western Europe.

Trouvères. Northern French counterparts of the troubadours. They composed in *langue d'oïl*, and in ideas and the technique of lyric composition they were often influenced by the troubadours.

Trouver (Provençal, *Trobar*). The art of composing words and music.

Valors (Provençal). Innate moral worth, often in a courtly or a knightly, and not necessarily a Christian sense.

Vergoigne. A proper sense of shame; a realisation of the fact that *mesure* is being flouted; embarrassment and shame caused by this.

Volantez. The will and desire to commit oneself to an individual, to a cause, or to Love.

Vouloir (Provençal, *Voler*). Generalised sexual desire, unaccompanied by mental desire for a particular person. See also *Desir*.

Abbreviations

AMid	*Annales du Midi*
AUMLA	*Journal of the Australian Universities Modern Language Association*
BBIAS	*Bibliographical Bulletin of the International Arthurian Society*
BGDSL	*Beiträge zur Geschichte der Deutschen Sprache und Literatur*
BRABLB	*Boletín de la Real Academia de Buenas Letras de Barcelona*
CCMe	*Cahiers de Civilisation Médiévale*
CL	*Comparative Literature*
CN	*Cultura Neolatina*
DVLG	*Deutsche Vierteljahrschrift für Literaturwissenschaft und Geistesgeschichte*
FiR	*Filologia Romanza*
FMLS	*Forum for Modern Language Studies*
FS	*French Studies*
MA	*Le Moyen Age*
MAe	*Medium Aevum*
MLN	*Modern Language Notes*
MPh	*Modern Philology*
NMi	*Neuphilologische Mitteilungen*
PL	*Patrologia Latina*
PMLA	*Publications of the Modern Language Association of America*
R	*Romania*
RPh	*Romance Philology*
RR	*Romanic Review*
SFr	*Studi Francese*
SP	*Studies in Philology*
Sp	*Speculum*
TLL	*Travaux de linguistique et de littérature. Centre de philologie et de littérature romanes, Strasbourg*
ZRP	*Zeitschrift für Romanische Philologie*

NOTES

1 THE INHERITANCE

1 For a useful introduction to the thought of the twelfth-century Renaissance, cf. Chenu, *Théologie*, pp. 19–51, and in translation, *Id.*, *Nature, Man and Society*, pp. 1–48. See also J. de Ghellinck, *L'Essor de la littérature latine; Id.*, *Le mouvement théologique;* Wetherbee, *Platonism and Poetry in the Twelfth Century;* Leff, *Medieval Thought.* For more general works on the subject, see Brooke, *The Twelfth Century Renaissance* – useful bibliography; Paré *et al.*, *La renaissance du douzième siècle;* Haskins, *The Renaissance of the Twelfth Century;* Southern, *The Making of the Middle Ages.* For scientific thought and discoveries see Haskins, *Studies in the History of Medieval Science;* the chapter by A. C. Crombie in *Medieval England*, ed. Poole, II, pp. 571–604.

2 Cf. Gilson, *The Mystical Theology of St Bernard.*

3 Cf. Chenu, *Théologie*, pp. 159–209 (*Nature, Man and Society*, pp. 99–145); Robertson in *SP*, XLVIII (1951), pp. 669–92; Misrahi in *RPh*, XVII (1964), pp. 555–69; and Bloomfield in *MPh*, LVI (1958), pp. 73–81...

4 *Policratici* . . . libri VIII, ed. Webb, II, p. 186, transl. Pike, *Frivolities of Courtiers and Footprints of Philosophers*, p. 167.

5 Cf. Bezzola, *Les Origines*, II, pp. 255–62, and Richard, *Histoire des comtes de Poitou*, I. Cf. also the probable influence in this connection of Gilbert de la Porrée, Platonist thinker and pupil of Bernard of Chartres. Born c.1076, Chancellor of Chartres from 1124 to 1141, he was Bishop of Poitiers from 1142 to 1154. William of Conches (1080–1145), another pupil of Bernard of Chartres, was also tutor to the young Count of Anjou who married Eleanor of Poitou and Aquitaine and became Henry II of England.

6 Cf. Bezzola, *Les Origines*, II, p. 260: 'cette amitié trouve dans les lettres de Pierre Damien une expression toute proche, non seulement du langage de saint Bernard, mais aussi de celui de l'amour courtois, dans sa phase même la plus idéalisée'.

7 Cf. 'Marcabru and Fin'Amors', in Topsfield, *Troubadours and Love*, pp. 70–107.

8 See Lejeune in *Mélanges Pierre Le Gentil*, pp. 485–503. Numbering of poems and quotations are taken from Jeanroy, *Les Chansons de Guillaume IX Duc d'Aquitaine.*

9 Cf. *Troubadours and Love*, p. 44.
10 Cf. Topsfield in *L'Esprit Créateur*, XIX (1979), pp. 37–53.
11 For folly as a courtly concept, see *Troubadours and Love*, ch. 1 *passim* and pp. 146 and 229.
12 Cf. p. 15–16.
13 For a summary account of the *Historia Regum Britanniae* see the chapter on Geoffrey of Monmouth by J. J. Parry and R. A. Caldwell in *Arthurian Literature*, ed. Loomis, pp. 72–93, especially pp. 79–89.
14 Cf. Wace, *Brut*, ed. Arnold; *La partie arthurienne du 'Roman de Brut' de Wace*, ed. Arnold and Pelan.
15 For the different styles used in troubadour poetry, cf. Paterson, *Troubadours and Eloquence*; for the effect of these styles on their vocabulary, see ibid, p. 229. Cf. also Mölk, *Trobar clus – trobar leu*.
16 Quotations and numbering of Bernart's poems are taken from Appel, ed., *Bernart von Ventadorn*.
17 Cf. Topsfield, *Troubadours and Love*, pp. 70–136; Id. in *Mélanges Rostaing*, pp. 1149–58.
18 See p. 320, n. 35.
19 Cf. Pelan, *L'Influence de Wace sur les romanciers de son temps*. For Eleanor's role as patroness of poets see Lejeune in *La Femme dans les civilisations des Xe–XIIIe siècles*, pp. 111–27, especially pp. 114–18; Id. in *CN*, XIV (1954), pp. 5–57.
20 For the Alexander romances, see Cary, *The Medieval Alexander*; *The Medieval French Roman d'Alexandre*, ed. Armstrong *et al*.
21 See *Flamenca*, ed. Lavaud and Nelli, ll. 621–705. Cf. p. 336, n. 14.
22 *Le Roman de Thèbes*, ed. L. Constans; ed. G. Raynaud de Lage. For sources cf. Faral, *Recherches*.
23 *Eneas, roman du XIIe siècle*, ed. J. Salverda de Grave; for Ovidian influences in *Eneas*, cf. Faral, *Recherches*, pp. 125–57.
24 Cf. Crosland in *MLR*, XXIX (1934), pp. 282–90.
25 Guillaume IX, ed. Jeanroy, XI, 23–4:
   Et ieu prec en Jesu del tron
   Et en romans et en lati.
26 Cf. Tobler-Lommatzsch, VIII, col. 1441–4.
27 See n. 21 above.
28 For a discussion of these influences, cf. Faral, *Recherches*; Lewis, *Classical Mythology and Arthurian Romance*; Ziltener, *Chrétien und die Aeneis*; Jones, *The theme of love in the 'Romans d'Antiquité'*; Hofer in *ZRP*, LX (1940), pp. 245–61; Guyer in *RR*, XII (1921), pp. 113–15, 125–6, 224–7; Robertson in *CL*, VII (1955), pp. 32–42; Micha in *Mélanges Hoepffner*, pp. 237–43; Hoepffner in *R*, LV (1929), pp. 1–16; Van Hamel in *R*, XXXIII (1904), pp. 465–89; Micha in *Neophilologus*, XXXVI (1952), pp. 1–10; Bruce, *The Evolution of Arthurian Romance from the Beginnings down to the year 1300* I; Zaddy in *CN*, XXI (1961), pp. 71–82; Gallais in *CCMe*, XIV (1971), pp. 69–75.
29 For the ways in which the medieval romances were 'performed' and their probable audience, cf. Gallais in *CCMe*, VII (1964), pp. 479–93, and XIII (1970), pp. 333–47.
30 Foerster, ed., *Kristian von Troyes. Cligés*.

31 For an introduction to this oral and written tradition, cf. *Arthurian Literature*, ed. Loomis, chs. 1–6; Loomis, *Arthurian Tradition*. On King Arthur in history, legend, literature and art, see Barber, *The Arthurian Legends*.

32 William of Malmesbury, *Historia*, I, 1, p. 11; Chambers, *Arthur of Britain*, p. 263; Loomis, *Arthurian Tradition*, p. 15.

33 William of Malmesbury, *Historia*, II, 3, p. 342.

34 Wace, *Brut*, ed. Arnold, II, 9747–60. Cf. Huet in *MA*, XXVIII (1915), pp. 234–49. Loomis, *Arthurian Tradition*, p. 62, agrees with Dr Laura Hibbard Loomis' view that Wace, in emphasising the equalitarian function of Arthur's Round Table, was influenced by the fact that pilgrims at Jerusalem were shown a marble round table declared to be that of the Last Supper (attested from 1102).

35 For Arthurian names in historical documents from the ninth century onwards, see Gallais in *Actes du VIIe Congrès national de littérature comparée*, pp. 47–79. Cf. also Pirot's *Recherches sur les connaissances littéraires des troubadours occitans et catalans des XIIe et XIIIe siècles*, pp. 515–25, for the importance of Poitou in the rediffusion of Celtic material in France and Spain; also Loomis in *Arthurian Literature*, ed. Loomis, pp. 52–63.

36 Cf. Bromwich in *MAe*, XXVI (1957), pp. 36–8.

37 Cf. de Riquer in *FiR*, II (1955), pp. 1–19.

38 The term Beroul is used here to denote the authorship of the 'Beroul' fragment of *Tristran*, despite the probability that it consists of two separate works. Cf. Raynaud de Lage in *MA*, LXIV (1958), pp. 249–70, and *MA*, LXVII (1961), pp. 167–8, and especially Reid in *MLR*, LX (1965), pp. 352–8.

39 For this mythology of the Celtic tradition, Loomis, *Arthurian Tradition*, and Marx, *Légende arthurienne*, are especially helpful. See also the relevant chapters in *Arthurian Literature*, ed. Loomis, including a discussion by Foster (pp. 192–205) of the relationship between the Welsh *Gereint*, *Owein* and *Peredur* and Chrétien's *Erec*, *Yvain* and *Perceval* respectively. Cf. Fourquet in *RPh*, IX (1955–6), pp. 298–312, and Loomis in *R*, LXXIX (1958), pp. 47–77.

40 See pp. 58 and 99–100.

41 See Vigneras in *MPh*, XXXII (1934–5), pp. 341–2.

42 Frappier, *Chrétien de Troyes. L'homme et l'oeuvre*, p. 9. In his *Le Roman Breton. Chrétien de Troyes; Cligès*, pp. 5–6, Frappier did, however, envisage the possibility, though with several reservations, that this Christianus of Saint Loup might be the poet Chrétien.

43 Boutière and Schutz, *Biographies*, p. 263. Bernart Marti (ed. Hoepffner, V, 31–6) names him as a canon. Peire Rogier, also contemporary with Chrétien, is named by his Provençal biographer as a canon of Clermont (Boutière, *Biographies*, p. 267).

44 Cf. Topsfield, *Troubadours and Love*, pp. 178–91.

45 *Parzival*, 827, 1 ff.: *von Troies meister Kristjân*. In *Willehalm* 125, 20, Wolfram also refers to a certain *Cristjâns* who has not been definitely identified but may be Chrétien de Troyes. I am indebted to Dr L. P. Johnson for discussion on this point.

46 Boutière, *Biographies*, p. 39.
47 For Chrétien's references to his earlier works in *Cliges*, see also p. 66. Cf. Johnston in MLR, LXXIII (1978) pp. 496–8, for the discussion and rejection of the attribution to Chrétien de Troyes of two further works. Cf. also Owen in R, XCII (1971), pp. 246–60.
48 On Guillaume d'Angleterre, cf. Foerster, ed., *Christian von Troyes. Sämtliche erhaltene Werke*, IV, pp. 255–475; Chrétien de Troyes, *Guillaume d'Angleterre, roman du XIIᵉ siècle*, ed. Wilmotte; Wilmotte in R, XLVI (1920), pp. 1–38; Tanquery in R, LVII (1931), pp. 75–116; Delbouille in *Mélanges Lecoy*, pp. 55–65; Lonigan in SFr, XVI (1972) pp. 308–14; Dubois-Stasse and Fontaine-Lauve, *Guillaume d'Angleterre*.
49 For the dating of Chrétien's works, see especially Fourrier in BBIAS, II (1950), pp. 69–96; Misrahi in BBIAS, XI (1959), pp. 89–120; Lejeune in BBIAS, IX (1957), pp. 85–100; Fourrier in BBIAS, X (1958), pp. 73–85; Zumthor in MA, LXV (1959), pp. 579–86. Shirt in FS, XXXI (1977), pp. 1–17.
50 For the mss., see Micha, *La tradition manuscrite des romans de Chrétien de Troyes* and revs by Hoepffner in RLR, LXIII (1939), pp. 503–8 and Roques in R, LXVIII (1944), pp. 211–19. See also Pauphilet, *Chrétien de Troyes. Le manuscrit d'Annonay*, and in R, LXIII (1937), pp. 310–23. Flutre in R, LXXV (1954), pp. 1–21; Misrahi in PMLA, LVI (1941), pp. 951–61; Jodogne in *Lettres romanes*, IV (1950), pp. 311–30. Roques in R, LXXIII (1952), pp. 177–99; Reid in MAe, XLV (1976), pp. 1–19; Hunt in FS, XXXIII (1979), pp. 257–71.
51 Cf. Faral, *Les Arts poétiques du XIIᵉ et du XIIIᵉ siècle*, pp. 76–7.
52 Trojel, ed., *Andreae Capellani regii. De amore libri tres*; Battaglia, ed., *Trattato d'amore Andreae Capellani regii francorum 'De Amore' Libri Tres*; Parry, trans., *Andreas Capellanus. The Art of Courtly Love*.
53 Cf. Topsfield in MLR, LI (1956), pp. 33–41; Id., *Troubadours and Love*, pp. 219–37.
54 For a short glossary of courtly and poetic terms associated with the genres of the romance and the love lyric of the troubadours, see pp. 313–16.

2 EREC ET ENIDE

1 Quotations and line references from Foerster, *Kristian von Troyes. Erec und Enide*. For the merits of Foerster's editions of Chrétien's work, and editions based on these, cf. the works by Reid and Hunt in n. 50, above.
2 Cf. Kelly in *Viator Medieval and Renaissance Studies*, I (1970), pp. 179–200 (p. 189); Id. in Sp, XLI (1966), pp. 261–78 (pp. 272–4).
3 For symbolical associations related to the medieval use of colours and numbers cf. Bezzola, *Le sens de l'Aventure et de l'Amour (Chrétien de Troyes)*; Chenu, *Théologie*, pp. 163–4, and selected chapters of this in English translation, Id., *Nature, Man and Society*, pp. 106–7; Curtius, *European Literature and the Latin Middle Ages*, pp. 501–13.

4   For the medieval symbolistic mentality cf. Chenu, Théologie, pp. 159–90, and Nature, Man and Society, pp. 99–145. Also Bloomfield in MPh, LVI (1958), pp. 73–81; Misrahi in RPh, XVII (1964), pp. 555–69.

5   For the difference between the thematic structure of Erec et Enide and Yvain and that of Lancelot and Perceval see p. 339, n. 1. Cliges conforms to a different structural pattern (see Ch. 3). On the question of structure in Chrétien cf. also Zaddy, Chrétien Studies, and Woods in SP, L (1953), pp. 1–15.

6   Cf. Saran in BGDSL, XXI (1896), pp. 253–420 (290–1); Kellermann, Aufbaustil und Weltbild Chretiens von Troyes im Percevalroman, pp. 11–13; Kelly, Sens and Conjointure, p. 169.

7   For the Classical ancestry, especially in Cicero and Quintilian, of the Prologue in medieval French literature, cf. Hunt in FMLS, VI (1970), pp. 1–15.

8   For the meanings of savoir, sen and science in courtly romance, cf. Koenig 'Sen/sens' et 'savoir' et leurs synonymes dans quelques romans courtois du 12ᵉ et du début du 13ᵉ siècle.

9   Cf. Holmes in SP, XXXIX (1942), pp. 11–14; Illingworth in MAe, XXXI (1962), pp. 176–87; Webster, Guinevere. A Study of her Abductions, ch. 6; Loomis, Arthurian Tradition, pp. 68–70.

10 For the theme of accidia 'sloth' and otium 'idleness' with particular reference to the Joy of the Court episode, cf. Nitze in Sp, XXIX (1954), pp. 691–701.

11 Cf. Nitze, ibid., who sees the Irish Imram Bran as a source for the story; Loomis, Arthurian Tradition, p. 178, who notes the legend of Virgil, repeated by Alexander Neckam, De Naturis Rerum, ed. Wright, p. 310, as a possible source for the Wall of Air imagery: 'How is it that the said prophet fortified and surrounded his garden, moveless air taking the place of a wall?' For Loomis, however, this image was probably suggested by the magic mist which, according to Irish legend, concealed the palaces of the gods, such as that of Manannan in the Adventures of Cormac in the Land of Promise. For the importance of mist in Celtic (Irish) mythology, see Jones in Llên Cymru, IV (1957), pp.208–27 (my thanks are due to Dr Charlotte Ward for this reference).

12 For the joy from the 'folly' of spontaneous feeling freed from courtly sen and mesura, cf. Topsfield, Troubadours and Love, pp. 26–36; Andreas Capellanus, Book I, 7th Dialogue, ed. Trojel, p. 147, condemns the excess of sexual passion, and its misuse, in marriage: 'This is an offence more serious in a wife than in another woman, for the lover who is too ardent, as the apostolic law tells us, is held to be an adulterer with his own wife.' For examples of this commonplace, cf. Peter Lombard, Sententiae, IV, xxxi (PL, CXCII, 921); St Jerome, Contra Jovinianum, I, 49 (PL, XXIII, 281); Alanus de Insulis, Summa de arte praedicatoria, XLV (PL, CCX, 193).

13 Among many suggested reasons for Erec's harshness towards Enide, cf. Loomis, Arthurian Tradition, p. 34 (the motive of suspected infidelity is stated in the Welsh Gereint); Frappier, Chrétien de Troyes, pp.

98–100 (Erec's wounded honour); Sheldon in RR, v (1914), pp. 115–26; Nitze in RR, x (1919), pp. 26–37; Press in R, xc (1969), pp. 529–38; Zaddy, *Chrétien Studies*, pp. 14–16.

14 A clear response to Enide's: *Con mar i fus* (2507) and *mar i fustes* (2575).

15 For the Celtic *geis* as a spell which acts as a summons, a veto or an instrument of compulsion, cf. Marx, *Légende arthurienne*, pp. 81–2 and *passim*.

16 Lancelot in Chrétien's romance loses his horse on two successive occasions immediately before his test of humility in the episode of the Cart. For the same hero in *La Queste del Saint Graal*, ed. Pauphilet (pp. 61–2) the loss of his helmet, sword and horse symbolises the laying aside of his worldly and sinful life; cf. also his acceptance of the slaying of his horse by the Black Knight, ibid., p. 146.

17 Cf. *La Chanson de Roland*, ed. Whitehead, Oliver addressing Roland (l. 1725): *Mielz valt mesure que ne fait estultie*. *Mesure* for Oliver involves wholeness of view, the welfare of Empire and Church, Charlemagne and the peers, and 'sweet France'. A similar width of view is what Erec must acquire through *savoir*, before his Coronation.

18 Enide, Chrétien is saying, is entirely human, with no trace in her of the traditional Celtic fairy mistress who enchants an earthly hero, an affirmation perhaps thought necessary in view of the Celtic overtones implied by the White Stag as a messenger, by the Dwarf as a guide to the Other World, and in Erec's journey to Laluth and his return to Arthur's court. Cf. also the magic arts of the Fourth Damsel in Lancelot's quest (p. 126–7). For Enide as an idealised projection of the 'Fair Unknown' in medieval literature, cf. Luttrell, *The First Arthurian Romance*, *passim*.

19 In Chrétien's work, the revelation of a name may imply realisation of a character's social identity. Such is the case with Yder, Mabonagrain, Lancelot, and here, Enide. For Perceval, this revelation brings the beginning of self-awareness. Yvain's assumption of the title *Le Chevalier au Lion* symbolises rejection of his earlier self moulded by the world.

20 The Count's courtly words belie his intention:

'Quant je d'amor vos daing requerre,
Ne m'an devez pas escondire.' (3328–9)

'Since I deign to woo you with words of love, you have no right to rebuff me.'

21 For the association of Celtic tradition with the Wall of Air, see n. 11 above. For the significance of the horn cf. Loomis, *Arthurian Tradition*, pp. 172–5.

22 For the commonplace of the *locus amoenus*, see Curtius, *European Literature and the Latin Middle Ages*, pp. 195–200.

23 For the Celtic Other World see pp. 208–10. Also Marx, *Légende arthurienne*, pp. 82–90; Loomis in *PMLA*, LVI (1941), pp. 887–936.

24 See n. 21.

25 In Celtic, and in feudal and courtly terms, this damsel, having

defined the terms of combat for her knight Mabonagrain (6075–8), is the instigator of conflict. In this role she resembles the Elder Sister in Yvain (p. 199) and in the Gawain adventures in Perceval (p. 273).

26 For the theme of the boon granted without restriction and its use in narrative, cf. Frappier in Amour courtois, pp. 225–64; also in TLL, VII (1969), pp. 7–46.

27 Chrétien allows himself a shaft of irony, touched with seriousness, at the plight of the king and his five hundred barons:

> Onques mes an nule seison
> Ne fu trovez li rois si seus.　　　　(6420–1)

28 For different interpretations, among others, of the Joy of the Court episode, cf. Philpott in R, XXV (1896), pp. 258–94; Sheldon in RR, V (1914), pp. 115–26; Nitze in Sp, XXIX (1954), pp. 691–701; Whitehead in BBIAS, XXI (1969), pp. 142–3; Frappier, Chrétien de Troyes, pp. 91–6; Zaddy, Chrétien Studies, pp. 39–56.

29 For the concept of communal courtly Joy as a social convention cf. Topsfield, Troubadours and Love, pp. 223–37; Id., ed., Les Poésies du troubadour Raimon de Miraval, pp. 59–62.

30 Cf. Topsfield, Troubadours and Love, chs. 1–3, and in Mélanges Boutière, pp. 571–87.

31 Quotation from A. Del Monte, ed., Peire d'Alvernha, Liriche, pp. 66–7. For sabers (savoir) seen as a guide to mental serenity, cf. Topsfield, Troubadours and Love, pp. 166–90.

32 Guilhem IX of Aquitaine (1071–1127), Marcabru (fl. c. 1130–50), Raimbaut d'Aurenga (c. 1146–73), Arnaut Daniel (fl c. 1180–c. 1210), all come within this category.

33 Cf. Topsfield, Troubadours and Love, pp. 183–6.

34 Cf. Etienne de Fougères, in his Livre des Manières, ed. J. Kremer; ed. also Lodge, who criticises the high-born lady whose sole concern is to devote herself to Amors. Implicitly Etienne is also attacking the troubadours who praise her for this quality:

> De tote cure se despoille
> Fors de sei faire belle et gente
> E sei peindre blance ou rovente,
> Et dit que mal fu sa jovente,
> Si en amor ne met entente.　　　　(1056–60)

For the deceitful and blasphemous method employed by the lady to meet her lover cf. ibid., 1061–76, and for Etienne's criticism of the vanity of knightly displays and tourneys:

> N'i a neant de bobancier
> De boherder, de torneier.　　　　(ibid., 633–4)

35 Policratici . . . libri VIII, ed. Webb. Cf. also Pike, Frivolities of Courtiers and Footprints of Philosophers.

36 Cicero, De officiis (Loeb), pp. 116–17.

37 Cf. Topsfield, *Troubadours and Love*, pp. 70–107 and 177–83; Id. in *Mélanges Rostaing*, pp. 1149–58.

38 Cf. nn. 11 and 23 above.

39 For John of Salisbury, *Policraticus* (book VIII), rational well-being leads to individual happiness and social well-being. For William of St Thierry, *De natura corporis et animae*, written between 1130 and 1138, rational well-being is the necessary preparation for spiritual well-being, cf. Déchanet, *Oeuvres choisies de Guillaume de Saint-Thierry*, pp. 151–62.

40
> I ot contes et dus et rois,
> Normanz, Bretons, Escoz, Irois;
> D'Angleterre et de Cornoaille
> I ot mout riche baronaille;
> Que des Gales jusqu' an Anjo,
> Ne el Mainne ne an Peito
> N'ot chevalier de grant afeire
> Ne jantil dame deboneire,
> Que les mellors et les plus jantes
> Ne fussent a la cort a Nantes.   (6645–54)

This is the version in W. Foerster's edn. Cf. also the variant readings in mss. CP, Irois, einglois, and C Nan alemaigne.

41 A *faudestués* was a folding stool or seat, a necessity for medieval rulers, who like Henry II, were perpetually on the move. A *faudestués* as ornate as those described here would clearly have the quality of a throne, and be prized in addition as an ingenious mechanical device (6714–7).
corcatrilles (6729) is translated by W. Foerster (1896 edn, Glossary, p. 198) as 'Drache'. Were such a translation permissible, the combination of dragon and (Angevin) leopard on these 'thrones' would encourage the assumption of a link in the Coronation scene between Arthur and Henry II. In the *Wörterbuch*, the translation is 'Krokodil' (med. lat. corcodrillu).

42 Cf. Arthur's words:
> Ce apartient a leal roi
> Que il doit maintenir la loi.   (1797–8)

For a discussion of the meanings of *leals*, cf. pp. 160–70.

43 For the contemporary affair of the Byzantine marriage project, cf. p. 100.

44 Cf. Frappier, *Les chansons de geste du cycle de Guillaume d'Orange*, II, p. 159–60; Id. in ZRP, LXXVIII (1957), pp. 1–19, reprinted in *Histoire, Mythes et Symboles*, pp. 1–19. Cf. Wace Brut, ed. Arnold, ll. 9006–33.

45 For the possible historical significance of the setting of the Coronation scene in *Erec et Enide* at Nantes on Christmas Day, see Fourrier in BBIAS, II (1950), pp. 69–96 (pp. 69–73). Misrahi in BBIAS, XI (1959), pp. 89–120 (pp. 93–9) doubts Fourrier's thesis and argues that Nantes is a deformation of Kaer Nant or Carnant, site of the castle of King Lac (*Erec*, 2315–17). See also Foerster, *Wörterbuch*, under Carnant.

46 If Fourrier's theory is correct, the inclusion of the Irish among the subjects of the king would indicate a date of composition for this passage in *Erec et Enide* after the conquest of Ireland (1169–70). Hence 1170, possibly before Becket's murder in December 1170, or a date after 1170. See also n. 40.

47 To judge from contemporary chronicles, the 'illegal' coronation of Henry the Young King by Roger of York and three other bishops, *cum principibus et magnatibus terrae suae* . . . *clero et populo consentientibus et assentientibus*, followed by the homage of the king of the Scots (*Chronica magistri Rogeri de Hovedon*, ed. Stubbs, p. 5), was a major historical event. The Pope, at the instance of the exiled Thomas Becket, Archbishop of Canterbury, excommunicated the prelates who had crowned the Young King (Hoveden, p. 6). King Louis VII of France, and the bishops of France, begged the Pope to excommunicate Henry II. (Hoveden, pp. 9–10). On 12 October 1170, Henry II made his 'peace' with Thomas Becket. This truce came after a tumultuous year in which Henry had kept Christmas at Nantes and subdued Brittany, had narrowly escaped death by drowning in March on his passage to England, had enforced the 'illegal' coronation of his eldest son as a gesture of defiance to the Church and Thomas Becket, Archbishop of Canterbury, had resisted the French invasion of Normandy, and falling seriously ill, had divided his estates among his sons. Recovered from this illness, he had gone on a pilgrimage to Rocamadour. The scene was now set for the killing of Thomas Becket in the following Christmas season. On 29 December 1170 Thomas Becket was slaughtered by four of Henry's knights. At the burial the corpse of Thomas Becket gave a blessing with the right hand which ensured his martyrdom as a saint. The possibility cannot be excluded that some of these momentous events may have been in Chrétien's mind when he composed the Coronation scene in *Erec et Enide*, especially the hope for the future implied by the crowning of the Young King, who was admired by Bertran de Born as a paragon of knighthood and courtly qualities. That ll. 6865–9 imply a criticism of Becket's absence from the crowning of the Young King (cf. A. Fourrier in *BBIAS*, II (1950), p. 74) is possible but not provable. Was it fortuitous that Becket assumed the name of Christianus during his exile in France, as Guernes de Pont Sainte-Maxence relates in *La Vie de Saint Thomas Becket*, written between 1172 and 1174? That he and Chrétien were acquainted is by no means an impossibility, given the interest at the Plantagenet court in skilled writers of romances. Did the murder of Becket contribute to Chrétien's later revulsion against knightly violence?

48 *Policraticus*, I, 6, transl. Pike, *Frivolities of Courtiers and Footprints of Philosophers*, p. 30.

49 Cf. Chenu, *Théologie*, pp. 19–51.

50 Cf. Topsfield, *Troubadours and Love*, ch. 3.

51 Cf. Zitzmann in *DVLG*, xxv (1951), pp. 40–53.

52 For the emerald as a customary symbol of constancy, patience and

longanimitas, cf. *La Queste del saint Graal*, ed. Pauphilet, p. 124: 'Soffrance si est semblable a esmeraude qui toz dis est vert. Car soffrance n'avra ja si fort temptacion que ele puisse estre vaincue, ainz est toz dis verdoianz et en une meisure force.' For Bede, it signified: 'animas semper fide virentes' and constancy in adversity (PL, XCIII, 198), and similarly for Rabanus Maurus in *De universo* (PL, CXI, 466 C–D). A sceptre, symbol of sovereignty, made from emerald could scarcely fail to augur well for Erec's reign.

53 Cicero, *De finibus bonorum et malorum* (Loeb), pp. 436–45.

54 Cicero, *De officiis* (Loeb), pp. 14–17 and 292–3.

55 Luttrell, *The Creation of the First Arthurian Romance. A Quest*, ch. 3, offers a late chronology for Chrétien's work which permits the thesis that he was influenced by Alanus de Insulis.

56 Cf. nn. 11 and 18 above.

57 There is almost certainly no need to see Manichcist or Cathar influence in Chrétien's almost Stoic acceptance of the pervasiveness of Evil in human life. For twelfth-century man Inimicus, the Devil, was omnipresent.

3 CLIGES

1 Quotations and line references from Kristian von Troyes. *Cligés*, ed. W. Foerster. Cf. also *die vierte verkürzte Auflage*, ed. Hilka and *Cligés*, ed. Micha in the series *Les Romans de Chrétien de Troyes édités d'après la copie de Guiot*, II. For recent critical work on *Cliges*, cf. Maddox in NMi, LXXIV (1973), pp. 730–45.

2 Cf. also in the *Tristan* of Thomas reconstituted by J. Bédier the description of the loves, trials and sorrows of Tristan's parents (*Le roman de Tristan par Thomas. Poème du XIIᵉ siècle*, ed. J. Bédier, I, pp. 2–26).

3 *Marie de France. Lais*, ed. Ewert, pp. 3–25.

4 *The Romance of Horn* by Thomas, ed. Pope.

5 Cf. Hauvette, La 'Morte Vivante'; Lyons in *Mélanges Mario Roques*, I, pp. 167–77.

6 Frappier, *Cligès*, pp. 43–6.

7 Cf. Micha in *Mélanges Hoepffner*, pp. 237–43; Robertson in CL, VII (1955), pp. 32–42.

8 For Petersen Dygve, *Gace Brulé. Trouvère champenois, édition des chansons et étude historique*, p. 136, the poem is 'évidemment de Chrestien de Troyes qui obtient deux voix (RTa et C)', i.e. the atttribution of the poem to Chrétien by two separate groups of mss., including the authoritative ms. I. Cf. also Zai, ed. *Les Chansons courtoises de Chrétien de Troyes*.

9 For the relationship of these two poems to each other and to the *Non chant per auzel* of Raimbaut d'Aurenga (ed. Pattison, XXVII), see Roncaglia in CN, XVIII (1958), pp. 121–37.

10 For the possible relationship between *Cliges* and the *Tristan* of Thomas see: Van Hamel in R, XXXIII (1904), pp. 465–89; Hoepffner

in R, LV (1929), pp. 1–16; Maranini in *Annali della R. Scuola Normale Superiore di Pisa*, XII (1943), fasc. IV, pp. 13–26; Frappier, *Cligès*, pp. 46–51; Micha in *Neophilologus*, XXXVI (1952), pp. 1–10.

11 *Les chansons de Guilhem IX Duc d'Aquitaine*, ed. Jeanroy, pp. 6–8; Pasero, ed., *Gugliemo IX d'Aquitania. Poesie*, pp. 85–112; for the theme of nothingness in troubadour poetry, cf. Topsfield, *Troubadours and Love*, pp. 29–41; Lawner in *CN*, XXVIII (1968), pp. 147–64.

12 Cf. *Troubadours and Love*, pp. 45–6.

13 Quotations and line references from Dejeanne, ed., *Poésies complètes du troubadour Marcabru*.

14 Quotations and line references from Linskill, ed., *The Poems of the troubadour Raimbaut de Vaqueiras*.

15 For the use of this device by Chrétien's contemporaries, Bernart de Ventadorn (edn Appel, XLIV, 1–12) and Raimbaut d'Aurenga (ed. Pattison, XXXIX), cf. Topsfield, *Troubadours and Love*, pp. 128 and 154–8. For its wider application, cf. Curtius, pp. 94–8.

16 Cf. the note to this line (4532) by Foerster, edn, p. 209. The phrase *li doit oster la plume* is related in meaning to *l'aplaingne* (4535).

17 Fenice is directing their love towards *Proesce* and hence away from the recreancy of *Mauvestié*, cf. p. 167.

18 Bernart de Ventadorn (edn Appel, XLIII, 54–6): *mort m'a, e per mort li respon*, 'she has slain me and through death I reply to her'.

19 For the importance of mutual desire in love in the poetry of Bernart de Ventadorn see p. 153.

20 Cf. *The Romance of Tristran by Beroul*, ed. Ewert, I, 1995–2012, p. 60.

21 *largesce* (201) 'generosity in giving'; 'wide and adventurous generosity of mind and spirit'; cf. p. 178 and p. 334, n. 3.

22 *La Chanson de Guillaume*, ed. McMillan, I, pp. 91–2.

23 Cf. Bezzola, *Le sens de l'Aventure et de l'Amour (Chrétien de Troyes)*, pp. 129, 194–7, for the symbolical value of colour in dress and horses in Chrétien de Troyes.

24 Ed. Dejeanne, XXX, 82–4 and 88–90; XIX, 64–6.

25 Cf. Topsfield in *MAe*, XXXVI (1967), pp. 119–33.

26 Cf. Fourrier in *BBIAS*, II (1950), pp. 69–96 (pp. 76–80).

27 See p. 66.

28 Cf. the frequent use in this connection of bawdy puns such as *lo faire, o faire*, in troubadour poetry.

4 LANCELOT

1 For fragmented and whole thinking in troubadour poetry cf. Topsfield, *Troubadours and Love*, pp. 73–107 and 185–91. For some of the ideas involved in this controversy, cf. Id. in *Mélanges Rostaing*, pp. 1149–58. For questions of style involved, cf. Paterson, *Troubadours and Eloquence*, pp. 87–144.

2 Kelly, *Sens and Conjointure*, pp. 36–68. Cf. Lyons in *SP*, LI (1954), pp. 425–30 (p. 428), and the Glossary, p. 313. On *sen*, cf. Robertson in *SP*, XLVIII (1951), pp. 669–92; on *sen* in *Lancelot*, cf.

Rychner in *Vox Romanica*, XXVI (1967), pp. 1–23; Shirt in MLR, LXXIII (1978), pp. 38–50.

3 For a summary account of this work of Swiss provenance (*c.* 1200) based on a French (*welschez*) book, 'an Arthurian romance in its most elementary stage', cf. *Arthurian Literature*, ed. Loomis, pp. 436–9.

4 Chrétien's sole use of the term *fin amant* occurs in *Lancelot* (ed. Foerster, 3980), applied to Lancelot himself.

5 Cf. Appel, ed. *Bernart von Ventadorn*, pp. 254–5 for extracts from *Can vei la lauzeta* quoted in langue d'oïl in the romance *Guillaume de Dole*, ed. Servois, 5198–213 and the *Roman de la Violette*, ed. Michel, 4192–201; also Seelheim, *Die Mundart des altfrz. Veilchenromans*, p. 14. Cf. also the close imitation of Bernart's poetry by Gui de Coucy, ed. Lerond, in poems such as *La douce voiz du louseignol sauvage* (III) and *L'an que rose ne fueille* (IV).

6 Cf. balanced situations in *Eliduc* and *Fresne* (man between two women), *Laustic* and *Chievrefueil* (symbols of 'distant' love), *Bisclavret* and *Equitan* (the guilty woman and two men); balanced but contrasting situations in *Guigemar* and *Yonec* (illicit love justified, with disparate results).

7 This reference to the bipartite structure of *Erec et Enide* and *Yvain* is concerned with the thematic division in these romances between the narrative section leading to the major crisis in which the three characters are found wanting and the subsequent period of their rehabilitation. It is not concerned with the episodic subdivision of the narrative into *premerains vers* and the rest of the romance. Cf. also p. 339, n. 1.

8 All line references and quotations are from Foerster, *Der Karrenritter (Lancelot) von Christian von Troyes*. There is a good translation of *Lancelot* by Frappier, *Le Chevalier de la Charrette–Lancelot*.

9 For a helpful analysis of the structure of *Lancelot*, cf. Kelly, *Sens and Conjointure*, pp. 166–203.

10 Frappier in *Amour courtois*, pp. 225–40; previously published in TLL, VII, (1969), pp. 7–46; Loomis, *Arthurian Tradition*, ch. 28: the motive of the rash boon in the Celtic tradition is regularly linked to the abduction of a queen from her consort and her subsequent recovery.

11 Cf. pp. 170–1. The possibility cannot be excluded that this episode represents the first intimation in the romance of the allegorical struggle between *Mauvestié* and *Leauté* which is a major theme in the second half of the work.

12 See p. 178.

13 Lancelot has clearly been humbled as Erec was before the major trial of the Joy of the Court, and his most probable conqueror is Meleagant. This may be an enigmatic indication that Lancelot's *Leauté* and devotion to the Queen are insufficient to withstand the *Mauvestié* of Meleagant. In this case, this combat prefigures the test of the Cart.

14 On the function of the cart cf. Shirt in R, XCIV (1973), pp. 178–95; Id. in *Studies . . . Whitehead*, pp. 363–99.

15 Cf. Harward, *The dwarfs of Arthurian romance and Celtic tradition*.
16 Cf. Brown in *PMLA*, XXV (1910), pp. 1–59 (pp. 23–4); Marx, *Légende arthurienne*, pp. 129–35.
17 Cf. Marx, *Légende arthurienne*, pp. 284–7, 325–6, 360; Loomis, *Arthurian Tradition*, p. 204: the bed adventure can be traced to the eighth-century text of the Irish saga *Briciu's Feast*.
18 Diverres in his valuable article, 'Some thoughts on the *sens* of *Le Chevalier de la Charrette*', *FMLS*, VI (1970), pp. 24–36, suggests that Chrétien is blaming the *folie* of Lancelot, especially in mounting the cart, and that he cannot exemplify the lover according to the Provençal idea. But *folie*, or Provençal *foudatz*, is an integral part of the *fis amaire* in the poetry of Bernart de Ventadorn, by whom Chrétien appears to have been influenced in the writing of *Lancelot*. Though Chrétien acknowledged the role of *folie* in *Fin'Amors* in depriving the lover of his reason, he also mocks it, the poem *D'Amors qui m'a tolu a moi*, attributed to Chrétien, appearing to be a direct riposte to Bernart's declaration of *foudatz* and loss of self-control in love in his *Can vei la lauzeta mover*. See also p. 68.
19 Cf. Dejeanne, *Poésies complètes du troubadour Marcabru*, XIX, 64–6.
20 For the Welsh seasonal myth in which Melwas, King of the Summer County, conquers the King of Winter, and for the Celtic background for the land of Gorre [Glastonbury?], the Water Bridge and Sword Bridge, see Loomis, *Arthurian Tradition*, pp. 218–27; Weston, *The Legend of Sir Gawain*, p. 74; Newstead, *Bran the Blessed in Arthurian Romance*, pp. 140–2.
21 *Les Chansons de Guillaume IX Duc d'Aquitaine*, ed. Jeanroy.
22 *Les Chansons de Jaufré Rudel*, ed. Jeanroy.
23 Cf. Perceval's indignation in the episode of the Three Drops of Blood in the Snow, p. 270.
24 Cf. Tobler-Lommatzsch, II, col. 706–7.
25 *La Queste del saint Graal*, ed. Pauphilet, pp. 108–10.
26 Cf. Nelli, *L'Erotique des troubadours*, pp. 199–209.
27 *Le Roman de Tristan par Thomas, poème du XIIe siècle*, ed. J. Bédier, I, 649–58, p. 286.
28 Cf. p. 81 for Fenice's lament in *Cliges*.
29 The use of *orguel* here is unexpected. Love and pride were considered incompatible by courtly poets: cf. Bernart de Ventadorn, 'love cannot keep company with pride' (XLII, 20). Chrétien may be implying that the pride in one's devotion and purpose which is inspired by *Fin'Amors* is wholly praiseworthy. Paradoxically he may also be implying to his courtly audience that *Fin'Amors* which rules through reason and *mesura* (see n. 30) may induce self-satisfaction and pride.
30 Cf. Roncaglia in *CN*, XVIII (1958), pp. 121–37; Topsfield in *Mélanges Rostaing*, pp. 1149–58; Id., *Troubadours and Love*, pp. 119–20.
31 Boutière and Schutz, *Biographies*, p. 369.
32 *Le Roman de Renart*, ed. Martin, II, pp. 311–35, branch XXIII, ll. 1155–2080, and IV (supp. vol.), pp. 94 ff.
33 Cf. edn Foerster, p. 377. Also Loomis, *Arthurian Tradition*, pp. 233–6

34 Edn Pauphilet, pp. 11–12.

35 Cf. Loomis, *Arthurian Tradition*, pp. 239–40.

36 The expression *noauz feire* (2663) foreshadows the tourney at Noauz where Lancelot's devotion to the Queen overcomes self-pride and keeps him from 'doing what is evil'.

37 Cf. Loomis, *Arthurian Tradition*, pp. 260–1.

38 For the importance of *desleaus/leaus* as key-words in this romance, see pp. 166–71.

39 Do the lions, apart from their magic significance, represent, like the lion in Yvain, the extra moral and physical courage needed for the crossing of the Sword Bridge? Loomis, *Arthurian Tradition*, pp. 225–7 (p. 225), refers to *Perlesvaus*, ed. Nitze, I, 114 f. in which the third of three bridges leading to the castle of the Fisher King is guarded by a 'ferocious-looking but actually harmless lion'.

40 Cf. Owen in *FMLS*, VI (1970), pp. 37–48. The suggestion that there is a burlesque intention in this imagery is not easily acceptable. Its purpose is more probably to increase awareness of Lancelot's suffering.

41 Cf. edn Foerster, p. 390, n. to l. 3374.

42 Transl. Parry, *The Art of Courtly Love by Andreas Capellanus*, p. 107.

43 This is the same word (*gas*) which Guenevere applies to her behaviour towards Lancelot (see p. 150).

44 See n. 29, above.

45 *enor an honte levent* (4404). For *lever* 'to raise up from the font after baptism' cf. K. Bartsch, *Chres*, 85a, 17, p. 266 and Gloss., p. 440.

46 Edn Bédier, pp. 336–47.

47 For the passion which finally transcends courtly controls cf. Arnaut Daniel, *Autet e bas*, edn Toja, VIII, 19–22:

> Merces, Amors, c'aras m'acuoills!
> Tart mi fo, mas en grat m'o prenc,
> car, si m'art dinz la meola,
> lo fuocs non vuoill que s'escanta.

> 'Thanks be, Love, that you now welcome me. The delay has been long, but gratefully do I accept this, for even if the fire is burning in my marrow I do not wish it to be put out.'

48 Cf. Seneca, *Epistulae morales ad Lucilium*, ed. L. D. Reynolds, LXXVIII.

49 Presumably, apart from the use of magic or supernatural means of communication, Guenevere had learnt of this from the dwarf.

50 Cf. Nelli, *L'Erotique des troubadours*, pp. 199–209.

51 *De amore*, I, ch. VI H, ed. Battaglia, p. 212. Translation from Parry, *The Art of Courtly Love*, p. 122.

52 Cf. Bernart de Ventadorn, edn Appel, XLIV, 57–8:

> domna, per vostr' amor
> jonh las mas et ador!

> 'my lady for love of you I join my hands together in adoration of you!'

53 *The Romance of Tristran by Beroul*, ed. Ewert, I, ll. 701–82, pp. 21–4.

54 Cf. the grief of the court, also for the distant imprisonment of a knight by a tyrant, in the Provençal romance *Jaufre*, ed. Lavaud and Nelli, in *Les Troubadours*, I, ll. 3151–70, p. 118.

55 *veez celui qui aunera!* Cf. edn Foerster, p. LI, note, and *Wörterbuch*, p. 36; Nitze in *MLN*, LVI (1941), pp. 405–6, 408–9; Kelly, *Sens and Conjointure*, p. 140, n. 49.

56 For discussion of this episode see pp. 225 and 272, and my article 'The tourney at Noauz and the Hermit Episode in the *Lancelot* and the *Perceval* of Chrétien de Troyes', *Miscellània d'homenatge a Ramon Aramon i Serra* (Barcelona, 1979), pp. 573–83, especially p. 579.

57 For the paradox of this festival of sensuality on St John's Day at Midsummer and the spirituality enjoined by the Gospel according to St John, cf. also *Les Troubadours . . . Flamenca*, ed. Lavaud and Nelli, ll. 725–77, pp. 680–4.

58 For courtly scorn of purposeless jousting cf. Sordello (c. 1250), edn Boni, XVII, 37–40:

> e vos irez cazen e derrocan,
> qu'ieu remanrai ab ma dompna baizan;
> e si be·us faitz dels ponhedors de Fransa,
> us douz baizars val ben un colp de lansa.

'and you will go around falling off your horse and knocking others off theirs while I shall stay and enjoy my lady's kisses, and even if you make yourself into one of the champion fighters of France, a sweet embrace is worth more than a lance's thrust'.

59 Cf. Diverres in *FMLS*, VI (1970), pp. 24–36 (pp. 34–5).

60 See p. 126.

61 For a fuller discussion of this problem cf. Topsfield in *L'Esprit Créateur*, XIX (1979), pp 37–53. These views were also contained in a shorter paper given on 2 April, 1979 to the *Conference on Medieval Occitan Language and Literature* held at the University of Birmingham.

62 For these two styles, cf. p. 8 and p. 319, n. 15.

63 It is the difference in meaning given to *natura* by the reflective and courtly poets which highlights the controversy between Peire d'Alvernhe and the detractors of Marcabru, among whom we may reckon Bernart de Ventadorn; cf. Topsfield in *Mélanges Rostaing*, pp. 1149–58.

64 In *Compaigno, no puosc mudar* (edn Jeanroy, II, 13–15) Guilhem gives solemn and learned warning to the guards of an imprisoned lady: 'for I never saw a woman of such great constancy, who, if her entreaty or her plea for mercy are not heeded, will not come to terms with *Malvestatz* if she is removed from *Proeza*'. For Guilhem's mockery of the learned interests of his aunts, cf. Lejeune in *Mélanges Pierre le Gentil*, pp. 485–503. For links between Chartres and the eleventh-century court at Poitiers see pp. 3–4 and p. 318, n. 5.

65 *Companho tant ai agutz* (edn Jeanroy, III, 10–12):

Pero dirai vos de con cals es sa leis,
Com sel hom que mal n'a fait e peitz n'a pres,
Si c'autra res en merma, qui.n pana, e cons en creis.

'Yet, as a man who has acted badly in this matter, and has suffered worse because of it, I will tell you about the natural law as it concerns the *con*: "As other things when they are robbed decrease, so does it increase".' Then follow mock-scholarly *exempla* and amplifications of this *leis* or natural law. For the natural law within all creatures, see Honorius of Autun, *Liber XII quaestionum*, II, (PL, CLXXII, 1179).

66 Edn Dejeanne (XI, 21–4):

Qu'usquecs crida 'fuec e flama!'
Via dinz e sia prisa!
Degolem Joi e Joven
E Proeza si 'aucisa'.

67 For these virtues see pp. 50–51.

68 For examples of this usage cf. Topsfield in *L'Esprit Créateur*, XIX (1979), pp. 37–53.

69 It is not without interest that Torquato Tasso in his *Discorsi sul poema eroico*, ch. 46, declares that Arnaut Daniel was the author of a *Lancelot*; cf. Lavaud, ed., *Les Poésies d'Arnaut Daniel*, p. 132, and Toja, ed., *Arnaut Daniel, Canzoni*, pp. 25–30. If this statement is true, it is just possible that Arnaut Daniel's use of *leautatz* in this connection may be related to Chrétien's emphasis on *Leauté* in his *Lancelot*.

70 Cf. p. 272.

71 For the contrary view, see Rychner in *Vox Romanica*, XXVI (1967), pp. 1–23, and *Mélanges offerts à Rita Lejeune*, II, pp. 1121–35. For a discussion of this question, see Kelly, *Sens and Conjointure*, pp. 69–76.

72 Cf. p. 131 for this controversy and p. 330, n, 29, for the possibility that Chrétien was using a speech by Lancelot in order to comment on this dispute.

73 Cf. pp. 8–9; also Topsfield in *Love and Marriage in the Twelfth Century*.

74 Cf. the implication of evil in the dwarf and the Cart (343–6) and in the Arrogant Knight as executioner in the Other World (2640–9).

75 Cf. Loomis, *Arthurian Tradition*, p. 192, who suggests the hypothesis that the Celtic forebear of Lancelot may have been Llwch, which in Welsh means 'lake', alias Llenlleawc the Irishman, and that his ultimate ancestor may have been the Irish god, Lug.

76 Cf. the monk's prophecy when Lancelot raises the tombstone (1980–6), the imagery of Lancelot's bleeding hands and feet in the crossing of the Sword Bridge (3126 and 3130), and the prayers of the prisoners for his success against Meleagant (3593–9). For the possible Christian *sen* of *Lancelot* and an interpretation which is probably out of keeping with the rounded quality of what appears to be Chrétien's *sen* in the work, cf. Ribard, *Chrétien de Troyes. Le Chevalier de la Charrette.*

5 YVAIN

1 For the chronology of *Yvain* and *Lancelot*, see p. 18 and p. 321, n. 49.

2 Line references and quotations from Reid, ed., *Chrestien de Troyes, Yvain (Le Chevalier au Lion)*.

3 Cf. Tobler–Lommatzsch, v, col. 173–4. Cf. also Whitney in *Vassar Medieval Studies*, ed. Fiske, pp. 181–215.

4   'Son seignor a mort li navrai,
        Et je cuit a lui pes avoir?'   (1430–1)

'And can I who will be in the position of having fatally wounded her lord imagine that I can live at peace with her?'

These lines foreshadow the conclusion of the romance: *Ore a mes sire Yvains sa pes*, where peace has the double meaning of reconciliation with Laudine after his recreancy towards her, and the peace of mind which Yvain has gained through his sufferings.

5 Cf. Ovid, *Ars Amatoria*, III, 573–5; and, with a slight change in the metaphor, Marcabru, XVIII, 13–18.

6 *la falso razo daurada* (XXV, 24).

7 For the use of this device by Kay in *Lancelot*, cf. p. 113, and p. 329, n. 10.

8 *Lanval*, l. 605 in Marie de France, *Lais*, ed. Ewert, p. 73. Also the lay of *Graelent*.

9 *Arnaut Daniel, Canzoni*, ed. Toja (X, 43–5); a personal crisis which Arnaut Daniel acknowledges in his later poems *Amors e iois* (XIV) and *Ans que* (XVI). Cf. Topsfield, *Troubadours and Love*, pp. 208–12.

10 Cf. Marcabru: V, 33–6, VIII, 26–30, XVI, 52–4; Arnaut Daniel: VIII, 21–2, XIII, 8–9, XI, 18–20.

11 Küchler in *ZRP*, XL (1920), pp. 83–99 (p. 92): 'Im *Ivain* ist keine Spur von These, Tendenz, Moral. Der *Ivain* is von Anfang bis zu Ende eine leichtbeschwingte Komödie.' Quoted by Whitehead who in 'Yvain's Wooing', *Medieval Miscellany presented to Eugene Vinaver*, pp. 321–36, sees no *beschwingte Komödie* in *Yvain* but an ironical diversion in which artistry and lightness of touch do not exclude cruelty and cynicism. Cf. also Frappier, p. 216: 'En choisissant le lion, Yvain a choisi la forme la plus haute de son destin. La rencontre du chevalier et du lion a été un événement spirituel.' See also Harris in *PMLA*, LXIV (1949), pp. 1143–63; Haidu, *Lion-queue-coupée. L'écart symbolique chez Chrétien de Troyes*.

12 Cf. Topsfield, *Troubadours and Love*, pp. 74–8.

13 Cf. Heloise describing Abelard's love for her: 'Concupiscentia te mihi potius quam amicitia sociavit, libidinis ardor potius quam amor. Ubi igitur quod desiderabas cessavit, quidquid propter hoc exhibebas pariter evanuit' (Epist. II; PL CLXXVIII, c 186 B).

14 Contrast this Grief of the Court, and Yvain's reaction to it, with the description of the Grief of Arthur's Court in *Lancelot*, ll. 5361–78, mentioned on p. 156.

15 For the chronology of the composition of *Lancelot* and *Yvain*, see n. 1 above.

16 With these words Chrétien is condemning Kay's attitude to the suppliant Guenevere; see p. 113.

17 The Virgin Mary becomes the damsel's mediatrix with God, and Yvain in her eyes becomes the Elect of God, of the Virgin Mary and the angels in the fight against the devil (*anemis*) incarnate in the giant.

18 Cf. *Farai un vers de dreyt nien* (IV) by Guilhem IX of Aquitaine; Scheludko in *Archivum Romanicum*, XV (1931), pp. 132–206 (p. 167); Topsfield, *Troubadours and Love*, pp. 30–5.

19 Lunete may not travel beyond the limits of Laudine's territory.

20 For the sources, mythical and Celtic, of *Yvain*, see Frappier, *Etude*, ch. 3, and for the castle of Pesme Aventure in particular, pp. 111–15. Cf. also Loomis, *Arthurian Tradition*, pp. 226–331 and for Pesme Aventure, pp. 320–6.

21 *De amicitia*, VI, 20 (Loeb), pp. 130–1 : *Est enim amicitia nihil aliud nisi omnivium divinarum humanarumque rerum cum benevolentia et caritate consensio, qua quidem haud scio an excepta sapientia nil quicquam melius homini sit a dis immortalibus datum.* 'For friendship is nothing else than an accord in all things, human and divine, conjoined with mutual goodwill and affection, and I am inclined to think that, with the exception of wisdom, no better thing has been given to man by the immortal gods.'

6 PERCEVAL

1 Among useful works on Chrétien's *Perceval*, and the theme of the Grail, see: Frappier, *Mythe du Graal*; Id., *Autour du Graal*; Id., *Chrétien de Troyes. L'homme et l'oeuvre*, pp. 170–209; Marx, *Légende arthurienne*; Id., *Nouvelles recherches sur la littérature arthurienne*; Loomis, *Arthurian Tradition* pp. 335–459; Id. in *PMLA*, LXXI (1956), pp. 840–52; Owen, *The Evolution of the Grail Legend*; *Lumière du Graal, études et textes présentés sous la direction de René Nelli*; Fourquet, ed., *Les romans du Graal dans la littérature des XIIe et XIIIe siècles*; Weston, *The Legend of Sir Perceval*; Id., *From Ritual to Romance*, inspired by Sir James Frazer's *The Golden Bough*, and inspiring, in turn, *The Waste Land* of T. S. Eliot. P. Imbs, 'Perceval et le Graal', *Bulletin de la Société Académique du Bas-Rhin*, LXXII–LXXIV (1950–2), pp. 38–79.

2 The word 'procession' in this context is not necessarily intended to carry with it any religious or ritual significance.

3 Line references and quotations from Hilka, *Percevalroman*.

4 For these Magic Objects, cf. Marx, *Légende arthurienne*, pp. 108–39.

5 Cf. Brown, *Origin of the Grail Legend*; Loomis, *Arthurian Tradition*, pp. 375–93; Marx, *Légende arthurienne*, pp. 117–18.

6 Newstead, *Bran the Blessed in Arthurian Romance*.

7 Nitze in *RPh*, VI (1952–3), pp. 14–22.

8 See Thompson, ed., *The Elucidation. A prologue to the Conte del Graal*. The other 'prologue' to *Perceval*, also written after the main work, explains why Perceval's widowed mother retired to the forest and

kept him in total ignorance of knighthood, cf. Wolfgang, ed., *Bliocadran. A Prologue to the 'Perceval' of Chrétien de Troyes*. See also Frappier, *Mythe du Graal*, ch. 4.

9   Cf. Marx, *Légende arthurienne*, pp. 159–81; Frappier, *Mythe du Graal*, pp. 163–212.

10 For the Chalice and the Lance in the Holy Land and Constantinople, cf. Peebles, *The Legend of Longinus and its connection with the Grail*, pp. 56–71; Hofer, *Chrétien de Troyes, Leben und Werke*, pp. 198–206; Imbs, 'Perceval et le Graal', pp. 44 and n. 5, 52, n. 10.

11 The phial was transferred to Bruges by Count Thierry of Flanders, father of Philip, and the cult of the Holy Blood spread to Fécamp, London and Glastonbury. Cf. Marx, *Légende arthurienne*, pp. 239–40 and 255.

12 For the theory of the Byzantine liturgy as a source and explanation of the Grail Procession and the function of the Lance in this procession, cf. Burdach, *Der Graal, Forschungen über seinen Ursprung und seinen Zusammenhang mit der Longinuslegende*, ch. 9; see also review of Burdach, op. cit., by Nitze in MPh, XXXVII (1940), pp. 315–20, and Id. in Univ. of California Publications in Mod. Phil., XXVIII (1949), pp. 281–332 (pp. 307–10); E. Anitchkof in R, LV (1929), pp. 174–94; Marx, *Légende arthurienne*, pp. 236–40.

13 Cf. Roques in R, LXXVI (1955), pp. 1–27; Frappier, *Chrétien de Troyes, L'homme et l'œuvre*, pp. 193–6.

14 At Flamenca's wedding-feast, the 'lays' of Perceval and of the Fisher King are performed quite separately (*Flamenca*, ed. Lavaud and Nelli, ll. 671–2 and 688–90). The original Perceval-story, without the addition of the Grail theme, may have been related to the account of his adventures in *Peredur* in the *Mabinogion*. Cf. also the middle-English *Sir Perceval of Gales*, ed. Campion and Holthausen.

15 Cf. Frappier's summary and review of these theories in RPh, XXIV (1971), pp. 373–440, reprinted in *Autour du Graal*, pp. 323–405.

16 Cf. Owen, *The Evolution of the Grail Legend*, and in R, LXXXIX (1968) pp. 31–53.

17 Cf. especially the valuable article by Hunt, 'The Rhetorical Background to the Arthurian Prologue: Tradition and the Old French Vernacular Prologues', FMLS, VI (1970), pp. 1–15.

18 Cf. Hilka, ed., *Percevalroman*, p. 617, n. 39.

19 For this analysis of St Bernard's thought I am greatly indebted to Gilson, *La Théologie mystique de Saint Bernard*, transl. Downes.

20 On these two theories, see M. de Riquer in FiR, IV (1957), pp. 119–47; Frappier in MA, LXIV (1958), pp. 67–102, reprinted in *Autour du Graal*, pp. 155–210; de Riquer in BRABLB, XXVII (1957–8), pp. 279–320, reviewed by Lecoy in R, LXXX (1959), pp. 268–74 (pp. 272–3); Köhler in ZRP, LXXV (1959), pp. 523–39; Frappier in R, LXXXI (1960), pp. 308–37, reprinted in *Autour du Graal*, pp. 185–210; Delbouille in TLL, VI (1968), pp. 7–35; Pollmann, *Chrétien de Troyes und der 'Conte del Graal'*, ch. 4. Summary of the discussion in Frappier 'Le Graal et ses Feux Divergents', RPh, XXIV (1970–1), pp. 373–440.

21 *De dilig. Deo*, x, trans. from Gilson, *Mystical Theology*, p. 132.
22 Owen, *The Evolution of the Grail Legend*, pp. 153–63, and in R, LXXXIX (1968), pp. 31–53 (p. 52). For the contrary view, see Hoggan 'Le Péché de Perceval' in n. 29 below.
23 See p. 332, n. 56 and p. 338, n. 46.
24 For similar examples of Chrétien's skilful use of vowel-sounds, and also his handling of the octosyllabic couplet, cf. Frappier, *Mythe du Graal*, pp. 257–72, and Johnston, 'Sound-related couplets in Old French', FMLS, XII (1976), pp. 194–205.
25 Cf. p. 145, for Chrétien's lament for *Proesce* in *Lancelot* (3184–96).
26 *mostiers*, 'minster' in the sense of 'monastery church' rather than 'cathedral'. Cf. Foerster, *Wörterbuch*, p. 169.
27 This line (598) is missing in ms. M.
28 This pessimism is no nostalgic commonplace but an essential part of Chrétien's *sen* in both *Lancelot* and *Perceval* (see p. 145).
29 Cf. the valuable article by Hoggan, 'Le Péché de Perceval', R, XCIII (1972), pp. 50–76 and 244–75.
30 In troubadour poetry *nesci* can mean 'ill-mannered, untutored in courtly matters', cf. A Kolsen. ed., *Sämtliche Lieder des Trobadors Giraut de Bornelh*, I, XXX, 9; XXXII, 28; LXXVI, 26 and XXIV, 66.
31 For the significance of the emerald as a symbol of constancy, see p. 326, n. 52.
32 *gasté*, almost certainly an ironical pun.
33 In Celtic tradition the essence of the man lies in his head and to have this cut off implies total destruction. Cf. pp. 139–41, for the Arrogant Knight who wishes to behead Lancelot and loses his own head.
34 Cf. Roland riding into battle:

Cors ad mult gent, le vis cler e riant.

La Chanson de Roland, ed. F. Whitehead, l. 1159.
35 *des mois*, can either mean 'for a long time to come', in this case 'never' (cf. Foerster, *Wörterbuch*, p. 168) or 'to play the fool'.
36 Cf. the knight in the forest describing Perceval:

Cis est aussi come une beste (245)

37 *noveliers* 'inquisitive', a 'rich' word which can mean: 'changeable, inconstant, cowardly, recreant, treacherous, gossipy'. Cf. Tobler-Lommatzsch, VI, col. 863–5.
38 Cf. edn Hilka, l. 2732, note, pp. 666–7, for reference to Dinas d'Aron, Dinas of Cornwall.
39 For this meaning of *mauves*, see pp. 166–71.
40 A *graal* was a flat serving dish. For its much discussed etymology cf. Frappier in RPh, XX (1966–7), pp. 6–8, n. 24. This article, and its predecessor in RPh, XVI (1962) are reprinted in *Autour du Graal*, pp. 205–305.
41 For the controversy whether *trestot descovert* means 'uncovered' or 'open or visible to the eyes of all present', cf. the major articles by

Frappier in R, LXXIII (1952), pp. 82–92 and R, LXXIV (1953), pp. 358–75, reprinted in *Autour du Graal*, pp. 63–72 and pp. 73–88 respectively.

42 See p. 2; Cf. Topsfield, *Troubadours and Love*, pp. 30–4.

43 *main* – a possibly intentional ambiguity of sound with *mahaint*, *mahaing* 'wounded' and the evocation of Perceval's father and the Fisher King?

44 See *Yvain*, ll. 279–313.

45 Cf. edn Hilka, p. 718, n. to ll. 4724–6 and allusion to *mons dolorosa*.

46 The sequence ABABA used by Chrétien as a structural device in the interaction of episodic scenes on a small scale has been discussed by Kelly, *Sens and Conjointure*, pp. 173–4, quoting the earlier works by F. Saran in BGDSL, XXI (1896), pp. 290–1, and Kellermann, *Aufbaustil und Weltbild Chrestiens von Troyes im Percevalroman*, p. 6. It also appears probable, however, that this sequence ABABA was applied by Chrétien to his thematic structure on the widest possible level. Cf. Topsfield, 'The tourney at Noauz and the Hermit Episode in the *Lancelot* and the *Perceval* of Chrétien de Troyes', *Miscellània Ramon Aramon i Serra*, pp. 573–83.

47 For the considerable controversy about the importance or otherwise of the Gawain adventures in *Perceval*, cf. Frappier, *Mythe du Graal*, pp. 213–54.

48 *Le Roman de Renart. Première Branche*, ed. Roques, ll. 652–68, p. 23.

49 *The Romance of Tristran by Beroul*, ed. Ewert, I, ll. 1251–6, p. 38.

50 Cf. Jeanroy and Guy, *Chansons et dits artésiens du XIIIᵉ siècle*.

51 Cf. ll. 6168–71.

52 See pp. 208–9.

53 for *memoire* 'mind, reason', cf. Tobler-Lommatzsch, V, col. 1382.

54 *Que je ne soi ou je me fui*. An alternative translation would be 'that I am not there where I was'. Cf. the anonymous Provençal religious riddle-poem: *Sui e no suy, fuy e no fuy . . .* and its counterpart: *Fuy e no suy senes peccatz, Suy e no fuy d'els tant lassatz . . .* (edn Appel, *Chres*, XLII, pp. 82–3).

55 See p. 337, n. 41.

56 For the 'Host' and the Grail, cf. Imbs, 'Perceval et le Graal', pp. 72–4; Frappier, 'Le graal et l'hostie', in *Les Romans du Graal dans la littérature des XIIᵉ et XIIIᵉ siècles*, pp. 63–81, reprinted in *Autour du Graal*, pp. 134–54.

57 As Enide, though married, was 'carried off' by Erec as a lure for rapacious knights.

58 Cf. *L'autrier jost' una sebissa*, edn Dejeanne, XXX, and Topsfield, *Troubadours and Love*, pp. 88–91.

59 For the Celtic antecedents of the *Male Pucele* and the adventures which befall Gawain, cf. Loomis, *Arthurian Tradition*, pp. 433–59. On the *Male Pucele*, see also Frappier, *Mythe du Graal*, pp. 231–9.

60 In this situation the role of the Male Pucele is in direct contrast to that of Perceval's cousin (3638–43) (see p. 264), and that of the damsel maltreated by Orguelleus (see p. 265).

61 For the sexual overtones of horse imagery in troubadour poetry,

cf. Guilhem IX, edn Jeanroy, poems I; II; IV, 6 and J. Rudel, edn Jeanroy, I, 26–8.

62 For a note on this crippled person, both rich and infirm, see Frappier, *Mythe du Graal*, p. 241, n. 27: Is he a counterpart of the Fisher King, or the displaced ruler of a domain, and governed by women who await a new lord? See also, quoted by Frappier, Loomis, *Arthurian Tradition*, pp. 445–7, and Fynn in MLR, XLVII (1952), pp. 52–5: Chrétien is using a survival in medieval art of a folkloric crippled figure representing the Devil or a pagan divinity of Hell.

63 For the tradition of the Dangerous Bed, cf. p. 330, n. 17.

64 *Chanpguin*. For ms. variant readings see edn Hilka, n. to 8817 and *Wörterbuch*, p. 279 under *Roche*.

65 Cf. edn Hilka, p. 414, and edn Roach, p. 303, l. 9234 note.

66 Cf. R. Lavaud, ed., *Poésies complètes du troubadour Peire Cardenal*, LXXX, p. 530.

67 Cf. Pauphilet, ed., *La Queste del Saint Graal*, pp. 53–4, in which Gawain is blamed by the *preudon* for the slaughter of the seven brothers previously spared by Galahad.

68 Cf. Topsfield, 'The tourney at Noauz and the Hermit Episode in the *Lancelot* and the *Perceval* of Chrétien de Troyes', *Miscellània d'homenatge a Ramon Aramon i Serra*.

69 Cf. edn Pauphilet, pp. 277–8.

7 THE LEGACY

1 *Erec et Enide* and *Yvain* are thematically bipartite. In the first part the hero is found wanting; in the second he finds rehabilitation as an individual and in a wider context. In *Lancelot* and *Perceval*, the hero is found wanting in the first section; in the second section he goes on a quest and is tested further in a major central episode; in the third section, his absolute victory over his former weakness is made clear – for Lancelot at Noauz and for Perceval in the Hermit episode – and his virtue is contrasted with the vice of the forces of Evil.

2 Cf. p. 131.

3 On Chrétien's style and tonality of language, cf. Frappier, *Chrétien de Troyes*, pp. 210–29, and *Mythe du Graal*, pp. 256–72; Johnston in FMLS, XII (1976), pp. 194–205. On use of monologue and dialogue: Hilka, *Die direkte Rede als Kunstmittel in den Romanen des Kristian von Troyes*; Nolting-Hauff, *Die Stellung der Liebeskasuistik im höfischen Roman*, pp. 30–93. Also T. Fotich, *The Narrative Tenses in Chrétien de Troyes. A Study in Style and Stylistics*; Colby, *The portrait in twelfth-century French literature: an example of the stylistic originality of Chrétien de Troyes*; Robson in *Studies in medieval French presented to Alfred Ewert*, pp. 26–70; Hunt in MLR, LXXII (1977), pp. 285–99.

4 Cf. p. 13, and p. 320, n. 31.

5 Cf. Topsfield in MAe, XXXVI (1967), pp. 119–33: the linear method in *Flamenca* is apparent in the balance of analogies and contrasts;

the expository method is evident in the set monologues; the allusive method, with courtly rather than metaphysical intention, is inherent in the closing tourney as a form of amatory contest.

6 G. W. Roach, ed., *The Continuations of the Old French Perceval of Chrétien de Troyes*.

7 See Nitze, ed., *Le Roman de l'Estoire dou Graal*.

8 See *Le Haut livre du Graal*, ed. Nitze *et al.*

9 See Sommer, ed., *The Vulgate version of the Arthurian romances edited from manuscripts in the British Museum*.

10 Cf. Lot, *Etude sur le Lancelot en prose*, and Frappier in *Arthurian Literature*, ed. Loomis, pp. 295–318.

11 See Pauphilet, ed., *La Queste del saint Graal*; *Id.*, *Etudes sur la Queste del saint Graal attribuée a Gautier Map*.

12 See Frappier, ed., *La Mort le Roi Artu, roman du XIIIe siècle*; M. B. Fox, *La Mort le roi Artu, Etude sur les manuscrits, les sources et la composition de l'œuvre*; Frappier, *Etude sur la Mort le roi Artu*.

BIBLIOGRAPHY

This bibliography of books and articles also includes works of general interest and editions of the romances of Chrétien de Troyes to which reference has not been made in the text or the notes.

Further bibliographical information about Chrétien de Troyes may be found in: the *Bibliographical Bulletin of the International Arthurian Society* (*BBIAS*); the relevant sections in *The Year's Work in Modern Language Studies*; F. D. Kelly, *Chrétien de Troyes; an analytic bibliography* (*Research Bibls and Checklists*, 17) (London, Grant and Cutler, 1976); R. Bossuat, *Manuel bibliographique de la littérature française du moyen âge* (Melun, 1951); *supplément* (1949–1953) (Paris, 1955); *second supplément* (1954–1960) (Paris, 1961).

Anitchkof, E. 'Le Saint Graal et les rites eucharistiques', R, LV (1929), pp. 174–94.

Appel, C. (ed.) *Bernart von Ventadorn* (Halle, 1915).
Provenzalische Chrestomathie, 6th edn (Leipzig, 1930) (Chres).

Armstrong, E. C., et al. (eds.) *The Medieval French Roman d'Alexandre* (Princeton, 1937–55), 7 vols.

Arnold, I. (ed.) *Le Roman de Brut, de Wace* (Paris, 1938–40), 2 vols (Brut).

Arnold, I. and Pelan, M. (eds.) *La Partie arthurienne du 'Roman de Brut', de Wace* (Strasbourg, 1960).

Barber, R. *The Arthurian Legends* (Woodbridge, Boydell, 1979).

Bartsch, K. *Chrestomathie de l'ancien français*, 10th edn (Leipzig, 1910) (Chres).

Battaglia, S. (ed.) *Trattato d'amore Andreae Capellani regii francorum 'De Amore' Libri Tres testo latino del sec. XII con due traduzioni toscane inedite del sec. XIV* (Rome, 1947).

Bédier, J. (ed.) *Le roman de Tristan par Thomas. Poème du XIIe siècle* (Paris, 1902) 2 vols.

Bezzola, R. R. *Le sens de l'Aventure et de l'Amour* (Chrétien de Troyes) (Paris, 1947).
Les Origines et la formation de la littérature courtoise en Occident (Paris, 1960), 3 parts (Les Origines).

Bloomfield, M. W. 'Symbolism in Medieval Literature', MPh, LVI (1958), pp. 73–81.

Boni, M. (ed.) *Sordello. Le Poesie* (Bologna, 1954).

Bossuat, R. *Manuel bibliographique de la littérature française du moyen âge* (Melun, 1951); *supplément* (1949–1953) (Paris, 1955); *second supplément* (1954–1960) (Paris, 1961).

Bibliography

Boutière, J. and Schutz, A. H. Biographies des Troubadours édn refondue . . . par Jean Boutière avec la collaboration d'I.M. Cluzel (Paris, 1964) (Biographies).

Bromwich, Rachel 'A note on the Breton lays', MAe, XXVI (1957), pp. 36–8.

Brooke, C. The Twelfth Century Renaissance (London, 1969).

Brown, A. C. L. 'The Bleeding Lance', PMLA, XXV (1910), pp. 1–59.
Origin of the Grail Legend (Cambridge, Mass., 1943).

Bruce, J. D. The Evolution of Arthurian Romance from the Beginnings down to the year 1300, 2nd edn (Göttingen, 1928), 2 vols.

Burdach, K. Der Graal, Forschungen über seinen Ursprung und seinen Zusammenhang mit der Longinuslegende (Stuttgart, 1938).

Campion, J. and Holthausen, F. (eds.) Sir Perceval of Gales (Heidelberg, 1913).

Cary, G. The Medieval Alexander (Cambridge, 1956).

Chambers, E. K. Arthur of Britain (London, 1927).

Chenu, M. D. La théologie au douzième siècle (Paris, 1957) (Théologie).
Nature, Man and Society in the Twelfth Century, transl. Jerome Taylor and L. K. Little (Chicago, 1968).

Cicero, De officiis (Loeb Classical Library, London/Cambridge Mass., 1968).
De senectute, De amicitia, De divinatione (Loeb Classical Library, London/Cambridge, Mass., 1964).
De finibus bonorum et malorum (Loeb Classical Library, Cambridge, Mass., 1967).

Colby, Alice The portrait in twelfth-century French literature: an example of the stylistic originality of Chrétien de Troyes (Geneva, 1965).

Constans, L. (ed.) Le Roman de Thèbes (Paris, 1890) 2 vols.

Crombie, A. C. see Poole, A. L.

Crosland, Jessie 'Eneas and the Aeneid', MLR, XXIX (1934), pp. 282–90.

Curtius, E. R. European Literature and the Latin Middle Ages, transl. W. R. Trask (London, 1953).

Déchanet, J. M. Œuvres choisies de Guillaume de Saint-Thierry (Paris, 1944).

Dejeanne, J. M. L. (ed.) Poésies complètes du troubadour Marcabru (Toulouse, 1909).

Delbouille, M. 'Chrétien de Troyes et le Livre du Graal', TLL, VI (1968), pp. 7–35.
'A propos des rimes familières à Chrétien de Troyes et à Gautier d'Arras', Etudes de langue et de littérature du moyen âge offerts à Felix Lecoy (Paris, 1973), pp. 55–65 (Mélanges Lecoy).

Del Monte, A. Peire d'Alvernha, Liriche (Turin, 1955).

Diverres, A. H. 'Some thoughts on the sens of Le Chevalier de la Charrette', FMLS, VI (1970), pp. 24–36.

Dubois-Stasse, M. and Fontaine-Lauve, A., Guillaume d'Angleterre. Concordances et index établis d'après l'édition M. Wilmotte (Liège, 1974).

Dygve, H. Petersen (ed.) Gace Brulé, Trouvère champenois, édition des chansons et étude historique (Helsinki, 1951).

Ewert, A. (ed.) The Romance of Tristran by Beroul, vol. I (Oxford, 1939).
(ed.) Marie de France. Lais (Oxford, 1958).

Faral, E. Recherches sur les sources latines des contes et romans courtois du moyen âge (Paris, 1913) (Recherches).
Les Arts poétiques du XIIᵉ et du XIIIᵉ siècle (Paris, 1924).

Bibliography

Flutre, L. 'Nouveaux fragments du manuscrit dit d'Annonay', R, LXXV (1954), pp. 1–21.

Foerster, W. (ed.) Christian von Troyes. Sämtliche erhaltene Werke (Halle, 1884–99), 5 vols.

Kristian von Troyes. Erec und Enide (Halle, 1896).

Christian von Troyes. Sämtliche erhaltene Werke. IV. Der Karrenritter (Lancelot) und das Wilhelmsleben (Guillaume d'Angleterre) (Halle, 1899).

Kristian von Troyes. Cligés . . . dritte umgearbeitete und vermehrte Auflage (Halle, 1910).

Wörterbuch zu Kristian von Troyes' Sämtlichen Werken, 5th edn, revised H. Breuer (Tübingen, 1973) (Wörterbuch).

Foster, I. L. 'Gereint, Owein, and Peredur' in Arthurian Literature, ed. R. S. Loomis, pp. 192–205.

Fotich, T. The Narrative Tenses in Chrétien de Troyes. A Study in Style and Stylistics (Washington D.C. Catholic University of American Studies in Romance Languages and Literature, XXXVIII, 1950).

Fourquet, J. 'Le rapport entre l'œuvre et la source chez Chrétien de Troyes et le problème des sources bretonnes', RPh, IX (1955–6), pp. 298–312.

(ed.) Les romans du Graal dans la littérature des XIIᵉ et XIIIᵉ siècles (Paris, CNRS, 1956).

Fourrier, A. 'Encore la chronologie des œuvres de Chrétien de Troyes', BBIAS, II (1950), pp. 69–96.

'Réponse à Mme Rita Lejeune', BBIAS, X (1958), pp. 73–85.

Fox, M. B. La Mort le roi Artu, Etude sur les manuscrits, les sources et la composition de l'œuvre (Paris, 1933).

Frappier, J. Etude sur la Mort le roi Artu (Paris, 1936).

(ed.) La Mort le Roi Artu, roman du XIIIᵉ siècle (Paris, 1936).

'Du "Graal trestot descovert" à la forme du Graal chez Chrétien de Troyes', R, LXXIII (1952), pp. 82–92, and 'Du "Graal trestot descovert" à l'origine de la légende', R, LXXIV (1953), pp. 358–75; also in Autour du Graal, pp. 63–72 and pp. 73–88 respectively.

Les chansons de geste du cycle de Guillaume d'Orange (Paris, 1955–65), 2 vols.

'Le graal et l'hostie', in Les Romans du Graal dans la littérature des XIIᵉ et XIIIᵉ siècles (Paris, 1956), pp. 63–81; also in Autour du Graal, pp. 134–54.

Chrétien de Troyes. L'homme et l'œuvre (Paris, 1957, revised edn 1968).

'Réflexions sur les rapports des chansons de geste et de l'histoire', ZRP, LXXIII (1957), pp. 1–19; also in Histoire, Mythes et Symboles (Geneva, 1976), pp. 1–19.

'Sur la composition du Conte du Graal', MA, LXIV (1958), pp. 67–102; also in Autour du Graal, pp. 155–210.

Le Roman Breton. Chrétien de Troyes; Cligès (Paris, Centre de Documentation Universitaire, 1958).

'The Vulgate Cycle', Arthurian Literature, ed. R. S. Loomis, pp. 295–318.

'Note complémentaire sur la composition du Conte du Graal', R, LXXXI (1960), pp. 308–37; also in Autour du Graal, pp. 185–210.

(transl.) Le Chevalier de la Charrette – Lancelot (Paris, 1962).

'Le Conte du Graal est-il une allégorie judéo – chrétienne', RPh, XVI (1962), and XX (1966–7); also in Autour du Graal, pp. 205–305.

343

'Le motif du "don contraignant" dans la littérature du moyen âge', TLL, VII (1969), pp. 7–46. Also in Amour courtois, pp. 225–64.

Etude sur Yvain ou le Chevalier au Lion de Chrétien de Troyes (Paris, 1969), (Etude).

'Le Graal et ses feux divergents', RPh, XXIV (1971), pp. 373–440; also in Autour du Graal, pp. 323–405.

Chrétien de Troyes et le Mythe du Graal (Paris, 1972) (Mythe du Graal).

Amour courtois et table ronde (Geneva, 1973) (Amour courtois).

Histoire, Mythes et Symboles (Geneva, 1976).

Autour du Graal (Geneva, 1977).

Fynn, Sheila M. 'The Eschacier in Chrétien's Perceval in the light of Medieval Art', MLR, XLVII (1952), pp. 52–5.

Gallais, P. 'Recherches sur la mentalité des romanciers français', CCMe, VII (1964), pp. 479–93 and XIII (1970), pp. 333–47.

'Bleheri, la cour de Poitiers et la diffusion des récits arthuriens sur le continent', Actes du VIIe Congrès national de Littérature comparée (Poitiers, 1965), pp. 47–79.

'De la naissance du roman. A propos d'un article récent', CCMe, XIV (1971), pp. 69–75.

Ghellinck, J. de L'essor de la littérature latine au XIIe siècle (Brussels/Paris, 1946).

Le mouvement théologique du XIIe siècle, 2nd edn (Bruges, 1948).

Gilson, E. La Théologie mystique de Saint Bernard (Paris, 1934); transl. A. H. C. Downes, The Mystical Theology of St Bernard (London, 1940).

Green, D. H. Irony and the Medieval Romance (Cambridge, 1979).

Guyer, F. E. 'The influence of Ovid on Crestien de Troyes', RR, XII (1921), pp. 97–134, 216–47.

Haidu, P. Aesthetic Distance in Chrétien de Troyes; Irony and Comedy in 'Cliges' and 'Perceval' (Geneva, 1968).

Lion-queue-coupée. L'écart symbolique chez Chrétien de Troyes (Geneva, 1972).

Harris, J. 'The Role of the Lion in Chrétien de Troyes' Yvain', PMLA, LXIV (1949), pp. 1143–63.

Harward, V. J. The dwarfs of Arthurian romance and Celtic tradition (Leiden, 1958).

Haskins, C. H. Studies in the History of Medieval Science (Cambridge, Mass,. 1924).

The Renaissance of the Twelfth Century (Cambridge, Mass., 1927, New York, 1957).

Hauvette H. La 'Morte Vivante' (Paris, 1933).

Hilka, A. Die direkte Rede als Kunstmittel in den Romanen des Kristian von Troyes (Halle, 1903).

(ed.) Kristian von Troyes. Cligés . . . vierte verkürzte Auflage (Halle, 1921).

(ed.) Der Percevalroman. Li Contes del Graal von Christian von Troyes (Halle, 1932) (Percevalroman).

Hoepffner, E., 'Chrétien de Troyes et Thomas d'Angleterre', R, LV (1929), pp. 1–16.

Hofer, S. 'Alexanderroman – Erec und die späteren Werke Kristians', ZRP, LX (1940), pp. 245–61.

Chrétien de Troyes. Leben und Werk (Cologne, 1954).

Hoggan, D. G. 'Le Péché de Perceval: pour l'authenticité de l'épisode de l'ermite dans le Conte du Graal de Chrétien de Troyes', R, XCIII (1972), pp. 50–76 and 244–75.

Bibliography

Holmes, U. T. 'A Welsh motif in Marie's *Guigemar*', SP, XXXIX (1942), pp. 11–14.

Holthausen, F. *see* Campion, J.

Huet, G. 'Le témoignage de Wace sur les "fables" arthuriennes', MA, XXVIII (1915), pp. 234–49.

Hunt, T. 'The rhetorical background to the Arthurian Prologue: Tradition and the Old French vernacular Prologues', FMLS, VI (1970), pp. 1–15.

'The Dialectic of "Yvain" ', MLR, LXXII (1977), pp. 285–99.

'Chrestien de Troyes: the Textual Problem', FS, XXXIII (1979), pp. 257–71.

Illingworth, R. N. 'Celtic tradition and the Lai of Guigemar', MAe, XXXI (1962), pp. 176–87.

Imbs, P. 'Perceval et le Graal chez Chrétien de Troyes', Bulletin de la Société Académique du Bas-Rhin, LXXII–LXXIV (1950–2), pp. 38–79 ('Perceval et le Graal').

Jeanroy, A. and Guy, H. *Chansons et dits artésiens du XIIIᵉ siècle* (Bordeaux, 1898).

Jeanroy, A. (ed.) *Les Chansons de Jaufré Rudel*, 2nd revised edn (Paris, 1924).

(ed.) *Les Chansons de Guillaume IX Duc d'Aquitaine*, 2nd edn (Paris, 1927).

Jodogne, O. 'Fragments de Mons', *Lettres romanes*, IV (1950), pp. 311–30.

Johnston, R. C. 'Sound-related couplets in Old French', FMLS, XII (1976), pp. 194–205.

'The Authorship of the "Chevalier" and the "Mule" ', MLR, LXXIII (1978), pp. 496–8.

Jones, R. H. 'Y Rhamantau Cymraega a'u Cysylltiad â'r Rhamantau Ffrangeg', Llên Cymru, IV (1957), pp. 208–27.

Jones, Rosemary, *The theme of love in the 'Romans d'Antiquité'* (London, M.H.R.A., 1972).

Kellermann, W. *Aufbaustil und Weltbild Chrestiens von Troyes im Percevalroman* (Beihefte zur ZRP) (Halle, 1936).

Kelly, F. D. *Sens and Conjointure in the 'Chevalier de la Charrette'* (The Hague, 1966) (Sens and Conjointure).

'The scope of the treatment of composition in the twelfth- and thirteenth-century Arts of Poetry', Sp, XLI (1966), pp. 261–78.

'The source and meaning of conjointure in Chrétien's Erec 14', Viator Medieval and Renaissance Studies, I (1970), pp. 179–200.

Chrétien de Troyes; an analytic bibliography (Research Bibls and Checklists, 17) London, Grant and Cutler, 1976).

Koenig, D. 'Sen/sens' et 'savoir' et leurs synonymes dans quelques romans courtois du 12ᵉ et du début du 13ᵉ siècle (Frankfurt a. M., 1973).

Köhler, E. 'Zur Diskussion über die Einheir von Chrestiens Le Conte del Graal', ZRP, LXXV (1959), pp. 523–39.

Kolsen, A. (ed.) *Sämtliche Lieder des Trobadors Giraut de Bornelh*, I (Halle, 1910).

Kremer, J. (ed.) *Etienne de Fougères, Livre des Manières* (Marburg, 1887).

Küchler, W. 'Über den sentimentalen Gehalt der Haupthandlung in Crestiens Erec und Ivain', ZRP, XL (1920), pp. 83–99.

Lavaud, R. (ed.) *Les Poésies d'Arnaut Daniel* (Toulouse, 1910), also publ. in AMid, XXII (1910) and XXIII (1911).

Poésies complètes du troubadour Peire Cardenal (Toulouse, 1957).

Lavaud, R. and Nelli, R. *Les troubadours*; *Jaufre, Flamenca, Barlaam et Josaphat* (Bruges, 1960).

Lawner, L. 'Notes towards an interpretation of the *Vers de dreyt nien*', CN, XXVIII (1968), pp. 147–64.

Lecoy, F. (ed.) *Le Conte du Graal. Perceval* (Paris, 1972–5), 2 vols.

Leff, G. *Medieval Thought* (London, 1958).

Lejeune, Rita. 'Encore la date du *Conte du Graal* de Chrétien de Troyes', BBIAS, IX (1957), pp. 85–100.

'Rôle littéraire d'Aliénor d'Aquitaine et de sa famille. 1: Aliénor d'Aquitaine', CN, XIV (1954), pp. 5–57.

'La Femme dans la littérature française et occitane du XIᵉ au XIIIᵉ siècle', *La Femme dans les civilisations des Xᵉ–XIIIᵉ siècles, Actes du colloque tenu à Poitiers les 23–25 septembre 1976* (Poitiers, 1977), pp. 111–27.

'L'extraordinaire insolence du troubadour Guillaume IX d'Aquitaine', *Mélanges Pierre Le Gentil. Mélanges de langue et littérature médiévales. Espagne, France, Portugal* (Paris, 1973), pp. 485–503.

Lerond, A. (ed.) *Chansons attribuées au Chastelain de Couci* (Paris, 1964).

Lewis, C. B. *Classical Mythology and Arthurian Romance* (Oxford, 1932).

Linskill, J. (ed.) *The Poems of the troubadour Raimbaut de Vaqueiras* (The Hague, 1964).

Lodge, R. A. (ed.) *Etienne de Fougères. Le Livre des Manières* (Geneva, 1979).

Lonigan, P. R. 'The Authorship of the "Guillaume d'Angleterre", a New Approach', SFr, XVI (1972), pp. 308–14.

Loomis, R. S. 'The Spoils of Annwn', PMLA, LVI (1941), pp. 887–936.

Arthurian Tradition and Chrétien de Troyes (New York, 1949) (*Arthurian Tradition*).

'The Grail Story of Chrétien de Troyes as Ritual and Symbolism', PMLA, LXXI (1956), pp. 840–52.

'Objections to the Celtic Origin of the Matière de Bretagne', R, LXXIX (1958), pp. 47–77.

'The Oral diffusion of the Arthurian Legend', in *Arthurian Literature* (ed. R. S. Loomis), pp. 52–63.

(ed.) *Arthurian Literature in the Middle Ages* (Oxford, Clarendon, 1967) (*Arthurian Literature*).

Lot, F. *Etude sur le Lancelot en prose* (Paris, 1918, 1954).

Luttrell, C. *The Creation of the First Arthurian Romance. A Quest* (London, 1974).

Lyons, Faith 'La fausse mort dans le *Cligés* de Chrétien de Troyes', *Mélanges de linquistique et de littérature romane offerts à Mario Roques* (Paris, 1950), 4 vols., I, pp. 167–77.

' "Entencion" in Chrétien's *Lancelot*', SP, LI (1954), pp. 425–30.

Mabinogion, The. Transl. G. Jones and T. Jones (Everyman's Library, London/New York, 1970).

McMillan, D. *La Chanson de Guillaume* (Paris, 1949–50), 2 vols.

Maddox, D. L. 'Critical trends and recent work on the *Cligés* of Chrétien de Troyes', NMi, LXXIV (1973), pp. 730–45.

Maranini, L. 'I motivi psicologici di un Anti-Tristano nel *Cligés*', *Annal della R. Scuola Normale Superiore di Pisa*, XII (1943), fasc. IV, pp. 13–26.

Martin, E. *Le Roman de Renart* (Strasbourg, 1885), 4 vols.

Bibliography

Marx, J. La Légende arthurienne et le Graal (Paris, 1952) (Légende arthurienne).
Nouvelles recherches sur la littérature arthurienne (Paris, 1965).

Micha, A. La tradition manuscrite des romans de Chrétien de Troyes (Paris, 1939).
'Eneas et Cligès', Mélanges de philologie romane et de littérature médiévale offerte à Ernst Hoepffner (Paris, 1949), pp. 237–43 (Mélanges Hoepffner).
'Tristan et Cligès', Neophilologus, XXXVI (1952), pp. 1–10.
(ed.) Cligès (Paris, 1957).

Migne, J. P. Patrologia cursus completus. Series latina (Paris, 1844–64) (PL).

Misrahi, J. 'Fragments of "Erec et Enide" and their relation to the manuscript tradition', PMLA, LVI (1941), pp. 951–61.
'More light on the chronology of Chrétien de Troyes', BBIAS, XI (1959), pp. 89–120.
'Symbolism and Allegory in Arthurian Romance', RPh, XVII (1964), pp. 555–69.

Mölk, U. Trobar clus-trobar leu (Munich, 1968).

Nelli, R. L'Erotique des troubadours (Toulouse, 1963).
(ed.) Lumière du Graal, études et textes présentés sous la direction de René Nelli (Paris, 1951).
see Lavaud, R.

Newstead, Helaine Bran the Blessed in Arthurian Romance (New York, 1939).

Nitze, W. A. 'Erec's treatment of Enide', RR, X (1919), pp. 26–37.
(ed.) Le Roman de l'Estoire dou Graal (Paris, 1927).
et al. (eds) Le Haut Livre du Graal; Perlesvaus (Chicago, 1932–7), 2 vols.
' "Or est venuz qui aunera". A medieval Dictum', MLN, LVI (1941), pp. 405–9.
'Perceval and the Holy Grail, An Essay on the Romance of Chrétien de Troyes', Univ. of California Publications in Modern Philology, XXVIII (1949), pp. 281–332.
'The Fisher King and the Grail in Retrospect', RPh, VI (1952–3), pp. 14–22.
'Erec and the Joy of the Court', Sp, XXIX (1954), pp. 691–701.

Nolting-Hauff, I. Die Stellung der Liebeskasuistik im höfischen Roman (Heidelberg, 1959).

Ovid, The Art of Love and other poems (Loeb Classical Library, London/ Cambridge, Mass., 1962) (Ars amatoria).

Owen, D. D. R. The Evolution of the Grail Legend (Edinburgh and London, 1968).
'From Grail to Holy Grail', R, LXXXIX (1968), pp. 31–53.
'Profanity and its purpose in Chrétien's Cligés and Lancelot', FMLS, VI (1970), pp. 37–48.
'Two more romances by Chrétien de Troyes?', R, XCII (1971), pp. 246–60.

Paré, G., Brunet, A., Tremblay, P. La renaissance du douzième siècle (Paris, 1933).

Parry, J. J. (transl.) Andreas Capellanus. The Art of Courtly Love (New York, 1959).

Parry, J. J. and Caldwell, R. A. 'Geoffrey of Monmouth', in Arthurian Literature, ed. R. S. Loomis, pp. 72–93.

Pasero, N. (ed.) Gugliemo IX d'Aquitania. Poesie (Modena, 1973).

Paterson, Linda M. Troubadours and Eloquence (Oxford, Clarendon, 1975).

Pattison, W. T. (ed.) The Life and Works of the Troubadour Raimbaut d'Orange (Minnesota, 1952).

Pauphilet, A. Etudes sur la Queste del saint Graal attribuée à Gautier Map (Paris, 1921). Chrétien de Troyes. Le manuscrit d'Annonay (Paris, 1934).

'Nouveaux fragments manuscrits de Chrétien de Troyes', R, LXIII (1937), pp. 310–23.

(ed.) La Queste del Saint Graal (Paris, 1949).

Peebles, Rose J. The Legend of Longinus and its connection with the Grail (Baltimore, 1911).

Pelan, M. L'Influence de Wace sur les romanciers de son temps (Paris, 1931). see Arnold, I.

Philpott, E. 'La Joie de la Cour', R. XXV (1896), pp. 258–94.

Pike, J. B. (transl.) Frivolities of Courtiers and Footprints of Philosophers (Univ. of Minnesota, 1938). See Webb, C. C. J.

Pirot, F. Recherches sur les connaissances littéraires des troubadours occitans et catalans des XIIe et XIIIe siècles (Barcelona, Memorias de la Real Academia de Buenas Letras, 1972).

Pollmann, L. Chrétien de Troyes und der 'Conte del Graal' (Tübingen, 1965).

Poole, A. L. (ed.) Medieval England (Oxford, 1958), II, pp. 571–604, chapter on medieval science by A. C. Crombie.

Pope, M. K. (ed.) The Romance of Horn by Thomas (Anglo-Norman Texts IX–X, XII–XIII) vol. I (Oxford, 1955), vol. II (revised and completed by T. B. W. Reid, Oxford, 1964).

Press, A. R. 'Le comportement d'Erec envers Enide dans le roman de Chrétien de Troyes', R, XC (1969), pp. 529–38.

Raynaud de Lage, G. 'Faut-il attribuer à Béroul tout le Tristan?', MA, LXIV (1958), pp. 249–70.

'Post-scriptum à une étude sur le Tristan de Béroul', MA, LXVII (1961), pp. 167–8.

Le Roman de Thèbes (Paris, 1966–8).

Reid, T. B. W. (ed.) Chrestien de Troyes, Yvain (Le Chevalier au Lion) (Manchester, 1948).

'The "Tristran" of Beroul: One Author or Two?', MLR, LX (1965), pp. 352–8.

'Chrétien de Troyes and the scribe Guiot', MAe, XLV (1976), pp. 1–19.

Reynolds, L. D. (ed.) L. Annaei Senecae ad Lucilium epistulae morales (Oxford, 1965), 2 vols.

Ribard, J. Chrétien de Troyes. Le Chevalier de la Charrette (Paris, 1972).

Richard, A. Histoire des comtes de Poitou (Paris, 1903), 2 vols.

Riquer, M. de 'La "Aventure", el "Lai" y el "Conte" en Maria de Francia', FiR, II (1955), pp. 1–19.

'Perceval y Gauvain en "Li contes del Graal"', FiR, IV (1957), pp. 119–47.

'La composición de "Li contes del Graal" y el "Guiromelant"', BRABLB, XXVII (1957–8), pp. 279–320.

Roach, W. (ed.) The Continuations of the Old French Perceval of Chrétien de Troyes (Philadelphia, 1950–5), 3 vols.

(ed.) Le Roman de Perceval ou Le Conte du Graal publié d'après le ms. fr. 12576, de la B.N. (Geneva/Lille, 1956).

Bibliography

Robertson, D. W., Jr 'Some Medieval Literary Terminology with special reference to Chrétien de Troyes', SP, XLVIII (1951), pp. 669–92.

'Chrétien's *Cligès* and the Ovidian spirit', CL, VII (1955), pp. 32–42.

Robson, C. A. 'The technique of symmetrical composition in medieval narrative poetry', *Studies in medieval French presented to Alfred Ewert* (Oxford, Clarendon, 1961), pp. 26–70.

Roncaglia, A. 'Carestia', CN, XVIII (1958), pp. 121–37.

Roques, M. 'Le manuscrit fr. 794 de la B.N. et le scribe Guiot', R, LXXIII (1952), pp. 177–99.

(ed.) *Erec et Enide*. Vol. I of *Les romans de Chrétien de Troyes édités d'après la copie de Guiot* (Paris, 1952).

'Le Graal de Chrétien et la demoiselle au Graal', R, LXXVI (1955), pp. 1–27.

(ed.) *Le Chevalier de la Charrette*. Vol. III of *Les romans de Chrétien de Troyes édités d'après la copie de Guiot* (Paris, 1958).

Rychner, J. 'Le prologue du "Chevalier de la Charrette"', *Vox Romanica*, XXVI (1967), pp. 1–23.

'Le prologue du "Chevalier de la Charrette" et l'interprétation du roman', *Mélanges offerts à Rita Lejeune* (Gembloux, 1967), 2 vols, II, pp. 1121–35.

Salverda de Grave, J. (ed.) *Eneas, roman du XIIe siècle* (Paris, 1964–8), 2 vols.

Saran, F. 'Uber Wirnt von Grafenberg und den *Wigalois*', BGDSL, XXI (1896), pp. 253–420.

Scheludko, A. 'Beitäge zur Entstehungsgeschichte der altprovenzalischen Lyrik', *Archivum Romanicum*, XV (1931), pp. 132–206.

Schutz, A. H. *see* Boutière, J.

Seelheim, K. *Die Mundart des altfranzösischen Veilchenromans* (Leipzig, 1903).

Servois, G. (ed.) *Guillaume de Dole* (Paris, 1893).

Sheldon, E. S. 'Erec's treatment of Enide', RR, V (1914), pp. 115–26.

Shirt, D. J. 'Chrétien de Troyes et une coutume anglaise', R, XCIV (1973), pp. 178–95.

'Chrétien de Troyes and the Cart', *Studies in medieval literature and languages in memory of Frederick Whitehead* (Manchester, 1973), pp. 363–99 (*Studies . . . Whitehead*).

'Godefroi de Lagny et la composition de la *Charrette*', R, XCVI (1975), pp. 27–52.

'How much of the Lion can we put before the Cart? Further light on the chronological relationship of Chrétien de Troyes' *Lancelot* and *Yvain*', FS, XXXI (1977), pp. 1–17.

'Chrétien's "Charrette" and its Critics', MLR, LXXIII (1978), pp. 38–50.

Sommer, H. Oskar (ed.) *The Vulgate version of the Arthurian romances edited from manuscripts in the British Museum* (Washington, Carnegie Institution, 1908–13); AMS reprint (8 vols. in 7) with new introduction by W. T. H. Jackson (1980).

Southern, R. W. *The Making of the Middle Ages* (London, 1953).

Stevens, J. *Medieval Romance, Themes and Approaches* (London, 1973).

Stubbs, W. (ed.) *Chronica magistri Rogeri de Hovedon* (London, 1869). See also William of Malmesbury.

Bibliography

Tanquery, F. J. 'Chrétien de Troyes est-il l'auteur de *Guillaume d'Angleterre?*', R, LVII (1931), pp. 75–116.

Taylor, J. and Little, L. K. (transl.) *see* Chenu, M. D.

Thompson, A. W. (ed.) *The Elucidation. A prologue to the Conte del Graal* (New York, 1931).

Tobler, A. and Lommatzsch, E. *Altfranzösisches Wörterbuch* (Berlin/Wiesbaden, 1925–), (Tobler-Lommatzsch).

Toja, G. (ed.) *Arnaut Daniel, Canzoni* (Florence, 1960).

Topsfield, L. T. 'Raimon de Miraval and the art of courtly love', MLR, LI (1956), pp. 33–41.

'Intention and Ideas in Flamenca', *MAe*, XXXVI (1967), pp. 119–33.

(ed.) *Les Poésies du troubadour Raimon de Miraval* (Paris, 1971).

'Three levels of love in the poetry of the early troubadours, Guilhem IX, Marcabru and Jaufre Rudel', *Mélanges de philologie romane dédiés à la mémoire de Jean Boutière* (Liège, 1971), pp. 571–87 Mélanges Boutière).

'The "natural fool" in Peire d'Alvernhe, Marcabru and Bernart de Ventadorn', *Mélanges offerts à Charles Rostaing* (Liège, 1974), pp. 1149–58 (Mélanges Rostaing).

Troubadours and Love (Cambridge, 1975; paperback edn 1978).

'The tourney at Noauz and the Hermit Episode in the *Lancelot* and the *Perceval* of Chrétien de Troyes', *Miscellània d'homenatge a Ramon Aramon i Serra* (Barcelona, 1979), pp. 573–83.

'Malvestatz versus Proeza and Leautatz', L'Esprit Créateur, XIX (1979), pp. 37–53.

'Fin'Amors in Marcabru, Bernart de Ventadorn, and the *Lancelot* of Chrétien de Troyes', in *Love and Marriage in the Twelfth Century* (Mediaevalia Lovaniensia, Leuven, in press).

Trojel, E. (ed.) *Andreae Capellani regii francorum. De amore libri tres* (Copenhagen, 1892) (De amore).

Van Hamel, A. G. 'Cligès et Tristan', R, XXXIII (1904), pp. 465–89.

Vigneras, L. A. 'Chrétien de Troyes rediscovered', MPh XXXII (1934–5), pp. 341–2.

Vinaver, E. *The Rise of Romance* (Oxford, Clarendon, 1971).

Webb, C. C. J. *Policratici sive De nugis Curialium et vestigiis philosophorum libri VIII* (Oxford, 1909). See also Pike, J. B. (transl.).

Webster, K. G. T. *Guinevere. A Study of her Abductions* (Milton, Mass., 1951).

Weston, Jesse *The Legend of Sir Gawain* (London, 1897).

The Legend of Sir Perceval (London, 1906–9), 2 vols.

From Ritual to Romance (Cambridge, 1920; New York, 1957).

Wetherbee, W. *Platonism and Poetry in the Twelfth Century. The literary influence of the school of Chartres* (Princeton, 1972).

Wheeler, J. A. 'Hartmann's *Iwein* and Chrétien's *Yvain* as seen by the Critics', *AUMLA*, II (1954), pp. 49–56.

Whitehead, F. *La Chanson de Roland* (Oxford, 1947).

'Yvain's Wooing', *Medieval Miscellany presented to Eugene Vinaver* (Manchester and New York, 1965), pp. 321–36.

'The Joie de la Cour episode in *Erec* and its bearing on Chrétien's ideas on love', *BBIAS*, XXI (1969), pp. 142–3.

Whitney, Marian P. 'Queen of Medieval Virtues, Largesse', *Vassar Medieval Studies*, ed. Christabel Forsythe Fiske (New York, 1923), pp. 181–215

Bibliography

William of Malmesbury, *De Gestis Regum Anglorum*, ed. W Stubbs (London, 1889).

Wilmotte, M. 'Chrétien de Troyes et le conte de Guillaume d'Angleterre', R, XLVI (1920), pp. 1–38.

(ed.) *Chrétien de Troyes, Guillaume d'Angleterre, roman du XIIe siècle* (Paris, 1927).

Wolfgang, Lenora D. (ed.) *Bliocadran. A Prologue to the Perceval of Chrétien de Troyes* (ZRP Beiheft 150) (Tübingen, 1976).

Woods, W. S. 'The Plot Structure in Four Romances of Chrestien de Troyes', SP, L (1953), pp. 1–15.

Wright, T. (ed.) *Alexander Neckham. De naturis rerum* (London, 1863).

Zaddy, Z. P. 'Chrétien de Troyes and the epic tradition', CN, XXI (1961), pp. 71–82.

Chrétien Studies (Glasgow, 1973).

Zai, Marie-Claire (ed.) *Les Chansons courtoises de Chrétien de Troyes* (Publs. Universitaires Européennes, sér. XIII, 27) (Berne, 1974).

Ziltener, W. *Chrétien und die Aeneis* (Graz–Cologne, 1957).

Zitzmann, R. 'Der Ordo-Gedanken des mittelalterlichen Weltbildes und Walthers Sprüche im ersten Reichston', DVLG, XXV (1951), pp. 40–53.

Zumthor, P. 'Toujours à propos de la date du *Conte del Graal*', MA, LXV (1959), pp. 579–86.

GENERAL INDEX

The name of Chrétien appears so many times that passing mentions of it have not been indexed. Persons and places named in the works of Chrétien have been indexed separately: see page 362.

Indexes

Chrétien de Troyes—*cont.*
contemporary coronation, 58,
59; on knowledge and need to
use talents, 60, 63; on divine
ordering, 60–3; begins to reveal
doubts about worldly existence,
64; discovers the story of
Cliges, 65, 301; masters theories
of love, 66, 100; develops four
themes in *Cliges*, 67; riposte to
Bernart by, 68; denigrates all-
consuming passion, 68, 69,
100; uses humour and irony,
72, 82, 85, 91, 97, 119, 129,
132, 183, 270; mocks
'nothingness', 77, 78; opposes
loveless marriage, 78, 91;
turns courtly love upside-down,
80–2, 100; mocks hypocrisy of
courtiers, 81; parodies 'death
through love', 86; and
adulterous love, 87, 91, 109,
110, 155, 157; praises
chevalerie and *clergie*, 90;
contrasts knightly and feudal
codes, 93; mocks preciosity and
colour symbolism, 97, 98;
juxtaposes opposites, 98, 107,
294, 295; bases political
marriage on real event, 99, 100;
turns to real life in *Cliges*, 101;
uses 'multiple incidents', 102;
makes comedy jostle tragedy,
102; and the quest for inner
peace, 105, 174, 205, 299;
treats conflict of Good and
Evil, 106, 112, 144, 145, 157,
165, 172, 215, 289, 299, 302;
instructs Godefroi de Leigni to
finish his work, 111; parodies
Bernart, 131; uses imagery of
Christ, 143; on mutual death
through love, 150, 193, 261;
and Art of Fin'*Amors* in
Lancelot, 165; relation to
Bernart's poetry of the *Lancelot*
of, 165; and four patterns of
thinking of troubadours,
165–71; emphasis on *Leauté* in
Lancelot, 170, 173, 304, 305; no
stranger to poetic controversy,
172; subsumes earlier themes
in *Yvain*, 176; depicts
conflicting ways of life, 176,

301, 302; possible mental
crisis of, 186; shows man's
isolation, 186, 213; and
Christian significances, 189,
209, 210, 219, 236, 296, 297,
306; uses lion as symbol of
moral courage, 189, 190, 191;
and theme of reciprocal
kindness, 203; inconclusive
endings by, 204, 205, 222;
and human reaction to sin and
suffering, 205, 206; associates
himself with Yvain, 205;
presents main elements of
Grail theme, 207; praises
Count Philip of Flanders, 211;
seeks truth and redemption in
Perceval, 212, 299; shows faith
in realist view of life, 213; on
theme of the right and left
hand, 216, 233; contrasts
caritas and *vaine gloire*, 217, 218,
233, 298, 299; and time
sequence in *Perceval*, 219; and
authorship of *Perceval*, 219, 220;
pessimistic view of, 229;
blends varying moods, 239,
240; startles with the Grail
Procession, 257, 258; on the
quality of knighthood, 272,
283, 299, 304; defines the
'madness' of a society, 276;
work on *Perceval* interrupted by
death of, 298; reverts to earlier
themes, 299; differences
between romances of, 301;
changes from 'clear' to 'close'
style, 303; sees life as a cosmic
unity, 303; deepens his
treatment of love and
knighthood, 304; on the
quality of intention, 304; as a
poet of *universitas*, 305;
establishes romance as major
genre, 305; influences later
romances, 305; emphasises
function of the Grail, 306;
does not accept absolutes, 307;
indicates the ideal which
escapes us, 307
Christ, *see* Jesus Christ
Christian ideas: and evolution of
literature in vernacular, 3, 4;
mingled with Celtic and

Indexes

Grail, the: as Chrétien's
imaginative high point, 1, 102;
influence of St Bernard on
theme of, 2; in *Perceval*, 207–300
passim; elements of the theme
of, 207–14; Christian symbolism
of, 211, 306; Christian
meaning of, 214, 306;
Perceval's quest for meaning of,
225, 233, 260, 271, 295–300;
Hermit enlightens Perceval
about, 278; Gawain excluded
from fellowship of, 294;
other writers inspired by
theme of, 305, 306; returned
to Jerusalem, 306; alluded to,
45, 54, 105, 176, 189, 304;
see also Grail Procession
Grail, Story of the, *see Perceval*
Grail Procession, 209–14, 219,
241, 257–9, 297–8, 303; *see
also* Grail
gravitas, 5
Greece, and twelfth-century
thought, 1, 11
Greek Church, liturgy of, 211
Guigemar, 14, 29, 65, 78, 91
Guilhem III, Count of Poitou (the
Great), 3
Guilhem VII, Count of Poitou, 3,
14; also IX, Duke of
Aquitaine: satirises scholarly
debate, 4, 166; and quest for
happiness, 5, 50; and
nothingness, 77; juxtaposes
opposites, 98; loses sense of
identity, 124, 269; alluded to, 7
Guillaume d'Angleterre, 18
Guillaume de Lorris, 48, 111

Hartman von Aue, 305
Henri I (Count of Champagne), 17
Henry I of England, 6, 9
Henry II Plantagenet: electrifies
French literature, 6; marries
Eleanor, 7; favours Benoît de
Sainte Maure, 9; new dynasty
of, 10; events in reign of, 45;
court of, 52, 58; John of
Salisbury secretary of, 53; as a
political animal, 93; and
Becket, 326; alluded to, 59
Henry of England ('the Young
King'), 59, 95, 326

Hermensent, aunt of Guilhem IX,
3, 5
Hero, 11
Hildegarius, 3
Hispano-Arabic thought, 1
Historia de excidio Trojae, 9
Historia Regum Anglorum, 13
Historia Regum Britanniae, 6, 11, 12
Horace, 1

Ille et Geleron, 14
Italy, 9

Jason, 11
Jaufre Rudel, 50, 77, 109, 124
Jesus Christ, 144, 210–12, 233,
277, 297
John, King of England, 7
John of Salisbury, 3, 5, 52, 60
Joie de la Cour, 29, 30, 45, 46, 48, 49
Jois: and Marcabru, 4, 19, 50, 51,
166, 167, 169; and Guilhem
IX, 4, 5; and Andreas
Capellanus, 18; and Raimbaut,
51; and Peire d'Alvernhe, 51;
and the troubadours, 166;
see also Appendix 2
Joseph of Arimathea, 144, 210, 306
Jovens, 4, 5, 19, 50, 51, 167;
see also Appendix 2
Le Jugement de Renart, 274
Julius Caesar, 11

'Knight of the Cart', *see Lancelot*
'Knight of the Lion' *see Yvain*
Kulhwch and Olwen, 13

lai, 14, 15, 49
'Lancan son passat', 170
Lancelot (or *Le Chevalier de la
Charrette*): commissioned by
Marie de Champagne, 17, 19,
107, 108, 110, 171; not
written before 1164, 17;
probably written between 1177
and 1181, 18, 106; manuscripts
of, 18; shared death of lovers
in, 86, 87, 150; comedy
jostles tragedy in, 102;
discussed, 105–74; lacks and
failures of a man, 105; the
quest for 'wholeness' in, 105,
106, 168, 172, 174, 307; and
caritas, 105, 142, 170, 173, 174,

357

Indexes

The Spoils of Annwn, 13
Statius, 10
Stephen (King of England), 6
Stoic ideas, 4

Thebais, 10
Thibaut, Archbishop of Canterbury, 53
Thisbe, 153
Thomas (author of Tristan), 14, 15, 65, 152
Thomas Becket, 52, 53, 58, 326
Thomas Malory, Sir, 305
tort sentier, 120, 121, 133
Tristan, 9, 12, 14, 66, 68, 69, 100, 155
Tristan, 14, 86, 95, 152, 155
Troubadours: quest for truth by, 2, 3; encouraged by Eleanor, 8; changes in style of, 8, 303; react against courtly values, 20; linked with Poitiers and Aquitaine, 50; and foudatz, 50; reject tyranny of mindless desires, 51; juxtapose opposites, 98; and Fin'Amors, 165, 166; four patterns of thought of, 165–9; allusive method of, 302; extra levels of meaning of, 302; alluded to, 1, 14; see also Bernart de Ventadorn; Guilhem VII, Count of Poitou, IX, Duke of Aquitaine; Marcabru; Peire d'Avernhe; Raimbaut d'Aurenga; Raimbaut de Vaqueiras; Raimon de Miraval and Appendix 2

Ulrich von Zatzikhoven, 108
'Una ciutatz fo', 293
universitas, 2, 18, 165, 167, 305

vaine gloire: in Erec et Enide, 35; in Lancelot, 111, 157, 171; in Yvain, 198; in Perceval, 217, 219, 225–36 passim, 263, 271, 276, 292; taints personality, 302
valors, 19, 50; see also Appendix 2
vergonha (or vergoigne), 167; see also Appendix 2
vertat vilana, 117
Victor, St, school of, 1
vilenie, 110, 195

Virgil, 1, 10
Vision of St Paul, St Patrick's Purgatory, 143
Vita Gildae, 13, 108
volanté (or volantez), 109; see also Appendix 2
voluntas communis, 217
voluntas propria, 217–19, 260, 264, 294, 299

Wace, 7, 9, 11–14, 58, 93
Waleran of Beaumont, 6
Walter, Archdeacon of Oxford, 6
Wauchier de Denain, 305
White Book of Rhydderch, 13
William of Malmesbury, 13
William of St Thierry, 4
Wolfram von Eschenbach, 17, 305

Yonec, 77, 78, 91, 184
Yseut, 9, 16, 66, 69, 75, 100
Yvain (or Le Chevalier au Lion): debt to Welsh tales, 13; probably written between 1177 and 1181, 18; manuscripts of, 18; structural pattern of, 25; shared death of lovers, 87; lacks and failures of a man, 105, 176, 189, 192, 198; discussion of, 175–206; social morality within marriage in, 175; richness of language and characterisation, 175, 302; sums up earlier themes, 176; and Fin'Amors, 176, 177, 186, 189, 203, 205, 206; and caritas, 176, 177, 198, 199, 203, 205; allusive method in, 176; conflicting ways of life in, 176, 179, 189, 204; wholeness in, 176, 177, 190, 191, 206; and mesure, 177, 186; isolation of a man in, 177, 186; Celtic tradition in, 177, 181, 184–6, 206; and niceté, 180, 182; pivots of the story of, 191, 192; and vaine gloire, 198; and savoir, 198, 199; theme of reciprocal kindness in, 203; unconvincing ending of, 205; human reaction to sin and suffering in, 205, 206; language of, 302; alluded to, 24, 106, 301

361

INDEX OF PERSONS AND PLACES NAMED IN THE ROMANCES OF CHRÉTIEN DE TROYES AND IN ASSOCIATED WORKS

Acorionde, 94

Alexander, father of Cliges:
marriage with Soredamors of,
64, 67, 110; knighting of, 66,
93; love of, 69–74, 80, 90,
133; deeds of, 72, 73, 92–6,
215–17, 247; addresses
Arthur, 92

Alier, Count, 187, 188

Alis, Emperor, 67, 73–8, 88–101,
124, 125, 136

Amangon, King, 209

Angres, 72, 92, 98

Anguigneron, 248, 249

Anjou, 56

Arrogant Knight, the: taunts
Lancelot, 138–40; and the cart,
140–2; beheaded by Lancelot,
141, 171; evilness of, 144;
alluded to, 134, 147, 161, 267, 289

Arthur, King: mentioned by
Geoffrey of Monmouth, 7, 13;
re-created in twelfth century,
11, 14; weaknesses of, 13, 96,
114, 145, 178, 202, 239; and
the White Stag, 29, 39; in *Erec
et Enide*, 36, 49, 56–9, 169,
177; and the crowning of Erec,
57–9; in *Cliges*, 69, 73; calls off
invasion, 89; learns the
treachery of Angres, 92; as
mighty ruler, 93, 94, 98; as
centrepiece of the court, 98,
178, 269, 270; rescues
Guenevere, 108; treats
Guenevere with scorn, 110;
challenged by Meleagant, 112,
113; in *Lancelot*, 147–9, 155–7,
165, 175, 177; friendship with
Lancelot, 164; ethics of, 169,
289, 299; beliefs of, 177; in

Yvain, 178, 181–5, 195, 199,
200, 205; in *Elucidation*, 209;
in *Perceval*, 223, 226, 228, 229,
237, 243, 275, 276, 291–4;
Scarlet Knight claims lands of,
237–42; and Robert de Boron,
306; and the *Mort Artu*, 306;
see also Arthur's world, Court of
King Arthur *and* knights of King
Arthur

Arthur's world: conflicting
demands on, 66; heroes
separated from, 105, 117;
Meleagant's threat to, 112;
Lancelot ostracised by, 120, 139,
147; narrow-mindedness of,
169; fragmented thinking of,
171; *fable* and *mançonge* of, 178;
self-indulgence of, 182;
rejected by Yvain, 188; tainted
by violence, 294; alluded to,
118, 163, 203; *see also* Arthur,
King; Court of King Arthur *and*
knights of King Arthur

Athens, 99

Avalon, 15, 208

Bade, 137, 147

Bademagu, King: court of, 111,
112; goodness of, 112, 144–9,
157, 159–61, 170, 173; stops
the fight, 156; despairs of
Meleagant, his son, 160; and
wholeness, 177; alluded to, 122,
135, 162, 163, 289

Ban de Gormeret, King, 229

Belrepeire: disrepair of, 245;
Perceval's defence of, 274;
Perceval's promise to revisit,
297; alluded to, 221, 222, 258,
286; *see also* Waste City